Fashion Buying

About the Author

Elaine Stone is associate professor of merchandising and marketing and coordinator of The Small Business Center at the Fashion Institute of Technology, a unit of the State University of New York, located in Manhattan's garment center. She is also a frequent lecturer on fashion marketing at colleges and universities throughout the United States and at professional seminars for trade associations in the fashion industry.

Professor Stone has worked under federal grants to aid fashion apparel manufacturers and retailers in determining their target customers and marketing their products. She has conducted independent marketing and merchandising consulting services for fashion industry clients both domestically and abroad.

In addition to teaching and consulting, Professor Stone has worked extensively in the fashion-apparel manufacturing industry, aiding manufacturers in the merchandising of their product lines. Her experience in fashion retailing includes holding positions of buyer, fashion director, merchandise manager, and corporate vice president in department stores, specialty stores, chain stores, and mass merchandising firms. She has been associated with Macy's New York, Allied Stores Corporation, and Mangels Stores Corporation in executive positions.

Elaine Stone is coauthor of *Fashion Merchandising: An Introduction.*

Fashion Buying

Elaine Stone
Associate Professor and
Coordinator of the Small Business Center
Fashion Institute of Technology
New York, N.Y.

GREGG DIVISION
McGRAW-HILL BOOK COMPANY

New York   Atlanta   Dallas   St. Louis   San Francisco
Auckland   Bogotá   Guatemala   Hamburg   Johannesburg
Lisbon   London   Madrid   Mexico   Milan
Montreal   New Delhi   Panama   Paris
San Juan   São Paulo   Singapore
Sydney   Tokyo   Toronto

Sponsoring Editor: Sylvia L. Weber
Editing Supervisor: Mitsy Kovacs
Design and Art Supervisor/Cover and Interior Design: Caryl Spinka
Production Supervisor: Mirabel Flores

Photo Editor: Rosemarie Rossi
Photo Research/Styling: Betsy Horan, Ellen Horan
Technical Art: Burmar Technical Corp.
Cover Photography: Bonnie West, Courtesy of The Limited, Inc., Courtesy of
 R.H. Macy & Co. Inc./© Alan Bolesta

Library of Congress Cataloging-in-Publication Data

Stone, Elaine.
 Fashion buying.

 Bibliography: p.
 Includes index.
 1. Fashion merchandising.   I. Title.
HD9940.A2S76 1986   687'.068'8   86-19507
ISBN 0-07-061746-5

ISBN 0-07-061746-5

Preface

Fashion Buying has been written to prepare students for enriching careers as retail buyers and merchandisers. I have spent over 20 years in the fashion-buying business and have loved every minute of it. I started my career as an executive trainee and followed a career path through the merchandising positions of branch store department manager, assistant buyer, buyer, divisional merchandise manager, and, finally, merchandising vice president. My days were exciting, challenging, and fun. They were also stressful and full of hard work. But the rewards, both emotional and financial, have always made me very happy with my career choice.

Because I have enjoyed the business so much, I felt it was important to write a book about the fashion buying and merchandising career path. This book introduces students to the full scope of the fashion buyer's responsibilities. It endeavors to present fashion merchandising principles and techniques logically and concisely and to help students learn accepted, proven practices that remain as pertinent today as ever.

Organization of the Text

Fashion Buying prepares students for a wide range of jobs. The text treats the subject matter in the context of fashion apparel and accessories. However, the concepts it develops are equally applicable to the buying and merchandising of other fashion-influenced goods, such as home furnishings, gifts, and linens.

Fashion Buying is structured according to a sequential learning order.

Unit 1—The Retail Buying Environment

The first four chapters acquaint the student with the position of the buyer and discuss the buyer's responsibilities in different retail establishments. They also show the role of the buyer in interpreting consumer demand and projecting the store image.

Chapter 1 introduces the traits and characteristics needed in order to become a successful buyer. This chapter shows the methods used by stores to evaluate a buyer's operation and explains how and why the buyer has to be accountable for the "bottom line." Chapter 2 shows how consumer demand can be analyzed and forecast and explores the buyer's role in interpreting consumers' needs and wants. Chapter 3 examines the ways various types of stores create and maintain their unique fashion personalities and how buyers can contribute to this image-building. The major types of retail organizations that operate as distributors of fashion merchandise are examined in Chapter 4. This chapter discusses the buyer's responsibilities in each of the various types of retail organization.

Unit 2—The Planning and Control Functions

The second unit examines in detail each of the merchandising activities of planning and control that a buyer might be expected to undertake. Because retailers are relying increasingly on computers to carry out planning and control tasks, these chapters are written on the assumption that these functions will be performed with the aid of a computer.

Chapter 5 leads the students through the preparation of a six-month merchandising plan and covers the elements that relate to dollar merchandise planning. Chapter 6 explains factors influencing assortment planning, methods of seasonal planning, and classification of merchandise assortments. The importance and value of strong control over merchandise are emphasized in Chapter 7, which discusses unit control. Chapter 8 focuses on dollar control. This chapter covers the forms and reports that management uses to evaluate merchandising operations.

Unit 3—The Buyer/Market/ Vendor Relationship

These four chapters deal with the activities involved in preparing for and actually making market trips. Criteria for analyzing and selecting vendors are examined in Chapter 9. Chapter 10 covers selecting the actual merchandise to implement the buying plan. The timing of domestic market trips and various services available in the domestic market are also discussed. A complete overview of foreign buying is presented in Chapter 11. Chapter 12 explains and illustrates the different types of buying procedures and covers the process of negotiating the terms of the sale.

Unit 4—The Buyer and Sales Promotion

The last four chapters examine the methods used to promote and sell fashion merchandise. They show the buyer's part in the teamwork that is needed to coordinate the promotional activities of related fashion departments in a store. Chapter 13 explains the objectives of advertising and the buyer's role in meeting these objectives. Visual merchan-

dising is discussed in Chapter 14, and Chapter 15 covers the tools of public relations and publicity. Chapter 16 explains the steps of a sale and the importance of personal selling in the success of a fashion department. The buyer's contributions to and benefits from these promotional activities are important topics in each chapter.

Special Features

Fashion Buying uses many special features to explain fashion buying and merchandising principles and techniques and to bring the subject matter to life. The book contains more than just theory; it is a practical book with real business situations used to illustrate each principle. The approach has been to state the material clearly and to make it interesting and easy to assimilate.

Focuses. A Focus is a vignette that shows how the information in the text is applied in the fashion-buying business. These vignettes highlight interesting people, places, and techniques related to the subject matter discussed in the chapters in which they appear. Each Focus is appropriate for class discussions and for a library research project.

Activities. Each chapter ends with a variety of activities that review and apply the concept discussed. The Buying Vocabulary lists all new terms defined within the chapter. Buying Review is a series of questions that can be used to generate discussion as well as to review information. Buying Cases provide an opportunity to apply the principles explained within the chapter. Each unit concludes with a case that integrates material from all four chapters of the unit.

Illustrations. Accurate records are essential to a buyer's job performance. Although business forms vary from one organization to another, the kinds of data they record are similar. *Fashion Buying* is heavily illustrated with forms used by real fashion retailers so that students can become familiar with the way buyers communicate in writing. Photographs taken in fashion showrooms and stores, both on the selling floor and in the offices, reveal the environment in which buyers work.

Appendices. The two appendices in this book fill very special needs for the student. Appendix A shows career paths in different retail organizations and describes the training programs that are used to help new employees advance in their chosen fashion career paths. Appendix B is a handy math refresher and reference for the basic mathematical formulas used in fashion buying and merchandising.

Glossary. Over 200 frequently used industry terms are included here. A student who has a working knowledge and understanding of fashion industry terminology is many steps further into a fashion career than others who do not have this knowledge. Correct use of the terms in the fashion business vocabulary will give a touch of professionalism to a student entering the world of fashion buying and merchandising.

Instructor's Manual and Key. An instructor's manual and key is available for use with *Fashion Buying.* Suggestions for teaching the course, with specific activities for each chapter, are provided. The manual also includes a bibliography, an answer key to the text activities, and an objective test and key.

Acknowledgments

The cooperation of many business professionals in the fashion industry helped me to keep the information in this book in line with current buying practices. I thank them all for their help. Much appreciated, too, is the advice of my colleague at F.I.T., Professor Jeanette Jarnow, who was so generous with her time. I am especially indebted to the following manuscript reviewers, whose expertise in fashion buying and in teaching was reflected in their helpful suggestions:

Dr. Karen R. Gillespie, New York University, New York, N.Y.

Sallie Hook, University of South Carolina, Columbia, S.C.

Meyer Karch, Mike Karch, Inc. and International Academy of Merchandising & Design, Ltd., Chicago, Ill.

Jean Samples, formerly of Houston Community College, Houston, Tex.

Elaine Stone

Contents

Unit 1
The Retail Buying Environment

Unit 2
The Planning and Control Functions

Unit 3
The Buyer/Market/ Vendor Relationship

Unit 4
The Buyer and Sales Promotion

Photo Credits

Fashion
Buying

Unit 1

The Retail Buying Environment

What are you going to be when you grow up? All of us have been asked this question from early childhood by relatives and friends and sometimes, in front of our own mirrors, by ourselves. What are you going to be? What are you going to do? What are you going to study?

You have begun to make that decision! You are here in school, in class, beginning to learn about the fashion business and particularly about the retail buying environment.

Up until this moment you have read papers, magazines, and books about the fashion business. You may have already worked in the retail world and want to learn more about it with the emphasis on retail fashion buying. You think you want to be a buyer. Good!

In this unit you will begin your study of what career paths are open for fashion buyers, how and why customer demand is important, what a fashion image is and how to develop it, and how retail companies are organized and where the buyer's responsibilities are located.

Each of the first four chapters will cover one aspect of the retail buying environment. Chapter 1 focuses on "The Career of Fashion Buying and Merchandising" describing the traits and attributes that are necessary for success in this field. The opportunities and challenges are also explored, so that you will be better prepared to make a career decision.

"Interpreting Customer Demand" is introduced in Chapter 2. This chapter explains the importance of knowing what your customers want, and how to make sure that you interpret these wants correctly into the "right goods at the right time." Remember, customers are an essential part of the merchandising process because without them there would be no business . . . . and you would not have a job.

In Chapter 3 we look at all the factors that work together to make a retail store's image. "Developing a Fashion Image" will cover the techniques that are used to maintain or to change a fashion image, and how important a role the buyer plays in implementing these techniques.

The final chapter in this unit covers "Retail Organization and the Buyer's Responsibility." It shows the place of the buyer in different types of retail organizations, how the responsibilities vary from one type to another, and the evaluation measures used to judge the success of fashion retail buyers.

Chapter 1

The Career of Fashion Buying and Merchandising

A great thinker aptly said, "Knowledge is always less expensive than ignorance." That axiom holds true in business as well as in personal planning; and for individuals about to launch themselves into the work world, the translation could read, "Having knowledge about a prospective career will result in greater success in that career."

This leads to the question: Where does the fashion merchandising school graduate find a job, knowing that the industry has been stricken with layoffs, bankruptcies, takeovers, retrenchment, relocation, consumer resistance, and competition from foreign markets? Answer: Despite all of the above, in the fashion industry!

Fashion, as you have learned, is a "style that is accepted by the majority of a group at any one time."[1] No matter what the economic climate of the times, fashion is and remains a part of our everyday life.

That means that there will always be a place for dedicated people who understand and direct their energies into the challenging world of fashion. You have already studied the different levels of the fashion business in *Fashion Merchandising: An Introduction* and learned that the fashion business has many areas of interest, expertise, and opportunity: the production of fibers and fabrics, the manufacture of men's, women's, and children's apparel and accessories, the distribution and retailing of fashion merchandise, and the supporting areas of advertising and promotion. However, anyone reading the operating figures of successful retailers knows that the largest rewards usually go to the merchandisers and buyers.

Buying and selling are the very life of any store, whatever the merchandise, and those who take the risks and are successful in planning and carrying out the buying and selling reap the rewards of their success. Among buyers, the greatest risks are usually taken by those in the fashion areas, and so to the fashion merchandisers usually go the greatest rewards, in both remuneration and acclaim, when they are successful. To be successful and profitable, a fashion business must be focused first, last, and always on fashion. The application of the fashion element changes and dominates the retailing process. Some fashion businesses succeed with small stocks, some need larger assortments; some work on small markups and some need larger ones; some turn their stocks many times, while others succeed with less turnover and frequently with lower markdowns; some spend much for advertising, others little. But none succeed, make a profit, and grow in business without fashion merchandisers who respond to the needs of their customers.

You have been thinking about a career, and many of you have always dreamed of being a "buyer." You have thought of the buyer as the person you saw in stores, regally surveying the selling floor and looking very glamorous. The buyer was the person who could take care of your problems and answer your questions about the merchandise. The buyer was the person who traveled to exciting and intriguing faraway places. The buyer had the best job in the whole world!

The leap from commencement to commerce can be challenging and awesome. To be part of "the real world of work" makes you change from student to practitioner in a very short time. The challenge of your job must be the focal point of your work life. What is it that made you want to be a fashion buyer? Did you think it was glamorous, exciting, lucrative, a stepping-stone to bigger and better

The buyer's job can be glamorous, exciting, lucrative, and a stepping stone to other positions.

positions? Well, it is all of those things—plus a great deal of hard work and dedication, and a solid background in the fundamental principles and techniques of fashion buying and merchandising.

One of the most interesting definitions of fashion buying is a little harsh, but it is certainly true: "Fashion buying gives you every chance to be successful, then it puts every pressure on you to prove that you haven't got what it takes. Although the pressure never eases, few jobs offer such a chance for a person to prove his or her mettle and become successful."

The ideal traits, characteristics, and competencies of a retail merchandising executive have been discussed, researched, studied, and reevaluated since the early days of commerce. A typical profile of the person who pulls ahead in the first five years of a retail merchandising career shows someone who is assertive, entrepreneurial, street-smart; someone who has self-confidence, is comfortable making decisions of significant dollar magnitude, is action-oriented and pragmatic rather than theoretical, is analytical and at ease with numbers, is able to deal effectively with many different types of people, and has a high mental and physical level. As you can see, the person we are talking about is faster than a fleeting fad, more powerful than a top resource in negotiations, and able to leap into advancement opportunities in a single bound. In short, the successful fashion buyer is a real champion of the American competitive spirit, a Superman or Wonder Woman ... a true merchandising whiz!

Traits of a Fashion Buyer

There is no doubt that a successful fashion buyer is a distinct breed of individual. As well as being able to cope with all the standard tasks and requirements of any retail position, the fashion buyer must understand and be able to act on the fleeting, often intangible concepts that determine what is fashion and what is convention. These merchandisers must cultivate what could almost be called a "sixth sense" about fashion directions—and then without hesitation make decisions based on that sense. There is no crystal ball to tell them when they will score a triumph and when they will fall flat on their faces, but they thrive on the challenge, and the greater the challenge, the greater their opportunity to shine, to stand out in the

A formal education in fashion merchandising provides the young buyer with a knowledge of the techniques needed to advance on the job.

crowd. Their goal is to be interpreters of the new. As stated by Peter Drucker[2]: "These are times of opportunity for those who can understand and exploit the new realities. The decision maker . . . must resist the temptation to base his decisions on 'what everybody knows.' These temptations are the certainty of yesterday. They are about to be the ancient superstitions of tomorrow."

For those who wish to jump into the world of fun and fancy that is fashion, the surest road to failure is to jump in unprepared. Training and experience are more important than ever, and a college education is becoming more and more the rule for fashion merchandisers on an upward career path. An increasing number of retail employers are looking for young people with an educational background in fashion merchandising, marketing, salesmanship, and retail business management, which gives them a knowledge of organization and techniques that could otherwise require years on the job to master. Most employers also look for some amount of actual experience in a store—during summer vacation or after school hours—and generally prefer some experience in sales, which gives the aspiring merchandiser a firsthand knowledge of comsumers' wants and tastes.

Whatever the background and training, it could never be said that all fashion buyers are identical, stamped out from the same cookie-cutter mold. If they were, the fashion image and merchandise from store to store would not be as wonderfully varied as it is. However, all fashion buyers share some very definite traits and characteristics to a degree, and you should recognize your own capacity before deciding to pursue the challenges and rewards of this career path. Some of these traits can be sharpened or developed through diligence and experience, but all must be present at least in some amount in the makeup of a prospective fashion buyer.

Dedication

Fashion buying is seldom, if ever, a nine-to-five job. There often may not seem to be enough hours in the day to accomplish all the many tasks of the position, especially at times when its demands are tied into seasonal peaks in purchasing, or into seasonal and promotional shifts in selling hours of the store. Since no one can dictate the timing of a new fashion trend's rise—or fall—buyers simply cannot put off until tomorrow what must be done today.

Because of the great investment of time necessary to do the job, fashion buyers must be strongly dedicated to their chosen career path. There is no such thing as being a buyer "halfway"; it is all or nothing. That kind of dedication must come from within, since much of a buyer's work is accomplished without direct supervision. Love of the challenge, willingness to sacrifice personal time during evenings or weekends, satisfaction at triumphs, and optimism even after temporary setbacks are all part of the dedication and drive that keep the fashion buyer on an upward spiral to success.

Enthusiasm

Coupled with dedication is a fashion buyer's need for undying enthusiasm about his or her job. As old-fashioned as it may sound, the ability of a buyer to stay excited about the job, the merchandise, and the merchandising of fashion is key to building a successful career.

That enthusiasm extends to all aspects of a buyer's task, ranging from a simple eagerness to get to work in the morning, to keeping an eternally fresh eye toward merchandise categories that may have been part of the scene for many seasons. Even if a buyer, for example, has been looking at notch-collar blouses for ten years, enthusiasm will enable him or her to go into the market and look at those blouses again, but with a fresh attitude that there might be something out there that is new and different—and wanted by consumers. Successful fashion buyers are never blasé, never bored by their task; they believe wholeheartedly in the "romance of retailing," and that perception keeps them eager and excited about their work every day.

Honesty

The personal characteristic of honesty is one toward which any individual should aspire in whatever the job position or career. Dealing with others in a business situation is always easier and more fulfilling when all parties perceive that they can trust each other not to act in a deceptive manner.

In the framework of a fashion buyer's position, honesty must take on additional dimensions as well. One of those aspects is the buyer's ability to maintain honesty and integrity in the very act of buying—that is, to give every vendor and every item a chance to succeed. Most buyers have particular vendors whose merchandise regularly meets their needs and specifications, and therefore they tend to give those vendors first consideration. But a good buyer will also be honest enough to view the lines of potential new sources with an open mind, and to recognize that those companies might have an item that could be the next "hot" trend.

It is not just in dealing with vendors that fashion buyers need to maintain a sense of integrity. They also must be honest in relation to their customers, in areas such as the quality of merchandise they are selling and the price for which they are selling it. Their honesty must also extend to an ability and willingness to purchase fashion goods which might not cater to their own personal preferences but which they recognize as styles that are liked and wanted by their customers. Honesty with their bosses and employees adds another dimension to this quality. Those with whom the buyer works must have the same trust as those customers and vendors who profit directly from the buyer's integrity.

Awareness

Some people seem to be born with an awareness of fashion. But whether it comes naturally or is developed through careful study, a constant alertness to all the elements of fashion is critical to succeeding as a buyer in this field. After all, the essence of fashion lies in *change,* and the more quickly trends rise and fall, the more quickly a fashion buyer must be aware of the cycle and act on it.

Someone truly and deeply devoted to the fashion field will not discover new fashion directions in the showroom alone but will be aware of those directions whenever and wherever they appear. A successful buyer will be able to recognize broad and specific trends from activities as varied as reading a newspaper or magazine, watching popular movies or television programs, attending a celebrity party, or simply walking down the street and noticing a change in the length of women's skirts or a particular color that lots of people seem to be wearing. Hand in hand with alertness goes a good memory for what was seen and heard, so that the observations can be retained and translated into action within the buying and mer-

Sometimes a buyer must roll up his sleeves and do strenuous physical work. The job requires stamina.

chandising activity. That constant and keen awareness of the world around them enables successful fashion buyers to identify not only a trend on its way up but also one on its way down—both of which are vitally important to keeping a department's merchandise selling. A buyer's powers of observation also enable him or her to communicate reasons for each selection to colleagues who are involved in selling the chosen goods or promoting their sale. The buyer must be able to identify for these colleagues the specific features that make each item a good buy for the store's customers.

Stamina

The long and hard hours a successful fashion buyer must devote to the job require a great amount of physical stamina.

Rarely do buyers find themselves sitting for hours behind a desk; rather, they are constantly on the go, helping to set out new merchandise on the sales floor, double-checking a delivery in the stock room, visiting a vendor's showroom to examine a new line, comparison shopping in a competitor's store, visiting a museum or gallery, or seeing a new show that might reveal new fashion directions. Possessing and maintaining good health are therefore prerequisites for this position.

But beyond the physical requirements of the job, a fashion buyer must also possess mental and emotional stamina. The ability to withstand criticism is crucial, since the blame for any failure on the sales floor will bounce right back to the buyer—who must be thick-skinned enough to take the criticism in stride and move right on to the next task at hand without letting disappointment dampen enthusiasm. That "stick-to-it-iveness" must also be called upon in situations of success, when everyone in the department jumps in to take credit for the triumph rightly belonging to the buyer—who in this case must not allow ego or frustration to lead to disheartenment with the job.

It is not just at the extremes of success and failure that fashion buyers must possess the ability to deal with stress. That type of stamina is a necessary quality virtually every day on the job, and it will enable a successful buyer to maintain equilibrium in an environment where everything, from merchandise styles to display, is constantly changing. It will also allow the buyer to handle competitive pressures, which may come from other buyers, other departments, or other stores, and to cope with constant pressure from supervisors to "make the figures" *today*—no matter how good those figures were yesterday!

Decision-Making Skill

Fashion buying is a business of taking gambles, and those who are not prepared to make decisions that represent a gamble will never win. A successful fashion buyer possesses a talent for making decisions quickly and decisively, and is not afraid to take a risk. Obviously, those decisions must be based on as many facts as can possibly be gathered, but expert buyers recognize that they will always have to rely a little on their intuition that what they have chosen will sell. Even the most successful buyers will be wrong from time to time, but then they must be prepared to make another decision—this time the decision to rectify the situation quickly, and to learn from the mistake so that it is not repeated.

All new buyers immediately become decision-makers on a small scale within their retail organization. Every task buyers undertake requires a decision. They alone are responsible for a distinct category of merchandise and must make constant decisions regarding new items, pricing, promotions, reorders, returns, markdowns, displays and selling. The results of those decisions can be seen clearly on a day-to-day basis in the sales figures from the selling floor, an almost instant feedback that can be tremendously gratifying when the decisions have been the right ones.

One of the most important things for buyers to do, however, is to resist the temptation to base their decisions on what is safe or on what "everybody knows." Instead they must call up all their expertise—including a thorough knowledge of the merchandise, knowledge of their customers, and knowledge of what is fashion—and make a decision that they feel is right for their store and their department. This requires tremendous self-confidence, and willingness to accept full responsibility for a decision, right or wrong. Without that willingness, a fashion buyer will never forge ahead and gain a reputation as being confident, and capable, and a leader in the field of fashion.

Mathematical Ability

Since the ultimate results of a buyer's work are measured in dollars, a buyer must have skill with figures and feel comfortable thinking in numbers—whether the numbers are markups to result in a particular price, tens of dozens of pairs of an item, or profits as a percentage of dollar sales for the department. Buyers must be adept at analyzing information presented in numerical terms, and translating that information into merchandising strategy. The buyer goes into the market-place armed with facts about the markup dollars and percentages needed. Vendors' prices are quickly translated into store prices in the buyer's mind. Whether buying for an off-price retailer with somewhat lower markups or a salon retailer with luxury prices, the buyer has the figures at hand to avoid confusion in buying.

The tremendous increase in retailers' use of computers in recent years has put even more numerical and statistical data into buyers' hands, and anyone entering the merchandising field today will be able to call up an enormous reserve of figures and information on which to base decisions. The key to success for a buyer lies not only in taking advantage of that electronic supply of information but also in cultivating the basic mathematical skills necessary to interpret and act on the wealth of numbers and statistics.

Communication Skills

Fashion buying involves constant contact with other people, from vendors and divisional merchandise managers to sales associates and customers, and being able to communicate effectively with all of those people is vital to doing the job well. Buyers need to be able to express themselves both orally and in writing, as the job often encompasses such tasks as making oral presentations to the sales staff, or writing fashion reports or bulletins.

The importance of communication can be felt throughout the fashion buyer's sphere of influence. Not only must buyers have a good eye and memory for detail, but they must be able to put design images and merchandise concepts into words, and to articulate merchandising ideas for their department to all who are involved in the purchasing, display, sales, and promotion of the goods.

Buyers must be able to express themselves in one-to-one conversations to communicate the most effective ways of presenting their selections.

Presentations to store personnel are one of the ways buyers share information about their merchandise.

Focus

Department Store Career Ladders: Starting at the First Rung

In the fast-paced world of merchandising, retailers are constantly seeking new recruits who will be able to learn and grow, and eventually join the ranks of management. For some department store companies, one of the best sources of new talent is the college campus: For instance, in 1984, The May Co. interviewed 3,700 students at 82 schools in order to hire 305, and Jordan Marsh selected 250 new trainees out of some 1,500 interviewed on 35 campuses.

What do these top retailers actually look for in an applicant? Howard Falberg, vice president-personnel for the Associated Dry Goods Corp., parent company of stores including Lord & Taylor, J. W. Robinson, and Joseph Horne, breaks the requirements into three segments: *marketing skills,* including such things as being attuned to consumer needs; *system skills,* which require awareness of the logistics of inventories and moving merchandise; and *people skills,* or the ability to work amiably with the public.

Falberg's assessment of necessary skills would certainly be common to most department stores. And another thing they have in common is that new employees are not simply thrown into the fray but rather are guided into their career path through intense training programs that generally last 12 weeks but are sometimes longer.

For instance, a leading midwestern department store recently developed a "master plan" for training buyers that analyzes all the competencies a buyer needs to have and then sets out to nurture those competencies over a three-year period—the average time it takes for a new recruit to become a buyer. Training is a combination of individual development planning, in which new employees learn what they're responsible for doing during the period to develop themselves, coaching instructions for their bosses over the period, and seminars.[1]

An important part of the on-the-job training is involvement in the floor work and floor management, which is one reason why department stores like new employees who have worked their way through college in retailing, or who have worked in a family business. Without that firsthand knowledge of the hard work and dedication involved, many trainees simply drop out. As Bill Goodlatte, Senior Vice President-Human Resources for Jordan Marsh, Boston, put it: "The first year is a killer: the hours; the physical work; the customers. There is no substitute for having gone through a Christmas in a department store. And some of these kids just can't hack it. Most of those who leave do not go to work for other retailers. They go into banking."[2]

But for those who do survive the rigors of training, the rewards can be great. As one personnel manager put it, "If the trainees can get past the obstacle of hard work, actual physical work, the truth of the matter is there is no other business where they can move more quickly into managing people, more quickly into having responsibility for a business."[3]

1 Jules Abend, "How Retailers Are Recruiting and Training People for the Fast Track," *Stores,* September 1985, p. 64.
2 Ibid., p. 68.
3 Ibid.
This Focus is based on information from the article cited above and from the following source:
Elizabeth M. Fowler, "Outlook for Jobs in Retailing," *The New York Times,* September 17, 1985, p. D-31.

Negotiation Skills

The ability to negotiate is a trait fashion buyers often need for successful dealing with vendors, especially in cases where pricing alternatives exist. In many instances, the actual prices for merchandise are standard, but there are other areas—such as delivery schedules, cooperative advertising, shipping allowances—for which a shrewd and persuasive buyer can sometimes bargain to make a better purchase and receive more value for the money.

Another aspect of negotiating with vendors depends on buyers' thorough knowledge of their merchandise area; only through that knowledge will they be sure that a vendor's quoted price is fair and reasonable for the quality, style, and general value an item will have in the market. Armed with that knowledge, a buyer is much more likely to be able to renegotiate a price that seems too high and, in that way, to ensure that the proper pricing will appear on the product for customers.

Managerial Skills

While a good portion of a fashion buyer's job relies on individual perceptions and decisions, an equal proportion relies on teamwork, so effective management skills are crucial to make sure other staff members follow through on the buyer's directives. Buyers themselves may be the ones to make the decisions and set the overall direction for a merchandise category, but without the ability to enlist the help and support of others in the department, buyers alone cannot guarantee that the merchandise will be sold effectively or profitably.

A successful buyer knows that managing is more complicated than simply giving orders. An important part of being a good manager is cultivating the talents of subordinates, so that certain tasks can be delegated to others who will perform them in a trustworthy and satisfactory manner. A successful manager is prepared with plans and can sell them to subordinates to win support in turning the plans into action. A successful manager will be fair, tactful, and impartial, and will seek to earn the *respect,* not the love, of his or her staff. Many buyers who are new to a managerial position make the mistake of wanting their subordinates, first, to like them, and they may bend over backward in that goal. The result is almost always a situation in which the buyer loses control of day-to-day operations because department considerations are placed after personal wishes. Invariably, efforts to win everyone's affection have no chance but to fail, since actions that please some will not please others. For successful buyers, it is far more important to earn respect, which they accomplish by always maintaining a professional attitude and by relying on their own self-confidence that they are worthy of their position of responsibility.

Challenges and Opportunities of a Fashion Buying Career

As we have just seen, it takes a lot of different skills and talents to be a success in the competitive field of fashion merchandising. And even for those who have what it takes to launch themselves into the profession, the challenges may be just beginning—but so are the opportunities for growth.

To stay successful, even fashion buyers with many years of experience under their belts can never permit themselves to lose the qualities that helped them succeed in the business in the first place—namely, the traits outlined above, plus a smatter-

ing of creativity, originality, imagination, and showmanship. Past experience will certainly guide an accomplished buyer's decisions, but even experience does not constitute a foolproof guarantee for sales. That challenge of second-guessing consumer taste—and the satisfaction when the "guess" is correct—is part of a devoted buyer's true love of the job. As one assistant buyer described her task: "If you make a mistake, the store will have to pay for it. The responsibility is considerable. However, picking out what you think your customer wants—and tracking its performance—is very exciting. If something doesn't sell, you must figure out why. Was it a fit problem? Was the item too expensive? Or was it poorly made?"[3]

Many of the challenging aspects of a fashion merchandising career are inherent in the characteristics that a buyer must possess to succeed: the willingness to work long hours, the ability to deal with competition and cope with constant pressure, and the capacity to accept criticism and responsibility for temporary failures. But there are other challenges fashion buyers must face and learn to handle, and as a result of their abilities, they will face new rewards and opportunities as well.

Challenges

Just as fashion retailing changes to reflect ongoing changes in style, so it changes to reflect developments and events in the world of which it is part. Many of those broader social and economic trends can have a profound influence on the way fashion merchandise is perceived and presented, and successful buyers must recognize and react to those events just as efficiently as they react to new fashion directions.

For instance, recent years have witnessed an increase in the birth rate, which

Whether you are the buyer of high fashion or staple goods in men's, women's, or children's wear, you must apply the same buying principles and techniques.

signals a growing number of young people gradually entering the consumer marketplace. The influence of those youthful consumers will surely be felt not only in the styling and colors of many fashion products but also in the assortments of merchandise that retailers will have to offer to attract the business of that segment of customers.

At the other end of the scale, many people are living to an older age, which means a greater number of consumers in the over-65 age category. Their specific wants and needs—often for more conservative fashions and conservatively priced goods—must also be addressed by fash-

ion merchandisers who wish to serve their total customer base successfully.

The influx of immigrants who have come to the United States from around the world has created an ethnic diversity that has greatly enriched our culture. These immigrants have sought many exotic styles and colors, and also a uniqueness in fashion that might otherwise have taken longer to develop. Retail store buyers have had to be alert to these culturally diverse requirements.

For many consumers of all ages, the pursuit of leisure-time activities now represents an important part of their day-to-day life and also accounts for a significant portion of their spending. An astute fashion merchandiser will always be aware of lifestyle trends of that type and will adjust merchandise mixes and presentations to reflect current consumer interests and activities.

Economic changes in society are another influence that can challenge a retailer's methods and buying habits. In periods of economic downturn, fashion buyers may find themselves passing up some "hot" new items in favor of more classic products for which consumers recognize a longevity. That type of situation presents a challenge to fashion merchandisers to keep their department new and fresh, without overextending themselves on too-trendy goods that consumers with less cash to spend may hesitate to buy.

Yet another challenge new and established buyers may face is that of unexpected competition from other retailers. Dramatic new specialty shops, antique boutiques, safari shops, and sports wear shops have sprung up almost overnight to add competitive challenges for the fashion buyer. The traditional lines separating department stores, specialty stores, discount stores and off-price stores have blurred in recent years, with so-called discounters trading up to what used to be department store lines, and so-called specialty stores branching out into new merchandise categories to broaden their base and shorten their risks in any one category. All of this means that fashion merchandisers may suddenly face new competition from unexpected sources, and may have to adjust their policies— from purchasing to pricing—to maintain their own customer base and loyalty.

Opportunities

While the challenges are many and varied, fashion merchandisers who are able to thrive and survive on those challenges are rewarded with opportunities for tremendous growth and advancement, both personally and professionally.

Right up at the top of the list is remuneration, which is almost always directly in proportion to a buyer's level of achievement. Many retail organizations pay their buyers' salaries on the basis of the sales/profit ratio of the department, so the rewards are tied directly to the buyers' own efforts and accomplishments. In general, the salary level of a buyer is considered above average as compared to similar positions in other industries.

A successful fashion merchandiser also holds one of the few positions in a business organization that allows for a great deal of self-expression. In fact, the more creativity the buyer exercises, the more opportunities for the store to set itself apart from others and build a more loyal customer base. The store's success obviously reflects back to the buyer, who could then be a candidate for even more responsibility and remuneration.

Fashion buyers also enjoy the benefit of travel, mostly within the United States when they are new, and later to exotic and exciting locations all over the world. Most buyers find the opportunity to mix pleasure with business on these trips, and consider the buying trips to be one of the most important fringe benefits of the job.

For women, the field of fashion merchandising is one industry that is remarkably free of sexual prejudice. Equal opportunity has long been a fact in the fashion field, opening to women every possible avenue for success. A recent survey of United States department store buyers showed that 64.4 percent were women![4]

What's more, individuals who have honed their skills in the field of fashion merchandising have the advantage of knowing that those skills can be parlayed into new and better job opportunities. A talented buyer who is willing to relocate should be able to change jobs and retail companies almost at will, and transferring to a new position frequently means being promoted. The expertise and knowledge gained in fashion merchandising are also transferable to other fashion industries, and a successful buyer may find him- or herself wooed by textile or fashion manufacturing firms for positions in marketing, sales promotion, or sales management.

In short, nothing is easy about being a successful fashion buyer—but then, nothing matches the rewards for those who work hard to succeed. If you are dedicated, enthusiastic, and talented, and feel you can thrive on challenges that may change from day to day, then this could be the career for you.

References

1 Elaine Stone and Jean A. Samples, *Fashion Merchandising: An Introduction,* 4th ed., McGraw-Hill Book Company, New York, 1985, p. 3.
2 Peter Drucker
3 Lorraine Gossett, assistant buyer, Carson Pirie Scott, quoted in *Business Week's Guide to Careers,* December 1984–January 1985, p. 57.
4 Myron Gable, Karen R. Gillespie, and Martin Topol, "The Current Status of Women in Department Store Retailing: An Update," *Journal of Retailing,* Vol. 60, No. 2, 1984, p. 91.

Buying Review

1. Name some of the personal traits considered necessary to be a successful fashion buyer.
2. Why do many retail employers look for some amount of in-store work experience in a prospective buyer?
3. Describe some of the activities that might require a fashion buyer to work beyond the normal nine-to-five business hours.
4. What are some of the ways in which fashion buyers must show honesty in their work?
5. Why is awareness of the world around them such a crucial characteristic for fashion buyers?
6. Describe a situation in which a fashion buyer must demonstrate mental or emotional stamina.
7. Name some specific fashion items or trends from the past for which fashion buyers might have had to use their "sixth sense" in predicting the items' success.
8. Why is mathematical ability an important skill for fashion buyers to possess?
9. What are some situations in which a fashion buyer needs to use good communications skills?
10. How can changes in demographic and world economy affect the fashion buyer's job?

Buying Case

You are the divisional merchandise manager for women's apparel in a medium-sized department store, and you have narrowed your choice for a new assistant blouse buyer to two applicants.

Helen, who majored in liberal arts at a state university, took several courses in business management and marketing, and also worked in sales part time during school and full time summers in a conservative women's boutique. She is soft-spoken and a conservative dresser, and says her long-term goals are to pursue either a fashion merchandising career or a career in retail marketing and promotion.

Joan attended a design school, where her primary focus was in textile design. Since high school, she has worked summers as assistant manager in her father's clothing store for children, overseeing inventory, orders, and sales. She is outgoing and wears young-looking fashions, and says her goal is to be a divisional merchandise manager in five years.

Which of these two applicants would you select? Explain your answer.

Chapter 2

Interpreting Customer Demand

The goal of all retail merchants is to have consumers buy the merchandise that they have selected. You can use a variety of innovative marketing techniques in an attempt to stimulate customer purchasing, but to do this successfully you must first understand that the merchandising of fashion is a procedure in which the democratic process is well established—the sellers nominate and the customers elect. Customers are an essential part of the merchandising process because without them there would be no business. The power of customers is exercised both individually and collectively—in the merchandise selections they make, on the one hand, and in their refusal to buy, on the other.

Retail buyers are in the catering business and will not meet with success if the people being catered to are not satisfied.

As the famed economist Dr. Paul H. Nystrom said, "Consumption and consumer demand constitute the basic foundation of the entire economic and business structure. As consumption goes, so goes business. Consumer demand is the guide to intelligent production and merchandising. There is no excuse or reason for the existence of any business enterprise other than its service directly or indirectly to consumers."[1]

The needs and wants of consumers are influenced by various economic, sociological, and psychological factors. These environmental factors constantly vary, and as they vary, so do the needs and wants of consumers. For instance, American consumers today are vastly different from consumers a few decades ago. They have a higher standard of living, are better educated, enjoy a wider range of interests, travel more, and have greater social mobility. And they are continuing to be transformed.

Because of the constantly different needs and wants of customers, the buyer's job of identifying those needs and wants and interpreting them in terms of specific items of merchandise is a continuing process. It cannot be a one-time or once-in-a-while research project; instead, it must be as much a part of day-to-day business operations as keeping sales or inventory records.

As buyers chart the trends in customer demand, they must be ready to alter their goods and services in accordance with important changes noted. Variations may require, for instance, the addition of new categories of apparel, such as ski wear, tennis outfits, and aerobic, jogging, biking, and exercise clothes. Or they may require the addition of designer-label or lower-price lines or the introduction of luggage in patterns and colors related to apparel fashions. As shifts occur in customers' interests or lifestyles, buyers must make corresponding modifications in their assortments.

To interpret customer demand effectively, you, as a fashion buyer, must first decide who your customers are, what motivates them to buy, and how they select the stores they patronize. This chapter will cover each of these elements of customer demand, and then it will focus on aids for determining customer preferences. These aids include information from store sources, outside sources, and customer advisory groups.

Elements of Customer Demand

In determining the potential demand for fashion merchandise among your store's customers, you must consider a number of important factors. First you must identify your target market group. Then you should study the buying motivations of people in your target market group and determine how these motivations are used when they select actual items of merchandise. Finally you should analyze the patronage motives of your potential customers to determine why they select your store for their fashion merchandise purchases.

Identifying Your Customers

Since no store can be all things to all people, it must select one or a few groups of customers that it wishes to attract. These customers are known as the store's **target market** or target group of customers. The selection of this group of customers and the determination of their needs and wants is aided by a process known as **market segmentation.**

To understand market segmentation, you must first know the meaning of the words "market" and "segment." In general terms, a market means a meeting of people for the purpose of buying and selling. Specifically, the market for fashion merchandise refers to people with money—some more, some less—and with the willingness to buy fashion-related goods. Within the market for fashon merchandise there are smaller, more specific markets such as the markets for women's ready-to-wear, cosmetics, and shoes. Fortunately, consumer fashion markets in the United States are so large that satisfaction of even a small percentage of a total market often is sufficient to ensure a company's profitable existence.

A segment is simply any part of a whole. Market segmentation, then, is the dividing of the total market into smaller customer parts which include those customers who have similar characteristics—

Identifying a target market is important. No store can be all things to all people.
Can you describe the target market this ad is seeking to attract?

Social Class Characteristics[1]

Social Class	Characteristics	Approximate Percentage
Upper-upper	These are the people in an area who represent "old families," who are locally prominent, and whose wealth is inherited. Such people usually occupy an old mansion and may have homes in other places. They are deeply interested in cultural events, usually travel extensively, serve on boards of charitable foundations, and are secure in their social position.	0.5
Lower-upper	The *nouveax riches* of the community constitute this class. Their wealth is not usually inherited but has been acquired by aggressive entrepreneurial activities. These people enjoy spending the wealth they have acquired, like publicity, and want to be seen at important events. They seek the newest in purchases and lifestyles.	1.5
Upper-middle	These are moderately successful doctors, lawyers, or other professional people, or owners of medium-size businesses, or middle managers in large firms. They are concerned with status, live well, are usually substantial members of their communities, and have an enormous drive for success.	10.0
Lower-middle	To this group belongs the large segment of people who teach, work in offices, are small-business owners, successful salespeople, and blue-collar workers with good jobs. As a group, these people strive for success, are relatively conservative and respectable, either own their own homes or aspire to do so, and contribute to the overall stability of the country.	33.0
Upper-lower	People with limited education who may have fairly substantial incomes that are derived from semiskilled work or from work in small factories or retail shops, from jobs as police personnel, fire department employees, or sanitation workers, or from work as office clericals are classified in this group. These people often live from day to day, enjoy spending money (easy come, easy go), attend sporting events, and hang out at neighborhood recreation areas.	40.0
Lower-lower	This group comprises unskilled, uneducated, unemployed, and unassimilated people who are very poor, often on welfare, and sometimes even homeless.	15.0

A subsequent study by the *Chicago Tribune* revealed that social class membership is a better determinant of buyer behavior than is the amount of income people have.[2]

1 Based on W. Lloyd Warner, Marchia Meeker, and Kenneth Eells, *Social Class in America*, Science Research Associates, Chicago, 1949.

2 James H. Myers, Roger R. Stanton, and Arne F. Haug, "Correlates of Buying Behavior: Social Class vs. Income," *Journal of Marketing*, October 1971, pp. 8–15.

for example, upper-middle-class suburbanites who enjoy jogging.

Customers may be classified in many different ways. Although we view America as a land of equality, varied social structures do exist. In the 1940s, W. Lloyd Warner, relying on extensive research, sorted people into a six-class system. Many different ethnic groups have added to the complexity of American society since that decade, but the six-class system still exists in most urban areas. Warner's groupings show small percentages of the population at the top, with increasing proportions reaching down to the middle groups, and a still-sizable percentage at the bottom of the class structure.

No grouping can be used to classify any one individual, but such categories are useful in helping to identify target markets. A summary of Warner's classification is given in the table shown on page 20.

Another theory of market segmentation indicates that there are four bases for segmentation; demographic, geographic, psychographic, and behavioral.[2]

DEMOGRAPHIC SEGMENTATION. When the market is divided into groups according to such characteristics as population, age, families, income, households, sex, occupation, and education, the segmentation is based on demographics. Although **demographic segmentation** can be useful in isolation, it is usually more helpful in identifying potential customers when it is teamed with another type of segmentation. Demographic segmentation is used in isolation when an increase in the number of potential customers who are senior citizens is identified. This type of growth usually suggests an added need for comfortable clothing, health care, special housing, and new types of recreational opportunities. Demographic segmentation might also identify people who have incomes over a specified amount of money per year. These people might be considered potential customers for luxury apparel, including fur coats if they live in the type of climate that requires the wearing of such garments.

GEOGRAPHIC SEGMENTATION. Dividing a market into cities, counties, states, regions, or rural areas, or **geographic segmentation,** is a very obvious form of segmentation, but it can also be a valuable marketing tool. Customer demand is often influenced by geography. Variations in the composition of the population and in the prevailing climate vary the demand for fashion goods in different parts of the United States. For instance, people in the western states are often quicker than most to adopt new styles, especially if they are casual and informal.

Sometimes climate is responsible for variations in demand. San Francisco, for example, is famous as a "suit city," whether or not suits are fashionable elsewhere. It is also known as a city whose women never store their furs. The city's climate makes a removable jacket comfortable for daytime wear. Chilly evenings make the warmth of a fur welcome even in summer.

Buyers have also found that fashion demand in suburbs is usually different from that in central cities. Too, there may be notable differences in demand among the various suburbs of a single city. Although branch customers may be in similar income brackets and have essentially the same taste levels as city customers, most retail stores find that apparel preferences of the two groups differ. Living is more casual in suburbs than in cities.

PSYCHOGRAPHIC SEGMENTATION. Dividing the market according to customer lifestyles is called **psychographic segmenta-**

Form 2-1. The first page of a questionnaire Honeybee used to pinpoint its customers demographically. Subsequent pages ask about education, job, and geographic location.

tion. **Lifestyle** refers to a person's overall living experiences. It includes the work a person does, social activities, leisure pursuits, and resulting decisions about needs and wants. Lifestyle changes occur throughout one's existence. Each person's lifestyle is shaped by personality, activities, interests, opinions, and self-concept. Although psychographics are hard to measure, the results are often worth the effort. One recognized way of measuring activities, interests, and opinions of consumers is by giving them an extensive series of statements and asking them to respond by selecting alternatives that range from "definitely agree" to "definitely disagree." The following statements are similar to those that might be presented during this type of research:

☐ A quiet evening at home with my family is the best kind of evening.

□ Television commercials cause people to buy items that they cannot afford and do not need.
□ Name-brand clothing is made better and lasts longer than store-brand clothing.
□ People should attend some type of religious service every week.

When a large number of consumers are asked to respond to hundreds of statements like these, the respondents can be grouped according to lifestyles. Those who have similar lifestyles can make up a target market group. Although as a buyer you may never be involved in this type of in-depth market segmentation, you may be better able to identify your own target market groups by studying the psychographic findings of professional market researchers.

BEHAVIORAL SEGMENTATION. When **behavioral segmentation** is used, consumers are grouped according to either their opinions of specific products or services or their actual rate of use of these products or services. For example, regular customers at hair salons may have measurable characteristics that make them different from infrequent customers and from people who never visit hair salons. Similarly, those customers who spend several hundred dollars on new designer clothing each month may differ measurably from those who seldom buy designer clothing and those who never buy designer clothing.

If you segment your market into user groups according to behavior, you might be able to identify the reasons for one group's refusal to use a service or buy a product. When these reasons are identified, you may be able to overcome them by providing a slightly different product or service or by promoting your product or service in a different way.

Determining Why Your Customers Buy

In determining why your customers buy, you will need to explore both buying motivation and traditional variations in customer demand.

BUYING MOTIVATION. The great philosopher George Santayana addressed himself to the elements which shape us and motivate us in our lives. He showed that each of us takes with us through life a history of causes and effects which makes us react differently from, or the same as, our friends, neighbors, and members of our own family. These causes and effects also motivate us in our fashion selections. If we want to determine why one item appeals to customers while another does not, we must study **buying motivation,** or why people buy what they buy.

One of the early marketing authorities to buying motivation was Dr. Melvin T. Copeland. He divided consumer buying motives into two classes: rational motives, or those based on appeal to reason, and emotional motives, or those originating in instinct and emotion, representing impulse or unreasoned promptings to buy.[3] Rational motives, according to Dr. Copeland, included such factors as durability, dependability, comfort, economy of operation, and price. Emotional motives were thought to include such factors as imitation, emulation, quest for status, prestige, appeal to the opposite sex, pride of appearance, the desire for distinctiveness, ambition, and fear of offending.

As a result of more recent market research and the findings of experimental psychology, it has become obvious that buying motives are neither as simple nor as easily categorized as was believed when the variety of consumer goods was considerably less than today.

A more recent marketing authority, Jon G. Udell, has developed a much more valid theory. He claims buying motives arise out of both conscious and unconscious reasoning and can best be measured along a bar scale of motives.[4] Udell's bar scale runs from **operational satisfactions,** which are those derived from the physical performance of the product, to **psychological satisfactions,** which are those derived from the consumer's social and psychological interpretation of the product and its performance.

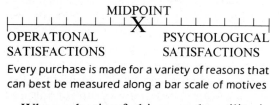

MIDPOINT
X
OPERATIONAL
SATISFACTIONS
PSYCHOLOGICAL
SATISFACTIONS

Every purchase is made for a variety of reasons that can best be measured along a bar scale of motives

When selecting fashion goods, utility is seldom the only concern of consumers.

The psychological satisfactions to be derived from ownership and use of the product play an important part in the buying decision.

When a woman buys a pair of shoes, for example, she may be concerned about a series of utilitarian product features that include workmanship, color, fit, and appropriateness. But this customer may also be concerned about the image that she will project when these shoes are worn. The customer's self-concept plays a role in the buying decision. A variety of shoe styles can be worn with the same business dress or suit and be considered equally appropriate. Different styles of shoes carry with them a different unspoken message about the wearer. The message might be "I am a practical, no-nonsense businesswoman who likes both style and comfort," or it might be "I am a progressive businesswoman who cares a great deal

Each customer seeks a unique personal set of operational and psychological satisfactions from each purchase he or she makes.
Drawing by Lorenz © 1983 The New Yorker Magazine, Inc.

"This might appeal. It's wrinkle-free, wash-and-wear, stain-resistant, and bulletproof."

about fashion," or possibly "I am a successful business executive who enjoys being feminine."

Now let's take a closer look at some of the specific **selection factors** that customers consider when making fashion purchases. A combination of these factors can influence a customer's decision to purchase a product or to pass it by.[5]

- ☐ **Silhouette** refers to the degree to which an item is considered moderate or extreme in form in relation to the currently popular shape or form of such products.
- ☐ **Decoration** or **trim** refers to the presence or absence of buttons, bows, piping, ruffles, or other types of ornamentation. Some customers prefer strictly tailored apparel, while others prefer various degrees of adornment.
- ☐ **Material** refers to the **fabric** or other substance from which the item is made. The "hand" or feel of a fabric involves its weight, its sheerness or opacity, its fiber content, and its durability (Will it stand up under hard wear? Is it easily snagged? How likely is it to "pill"?).
- ☐ **Surface interest** refers to the roughness or smoothness of the material, the degree to which the material is dull or shiny, whether the surface is patterned (as in jacquard), plain, or plush (as in velvet or corduroy).
- ☐ **Color** refers to the actual hues used and the lightness or darkness of each, the intensity of color, whether the item is solid or multicolored, whether the tones are complimentary to the wearer, and whether the colors blend with, mix with, or match accesories or wardrobe items already owned.
- ☐ **Workmanship** refers to the degree of quality in construction, stitching, shaping, finishing. Subjective judgment is often involved here. Not all customers have the same standards relating to workmanship.
- ☐ **Size** refers to preciseness of fit, degree to

which the graded measurements of ready-to-wear apparel correspond to the actual body measurements of customers, and the relative size of accessories to the size and shape of the apparel with which they will be worn.

- ☐ **Sensory factors** refer to touch, taste, smell, sight, and hearing. Odors such as the pleasant scent of leather or perfume, or the unpleasant scent of some leather substitutes; sounds such as the pleasant crackle of taffeta, the unpleasant squeak of a poorly made pair of shoes; touch, such as the sensation of caressing velvet, furs, or suede; and the enjoyment of seeing dramatic outlines, colors, and textures affect our reaction to merchandise.
- ☐ **Ease and cost of care** refers to such easy-care and economical features as wash-and-wear and permanent-press finishes, as well as consideration of future expenses involved in taking care of fabrics or leathers that have to be dry-cleaned or furs that have to be both cleaned and stored.
- ☐ **Brand** refers to the identity of a manufacturer or distributor of an item. Customer confidence or lack of confidence in a brand name because of previous experience with it, familiarity or lack of familiarity with the brand, and its status or lack of status make brand a selection factor.
- ☐ **Utility** refers to the extent of usefulness and service of an item (such as the degree of warmth and protection provided by a coat, the support provided by a well-fitting shoe, the capacity and carrying devices of a handbag), the number of different uses for such an item, and its durability.
- ☐ **Appropriateness** refers to the degree of suitability and acceptability of an item for specific occasion use.
- ☐ **Price** refers to the value placed by an individual customer upon the above factors, plus any other features that a customer may consider important, in relation to the retail price of the item. For example, in a

child's swimsuit, a high quality of workmanship may not be as important as price. The suit may be worn only a few times one summer, outgrown in the following season, and discarded. On the other hand, a high quality of workmanship is usually important when purchasing work shoes, since they are likely to have to withstand long, hard wear.

Udell's theory of operational and psychological satisfactions can be applied to analyzing the ways in which consumers might use these selection factors.

When a man buys a business suit, for example, several suits might meet the criteria of having the right silhouette, color, workmanship, size, or ease of care. These criteria are all toward the operational satisfactions end of Udell's bar scale. If the customer is a businessman, there may be a point at which the buying decision passes the midpoint toward the psychological satisfactions of the product. Let's assume, for example, that the average price for a good quality business suit to be worn by a businessman in middle management is $250. The customer has found several handsomely styled $250 suits that have good workmanship, are the right color and fabric, and fit well. The satisfactions derived from the purchase of any of these suits could probably be considered more operational than psychological. If, however, the customer passes up these suits in favor of a $350 suit that quite obviously has superior quality fabric, workmanship, and detailing, the decision has probably passed the midpoint toward psychological satisfactions.

TRADITIONAL VARIATIONS IN DEMAND. In areas where the change of seasons is strongly marked, the demand for warmer or cooler apparel follows the calendar. In regions like southern Florida, Puerto Rico, or Hawaii, however, there is practi-cally no seasonal climatic change. Thus there is little reason for seasonal variations in the weight or type of garments offered for sale. Some northern parts of the country have short springs and summers, and most of their fashion demand is for cold-weather clothes. In the South and Southwest the reverse is true; there is only a short winter season and little demand for warm clothes. As a result, fashion interest concentrates mainly on styles, materials, and colors that provide summer comfort.

Seasonality has once again become an important factor in consumer demand for fashion goods. However, the demand for clothes designed specifically for hot or cold weather had diminished in the 1960s and early 1970s because of improved heating and air-conditioning systems in offices and homes. This changed with the energy conservation initiated in the late 1970s and early 1980s. Outdoor climate became a factor in the type of clothing the consumer chose. Styles and fabrics that help the consumer face differences in seasonal variations are important now to meet consumer demand.

A factor that upsets the traditional impact of the calendar upon fashion demand is the ease and speed of travel. Consumers can take a brief vacation—even a weekend trip—and quickly reach a climate radically different from the one at home. Today, customers who live in a mild climate turn to the stores they regularly patronize in search of warm clothing for a ski weekend. Customers who live in a cold climate and are planning a quick trip south descend upon their favorite store in midwinter looking for cool, lightweight apparel and accessories to wear with that apparel.

Successful merchants must provide at all times what their customers want. The timing and nature of customer demand

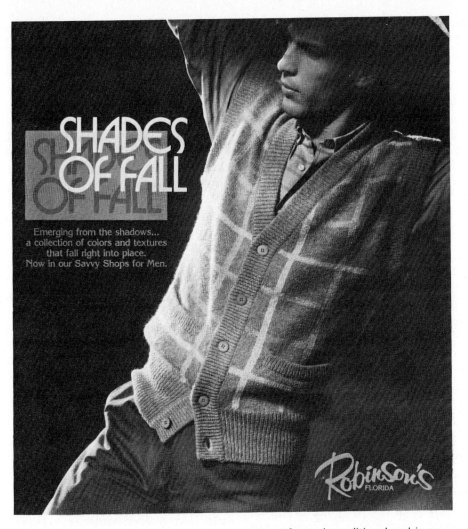

Featuring certain fashion items at certain times of year is traditional and is expected by customers.

today is subject to constant change. It requires that fashion assortments include the various types of merchandise that customers want, no matter when they want them.

In every part of the country, regardless of climate, certain periods of the year have gradually become traditional for the selling of certain fashions. Also, customers have come to expect special sales at certain times of the year.

Special Occasions and Holidays. In the torrid days of late August, parents across much of the nation are busy outfitting their school-age children in warm pants, sweaters, skirts, and coats. The calendar shows that school days are fast approaching, and parents become aware that new clothes are needed for the fall term. This is a natural peak in fashion demand that is completely determined by the calendar, and stores are quick to satisfy it. The back-to-school period represents the single largest selling period of the year for clothing for all students from first grade through college. Therefore, stores traditionally offer greatly enlarged assortments and usually run special-price promotions on selected merchandise.

With year-in and year-out regularity, May, June, September, and December are the traditional wedding months. Stores peak their assortments of gowns and accessories for the bride and her attendants at specific periods in advance of those months to accommodate this demand. Such preplanning also takes place in order to provide suitable clothing for the social events that are part of such holidays as Christmas, New Year's, and Easter.

Although travel today is practically an everyday affair, vacation needs are still a seasonal spur to fashion selling. Summer travel clothes and accessories are still the basis of vacation fashion planning. There is an ever-growing demand for winter vacation fashion needs as well.

Special Sales Events. Because stores have established an annual pattern of promotions, customers have come to expect and patronize special preseason or postseason sales. These have little relation to the natural pattern of demand but have become traditional off-price sale periods. Merchants need to stimulate sales during normally slow periods and to clear out odds and ends of old stock before bringing in styles for the new season. This has led to a traditional pattern of special sales events in many merchandise categories, ranging from bed linens to furniture and including such fashion items as apparel, lingerie, and shoes. Even elegant shops whose policies are firmly against off-price promotions find it necessary to stage semiannual or annual clearances.

Another example of artificially stimulated demand is the summer preseason sale of winter coats and furs. The history of such sales goes back to the 1920s and perhaps even earlier. Coat factories had long layoffs between peak selling seasons and periods of intense activity and expensive overtime work. To reduce the need for overtime work and provide their workers with more regular employment, manufacturers made concessions in price to retailers who ordered and accepted delivery of goods in advance of the normal selling period. This enabled the retailers, in turn, to offer winter garments to their customers at lower than regular prices if they bought such garments in the summer. In the days before air-conditioning, a considerable price inducement was necessary to entice women into stores to try on winter coats in midsummer heat. Nonetheless, customers came and made their selections, and summer coat and fur sales became a tradition.

While early sales continue, promotional stores often offer bargains throughout the season. Off-price stores that offer name-brand articles at lower-than-regular prices promote year round. Thus, Burlington Coat Factory, a retailer, is never without special low prices on the famous-brand coats it offers customers.

Understanding Why Customers Shop Where They Do

Patronage motives is the name given to the reasons that induce customers to shop in one store rather than another—it refers to "why we buy where we buy."

For such "pickup" items as cosmetics or inexpensive hosiery, people often depend on the neighborhood drugstore or supermarket, or any other nearby store, even if its selection is limited. For fairly routine fashion merchandise, such as moderately priced blouses, slacks, and sweaters, the suburban shopper is likely to go to a nearby shopping center for a good selection of such items. For the more important fashion purchases, such as furs, fine jewelry, or designer clothes, it may be necessary for people who live in the suburbs or in small towns to go to stores in the nearest large city or in a not-too-distant high-fashion shopping center.

There are countless reasons why a customer chooses one store over another when the locations and merchandise offerings are comparable. A store's fashion reputation, its assortments, and its price ranges all come into play. So do the services offered (such as credit, delivery, adjustments, and parking) and the attitudes of the salespeople. Each of these factors can help to sway a customer toward one store and away from another. Even the size of a store and the way it is laid out have a bearing on whether or not a customer chooses to shop in it. A customer will award fashion patronage to the store that best fills a need and supplies the motivation that results in a purchase.

All of these factors are a part of the **store image,** the character or personality that a store presents to the public. Store image will be covered in detail in Chapter 3.

Aids in Determining Customer Preferences

The fashion sense of successful buyers is the fruit of hard work. These buyers check their own stores' past merchandising records. They determine general trends in consumer demand through every available source. And on occasion they solicit information on local demand from representative groups of their own customers. In fashion merchandising, instinct and intuition are no match for facts and conscientious research.

Although most stores base their fashion merchandise selections on systematic research, such research is particularly important in larger stores. In a small specialty store, the owner is usually also the merchandise manager and the buyer. He or she can collect customer preference information by studying stock and sales records, talking with customers, and listening to vendors. In larger stores, determining customer preference is a more complex research job. The customers served may number in the hundreds of thousands instead of just the hundreds. The number of fashion items offered and vendors involved may be multiplied proportionally. Smaller stores may need only pencil and paper to do a good customer research job from their sales and stock records. Larger stores use computerized systems to collect and analyze customer demand information on a continuing basis.

Information from Store Sources

Any store that has been in business for more than a season has in its records a treasury of information about its customers' responses to previous merchandise offerings. This information, properly interpreted, shows what customers have bought and what has not interested them. It also indicates what fashion trends may be developing and what trends may be passing their peak.

Of course, one can assume that the store or department being studied has a clearly defined target group of customers. These are not necessarily the same individuals month after month or year after year, but they are people of similar incomes and taste levels who prefer styles at approximately the same point in time. Store source information is less reliable for future planning if a store's customers are too heterogeneous a group, or if a store has been shifting its sights, aiming first at one and then at another type of target customer.

PAST SALES RECORDS. It can be assumed that those items which sold at the fastest rates in the past had the strongest natural appeal to customers. If fast sellers have some features in common, such as color, price, detail, or texture, these features can be an important indication of the nature of customer demand. For example, if the padded shoulder is a feature of nearly all best-selling suit jackets at several prices and in several colors, it can be assumed that the padded shoulder is gaining in demand over other types. On the other hand, if beige jackets are the best-sellers, regardless of neckline or sleeve treatment, then it is color that is influencing the customers, beige being the most important color in the tide of demand.

PRETESTING. New styles are first bought in wide variety but in small quantities in advance of the season. For example, in December, designer spring rainwear may be shown in small selections. From gift sales would come clues for early spring reorders. Customer reaction and sales are then observed. Styles that sell promptly are reordered. Other similar styles are ordered, and slow sellers are dropped.

There are many other ways to pretest new styles. One way is to stage fashion shows early in the season, observe customer reactions, and note their purchases. Another way is to show vendors' lines to salespeople and invite their comments. Still another is to hold preseason sales,

such as summer coat sales, in order to determine which styles are most popular.

The trunk show, as discussed in Chapter 17, is a dramatic form of pretesting new season styles. Samples of the producer's lines are exhibited at scheduled, announced showings. People who attend see every style the producer has available, not just those styles the merchant has already chosen to stock. If customers see a style they want that is not carried by the store, they can order it. Buyers, meantime, have a chance to see how their selections from the producer's line compare with those that interest their customers. Retailers thus can tailor their assortments to more adequately reflect their customers' wants.

MARKDOWNS. Downward revisions in the selling prices of merchandise are **markdowns.** Good retail practice requires that all markdowns be entered on a store record and a reason given for each markdown. Since markdowns are often used to clear out slow-moving stock, an analysis of the styles that had to be reduced often shows what merchandise features failed to attract sufficient customers. This indicates how the merchant should readjust the assortments in the future. For example, a line of vividly colored leather jackets may do well in a high-priced version in a boutique setting and in a low-priced vinyl version in the budget department. A moderate-priced leather and vinyl version offered in the regular sportswear department, however, may be such a slow seller that most of the stock ends up on the markdown rack. A logical assumption, then, is that the extreme in leather or vinyl sport jackets, properly priced, is acceptable to the top and bottom strata of the store's customers. But the group in the middle, who are traditionally conservative, are interested only in a modified version of this type of merchandise.

Focus

Leslie Wexner: Unending Research for The Limited

Leslie Wexner, chairman of The Limited, Inc. believes that "Great merchants are great researchers,"[1] and he practices what he believes! The Limited identifies particular segments of the women's-wear market and sets out to capture them. Wexner also believes that all fashions are decided in a give-and-take between the fashion professional and the consumer. The professional's job is to identify customers' needs and fill them—and not to try to dictate trends and get customers to follow them. Today The Limited sells more women's clothing and accessories than any other merchant in the world, including such giants of retailing as Sears, J.C. Penney, and K mart.[2]

Specialty chains like The Limited are the new wave in retailing. Others include The Gap, a California chain, and Benetton, an Italian franchiser. They cater to the taste of younger Americans—for fresh, affordable fashion apparel.

The Limited, unlike most fashion retailers, test-markets its clothing much the same way that Procter & Gamble researches a new toothpaste. The procedure is: Identify the market, identify the need, and then supply the goods to fill it. Adhering to this credo, The Limited has been able to satisfy the needs and wants of its customers for many years.

In the 1980s the baby boomers that had been The Limited's customers as teenagers were now adult working women with elevated fashion tastes and incomes. The Limited had to adapt to their changing needs. To meet its customers' new demands, The Limited upgraded the quality of the merchandise in its stores. Besides its private label merchandise the company signed up big-name designers, such as Kenzo, Mariuccia Mandelli of Krizia, and Carol Horn, to create exclusive collections for this changing market.

But management did not forget the target audience of 15 to 25 year olds. A new generation, that likes funky fashion, is served by Limited Express stores, a chain that has grown to 218 stores in a short time.[3]

In his acquisitions, as in the stores he founded, Wexner stays close to his credo of segmenting the marketplace—researching a target market and serving its needs. He has acquired Victoria's Secret, boutiques of designer lingerie; Lane Bryant, the formost retailer of apparel for large-size women; Brylane, the largest catalog retailer of women's special sizes; Lerner Stores, a budget-priced apparel chain; and Henri Bendel, a New York specialty store whose customers are upper-income women at the introductory phase of the fashion cycle, women who rarely wear a size larger than a 10! Each acquisition has reinforced his belief in serving a target market and serving it well.

"Regardless of the individual differences among the companies, they all share one simple but vital belief: nothing happens until the customer buys something," Wexner explains. "This company-wide focus on the customer is spearheaded by our chief executives, division leaders who set the highest standards, standards that are responsible for The Limited's continued growth."[4]

1 Brian O'Reilly, "Leslie Wexner Knows What Women Want," *Fortune Magazine,* August 16, 1985, pp. 154–56, 58–60
2 William H. Myers, "Rag-Trade Revolutionary," *New York Times Magazine,* Part 2, The Business World, June 8, 1986, pp. 41–43, 119–120, 122.
3 Ibid.
4 Leslie H. Wexner, To Our Shareholders. The Limited, Inc. 1985 Annual Report, April 7, 1986.

This Focus is based on the articles cited above and the following articles:
Isadore Barmash, "Market Place-Specialty Shop: Allure Grows," *The New York Times,* Wednesday, April 2, 1986.
"The Limiting of Lerner" *Apparel Merchandising,* April 1986, pp. 29–31.
Dennis Holder, "Business Watch, Real-People Trends," *Working Woman,* May 1986, pp. 61–62.

WANT SLIPS. When a customer requests something that is not in stock, salespeople should be encouraged to report the situation on forms that are known as **want slips.** (See Form 2-2.) These forms include the salesperson's name, department number, and date, and spaces for information the buyer needs to determine accurately what customers seek. These can be particularly interesting as a means of studying current customer demand, for they are one of the few indications a store has of what customers would buy if it were available. Study of these unfilled customer wants helps a buyer correct possible errors in filling demand for particular sizes, prices, colors, or types of items. A dress department, for instance, might stock only conservative styles in larger sizes. But want slips might show that customers wearing these sizes would like to find more lively colors and youthful styles.

ADVERTISING RESULTS. Stores try to determine the amount of business that results directly from advertising. This is often hard to determine unless a customer arrives at the store with ad in hand or mentions the ad to a salesperson. However, if an ad promotes a particular line or item, increases in sales immediately after the ad appears are usually attributed to the promotion.

The response to the advertising of a specific style is usually an indication of the degree of customer interest in the style. This is particularly true if several styles receive equal advertising emphasis but show considerable difference in generating customer purchases. In a departmentalized store, a buyer for one department, in addition to the results of his or her own ads, sometimes can obtain valuable guidance from the results of advertising done by related departments.

MERCHANDISE WANT SLIP

Department No. _42_   Name _Sara Davies_

Date _8/17_

The following Requested Merchandise is not in Stock:

Description (Item, Color, Size, Price)	No. of Calls	Buyer's Remarks
Poly/cotton shirtwaist, blue/white stripe w/white collar; size 10, 12; $52	2	Order placed for #417 with Silhouette Dress Co. on 8/20

The following Stock is getting low:

Mfr., Style, Color, Price	Pieces On Hand	
Jacobs #6192, red, $46	4	Discontinued
R & K, #1001, 2/10, 1/14 $82	3	Reordered 24 pieces

SUGGEST A SUBSTITUTE

Form 2-2. Want slips tell what merchandise needs to be ordered to fill unmet customer demands. In small stores, want slips are also used to alert the buyer when stock is running low.

RETURNS, COMPLAINTS, AND ADJUSTMENTS. When a store accepts a return from a customer or makes an adjustment on goods that failed to give satisfaction, all the details about the transaction should be recorded. These records are warnings for store buyers, telling them which goods have not been found acceptable by customers and why. For example, if customers return wool sweaters because they pill after one washing or cleaning, the buyer should consider finding a sweater source that provides higher quality merchandise. In addition, the buyer would have to accept the fact that a certain degree of prejudice might have developed against the purchasing of any wool sweaters at the store thereby influencing customer demand. Additional promotion, stressing the quality of the new sweaters, might be needed.

CUSTOMER SURVEYS. Many customers are quite willing to tell a retailer what they like and what they do not like about the store. They will point out what does and does not interest them in the merchandise assortment. Such customer surveys can be quite informal and yet provide a clear indication of trends. The buyer or store owner who talks with customers on the selling floor, observes expressions, and listens to remarks made by customers learns a good deal about the nature of customer demand and how the store's assortment is viewed by the customer. Formal surveys can be made by mail or personal interview to determine, for example, what price lines are favored, what types of merchandise are wanted by regular or potential customers, and what services are expected.

SALESPEOPLE. Because of their constant, direct contact with customers, salespeople usually can provide valuable information about what customers want. In larger stores, salespeople are really the stores' only links with their customers, for buyers seldom can spend much time on the selling floor. Salespeople can report whether customers bought certain styles eagerly or reluctantly and whether they asked for any particular items that were not immediately available. Sometimes the information gathered from salespeople is the first indication a store may have of a change in trend. At other times, what the salespeople report will reinforce and amplify what a buyer may already have suspected from observations and from store records.

Information from Sources Outside the Store

Fashion buyers also look beyond their own doors for indications of consumer demand. What they learn from outside sources may confirm what they deduce from their own experience—or it may indicate points they have missed or perhaps misinterpreted. A typical case would be one in which certain styles or items are not yet stocked in a store but are enjoying good acceptance in other stores.

There are many specific sources to which merchants turn for information, including their competitors and suppliers. To alert retailers, however, almost everything has fashion significance. What people wear to the theater and restaurants, what important local people are wearing, and what national celebrities are wearing are among the many guides that help a fashion merchant identify current trends in customer demand.

COMPETITORS. One method of obtaining reliable information is by studying the advertising of other stores. It is relatively simple to visit the selling floor of competing stores to see what is stocked, what is featured in displays, and what appears to be selling. Some stores rely on their buyers and merchandise managers to do this job. Others prefer to set up a separate comparison bureau or office, believing that its staff can perform the work involved more extensively and more objectively than can the store's merchandising executives. These comparison shoppers visit the stores of local competitors, check prices, assortments, services, and customer response. They then report their findings to executives in their own store for appropriate action.

RESIDENT BUYING OFFICE. A **resident buying office** is a business organization, located in a major market area, that supplies its noncompeting client stores with many market-related services. It provides those stores with a steady flow of current information on general trends in consumer demand. Such information takes the form of market bulletins, reports on new items, fashion forecasts, and lists of styles and items that are best-sellers in other client stores. During periods when store buyers are in the market to view producers' lines, the resident buying offices hold clinics, or meetings, at which buyers from the buying office's various client stores can discuss fashion, merchandise, and merchandising. Separate clinics are held for buyers specializing in each category of merchandise, so that the discussions can be detailed. There are also group meetings for heads of stores and for merchandise managers.

In addition, individual store managers and their buyers may consult the market representatives of the buying office about vendors and best-selling items. At the resident buying office, store buyers meet informally and frequently compare notes on consumer demand.

MANUFACTURERS AND THEIR SALES REPRESENTATIVES. The producers with whom a store deals can contribute information in discussing why they sponsor certain styles and trends. Their lines have been planned to meet anticipated consumer demand and tested against the reactions and sales experience of many retail buyers. Well-prepared sales representatives usually are eager to furnish retail buyers with detailed information about their line and also about response to it.

Some of the most accurate information about consumer demand comes from producers. Today, major producers in each branch of the fashion business are large enough to use modern electronic equipment in collecting and analyzing information about sales trends quickly. Such producers thus are in a position to tell merchants what styles are selling at what rate in each part of the country. They can give advice about the styles that might prove to be best for each store and when they should be offered. They can also give the buyer helpful details about ways other stores have presented similar merchandise and what the results have been.

RESEARCH STUDIES AND SURVEYS. Individual manufacturers, industry associations, publications, and government agencies occasionally conduct research studies in which consumers are polled about what they want to buy, where and when they prefer to buy, and their reasons for buying or not buying. The purposes of these surveys are varied, but each contributes some useful information about customer buying patterns.

One typical survey was made by a foundation and lingerie producer to ascertain ages, heights, weights, and dress sizes of customers. This survey also gathered information about the kinds of foundations, lingerie, and sleepwear customers preferred.

CONSUMER AND TRADE PUBLICATIONS. Fashion merchants obtain insights into consumer demand from publications—both those that are intended for the general public and those intended for readers within some specific sector of the fashion business.

Fashion news is reported in almost all consumer newspapers and magazines. Merchants keep track of this news. They also follow the fashion advertising in such publications, so that they will know what influences may be creating or discouraging demand for certain fashion products among their customers. Magazines that give special emphasis to fashion, such as *Vogue, Harper's Bazaar,* and *Elle,* or to fashions for specific groups of customers, such as *Glamour* or *Mademoiselle,* make considerable efforts to keep fashion merchants informed about the merchandise to be featured in future editions. These publications also can provide merchants with assessments of fashion trends among particular segments of the public and with information about how merchants can best influence them. Many consumer magazines spend enormous amounts of money on research in order to know their readers better. They are usually more than willing to share these studies with merchants.

One type of survey used regularly by some consumer magazines and sporadically by others determines how many of certain items their readers buy per year and what they pay for each.

Trade publications are expert in assessing fashion and market developments. Some of these publications are directed primarily at retailers, telling them what merchandise is new and good, and how stores are promoting it successfully. Examples are *Body Fashion/Intimate Apparel, Fashion Accessories, Jewelers' Circular-Keystone,* and *Footwear News.* Others, like *Women's Wear Daily,* address themselves to all branches of an industry, from the retailers to the primary sources of materials used in manufacturing the products concerned. From both types of trade publications, a fashion buyer can get a highly professional assessment of consumer demand and the influences that are being exerted upon it.

REPORTING SERVICES. Retailers can subscribe to many services to keep up-to-date on store happenings, ideas, trends, and market news. For example, Retail News Bureau supplies regular reports on the ads run by New York stores. Its other services include market forecasts, hot-item bulletins, general market news, a merchants' newsletter, and a variety of other bulletins and news releases about women's apparel and accessories. Another example is the *Fashion Calendar,* published weekly and available on a subscription basis. It lists and gives details about all important fashion events. The same source also publishes a monthly fashion newsletter for retail executives called *Fashion International.* Similar market information is also available on a fee basis from Tobé Associates, Inc., one of the older services in the field.

FASHION CONSULTANTS. Independent fashion consultants sell their expertise to merchants to supplement that of a firm's own executives. Fashion consultants may be hired by merchants on a regular retainer basis or to assist with a single project. Some consultants specialize in certain areas of fashion, while others offer a wide range of fashion services. Most of these experts have had years of experience in the fashion business.

Customer Advisory Groups

A third source of useful information for retailers is supplied by various customer groups organized by some stores. These groups give retailers a consumer's point of view of store policies, services, assortments, and fashions. In addition, they assure the store of a flow of favorable publicity among the circles in which group members move. If group members or their activities are considered newsworthy, they also provide the store with publicity in the news media.

College boards, composed of selected college students, and **teen boards,** which involve leading high school students or DECA (Distributive Education Clubs of America) members, also serve as customer advisory groups for stores that carry clothes for those age groups. Career women, the newest special group to be identified, are also increasingly sought for membership on advisory boards.

Retailers now realize that the ranks of working women are going to swell in the next decade. In fact, stores such as Alcott and Andrews, Incorporated and Streets & Co., both based in New York City, whose entire stock of merchandise is devoted to the career woman, have been established during the mid-1980s. This extremely valuable market has placed its demands for recognition squarely in front of the country's retailers, who have responded with new departments and promotional programs.

References

1 Paul H. Nystrom, *Economics of Consumption,* Ronald Press, New York, 1929, p. iii.
2 Richard L. Lynch et al., *Introduction to Marketing,* Gregg Division, McGraw-Hill Book Company, New York, 1984, p. 61.
3 Melvin T. Copeland, *Principles of Merchandising,* A. W. Shaw Company, New York, 1924, pp. 155–167.

4 John G. Udell, "A New Approach to Consumer Motivation," *Journal of Retailing,* 40: 6–10, Winter, 1964–65; pp. 8–9.
5 Based on John W. Wingate and Joseph S. Frielander, *The Management of Retail Buying,* Second Edition, Prentice-Hall, Inc., Englewood Cliffs, N.J., 1978, p. 92.

Buying Vocabulary

Define or briefly explain the following terms:

Behavioral segmentation

Buying motivation

College boards

Customer demand

Demographic segmentation

Geographic segmentation

Markdowns

Market segmentation

Operational satisfactions

Patronage motives

Psychological satisfactions

Psychographic segmentation

Reporting services

Resident buying office

Selection factors

Store image

Target market

Teen boards

Want slips

Buying Review

1. Why is it important to identify your customers?
2. What is meant by "customer segmentation"?
3. Why do customers buy?
4. How can you encourage your target customers to buy from your store(s)?
5. What types of stores might attract customers from the top five social classes?
6. Is it possible for your selection of merchandise to be just what the customer requires?
7. What sources, within the store, are available to determine customer preferences?
8. Are there sources outside the store that can provide information about customer preferences? What are these outside sources?
9. How do customer advisory groups help you decide on your merchandise assortments?
10. What, in your opinion, is the best single source of in-store information?

11. Why are the in-store information sources the best?
12. If you have effectively interpreted the customer demand, what can be the optimum results of this knowledge?

Buying Case

Congratulations, you have been selected as a buyer for a moderate-priced sportswear shop. You will be going to buy your first selection of merchandise for the next season in 45 days.

Before going to market please prepare for your merchandise manager a segmented analysis of your customers and a list of the special occasions, holidays, and special sales events planned for the next season.   Fall 1989

Indicate the in-store sources of customer preference information neccesary to aid you in your buying.

Report on your competitors' selection of current moderate-priced sportswear.

What is the Career Women's Advisory Board suggesting for the next season's sportswear assortment?

Feb → July   6.mo.
Aug → Jan   6 mo.

Chapter 3

Developing a Fashion Image

When you hear the name Neiman-Marcus, what image comes to your mind? Exclusive merchandise? Plush surroundings? High prices? Shopping with the *haute couture* crowd?

The character or personality of Neiman-Marcus in the eyes of the public is called its store image. Store image is not reserved for exclusive stores such as Neiman-Marcus. All stores, regardless of what they sell, have a store image. Your local variety store may have the image of a store with friendly salespeople, reasonable prices, and a limited selection of just about any household item you might need.

Any store that sells fashion merchandise has a **fashion image,** which reflects the store's fashion reputation in the eyes of the public. There is no simple formula for developing what could be considered a favorable fashion image. An image that is seen as favorable by one store may be considered totally unacceptable by another.

A store's fashion image is not something that can be "created" by the store's management team and presented to the public for admiration. It is a give-and-take effort, and the customers are definitely a part of the image-creating process. At each step of the process they either approve or disapprove of the store's decisions by "casting their votes" in the form of purchases.

In this chapter we will look briefly at each of the factors that work together to make up a store's fashion image: the store's understanding of its target customers, its **merchandising policies** (established methods of doing business on such matters as price range and quality stan-

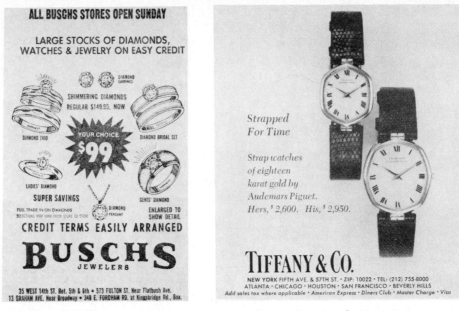

A store's image tells customers what to expect. Contrasting store images are reflected in these ads.

dards), its sales promotion and selling techniques, and the atmosphere created by the store's design, layout, and decor. Then we will examine the techniques that have been used by a number of different stores to change their image, and the image-building tools frequently used by various sizes and types of organizations.

Identifying Target Customers

Before a store can create a successful fashion image, it must understand its target customer group—those people it wants to attract as customers. In Chapter 2 you learned that there are a variety of techniques that a store can use to identify its target customer group. After they have been successfully identified, the store relates its merchandising policies, promotion decor, selling techniques, services,

participation in community affairs, and even its housekeeping to that target customer it seeks to serve. Elegant fashion merchandise cannot be offered against a background of dusty displays and untidy fitting rooms, nor do customers expect to find bargain-priced shirts or skirts where many thousands of dollars have been spent on a dramatic fashion decor.

Homogeneous Target Groups

Stores serving areas in which the preferences of potential customers are fairly similar tend to adopt somewhat similar fashion images, but stores with diversified target groups to choose from have a wide range of fashion image possibilities open to them. For instance, a small town in which a university is located probably would have two basic customer groups— the younger university students and the more adult faculty and townspeople.

A small city serving as the only metropolitan center in a large geographic area, and with limited business and industrial interests, would likely be dominated by people who have fairly similar general interests and thus form a homogeneous target group of customers.

Diversified Target Groups

In large metropolitan areas, however, the diversity of business and industrial interests and of lifestyle create a number of different customer groups to be served, each with distinct and separate needs and wants. A sampling of some of the fashion images projected by stores in the New York City area shows how diverse that variety can be.

Macy's New York, which has had the distinction of being the "world's largest department store" for many years, made a tremendous change in its image a little more than a decade ago. What was once the famous budget basement became The Cellar, stocked with exciting, innovative merchandise for kitchen and bath. This change was the first of many throughout the entire store. Macy's had changed its image to attract a new group of target customers: young, working, married or single New Yorkers, who find the merchandise in The Cellar tailored to their wants and needs. Macy's also changed its assortments of fashion ready-to-wear to project an image of youth and excitement at a moderate price. The scope and size of the store and the merchandise assortments presented to the customer since the change of image have been large and varied, but always tailored to the new target customer.

Henri Bendel has become a classic example of a very different kind of store, devoted to the concept that "small is beautiful." The store's target customers are small-sized, and eager for fashions in the early stages of their cycles. Bendel's has been the leader in introducing sizes 1 and 2 into fashion apparel. It has been the first to present certain unique and intriguing designs from such designers as Zandra Rhodes and Jean Muir of London and Stephen Burrows of the United States.

The Lane Bryant stores serve women of all ages who have fuller figures. The store assures these target customers that whatever the fashion, Lane Bryant will have it in their sizes.

Bloomingdale's, or "Bloomie's" as it is affectionately known by its customers, is an outstanding example of a store that has determined who its target customer would be and successfully tailored its fashion image to this customer. Young, trendy, upper-income customers consider Bloomingdale's an innovator for all types of fashion-influenced merchandise. Furniture, home furnishings, and gourmet foods are areas other than fashion ready-to-wear in which Bloomingdale's projects a fashion leadership image to its target customer. Many people are surprised to learn that for the first 75 years it was in business, Bloomingdale's was a price-conscious, bargain-basement type of store catering to lower-income customers who were certainly not fashion-conscious. With careful planning, Bloomingdale's evolved from this less-than-distinctive beginning to its current position as the fashion leader for the "in crowd."

The Lerner chain once determined that its target customers wanted fashions at their peak, and this was the image conveyed to customers by Lerner stores across the country. When print fabric skirts were popular, Lerner's offered its customers print skirts in every available print, color, and size. When classic blouses were wanted, Lerner's stocked them in every possible color and size. Lerner was purchased in 1984 by The Limited, a large merchandising chain, and is changing its image. Lerner's is becoming known for spotting new, young, trendy merchandise.

Each store or group of stores in these examples develops its own character through such things as merchandise assortments, decor, advertising, and display. It would not be difficult, given the descriptions above and time in which to inspect these stores and review their assortments and advertising, for someone completely new to the city to identify the image of each by its merchandise, its ads, its windows, and the behavior of the sales staff. Not only is the merchandise different in each store but the atmosphere is different. Each store has developed the atmosphere most natural and most comfortable to the target group of customers that the store wants to attract.

Establishing the Store's Merchandising Policies

When the target customer group has been clearly identified, the store management must consider many essential elements in establishing merchandising policies:

☐ Price range offerings—high, moderate, low, or very lowest
☐ Quality standards—finest available, serviceable, unspecified quality, or imperfect
☐ Breadth and depth of assortment—narrow and deep or broad and shallow
☐ Brand offerings—private, national, or unbranded
☐ Exclusivity—emphasized or not emphasized
☐ Fashion leadership—fashion leader, middle-of-the-road, or fashion follower
☐ Maintenance of basic assortments—always in stock, usually in stock, or basic stock unimportant

Each of these policy decisions must be in harmony with the character or image the store wishes to create and maintain. But just as the policies are aimed at the target group of customers, so the policies themselves determine the groups that will patronize the store. These policy decisions are made by the top management of a retail company. In the giant companies, the board of directors, presidents, and vice presidents make them; in smaller retail companies, it is usually the owner—but no matter how large or small the company, the buyer's job is to *follow* these policies and make them work to the best advantage of the company. Buyers should never make or change store merchandising policies on their own. It is only through the complete adherence, in every department, to these policies that a company builds and maintains its desired image.

Price Range Offerings

Since consumer income is a major factor in market segmentation, pricing policies are very much a part of a store's strategy to attract targeted customers. Although there is no direct correlation between prices and quality (since often the most serviceable quality is not the most expensive), price ranges do generally equate with quality standards. A "top quality" policy is usually associated with high price lines, whereas "serviceable" quality standards generally impose a limit on the bottom price lines to be carried. Stores which emphasize the lowest prices available generally do not set quality standards since goods at the very lowest price lines are likely to be shoddy.

A further factor in determining pricing policies relates to the nature of the business the top managers have decided to establish—for example, will it be a fashion leader with "traditional" prices or will it emphasize "underselling"?

A discounting price policy will, of necessity, affect the merchandise to be bought, the customer services to be offered, the layout of the store, the type of advertising to be run, and all other activities within the store. Thus the pricing policies which are set by top management impose limitations on merchandisers' freedom in many other policy areas.

Quality Standards

The merchandise to be carried can be a product of the finest available materials and workmanship, can embody the most serviceable quality consistent with low price lines, or can conform to a set of standards in between. In prestige stores, for example, durability of merchandise may be a minor consideration but fineness of materials and care in workmanship are usually of major importance. Stores emphasizing bargain prices may have no set standards of quality other than that the goods be represented honestly. Store policies may also exclude anything except perfect goods or, depending upon its clientele, may permit "irregulars" to be offered in special promotions.

Depth and Breadth of Assortment

There are two types of (fashion) assortments used by retailers. One is known as "narrow and deep" and the other as "broad and shallow." A **narrow and deep assortment** is one in which there is a relatively limited number of styles, but those that are selected are stocked in all available sizes and colors. A **broad and shallow assortment** is one in which there is a wide variety of styles, but only limited sizes and colors are carried in each style. Since space and money are major limitations, a policy of broad assortments usu-

The broad and shallow assortment shown at the top includes a wide variety of styles, but limited sizes and colors are carried in each one. The display at the bottom reflects a narrow and deep assortment. There are not many styles, but those that are offered are stocked in all available sizes and colors.

ally limits the average depth to which items can be stocked and conversely, if depth is desired, variety must be limited.

Broad-shallow assortments presenting a large range of styles, colors, and sizes, but not a large stock of any of these, are fairly characteristic of prestige stores and departments. In stores catering to the middle group of customers, assortments are usually broad and shallow early in the season when new styles are being tested, but relatively narrow and deep later in the season, once the trend of demand has become clear. Mass merchandisers concentrate on narrow-deep assortments of proven popular styles. Some large stores, with the space to carry wide assortments, may have broad-shallow stocks in the outer fringes of demand and narrow-deep stocks where demand is clearly defined.

Brand Offerings

A **brand** is a name, trademark, or logo which is used to identify the products of a specific maker or seller and to differentiate them from those of the competition. Some brands or names—especially those that are sold at very high prices—have become associated with status symbols.

TYPES OF BRAND OFFERINGS. There are several types of branded offerings that can be sold by each store: national, private (or store), signature, and designer. These are often referred to as "labels."

A **national brand** is one which identifies the producer of that product and is generally found in many stores across the country. National brands for blue jeans, such as Levi's, Lee, and Wrangler, can give stores and customers alike a consistent standard of quality and are the backbone of the jeans assortments in many stores. Hanes for hosiery, Lark for luggage, Cole of California for swimwear and

Nike for athletic footwear are all examples of famous national brands that have special appeal for many types of customers.

A **private** (or store) **brand** is one that meets the standards of the retail store where it is sold. Some stores offer private label products that are of better quality than products with national brands and are sold at comparable prices. Others sell comparable products at more reasonable prices. Private label merchandise may also be an effective way of achieving exclusivity for certain products. One means for doing this is through a **signature brand,** which is private label merchandise that has been endorsed by a well-known personality. This person is someone that the store believes to be influential with the store's target group of customers.

A **designer brand** is one that is associated with a "name" designer such as Oscar de la Renta, Bill Blass, or Diane Von Furstenberg. For many customers these designer names have a value quite distinct from the intrinsic value of the products themselves. But the names of some fashion designers have become so well known that they can almost be considered national brands.

Unbranded merchandise is the type that is sold without a label of established significance. Often there is no manufacturer's name on the label. Customers who buy this merchandise do so because of the reputation of the retailers who offer it or because of the price appeal, appearance, or fit of the merchandise itself.

USE OF BRAND OFFERINGS BY STORES. Traditionally, prestige stores tended to feature both their own labels and designer labels, department stores featured nationally branded merchandise, and mass merchandisers featured either unbranded merchandise or private label merchandise. In the early and middle 1980s many

Allen Solly is a private-label line found in the Sanger Harris stores. The same stores also have departments featuring designer brands like the Liz Claiborne department shown on the right.

department stores, mass merchandisers, and even discount stores began using brand offerings as a means of upgrading store image.

Spiegel, the fourth largest mail-order company in the country, was once known as a store that featured polyester pull-on pants and supplied refrigerators to *Let's Make a Deal*. It evolved into a leader in the high-fashion catalog business when management successfully negotiated with top designers such as Liz Claiborne, Ralph Lauren, Anne Klein, and Perry Ellis, who agreed to appear in the catalog. At the same time they changed their target market group from rural mail-order customers to fashion-conscious, sophisticated working women who have money to spend on fashion goods.

After Spiegel had built confidence in itself as a fashion catalog house, it was able to introduce its own private label fashion goods. The new image attracted people who were willing to buy from the "new" Spiegel because of the store's fashion image and not because of the designer names in the catalog.

In a later section of this chapter we will examine the ways in which brand offerings helped to change the fashion image of several other stores.

Exclusivity

All stores would like to feature exclusive products, but this goal is often very hard to attain. It is most difficult to keep manufacturers' lines and styles out of a competitor's stock since the lifeline of most manufacturers is the broad distribution of their products. For most stores, the policy is to carry nationally distributed merchandise along with their own private brands which measure up to national brands in all respects except nationally known identification and sometimes price.

ATTAINING EXCLUSIVITY. Some retailers consider exclusives so important that their buyers are expected to work with producers toward this end. A store may attain exclusive products in several ways:

☐ By prevailing upon vendors to confine one or more styles exclusively to their store within their trading area for a given period of time.
☐ By becoming the sole agent within their trading area for new young designers.
☐ By buying domestically or abroad from sources of supply not yet tapped by competitors.
☐ By buying from producers who will manufacture goods (usually in very large quantity) to the buyer's private design and other specifications.
☐ By associating with a resident buying office that is able to negotiate exclusive licensing for its member stores. (This type of arrangement is enjoyed by Frederick Atkins stores through an exclusive license with Christian Aujard.)

IMAGE BUILDING THROUGH EXCLUSIVITY. Both Sears and K mart have creatively combined the image-building benefits of brand offerings with exclusivity. The Cheryl Tiegs Collection for Sears and the Jaclyn Smith Collection for K mart feature "signature" labels that are exclusive with their respective stores.

The Sears agreement with Cheryl Tiegs was closely followed by a concentrated effort to bring a fashion image to the Sears catalog. This effort included television commercials devoted specifically to telling fashion-oriented women who were not originally a part of their target market group that the Sears catalog was an important source of fashion for them. In support of this claim, actress Stephanie Powers was the featured model on the catalog cover and on several pages of the catalog. In the same issue of the catalog, the store introduced its "first true designer collection" of men's fashions—Boston Athletic Club by Gil Truedsson.

K mart entered the licensing agreements for these exclusive Jaclyn Smith offerings with its own target customer groups in mind. They conducted carefully structured customer research and found that Smith evoked the all-American image that their customers identified with. Signing Smith was the first step in building a fashion image for the store. Their objective was to convince customers who were already loyal K mart customers that the store was also a source of quality fashion merchandise.

Fashion Leadership

Timing in the introduction of new fashions is a vital element of policy. All current styles move in and out of the fashion limelight. This movement, called the **fashion cycle,** refers to the rise, the wide popularity or acceptance by masses of people, and then the decline in the acceptance of that style while a new style is emerging to attract the buying public. These waves of fashion importance of certain styles swell and recede, but they do not follow each other in regular order. Some ripple in and ebb quickly while others have a sudden surge and remain at a peak for a substantial period of time before they lose their appeal. A store must determine what role it wishes to play—whether to undertake fashion leadership, to be a close second, or to wait until new trends have become widely accepted fashions. Naturally, the store's role must be directly related to the targeted customers' concept of what is fashionable.

The distinctive image of Banana Republic involves careful coordination of merchandise selection, display, and advertising in newspapers and catalogs.

Focus

The Forgotten Woman: Big Really Can Be Beautiful

Anyone who thinks that fashion stops at size 12 should think again. Or ask retailer Nancye Radmin, who will surely tell you that just because a woman may be on the large side does not mean she does not want to look her best. It is on that premise that Radmin started and built a growing chain of Forgotten Woman stores—specifically for women size 16 and larger.

It all began in 1977, when Radmin (a size 6) had a baby boy and gained 80 pounds. She went looking for clothes in her new size of 16 to 18, and she was frustrated and furious to find none—"no gabardine wool pants, no cashmere sweaters," she said[1]—nothing but polyester pantsuits. So she went home, asked her husband for a loan of $10,000, and set out to create her own clothing store to cater to other "forgotten women" like herself.

Targeting that specific segment of the population and building a fashion image for the store was not easy. Not because there weren't plenty of willing customers around; on the contrary, studies show that about 30 million American women, or one in three, now fit into a size 16 or larger. And those women are estimated to spend around $8 billion a year on clothing, four times what they spent in 1978.

The problem Radmin faced was in finding suppliers for clothes that fit the stylish look she knew her customers wanted. Most of the top designers refused even to think of having their names associated with wider garments, and many traditional apparel manufacturers had simply never dipped their toes into the big market. So Radmin proceeded to have clothing specially tailored to her own specifications and designed for the fashion-conscious larger customer. The stores' assortment now includes items ranging from a $49 T-shirt to a $16,000 fur coat.

As Radmin's Forgotten Woman stores have grown (there are now a dozen of them, from New York to Washington to Florida, and doing about $20 million a year in sales), so has the concept of providing fashion for big women. Both Macy's and Bloomingdale's have expanded their large-size departments, and Lane Bryant has upgraded its merchandise.

> But there are still customers who are looking for fashion in bigger sizes and who are lured by the image Radmin has cultivated. "This woman flew in from Cleveland," Radmin related, "had her driver park the limo outside the store, came in and shopped, got back in the limo, drove to the airport, and flew back to Cleveland. She couldn't get what she needed there. So she came here."[2]

1 N. R. Kleinfield, "Making Size 22 Posh and Profitable," *The New York Times,* October 6, 1985, p. D-1.
2 Ibid.

Regardless of type or size, fashion direction is needed in all stores to establish a fashion image that reflects the degree of fashion expertise the store seeks to project.

Although the degree of fashion leadership that retailers choose to assume represents one of many possibilities, fashion images tend to fall into three loosely defined categories:

1. Retailers who elect to cater to customers who want to be in the forefront of fashion seek leadership by featuring new and prophetic styles, designer names, and high-quality merchandise. There are fewer of these stores than of other types because the percentage of customers who can afford to buy high-quality, high-priced merchandise is relatively small. For example, Saks Fifth Avenue defines its average customer as having an income between $30,000 and $50,000 a year, a group that makes up only 10 percent of the total population.

2. Retailers whose fashion images fall midway between the leaders and the followers aim to attract middle-income consumers who accept a new fashion as its popularity grows. Retailers such as these are the most numerous because they cater to the largest segment of the population. However, some middle-of-the-road fashion image retailers are so large and sell to such a broad range of the public that a wide range of fashion can often be found in their stores. Their large size permits them to establish specialized departments or units which aim to attract customers who are interested in the newest fashions.

3. At the lower end of the price and fashion scale are the retailers who focus on widely accepted and proven fashions at a bargain price or off-price from better makers. New looks in fashion reach these stores later than the others and are generally bought from mass producers of lower-priced merchandise.

The degree of fashion leadership will affect the type of media and advertisements used by the sales promotion division. If the policy is to emphasize bargains, there may be numerous price promotions in mass media and general assurances that the store will not be undersold. Merchandising policies therefore affect almost every activity of the business so that the image or character presented to the public is consistent throughout.

Maintenance of Basic Stock

An item of merchandise is described as **basic stock** if it enjoys such consistent demand that it should be in stock in a complete range of sizes and colors throughout the year or season. Even fashion departments must carry certain basic stock items. Management in some high-fashion stores consider basic stock an unnecesary restriction on their buyers' ability to obtain the most fashionable offerings for their target group of customers. Managers in other stores consider the maintenance of basic stock a service to their target group of customers, who expect to find such items as women's pantyhose in neutral shades, black cocktail dresses, and men's white dress shirts in stock at all times. In Chapter 6 these merchandising policies are applied to the planning of the store's fashion assortment.

Identifying Sales Promotion and Selling Techniques

Sales promotion and personal selling techniques are both important factors in creating and maintaining a store's fashion image. If they are planned correctly, these factors can turn the target group of consumers into loyal customers.

Stores known for their fashion leadership are usually the first to introduce new trends, either in styling or in color. The ads that these stores run emphasize new themes and looks, and both window and interior displays reinforce these themes and looks. When possible, designer names are featured, exclusives are introduced, and fashion newness is underlined. It is very rare that price becomes a focal point in any of these ads or displays.

Stores whose target customers seek fashions at the peak of their cycles avoid extremes in styles or themes in their advertising. In general, their advertising and display stress the fashion rightness of the promoted styles rather than the newness. Price is given prominence only to the degree that it is important to the particular group of customers.

Stores in the mass-merchandising category give strong prominence to price in their advertising. Since the fashion leaders and the middle group have already proved the importance of the fashions concerned, these stores concentrate on promoting their availability at budget prices. Their assortments usually contain large quantities of nearly identical merchandise, thus reinforcing the idea that a particular fashion has made its mark. In Chapter 15 you will learn more about the advertising techniques that are used by fashion stores.

Selling techniques are keyed to the fashion image the store wants to project in much the same way. In prestige stores, salespeople are coached to speak with authority about fashion, to present new ideas with confidence, and to give full service to the customer. Salespeople in department stores and mass merchandise stores must also be knowledgeable about fashion.

Many experts believe it is at the point of sale that a store either succeeds or fails in its attempt to establish a particular fashion image—and that the salespeople are the key to that success or failure. The explanation by Herbert Wittkin, former Allied Stores executive, still holds true:

We can spend literally millions of dollars in merchandise investments; we can spend many millions more on display and merchandise presentation and advertising; we can spend unlimited energy and time trying to influence people to think well of us—only to have it all go down the drain because of a surly sales clerk. . . . Our salespeople talk to our customers and convey a feeling with everything they do—in the way they look— the way they smile—the way they shrug their shoulders—in short, they project our image more forcefully than any other element in the store. If they are warm, friendly, alert, fashionable, efficient people, our customers make the equation that our store is all of those things. If they are brusque, short-tempered, curt, unpleasant, their impact is deadly and frequently permanently damaging . . .[1]

In Chapter 16 you will learn more about the personal selling techniques that can either make or break a store's fashion image.

Creating a Fashion Image Through Store Atmosphere

Store layout, store design, fixtures, lighting, mannequins, merchandise arrangement, and display can all work together to create an atmosphere that either supports or detracts from the fashion image you are trying to create for your store. The carefully coordinated effort that encompasses these functions is called **visual merchandising.** It can be defined as the presentation of merchandise and services to their best selling advantage for maximum customer acceptance. In Chapter 14 we will discuss how visual merchandising is used to support desired store image.

Changing a Fashion Image

Stores sometimes find it either necessary or advantageous to shift their sights and to aim for a different target group of customers from the one for which their fashion image was originally created. Such a change may be necessary if the character of the community the store serves undergoes a marked change. Such change may be advantageous if the store wants to reach out for additional groups of customers not previously served, or to fill a mer-

chandising need temporarily left unfilled by competing stores, or even to retreat from a merchandising area in which the competition has become too fierce.

The classic case of the necessity to change an image is that of the neighborhood store whose original customers have moved out of the area and have been replaced by people of other income or ethnic groups. If the store is to continue to do business at its old location, it must adjust its fashion image to attract the new potential clientele flowing into the area. If, on the other hand, the store wants to retain its original image, it must move to a different area where it can find enough customers of the original type to support it.

Image-Changing Techniques

Changing an image, once it has been established, is not easy and should be a gradual process. In fact, it is more difficult to change an image than to build one from the start. Building an image can sometimes be done in a relatively short period of time, while some stores that have successfully changed their image have taken a decade or more to complete the process. Image changing should be evolutionary, not revolutionary. If you are not successful in reaching your newly targeted customers, a too-drastic change may cause you to lose your regular customers and suffer a reduced volume. J. C. Penney attempted in 1983 to transform its stores from a "drab, middle-market retailer" into an upscale retailer with more name brands and some expensive designer clothes. By late 1985, sales had declined substantially. Some Penney executives were worried that some long-time Penney customers were lost. However, William R. Howell, Penney's chairman, acknowledged that the change was traumatic, but that they (the executives) believed they would eventually show positive results.[2] Changes in fashion merchandise assortments, in promotion and advertising techniques, in quality standards, and in pricing all help to gradually change an image and permit a store to replace customers it has lost or no longer wishes to serve with new customers. The trick is to retain enough of the old customers while courting new ones to maintain volume and avoid losses.

Image-Changing Examples

Among the stores that have initiated carefully planned programs to change their fashion images are J. C. Penney, Carson Pirie Scott, Barneys, Weiboldt's, and Neiman-Marcus.

J. C. PENNEY. At one time J.C. Penney was perceived by potential customers as a discount store. In a mammoth effort to upgrade this image, they launched a five-year, billion-dollar campaign to modernize their stores. This was accomplished by the upgrading of their branded merchandise to include such names as Halston, Santa Cruz, Lee Wright, and Stafford, and the introduction of a $22 million-plus advertising campaign.

Penney's used the theme "There's a change in Penney's because there's a change in you," emphasizing that it was not abandoning its old target customers in favor of new, more fashion-oriented ones. Instead, it was addressing the new needs and wants of its already loyal customers.

CARSON PIRIE SCOTT. Chicago-based Carson's could be described as having had an "inferiority complex" next to Marshall Field. In a carefully designed program to improve the fashion image of Carson's, top managers first placed a major emphasis on customer service. Then they launched a 50,000-square-foot Corporate Level in the remodeled basement of their flagship store. Tailored to the needs and wants of executive and professional women, the Corporate Level provides a separate entrance to the store, features 7:30 a.m. to 7:30 p.m. hours, and offers a variety of apparel, gifts, luggage, stationery, books, and magazines found in no other department in the store. And in keeping with their emphasis on customer service, the Corporate Level offers the services of a florist, wardrobe consultant, beauty salon, shoe repair, dry cleaning, watch repair, quick print, ticket master, monogramming, executive delivery service, and take-out/eat-in salad, cheese, and wine area. The Corporate Level Board Room features special events for executive women and is available for use by customers who elect to join the Corporate Level Club.

BARNEYS. Barneys New York, well known as a menswear store, decided to change its image by venturing one step at a time into women's wear. Located on 17th Street and Seventh Avenue, Barneys was many blocks from the midtown area where most fashionable stores are located. Through a well-thought-out plan, management began introducing women's fashions into the store nine years before its major move into the women's wear field. Devoting two of its seven floors to women at that time, it developed an image apart from that of other Manhattan retailers by importing 80 percent of the women's merchandise. After nine successful years, management decided to devote a full 70,000 square feet of additional selling space to women. This additional space "rewarded" women for traveling all the way to Barneys by featuring free parking, a cosmetics department, a restaurant, and

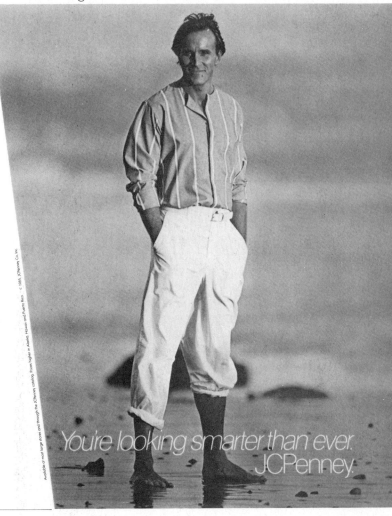

The Wright Attitude

Coty Award Winner Lee Wright: "Do you know what you'll like most about my clothes? You can be yourself in them. In my spring sportswear collection everything works together. The colors. The patterns. Even the textures. This means you can put together great-looking outfits that express your individuality, not mine. That's my idea of fashion." Slacks $35. Shirt $32.

Available at most large stores and through the JCPenney catalog. Prices higher in Alaska, Hawaii and Puerto Rico. © 1985, JCPenney Co, Inc.

You're looking smarter than ever. JCPenney.

To change its image, J.C. Penney launched a $22 million plus advertising campaign with a theme that emphasized that Penney's was not abandoning its old target customers. Rather, it was addressing their new needs and wants.

an enlarged version of the already popular Chelsea Passage gift shop. Print advertising featured a single model dressed in designer clothes moving across the page with a simple advertising message stressing both the merchandise and the services offered by the store.

WIEBOLDT'S. For most of its 101 years the Chicago-based Wieboldt's department store chain consisted of neighborhood stores that concentrated on blue-collar families. With the opening of Neiman-Marcus and Bloomingdale's and the addition at Carson Pirie Scott of the Corporate Level, Wieboldt's felt that its efforts were being overlooked. But rather than join the movement away from its blue-collar target customer group, Wieboldt's capitalized on the distinction of being the only department store that actively targeted the blue-collar market. Management changed the complete advertising program, introduced the slogan "Watch Wieboldt's", broadened its brand offerings into more fashionable merchandise to attract some young career women, and added more private label merchandise.

NEIMAN-MARCUS. Dallas-based Neiman-Marcus certainly had no need to upgrade its store image as many other stores did. Nevertheless, the store joined others in initiating a carefully planned program to broaden its customer base. The customers it was targeting were those people who did not buy *couture* but were shopping at higher price points for somewhat less exclusive fashions at competing stores.

The plan to attract a broader target customer group included the introduction of a large collection of private label merchandise priced somewhat lower than the *couture* merchandise. Included in the selection were shoes, women's sportswear, and men's sport coats, suits, and tuxedos. The broadening of its customer base was done carefully, however, in order not to dilute their highly successful fashion image.

Image-Building Tools Used by Various-Size Stores

While the examples in the preceding section give you an idea of the types of tools that can be used to change and/or build a fashion image, these are specific isolated examples. In the following section we will examine the image-building tools that are typical of large stores, small independents, and chain organizations.

The Giants

Giant retailers have special image considerations because of their size. Some of them sell to such a broad range of the public that they need to segment their overall image, presenting one face to those customers who are fashion leaders and another to those who are fashion followers. They often handle this through special departments or shops, each one establishing an image for a specific group of customers: teens, tall girls, expectant mothers, sport enthusiasts, wearers of country clothes, and career or college people. Giant retailers also represent buyer power since by dint of their large orders they are able to obtain better prices, take earlier deliveries of the newest fashions, and make direct import purchases at lower costs. The huge size of such stores permits them to engage in shop merchandising, whereas smaller stores, with more limited floor space and assortments, cannot set up such shops quite so freely.

Large stores often capitalize on their bigness. They stage promotions on a spectacular scale. Instead of devoting one or two windows to a new fashion, they devote block-long batteries of windows to an idea. They hire display executives who are highly creative and whose windows and interior displays are remembered for years. They turn their main floors into flower shows, as Macy's in New York City, and Hess Brothers in Allentown, Pennsylvania, do each spring. Or they regularly run ads that stress the vastness of their assortments.

Many large stores have special facilities, such as auditoriums, that they lend to civic groups for community events. Often the auditorium is used by the store for a fashion show or demonstration that is expected to draw large crowds.

The Small Independent

At the opposite end of the size scale is the small, independently owned shop in which the proprietor is likely to be the merchandiser, policymaker, and promotion expert. Such stores, even though they may employ several salespeople, cannot afford and may not need the amount of advertising that large stores use to enhance their image.

Small operations have their own special tools for image building, based on the personal approach. Salespeople and proprietors know customers by name, they suggest apparel to coordinate with what is already owned, and they send personal notes to customers when new merchandise of suitable type has arrived. They have coins readily available for parking meters, they gift wrap beautifully and individually, and they provide innumerable friendly, person-to-person services that cannot be offered practically by large stores.

In their merchandising, some small stores can capitalize on their smallness. They can be more flexible in their purchases, catch early fashion trends, and out-merchandise larger, less mobile operations. For example, Lina-Lee, a small high-priced specialty shop chain, has intimate knowledge of each of its regular customers and can service them whenever new garments that meet their demands arrive. They buy only a few pieces, or even single pieces, of a style. The customer who purchases a dress or coat from such a store can be certain that she will not meet herself on the street, at the bus stop, or at the club luncheon.

Chain Organizations

Units of apparel chains and general merchandising chains often use the image-building tools of both large and small stores. Among the large-store techniques a general merchandise chain could use, for example, might be the establishment of special shops within its stores to feature a particular look, such as country casuals. Or an apparel chain may create a series of ads and promotions devoted to the special needs of its customers, no matter in what part of the country they are located.

Other chains find ways to offer some of the personalized service characteristic of small stores. Salespeople may be encouraged to obtain customers' names for notification of special sales or new merchandise. Although the merchandise in one unit of a chain may not differ markedly from what is offered by another unit of the same organization, it is possible for the staff of each unit to develop warm, friendly relations with customers. In this way, all customers feel they are receiving personal attention and advice when making fashion purchases.

References

1 Herbert Wittkin, "An Image Is a Multi-Faceted Thing," *Readings in Modern Retailing,* National Retail Merchants Association, New York, 1969, p. 230.
2 Hank Gilman and Steve Weiner, "Penney's Plan to Tap Upscale Market So Far Is Failing to Improve Earnings," *The Wall Street Journal,* August 28, 1985, p. 4.

Buying Vocabulary

Define or briefly explain the following terms:

Basic stock

Brand

Broad and shallow assortments

Designer brand

Fashion cycle

Fashion image

Merchandising policies

Narrow and deep assortments

National brand

Private brand

Signature brand

Unbranded merchandise

Visual merchandising

Buying Review

1. Why is it important to target your customers?
2. Explain why you must establish price range offerings.
3. What is meant by quality standards?
4. How can the store policy affect your assortments?
5. When are "broad-shallow" assortments appropriate?
6. Do narrow-deep stocks have a place in your planning? Why?
7. How do you obtain "exclusive fashions"? Why?
8. What is the importance of fashion leadership?
9. Should a fashion image be changed rapidly? Why or why not?
10. Describe briefly how Barneys New York changed its image.
11. Is the principle that "image change must be evolutionary, not revolutionary" correct? Why?

Buying Case

You are the buyer for a new suit department in the women's wear division of your store. You are asked to develop merchandise ideas to promote your department. Tell how you would feature and help promote suits for professional and executive customers. Prepare suggestions to management for appealing to affluent career women. What merchandising policies could you follow to beat your competition?

Chapter 4

Retail Organization and the Buyer's Responsibility

Within every business, the arrangement of work and the people who do that work should be clearly defined. This arrangement is referred to as the **organizational structure** of the business, and it includes a clear understanding of the authority and responsibility for each job to be done.

Different types of retail businesses seldom have exactly the same organizational structure or system. The type of organization, the size of the retail firm, different types of merchandise lines, and different target customers lead to somewhat different organizational systems. In a small firm with few employees and a relatively low volume of sales, all employees (including store executives) will have varied responsibilities. As the size of the retail firm and the volume of sales get larger, the responsibilities of the employees become more specialized.

However, there are many similarities in the organizational structures of retail businesses. In this chapter we will examine the organizational structure of various types of stores and identify the similarities and differences that exist. Then we will look at the responsibilities of the buyer within the retail organization.

Organizational Structure of Retail Firms

A retail organization may adopt an organizational structure with anywhere from two to six major areas of responsibility, or **function.** Each of these functions is headed by an executive who is responsible to the chief executive of the firm. This person is usually called the president, general manager, owner, or executive vice president.

We will look first at the organizational structure of most medium-size department stores, which is based on a four-function plan. Responsibilities of the major divisions are as follows:

☐ The Merchandising division is responsible for buying, selling, merchandise planning and control, and often fashion coordination.

☐ The Sales Promotion division is responsible for advertising, visual merchandising (display, store layout, and store decor), special events, publicity, and public relations.

☐ The Finance and Control division is responsible for credit, accounts payable, and inventory control.

☐ The Operations division is responsible for maintenance of facilities, store and merchandise protection, personnel, customer services, and receiving and marking of merchandise.

Many firms find it necessary to increase the number of major functions from four to five when the sales volume, the number of employees, and the number of branch stores reach a large enough size. These stores generally remove responsibility for personnel from the Operations division and make a separate division devoted exclusively to personnel. The Personnel or Human Resources division is then responsible for such areas as employment, training, employee records, executive recruitment, and executive development.

In retail firms with the largest sales volume and number of employees, usually with more than six branches, there is often a sixth major function: the Branch Store division. The executive who is responsible for this division serves as a link between the branch store executives and the parent store, and sees that the public relations, merchandising, and personnel policies established by the firm are carried out in the branches.

An **organization chart** is a visual presentation of the firm's organizational structure. An organization chart of a large retail operation with six divisions is shown on page 59. The responsibilities of each division are shown on the chart.

Organizational Flexibility

Many retail fashion firms owe their success to their ability to anticipate and adapt to change. In a field of never-ending change, they depend upon a flexible organizational structure to allow them to function. Much of this change is prompted by increased competition and the increased sophistication of shoppers.

Retailing is a "people business," and retail firms often have lines of authority and responsibility that are less rigid and tightly structured than many other types of businesses. It is this flexibility that enables retail executives to use their creativity as they react to the rapidly changing retail environment.

It is not uncommon for authority and responsibility to overlap in the retailing field. For example, salespeople may be trained by the personnel department in ringing up sales, writing up sales checks, and handling delivery requests. But they may be given merchandise and fashion training by the buyer and sometimes by the fashion coordinator.

Organizational Structure Within Various Retail Businesses

No two retail organizations are alike. They differ in size and in the direction necessary to achieve their goals. In this section we will look at the basic structure of various types of retail businesses and the merchandising responsibilities within those businesses. We will look at the small single-unit store, in the multiunit department store, the specialty store, and the chain organization.

The Small Single-Unit Store

This type of store is the most common in the United States. It is usually owned and operated by one individual, alone or with family members. The basic organization includes a store manager who is usually

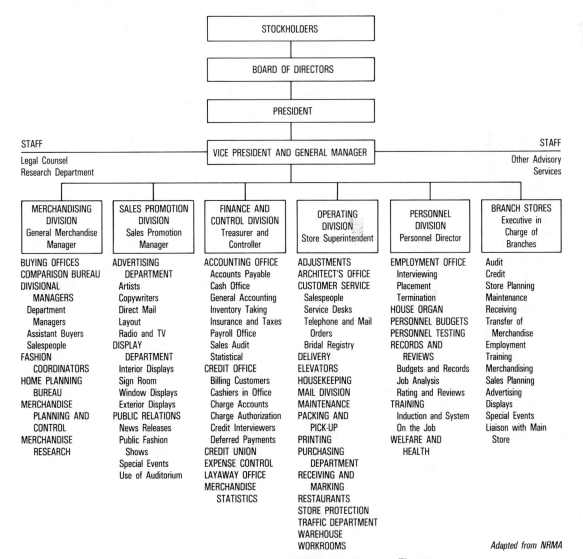

An organization chart visually presents a store's organizational structure. The one shown here charts a large retail organization with six divisions.

In a small store with few employees, a buyer has varied responsibilities.

the owner, a bookkeeper who handles the accounting aspects of the store, a stock clerk who checks and marks stock and helps maintain the store, salespeople, and sometimes a senior salesperson. In these types of stores many of the functions may overlap. During busy seasons, the manager and other employees will be busy on the selling floor taking care of customers. At other times, everyone handles the stock, clerical, and maintenance duties.

In a small store the owner-manager may purchase all the merchandise for that store. As the buyer, he or she determines what to buy, how much to buy, and when to buy it. Since the owner is also on the selling floor most of the day, he or she will supervise all the activities involved with setting up the merchandise on the selling floor for presentation to the customer. Once this is done, the selling activity can begin. In a small store there is a big advantage to having the buying/selling activities combined. Because the owner is responsible for all phases of the business, he or she is able to have control over its profitability.

The Multiunit Store

As an organization grows, it becomes necessary for the firm to divide and delineate job responsibilities. The growth of a firm into a large multiunit company requires a different form of organization. The most common forms are functional, geographical, and product, or a combination of these groupings.

As you learned earlier in this chapter, many department stores are organized by the functions of merchandising, sales promotion, finance and control, operations, and personnel or human resources.

Because of the expansion of most major large firms into far-flung areas of their market, geographical organizational structure has become very important. Here the merchandising activity is organized on a geographical basis because of the importance of structured buying activity. Such an organization has regional or district managers as well as branch store managers and merchandising coordinators.

Organization by product line means that a business is organized according to

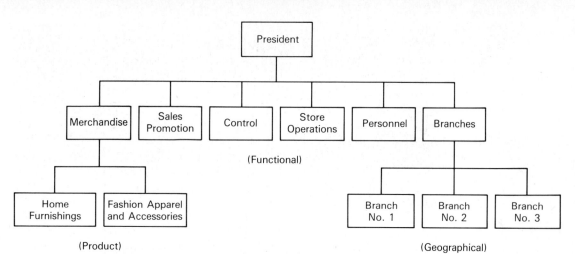

```
                        ┌───────────────┐
                        │   President   │
                        └───────┬───────┘
     ┌──────────┬──────────┬────┴─────┬──────────┬──────────┐
┌─────────┐┌─────────┐┌─────────┐┌─────────┐┌─────────┐┌─────────┐
│Merchandise││  Sales  ││ Control ││  Store  ││Personnel││Branches │
│         ││Promotion││         ││Operations││        ││         │
└────┬────┘└─────────┘└─────────┘└─────────┘└─────────┘└────┬────┘
     │                    (Functional)                      │
  ┌──┴──┐                                         ┌──────────┼──────────┐
┌──────┐┌──────────┐                        ┌──────┐┌──────┐┌──────┐
│ Home ││ Fashion  │                        │Branch││Branch││Branch│
│Furnish││ Apparel  │                        │No. 1 ││No. 2 ││No. 3 │
│ ings ││and Access│                        └──────┘└──────┘└──────┘
└──────┘└──────────┘
   (Product)                                      (Geographical)
```

This organization chart shows how a store can be organized according to function, products, and geography.

the various types of merchandise it sells. A merchandising division may be departmentalized into two major areas: fashion and accessories (soft lines) and home furnishings (hard lines). The fashion area may be further subdivided into various kinds of clothes and could be further subdivided into men's, women's, and children's clothes.

Since both department stores and chains have expanded their merchandise mix and their locations, many are organized by using a combination of functional, product, and geographic structures.

In the traditional department store the merchandising division is responsible for both buying and selling. (The chart on page 59 illustrates how the merchandising function is organized in such a store.) Often the buyers are located in a main store and perform the merchandising activity for that store as well as all the branches. Some large department stores with branches have separated the merchandising and buying activities by placing those personnel in a different location

to service the main store and the various branches, much as a chain organization does. When, under such an arrangement, the buyer is responsible for purchases for all the different stores, that buyer indicates on the order the amount of merchandise to be allocated to each store. This procedure speeds the delivery of the goods to each store's stocks.

The merchandising division may be supervised by a vice president or a **general merchandise manager.** In most large department stores there are usually at least two of these executives—one for soft lines and one for hard lines. Because each of these divisions contains a great many different product lines, a number of **divisional merchandise managers** have responsibility for a group of departments that are generally related, such as menswear, children's wear, ladies' apparel, or ladies' accessories. Therefore each divisional merchandise manager supervises the activities of a number of buyers. Each buyer is responsible for a particular classification of merchandise. Depending on volume of a department, ·

and also the type of merchandise carried, the number of merchandise classifications assigned to each buyer varies. In a smaller department store there may be only one ladies' sportswear buyer, while a larger department store may have separate buyers for different categories of ladies' sportswear, such as junior, misses', and women's. In the largest volume department stores, the categories may be further subdivided, for example, into junior active sportswear and misses' tailored sportswear.

The Specialty Store

Organized much like a department store for its merchandising function, the specialty store does not carry as full a range of merchandise classifications. It usually deals with limited merchandise categories—for example, apparel and accessories for women and men, or more specialized, for women or for men only. Some specialty stores may specialize in age or size groups—for example, children, teens, and preteens—or in sizes for large or petite customers. By the very nature of their specialization, specialty stores usually have a broader coverage of all segments of the market in which they specialize. Also, the breakdown of the responsibility of each buyer is more defined. In a large specialty store catering to women's apparel, the buying responsibility may be divided not only by classification but also by price and/or vendor.

The Chain Store

In a chain store operation, merchandising is conducted from a central headquarters and the selling activity is separated, with selling responsibilities given to the store manager of each store in the chain. The organization chart on page 63 shows the organizational structure of one apparel chain. Notice that merchandising is an entirely separate division from operations and sales. This separation of the buying/selling activity is the most important difference, in merchandising theory and practice, between multiunit department and specialty stores, on the one hand, and chain stores, on the other. Because central buying is a distinct and separate type of merchandising organizational structure, it is discussed in more detail in the following section.

Central Merchandising Organizations

Central buying means that all merchandise buying activity is performed from a central headquarters, with the authority and responsibility for the selection and purchase of merchandise in the hands of the central buying staff. Central buying should not be thought of as synonymous with chain store buying. It is only because so many of the chain stores organize in this manner that this confusion of terms occurs. Any type of store that is part of a group—department store groups, specialty store groups, discount department store groups—can use a central buying organization.

Central buying may take one of three forms: (a) the **central merchandise plan,** (b) the **warehouse and requisition plan,** and (c) the **price agreement plan.**

THE CENTRAL MERCHANDISE PLAN. With this system, once the merchandise is ordered by the buyer, distribution to the individual stores is made by the distribution division. Under the leadership and supervision of a **planner,** each store's needs are planned and the buyer purchases merchandise according to this plan. When these goods are received, a

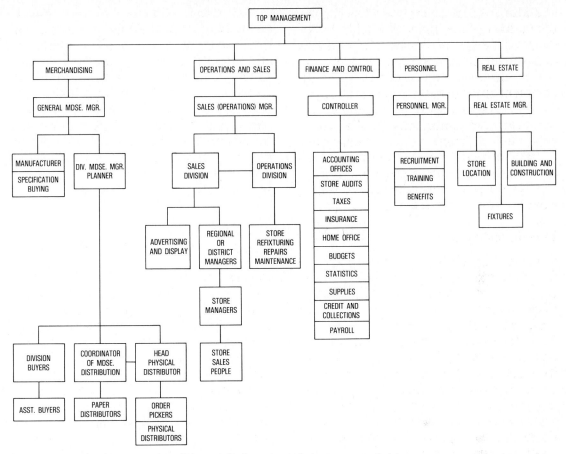

```
                              TOP MANAGEMENT

      MERCHANDISING     OPERATIONS AND SALES   FINANCE AND CONTROL   PERSONNEL      REAL ESTATE

   GENERAL MDSE. MGR.   SALES (OPERATIONS) MGR.    CONTROLLER      PERSONNEL MGR.  REAL ESTATE MGR.
```

MANUFACTURER / SPECIFICATION BUYING

DIV. MDSE. MGR. PLANNER

SALES DIVISION

OPERATIONS DIVISION

ACCOUNTING OFFICES
STORE AUDITS
TAXES
INSURANCE
HOME OFFICE
BUDGETS
STATISTICS
SUPPLIES
CREDIT AND COLLECTIONS
PAYROLL

RECRUITMENT
TRAINING
BENEFITS

STORE LOCATION

BUILDING AND CONSTRUCTION

FIXTURES

ADVERTISING AND DISPLAY

REGIONAL OR DISTRICT MANAGERS

STORE REFIXTURING REPAIRS MAINTENANCE

STORE MANAGERS

DIVISION BUYERS

COORDINATOR OF MDSE. DISTRIBUTION

HEAD PHYSICAL DISTRIBUTOR

STORE SALES PEOPLE

ASST. BUYERS

PAPER DISTRIBUTORS

ORDER PICKERS

PHYSICAL DISTRIBUTORS

In some organizations, merchandising and sales are entirely separate divisions.

distributor actually divides the quantities according to the needs and wants of each store. This is done according to plans and requirements predetermined between the buyer and the planner. It is the job of the distributor to make sure that all stores are given the right amount of merchandise from the shipments that have been received. Most planners and distributors are specialists in this function of distribution. The buyers who use this type of merchandising are also specialists, with the primary job of covering thoroughly the market segment for which they are responsible.

The central merchandising plan also lends itself to specification buying because of the expertise and narrow responsibility of the buyer. Not being responsible for the selling activity, the buyer is able to spend more time in the market.

Of course there are some limitations and disadvantages to the central merchandising plan. With the selling activity concentrated in the hands of the store manager and the salespeople, sometimes hundreds or thousands of miles away from the central office, it is very easy for these store people to be critical of the merchandise they receive from that office.

Chapter 4 □ Retail Organization and the Buyer's Responsibility **63**

Conversely, if the merchandise is slow-selling, there is a tendency for the buyer to blame the people at the selling store level.

THE WAREHOUSE AND REQUISITION PLAN. This type of central merchandising attempts to overcome the limitations of the central merchandise plan. The store manager, many times in accord with his or her selling staff, is given an opportunity to request and control the quantity and type of merchandise that is shipped to the individual store unit for sale to its customers.

Most of the time, the warehouse and requisition plan is used for basic or staple stock. The buyer usually purchases great amounts of this type of merchandise, and individual store managers are allowed to requisition the type and amount of these goods that each of them wants. This plan helps to eliminate some of the unhappiness that can be brought about by the central merchandise plan. Also, it gives the store people a better incentive to sell goods that they themselves have requisitioned.

THE PRICE AGREEMENT PLAN. Here the central buying office prepares catalogs in which merchandise that has been purchased is sketched or photographed and described in detail. This list of merchandise has been chosen by the central buyer after researching past sales and current trends. The manufacturer produces this merchandise and awaits shipping instructions. The merchandise is now owned by the central chain. The individual store managers, after receipt of the catalog, can order directly from the manufacturers listed, at the prices and terms agreed upon by the central buyer and the manufacturer. The central buying office gets a copy of the store's order so as to keep track of these "purchases" against the initial order. The manufacturer then ships the goods directly to the store. This is known in the trade as **drop ship.**

As you can see, the organizational structure of retail stores takes on different forms according to the merchandising necessities of the stores. They will differ in their organizational pattern depending upon their objectives, their merchandising philosophies, and their ability to remain competitive in the ever-changing world of fashion merchandising.

The Buyer's Job

Now that you have an understanding of the ways in which retail businesses are organized, we will look in depth at the buyer's actual job responsibilities. They fall into three main categories in any type of retail organization—planning, buying, and selling.

Planning

Working with the merchandise manager, the buyer must plan stocks so that the store image is reflected in the merchandise. The buyer is also responsible for the preparation of the six-month buying plan. This responsibility requires a knowledge of fashion trends, market conditions, and economic factors, and an analysis of the departments' unit control and other records of past seasons.

The most important factor in planning is flexibility. Every store tries to appeal to and attract a desired segment of customers. Buyers are made aware of the store's goals, established by top management, and must stay within these goals.

The planning is in reality an estimate, or forecast, and it includes provisions for constant adjustment to actual results. The planning is based on two major factors—how much the store expects to sell, and

Planning is an important part of the buyer's job. Plans are developed in cooperation with executives from other store divisions.

how much inventory is needed to achieve that sales goal. In Chapter 5 you will learn in detail about the six-month merchandise plan.

Buying

The second responsibility in a buyer's job is the actual buying. The planning established the amount of money that should be invested and the quantity of actual merchandise that the store needs in order to secure a profit. The planning process is the basis on which stock is purchased. Buying is done by classifications, price lines, sizes, colors, and quantities up to the dollar figure which has been approved in the plan.

Because buying is dependent on customer demand, research and study of customer wants and needs are the basis of buying decisions. The successful buyer knows what the customers want, when they want it, and how much they want to pay for the goods. Part of the buying func-

tion is deciding when assortments will be delivered and when and what should be reordered. Choosing the resource, selecting the merchandise, securing the best terms, and actually placing the order are all part of the buying responsibility. The buyer is responsible for determining not only what to buy and when to buy, but also where to buy and how much to spend. Buying responsibilities include the following:

☐ Establishing and maintaining effective buying relationships with vendors
☐ Obtaining the participation of resources for special events
☐ Securing vendor's selling aids, such as informative brochures, and credits in a resource's national advertising
☐ Adequately stocking the department's price lines and securing the best possible markup on all purchases
☐ Supervising the physical inventory or stock counts to verify the accuracy of stock records

Selling

Because buying is dependent on customer demand, and that is best determined from actual customer response to goods made available by the buying function, it means that buying cannot exist without involvement in the selling function. This function includes communication and promotional activity.

In fashion buying and merchandising, the selling function includes dramatic promotions, because selling fashion involves selling emotion, excitement, and change.

In the past few years there has been a great deal of movement in retailing companies to separate buying from selling, particularly in stores with multibranch operations. However, the buyer is still responsible for department sales. A truism of retailing is the expression that "goods well bought are half sold."

Nothing has created more controversy than the separation of the selling function from the buying function. Certain selling or promotional responsibilities should logically remain the prerogative of the buying function. These include determining the selling features of the merchandise for promotion purposes and the timing of those promotions. The buyer is keenly aware of the selection factors that will appeal most to customers. Timing is also an important element, and the buyer, as the specialist who determines this in purchasing, should also influence the timing of the promotion of the merchandise he or she has bought. Promotional, as well as creative, ideas are a vital part of successful buying.

With the trend toward central buying, merchandise presentation to the customer is becoming a function of sales management rather than of buying. Buyers who

Many large retailers offer formal executive training programs.

work within such an organization must be able to communicate to sales management the features that caused the buyer to select certain goods. Such buyers must rely on persuasion to implement their decisions about how the merchandise can best be presented to the customers.

Career Paths for Buyers

Because of the unique responsibilities of a fashion buyer, retailers demand that the prospective candidate for a buying career have certain personal characteristics. These attributes of successful buyers have been discussed in Chapter 1. Experienced retailers know that cultivating these talents in promising new employees through executive training programs benefits the firm as well as the aspiring buyer. Some typical career ladders are discussed in Appendix A.

Sanger Harris: Reorganization Responds to New Challenges

The nature of retailing requires flexibility in its organizational structure, and occasionally it may require a full-fledged overhaul to make sure each position is best fulfilling its function. At Sanger Harris, the Dallas-based department store, the latter was in order when the retailer recently set out to redefine three key jobs; buyers, branch store department managers, and sales associates.

One reason for the adjustment in the buyer's job was that Sanger Harris had added a number of branch stores, and it became impossible for buyers to fulfill all their responsibilities. Traditionally, they had handled not only buying but also advertising, presentation, accounts payable, downtown store floor supervision, and order distribution, among other duties. What's more, they often did not receive accurate or timely enough information to handle their decision making in a professional way, said John D. Miller, chairman of the store.

The restructuring of the buying job was accomplished over a number of years, beginning with the removal of sales floor responsibilities from their roster of tasks. They were also relieved of distribution of goods, developing financial plans, communicating information to the stores, and initiating advertising and promotional programs. In place of those, buyers were given specific responsibilities for achieving volume objectives and financial goals, managing gross margin elements, and developing assortment plans—all toward the end result of increasing sales and gross margin, and "maximizing their entrepreneurial talent," said George Wilson, personnel vice president.[1]

As backup to its new buying function, Sanger Harris initiated a new systems support program, including advanced on-line interactive systems to support the buyers' need for information; a planner/distributor organization, designed to be a financial partner with the merchants in the departments' growth; a fashion services and product development program, to assist buyers in their merchandise mix selection and private label programs; and a buyer administrative service department, to handle financial matters for both the buying and store organizations.

Evaluation Measures for Buyers

Fashion buying and merchandising do not rely on guesswork. There are standards to measure the efficiency of every department and buyer. Although the ultimate success of a buyer depends on both meeting these standards and demonstrating the personal qualifications discussed in Chapter 1, management judges and evaluates on objective results rather than on personal qualifications per se. The measures commonly used are sales, inventory, and profit results.

Sales Results

Sales may be measured in (a) dollars, (b) units of merchandise, and (c) sales per square foot of selling space. Many stores prefer to measure increase rather than actual volume in evaluating performance. The buyer is expected to achieve planned sales goals that are based on information from inside and outside sources already established. Public and private reports of sales results for different types of stores are found to be useful in evaluating the sales results in a given department. Government agencies and trade associations provide a large part of these comparative data.

Inventory Results

Inventory results may be measured by (a) **stockturn** (the sales divided by the average inventory for a given period), (b) **prior stock** (proportion of old goods versus new goods), and (c) **percentage of stock shortage to sales.** Management usually sets stockturn goals for each department and goals for the percentage of ending inventory that should be less than a certain number of months old. Trade associations, particularly the National Retail Merchants Association and the National Mass Retailers Institute, provide standards of comparison. Stock shortage percentages are established once a physical inventory is taken and compared with the book figure inventory. (In later chapters we will discuss all these factors in greater depth.)

Profit Results

Profit results are analyzed and measured on (a) initial markup, (b) maintained markup, (c) gross margin, and finally (d) net operating profit. Which of these criteria are used depends on the degree to which management holds the buyer responsible for the factors that affect each level of profit results.

Outcome of the Buyer's Evaluation

Buyers are usually reviewed on a seasonal or annual basis. Management's evaluation of the buyer's accomplishments can be an incentive for the buyers to do their job better. Favorable performance normally leads to a raise in salary or a bonus. Where special skills are evidenced, the buyer may be promoted to the position of merchandise manager. Unfavorable performance may result in a transfer to another department, not as fast-moving or fashion-oriented; in more careful supervision by the merchandise management; or, if these measures do not seem likely to improve performance, in an opportunity to resign. However, very often, a buyer with the right personal characteristics can apply what is learned from an unsuccessful experience to the new challenges and surroundings offered by a different employer.

Buying Vocabulary

Define or briefly explain the following terms:

Central buying

Central merchandise plan

Distributor

Divisional merchandise manager

Drop ship

Functions

General merchandise manager

Organization chart

Organizational structure

Percentage of stock shortage to sales

Planner

Price agreement plan

Prior stock

Stockturn

Warehouse and requisition plan

Buying Review

1. Explain briefly why you have selected retailing as a career.
2. Would you prefer to begin your business life in a large organization or a specialty firm? Why?
3. What are the advantages of working in a single-unit store?
4. Which division of a department store appeals to you? Why?
5. Describe the responsibilities of the division merchandise manager (DMM).
6. How does a "product line" organization operate?
7. Describe the place of the specialty store in the retail world.

8. In a central merchandising operation how does the warehouse and requisition plan function?
9. What are the three major job responsibilities of a buyer?
10. How does management evaluate the efficiency and success of a buyer?
11. Do you believe that retail buyers work a 40-hour week?

Buying Case

You are the buyer of the fashion jewelry department in a large specialty store, and one of ten buyers that report to the divisional merchandise manager of accessories and cosmetics.

List the different situations that might necessitate a meeting between just you and the divisional merchandise manager. List them in the order of importance for helping you operate your department at its most efficient and profitable level.

Under what circumstance would you and your divisional merchandise manager need to meet with the general merchandise manager? As the buyer, how much input do you think you would be permitted in the meeting with the general merchandise manager?

Case For Unit 1

You are about to graduate from the fashion merchandising program in which you are now enrolled. Your professor has announced that a leading department store in your region, a famous specialty store, and a national chain store company will all be on campus to recruit for their executive training programs. Your professor will tell you the names of the retailers who will be visiting your school.

The professor suggests that it would be extremely helpful for you to know in advance about the company with which you want to have an interview. By researching the company you will be able to ask pertinent questions of the executive recruiter and demonstrate your interest in, and knowledge of, the organization. The following points should be addressed in your research:

1. Brief history of the company: who founded it, where, and when, the number and location of retail units.
2. Fashion image and position on the fashion cycle.
3. The market segmentation done by the company and whom it perceives to be its target customer.
4. Prerequisites for the position of buyer after completion of the formal executive training program (personal and educational experience required).
5. Job description for position of buyer.
6. Major areas of concentrated activities (when, where, and with whom are the buyer's skills most needed and utilized?). *Which* skills are the most important?
7. Unique character of the specific buying responsibility.
8. Career advantages and disadvantages of working for this retailer.

Unit 2

The Planning and Control Functions

Most people resist the idea of control of any kind. It conjures up restraint, restriction, and lack of creativity. Equally tedious is the thought of planning, because planning takes time, and most of us think we can better use our time *doing* something. Most of us have been taught that the road to success is traveled fastest by people who are "busy" and "doing things."

The thinking that goes into developing a plan does not involve much physical activity. Therefore, many people do not appreciate the need to sit quietly and patiently in order to plan the movement of dollars and merchandise. This unit explains the reasons for planning and control and demonstrates in detail just how to plan and control a fashion business to make a profit.

Chapter 5 discusses the steps used to formulate the dollar merchandise plan and its impacts on the profit of your business. It is the platform upon which your talents as a buyer can be displayed. The "Fashion Merchandise Assortment Plan," Chapter 6, focuses on planning the amount and type of merchandise to buy and explains the steps used for planning the right assortment for your customers. In Chapter 7, the basics of unit control are discussed, and all the factors that affect the control of your merchandise are analyzed. Finally, Chapter 8, "Dollar Control," shows you how you can control every dollar you, as a buyer, spend and how you can keep within the guidelines of your dollar merchandise plan.

Chapter 5

The Dollar Merchandise Plan

As a fashion buyer, you are responsible for investing many thousands of your store's dollars in acquiring stock for resale. The objective of your buying is twofold (1) to satisfy the needs and wants of your customer, and (2) to make a profit for your company. Buyers cannot meet these goals by mere chance. It takes careful and creative planning. In Chapter 2 you learned how to determine the needs and wants of your prospective customers. In this chapter and the three that follow, we will discuss how to plan and manage the finances of buying to make a profit.

Many experienced buyers believe that planning is the most important function of merchandising. They often quip, "Success in merchandising is composed of three important factors: planning, planning, and planning." A merchandising plan, like the itinerary for a vacation, tells you where you are going and how you will get there. If you were traveling, you would not board the first plane that left the airport, no matter where it was going. You would check schedules for flights to your destination, and you would try to plan far enough in advance to save money as well as time. Similarly, you don't select merchandise randomly. You use a merchandising plan to guide you toward your objectives of supplying the right merchandise for your customers and meeting your profit projections. Customers who find a good selection of fashions in desirable colors in proper sizes, and at acceptable prices enjoy the results of effective planning.

Earning a Profit

Your reward for careful planning is the profit you will make for your company. **Profit** is the amount of money that is left over after all of the merchandise that is offered for sale has been purchased and all of the expenses of running the business have been paid. These expenses include such things as advertising, salaries, rent, utilities, equipment, supplies, and taxes.

If you know know to play ticktacktoe, you can calculate the amount of profit you have earned. First draw the ticktacktoe diagram.

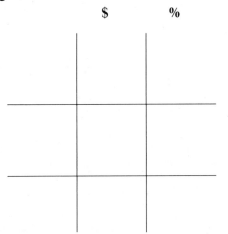

The diagram you have just made has nine sections. You will use the three on the left to write the profit formula shown below.

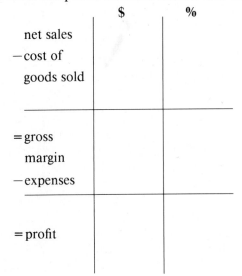

In the first section of the diagram you see "net sales − cost of goods sold." **Net sales** are all of the sales that have been made for a specific period of time minus **customer returns and allowances** (or adjustments), which are refunds or partial refunds that are made to customers when merchandise is returned. **Cost of goods sold** is the amount of money you have paid for the merchandise (including freight, discount, and workroom charges) that your store has sold during the same time period.

In the second section of the diagram you see "= gross margin − expenses." **Gross margin** is the amount of gross profit you have made before expenses are deducted. This gross profit is the margin of dollars between what the merchandise cost and what it was sold for. It lets you know what amount can be planned for expenses. **Expenses** is the term used to describe the money you have spent to run your business. Expenses include such items as salaries, advertising, rent, heat, and light.

In the bottom section of your diagram you see the word "profit." You already know that profit is the amount of money that is left over after you deduct your expenses from your gross margin. If your expenses exceed your gross margin, this "bottom line" number will show a loss rather than a profit.

In the middle three sections of your diagram you can indicate the *dollar* amounts of each of these items. Let's "plug in" the figures for the month of December. The diagram below shows that net sales are $70,000 and the cost of goods sold is $42,000. When you subtract $42,000 from $70,000, you find that the gross margin is $28,000. When you subtract expenses of $24,000, you find that your profit is $4,000.

	$	%
net sales	$70,000	
−cost of goods sold	−42,000	
=gross margin	28,000	
−expenses	24,000	
=profit	4,000	

	$	%
net sales	$ 70,000	100
−cost of goods sold	−42,000	−60
=gross margin	28,000	40
−expenses	24,000	34.3
=profit	4,000	5.7

The three right-hand sections of your diagram are for *percent* figures. Businesses convert the dollar figures they use into percents because they are easy to compare on a month-by-month or year-by-year basis. When you convert the dollar amounts in your profit diagram to percents, remember that *net sales always equal 100 percent.* All of the other factors are a part of the 100 percent (net sales) and are related as parts of a whole.

In the next diagram, it is clear that the cost of goods sold equals 60 percent of net sales ($42,000 divided by $70,000), gross margin equals 40 percent ($28,000 divided by $70,000), expenses equal 34.3 percent ($24,000 divided by $70,000), and profit equals 5.7 percent ($4,000 divided by $70,000).

$$\frac{\$\text{ cost of goods sold}}{\$\text{ net sales}} = \%\text{ cost of goods sold}$$

$$\frac{\$\text{ gross margin}}{\$\text{ net sales}} = \%\text{ gross margin}$$

$$\frac{\$\text{ expense}}{\$\text{ net sales}} = \%\text{ expense}$$

$$\frac{\$\text{ profit}}{\$\text{ net sales}} = \%\text{ profit earned}$$

Virtually every store calculates profit by using the basic formula shown in the ticktacktoe diagram. But instead of using the diagram, they use a **profit and loss statement,** which is a summary of the transactions that occurred over a specific period of time. The profit and loss statement is also called the **income statement.**

The profit and loss statement (Form 5–1) on page 77 shows the same basic figures that you used in your ticktacktoe diagram. In addition, you will see some figures that indicate more detailed information about the expenses that were incurred during the month of December.

Planning for Profit

To earn the best possible profit, you will need to plan both the amount of money you need to finance your purchases and the amount of revenue you expect to realize from sales. The basic tools for this planning are the dollar merchandise plan and the open-to-buy. The **dollar merchandise plan,** which will be discussed in this chapter, is the specific budget that you use to project both sales goals and the amount of stock that is required to achieve those

INCOME			
Gross sales		$140,000	
Customer returns and adjustments		8,600	
Net sales		$131,400	$131,400
COST OF GOODS SOLD			
Open inventory (cost value)		$118,000	
Purchase costs	$50,000		
Shipping costs	2,000		
Total purchase costs	52,000	52,000	
Total purchases		$170,000	
Closing inventory (cost value)		$100,000	
Gross cost of goods sold		70,000	
Cash discount		3,000	
Net cost of goods		$ 67,000	$ 67,000
Gross margin			$ 63,600
OPERATING EXPENSES			
Buyer's salary		3,000	
Sales help salaries		24,000	
Advertising and promotions		4,000	
Rent		18,000	
Utilities		5,000	
Total operating expenses		$ 54,000	$ 54,000
NET PROFIT			$ 9,600

Form 5-1. A profit and loss statement.

goals. **Open-to-buy,** which will be discussed in Chapter 7, is the amount of money you are permitted to spend for merchandise within a specific period of time, as determined by the dollar merchandise plan. The open-to-buy is like your bank checking account. Your checks (purchases) are deducted from your account balance. The ability to write checks (purchases) stops when no money is left in your account. Added sales, however, restore money to the account for more open-to-buy. Lower sales reduce the open-to-buy even more.

The major goals of careful, scientific planning in retail merchandising are:

☐ To maintain an inventory that is neither too large nor too small for anticipated customer demand

☐ To time the delivery of purchases so that merchandise is available for sale neither too early nor too late for customer demand

☐ To keep purchases in line with the store's ability to pay for them

☐ To have funds available for the purchase of new goods when they may be needed

Use of Retail Figures

The majority of department and specialty stores operate under an accounting system known as the **retail method of inventory.** In this system, all transactions affecting the store's inventory, such as sales, purchases, markdowns, transfers, and returns-to-vendor, are recorded at their retail prices. Stores that operate under the retail method also plan their merchandise budgets and assortments entirely on the basis of retail prices. All of the figures used in the following discussion of financial planning are at retail, unless otherwise indicated.

The Dollar Merchandise Plan

At the beginning of this chapter, we compared the merchandise plan to the plans you might make for a vacation. Before you leave home, you make a series of decisions that are very important to the success of your trip. You decide where you are going, how you plan to get there, when you plan to get there, how much the trip will cost you, and how much spending money you will have while you are there.

After you make your plans, you check them to see if things are progressing as you thought they would. Sometimes everything goes just as expected, but at other times you have to adjust your plans. If, during the first four days of your vacation, you spend $75 more than you planned to spend, you find a way to cut your spending on the following days. If you planned to drive on Route 45 but find that it is under construction, you find an alternate route. If you planned to stay at the River Plaza Hotel but learn that there is a newer and better hotel where you can stay more economically, you change your plans.

In a similar way, the dollar merchandise plan must be checked to see if everything is progressing as you projected. If you find that sales are below those that were planned or if you find that sales are much better than planned for a particular item, you adjust both your planned inventory and your planned sales figures. If you discover a "hot" item of merchandise that was unavailable to you when the plan was made, you make adjustments to work it into your plan.

In a small store, where the owner is in constant touch with all operations, the merchandise plan may be somewhat informal. But because most small stores have a limited amount of capital resources, the owner-buyer must do some preplanning of purchases and expenditures.

In large retailing organizations a more elaborate plan or budget is essential. The very size of the establishment means that merchandising responsibilities are distributed among many different buyers. The merchandising plan provides a guide for these buyers in their attempt to secure the desired level of sales and earn a good profit. The plan also serves as a guideline or standard against which the buyers' performance can be measured.

In a retail store many people have responsibilities—the delivery staff, the office staff, the display personnel, the housekeeping staff. The buyer also has responsibilities, but there is a difference. The buyer has both responsibility and accountability. This means that the store's management can check on the buyer's performance and measure it against the desired outcome of that performance, namely, profit.

Procedures for Preparing the Plan

Although the period of time covered by the dollar merchandise plan may vary from one month to a year, the usual planning period is for six months. The spring season—February through July—is usually planned in one budget. The fall season—August through January—is planned in another budget.

In a small organization, the dollar merchandising plans for the store as a whole are usually drawn up as one comprehensive plan. In larger stores, separate budgets are first developed for each department. Later these budgets are incorporated into a master plan at the divisional level or the storewide level, or both. While the format of the plan may vary considerably from store to store, the plan should be presented in the simplest form possible and in terminology that is familiar to everyone who must use it.

THE BUYER'S ROLE. Buyers play an active role in developing merchandise plans. First, the store's accounting department will supply you with a planning form several months in advance of the start of the actual buying season. On it are the figures from your department's merchandising operation during the corresponding season of last year. The plan may also include last year's actual sales and this year's projected goals. These projected figures include the gross margin desired, certain department operating expenses, and the number of stock turns desired. (Later in this chapter you will learn why stock turns are important and how to calculate them.) The projected goals are established by store management, not by departmental buyers.

Using the planning form and your specialized knowledge of market conditions, trends, and demand cycles, you will then prepare figures on anticipated sales, stock, markdowns, and purchases for your department for the upcoming six months.

MANAGEMENT'S ROLE. When you have completed your work on the plan, it is reviewed by your divisional merchandise manager, who may make revisions before approving it. Next, the merchandise manager consolidates your plan and plans from other buyers in your division into a divisional plan and submits it to the general merchandise manager for approval. Finally, all plans are subject to review by both the store's controller and the general manager or president. When approved, departmental plans are combined into a master plan for the whole store. If you own your own store, or work in a small organization, you and the owner will perform all these tasks.

Elements of the Plan

Although dollar merchandise plans vary from store to store, there will probably be four basic elements in your merchandise plan: *sales, stocks, markdowns,* and *purchases.* For this reason, each of these major planning elements will be covered in detail in the following sections of this chapter. Your plan may also include both seasonal goal figures and planned expense figures. The discussion of these figures, which will include initial markup, gross margin, stock shortage reserves, cash discounts, stock turnover, selling salaries, and advertising expenses, will be at the end of the chapter.

PLANNING SALES. The first step in the preparation of a merchandise plan is to make a realistic estimate of prospective sales during the upcoming season. To make this estimate, you will want to review past sales figures, examine both external and internal factors that may effect sales, and study general fashion trends that may influence your department's sales. After you have estimated planned sales for the season, you will break them down into sales goals for each of the six months of the season.

Sales Figures. You will begin your estimate by reviewing the sales figures for the store as a whole and for your particular department. Last year's figures are important, but you will also want to review the figures for the two or three years before last. Calculate the amount your department contributed to the total sales effort for each year, and look for trends that will help you in your estimating.

If you find, for example, that your sales have been increasing at the rate of 7 percent every year, you can assume that they will probably continue to increase at that rate. Or let's say that you learn the sales in your department have generally accounted for about 9 percent of the store's total sales but last year they accounted for a full 12 percent. With the aid of your merchandise manager, you can use this information as you attempt to determine the reason for the increase and capitalize on it for this year's sales. Smart buyers always press for continued growth in sales. This sales growth also boosts the buyer's salary or bonus. Optimism pays off for the aggressive buyer.

A good merchandise plan is both specific and flexible. Since the plan is an attempt to forecast customer demand and develop strategies far in advance of the period covered, the plan cannot be completely rigid. As the season actually gets under way, you will want to review your figures frequently, both in relation to the actual results and in relation to more current information about the balance of the season. For example, if you are buying handbags and learn that the supply of one particular type of popular bag will probably be threatened by a lengthy strike, you might decide to increase your stocks of these bags immediately, rather than waiting for the previously planned purchase time. All plans are subject to changes that may occur for a variety of reasons.

After you have made your best estimate of sales for the season on the basis of past sales records, you will want to check both external and internal factors that might affect that estimate, as well as general fashion trends that could either increase or decrease sales in your department.

External Factors. External factors are those outside of your store or its control, such as the pending strike that would affect handbag deliveries, mentioned above. They also include employment prospects, general economic conditions, population changes, and the competitive situation. The opening of a new plant in an area, for example, is likely to increase spending power in the community. Conversely, the possibility of strikes or shutdowns among local employers means a potential loss of spending power in the trading area.

Optimism about the future encourages consumer spending, whereas threats of new taxes, higher interest rates, or declines in economic activity tend to discourage spending, or delivery of goods if ordered from these firms.

Your sales prospects will be affected by the growth or lack of growth in an area's population. They will be affected by changes in the proportion of high-income to low-income families and by changes in the age composition of a population. A new housing development for young families, for example, provides a potential increase in sales in children's, juniors', young women's, and young men's departments. A new retirement condominium may favor departments selling higher-priced, more conservative apparel and accessories, as well as home furnishings.

You should also evaluate the competitive effect of new or expanded stores and shopping centers in your trading area. Stores in other communities within easy traveling distance may be gaining or losing power to draw off some of your retail business. On the other hand, if any local competitors have closed up shop, or if new highways or parking facilities have made it easier for customers to get to your store, there is reason to anticipate sales growth.

Internal Factors. Internal factors are those within your store or its control. They include physical changes within the store that either enhance or diminish the sales prospects of individual departments. They also include the opening of new branches, the general trend in store sales, and the number and extent of promotions your store's management expects to undertake during the season being planned.

Physical changes within a store can affect the sales prospects of various departments within the store. For example, if new escalators are being installed with landings at the entrance to the better dress department, sales of that department will probably benefit. On the other hand, if the accessories department had to be moved to a less prominent location or perhaps had its floor space reduced because of the alteration, sales of accessories may suffer. Relocation, expansion, or contraction of your department's selling space aren't the only physical changes that affect your sales. The acquisition or elimination of display fixtures, a change of decor, and any change in your department's proximity to other departments carrying related merchandise can also affect sales.

If a new branch of your store is to be opened nearby within the planning period, it is probable that some of your customers will transfer their patronage to the new branch, thus affecting your branch adversely.

If your store as a whole is enjoying expanded sales, each department within the store is likely to profit from the increased customer traffic. The reverse is true if your store as a whole is attracting less traffic. Your department's sales will also be affected by the amount of promotion the store plans in its behalf. Its sales opportunities will be enhanced if the store as a whole plans increased promotional effort, since this usually will bring increased customer traffic. These promotional efforts may be general, intended simply to bring more people into the store. Your store may also plan a special promotion aimed at a specific group of customers, such as career women, young mothers, or teenagers. If your department offers merchandise that has particular appeal to the group being courted, you can expect significant sales benefits.

Fashion Trends. Fashion trends are probably the most important factor influencing sales. They usually affect the sales of several departments at one time, pushing up the sales potential of some and depressing the sales prospects of others. For example, if the trend is toward dressier apparel, dress departments can budget optimistically. But departments selling sportswear and other casual attire will plan more cautiously. Similarly, fashion trends in ready-to-wear affect the sales planning of other fashion departments. For example, a trend toward skirts rather than pants will increase the sales potential of the hosiery department.

Monthly Sales Goals. As you plan sales for the season, you will look at each month within the season separately. Although you will be required to come up with a sales figure for the whole season, you will also need to set a firm plan for each of the six months.

One very helpful estimating tool is your ability to work with percentages. You will want to compare your estimated sales plan for each month with the corresponding month last year. The best way to do this is by using percentages. It is much easier, for example, to understand an increase of 4.95 percent in sales than an increase from $24,200 to $25,400.

Through your use of percentages, you will also be able to look at the amount each month's sales have contributed to the annual sales for your department. You can use those figures and percentages as guidelines in setting your monthly sales goals.

In setting goals, you should give careful consideration to the previous year's sales for the same month, to the percentage each month has contributed to total annual sales, and to any other factors influencing a department's sales potential.

You must also take into account the fact that consumer demand varies both seasonally and monthly. If there were no such variations, each month would contribute an equal number of dollars to the year's total sales volume. But this is virtually never the case. Another consideration is the fact that the number of business days changes from month to month. And in some of those months, customers buy more freely than in others.

Monthly sales volume, as a percentage of the total year's sales, also fluctuates from department to department. This is explained by the seasonality of the merchandise that each handles as well as the curve of customer demand for that merchandise. For example, toy departments and often fur departments do the bulk of their annual business in just a few months of the year.

Holidays and other special days such as Valentine's Day, Mother's Day, and Father's Day also give rise to variations in demand. The extent to which each influences monthly sales planning depends upon the nature of the merchandise and the extent of the department's promotional plans.

In estimating the sales potential for each month, you should also consider any special circumstances that may have affected sales last year but that can be ignored in this year's planning. For example, some sales may have been lost last year because of delivery delays. If no delivery problems are anticipated this year, sales may be appreciably better because of this one factor alone. Other factors affecting sales in previous years such as unseasonable weather, special promotions held in competing stores, and special attractions that drew customers to your store should also be taken into account when you set your goals on a month-by-month basis.

Most buyers keep some kind of personal notebook in which they list special conditions that have affected sales. Weather, their own advertising and that of their competitors, and changing market conditions are some of the factors noted.

Another familiar device is a departmental Beat-Last-Year book, in which comparative daily sales are recorded for as many as five successive years. Notes like "rain," "parade," and "half-page ad" (noting the item advertised) remind the buyer of the story behind sales figures for each day.

If you must plan sales for a new store, a new branch, or a new department within an established store, past sales records will not be available to use as a guide. Research—formal or informal—combined with careful judgment must take the place of past experience. Market studies, consultations with other merchants or other buyers, and discussions with bankers and vendors will all help you in arriving at sales goals for the new enterprise.

Form 5–2 indicates how the seasonal merchandise plan looks when seasonal and monthly sales goals have been set.

PLANNING STOCK. Since sales during any month can be realized only if there is stock to sell, the next step in dollar merchandising planning is to estimate the amount of stock that will be needed to support the planned monthly sales.

For each month in your six-month plan, you will estimate the beginning-of-the-month (BOM) stocks that you need to support planned sales.

Two major considerations influence your planning of BOM stocks. First, there must be an adequate opening assortment on hand, in sufficient quantity, to meet anticipated customer demand until stock replacements for goods sold can be secured. The best dollar stock plans for fashion departments are those in which minimum quantities of each item needed are detailed by classifications, price lines, types, colors, and sizes. (Assortment planning is discussed in detail in Chapter 6.)

Your second consideration in planning BOM stocks is anticipated sales. The planning must be such that the desired seasonal stock turnover may be realized, markdowns minimized, and a steady flow of new, interesting merchandise assured throughout the month.

Variations in Monthly Stock Goals. In planning monthly stock goals, stocks should be brought to a peak just prior to the time when sales are expected to reach their peak. By peaking stocks before consumer demand reaches its crest, you will be able to present maximum assortments in needed styles, sizes, and colors when the public is in the mood to buy.

Similarly, the beginning-of-the-month (BOM) stock plans should be reduced as a

			PLAN (This Year)	ACTUAL (Last Year)
SIX MONTH MERCHANDISING PLAN		Initial markup (%)	48.5	47.5
		Gross margin (%)	42.3	41.8
		Cash discount (% cost purch.)	8.0	7.8
		Season stock turnover (rate)	2.8	2.6
		Shortage reserve (%)	1.5	1.8
		Advertising expense (%)	2.8	3.0
		Selling salaries (%)	8.0	8.5

Dept. Name: Junior Sportswear   Dept. No. 145

SPRING 198—		FEB.	MAR.	APR.	MAY	JUNE	JULY	SEASON TOTAL
~~FALL 198—~~		~~AUG.~~	~~SEP.~~	~~OCT.~~	~~NOV.~~	~~DEC.~~	~~JAN.~~	
SALES	Last Year	24,200	28,400	34,600	31,000	28,200	21,600	168,000
	Plan	25,400	35,400	33,000	34,000	31,000	23,200	182,000
	Percent of Increase	4.95	24.6	−4.6	9.7	9.9	7.4	8.3
	Revised							
	Actual							
RETAIL STOCK (BOM)	Last Year	69,000	71,000	78,000	70,000	68,000	58,000	42,000 *
	Plan							
	Revised							
	Actual							
MARKDOWNS	Last Year	4,000	5,000	5,600	4,400	4,400	4,200	27,600
	Plan (dollars)							
	Plan (percent)							14.0%
	Revised							
	Actual							
RETAIL PURCHASES	Last Year	30,200	40,400	32,200	33,400	22,600	9,800	168,600
	Plan							
	Revised							
	Actual							

Comments
*Represents stock end of period.

Merchandise Manager _____   Buyer _____

Controller _____

Form 5-2. A six month merchandising plan showing the plan for sales.

selling season approaches its close and demand decreases. Two other factors can help you to reduce inventory as the season ends. You can mark down unsold seasonal goods and bring in new goods that are offered as manufacturers' closeouts. These are usually purchased and resold at prices lower than earlier in the season.

Dept. Name __Junior Sportswear__   Dept. No. __145__

SIX MONTH MERCHANDISING PLAN

	PLAN (This Year)	ACTUAL (Last Year)
Initial markup (%)	48.5	47.5
Gross margin (%)	42.3	41.8
Cash discount (% cost purch.)	8.0	7.8
Season stock turnover (rate)	2.8	2.6
Shortage reserve (%)	1.5	1.8
Advertising expense (%)	2.8	3.0
Selling salaries (%)	8.0	8.5

SPRING 198—		FEB.	MAR.	APR.	MAY	JUNE	JULY	SEASON TOTAL
~~FALL 198—~~		AUG.	SEP.	OCT.	NOV.	DEC.	JAN.	
SALES	Last Year	24,200	28,400	34,600	31,000	28,200	21,600	168,000
	Plan	25,400	35,400	33,000	34,000	31,000	23,200	182,000
	Percent of Increase	4.95	24.6	-4.6	9.7	9.9	7.4	8.3
	Revised							
	Actual							
RETAIL STOCK (BOM)	Last Year	69,000	71,000	78,000	70,000	68,000	58,000	42,000*
	Plan	65,000	79,000	74,000	72,000	68,000	52,000	42,000*
	Revised							
	Actual							
MARKDOWNS	Last Year	4,000	5,000	5,600	4,400	4,400	4,200	27,600
	Plan (dollars)							
	Plan (percent)							14.0%
	Revised							
	Actual							
RETAIL PURCHASES	Last Year	30,200	40,400	32,200	33,400	22,600	9,800	168,600
	Plan							
	Revised							
	Actual							

Comments

*Represents stock end of period.

Merchandise Manager _____   Buyer _____

Controller _____

Form 5-3. The six month merchandising plan showing the plan for retail stock.

Stock-Sales Relationships. Stores are guided in their stock planning by two stock-sales relationships: monthly stock-sales ratios and a desired ratio of seasonal stock turnover.

The **monthly stock-sales ratio** uses the number of months that would be required to dispose of a beginning-of-the-month inventory at the planned rate of sales for that month. The formula for calculating this relationship is:

$$\text{stock-sales ratio} = \frac{\$ \text{ BOM stock}}{\$ \text{ sales for month}}$$

Applying this formula to the February planned sales and stock figures appearing in Form 5-3:

$$\text{stock-sales ratio} = \frac{\$65,000}{\$25,400}$$

$$= 2.56$$

The stock-sales ratio is an important tool in stock planning since it directly relates stock requirements to planned sales. You can then compare stock-sales ratios with those your store has experienced in the past. Or you can compare them with the sales-stock ratios experienced by other stores as compiled by such trade associations as the National Retail Merchants Association. The compilation of these figures is known as the **MOR** (Merchandising and Operating Results) report. Ratios will vary from month to month, from department to department, from one type of retail operation to another, and from one type of merchandise to another. They depend primarily upon the cycle of demand for various types of merchandise and the merchandising policies of an individual store.

Once you have set a sales goal and established a desirable stock-sales ratio, you can determine the stock needed at the be-

Table 5-1

Typical Monthly Stock-Sales Ratio

Month	Women's Dressy Coats	Lingerie	Mens-wear
Jan.	2.1	4.7	6.3
Feb.	2.6	4.6	6.7
March	2.3	5.5	5.7
April	2.4	5.2	6.3
May	3.8	3.8	6.2
June	4.7	4.3	3.8
July	3.9	4.3	6.0
Aug.	4.5	3.9	5.6
Sept.	5.0	5.0	5.1
Oct.	3.3	4.7	5.6
Nov.	2.7	4.0	3.6
Dec.	1.9	1.8	1.5

ginning of any month by using the following formula:

$$\$ \text{ BOM stock} = \$ \text{ planned sales}$$
$$\times \text{ stock-sales ratio}$$

Table 5-1 shows typical monthly stock-sales ratios for three different departments. Using the figures from the table as an illustration of the application of this formula, assume that you plan February sales at $2,000 in each of the three departments: Women's Dressy Coats, Lingerie, and Men's Furnishings. If you apply the February stock-sales ratios listed in the table, the amount of stock at retail value that should be on hand February 1 in each of these departments would be:

Women's Dressy
Coats $2,000 × 2.6 = $5,200

Lingerie $2,000 × 4.6 = $9,200

Men's Furnishings $2,000 × 6.7 = $13,400

A second stock-sales relationship that will help you plan stocks is stock turnover. Unlike the stock-sales ratio, which is used in planning beginning-of-the-month stocks, **stock turnover** refers to the number of times that an average stock of merchandise (inventory) has been turned into sales during a given period. Put another way, stock turnover is bringing goods in, turning them into cash, and going out to buy more goods. The formula for determining the rate of stock turnover during any given period is:

$$\text{stock turnover} = \frac{\$ \text{ net sales}}{\$ \text{ average inventory}}$$

For example, using the dollar merchandise plan shown as Form 5–4, we can find that the average stock for the spring season being planned is $64,571. This figure is obtained by adding all six beginning-of-the-month stocks (February–July) to the end-of-season stock ($42,000) and dividing that sum by 7 (the number of inventory figures used):

	BOM Stock
February	$ 65,000
March	79,000
April	74,000
May	72,000
June	68,000
July	52,000
July (EOM)	42,000
Total	$452,000

$$\frac{\$452,000}{7} = \$64,571 \text{ average inventory}$$

Then, by dividing the season's total planned sales of $182,000 by the average stock of $64,571, a stock turnover rate of 2.82 is found for the six-month period:

$$\frac{\$182,000 \text{ planned sales}}{\$64,571 \text{ average stock}} = 2.82 \text{ stock turnover}$$

On a storewide basis, the typical stock turnover figure for all department stores is somewhat better than three turns a year (3.00). Rate of stock turnover, however, varies widely from one department to another within a given store. The rate depends upon the type of merchandise handled, its price ranges, and the depth and breadth of assortments carried.

In general, the rate of stock turnover is higher in women's apparel than in men's clothing or home furnishings. It is also higher in departments featuring lower price ranges than in those featuring higher price ranges. And in departments such as shoes, where many colors and sizes must be carried in each style, the turnover is low. The following average turnover figures illustrate how the annual stock turnover varies on the basis of type of merchandise handled:

Sleepwear and robes	7.8 turns
Millinery	6.5 turns
Misses' dresses	4.5 turns
Men's clothing	2.5 turns
Women's shoes	2.0 turns

The rate at which your stock is turned into sales directly affects your profit since you can receive no income until merchandise is sold. Exceptional buys of wanted items that sell fast can increase turnover and maximize profits. If you purchase 100 dressy coats at 50 percent off their usual cost and sell them within a few weeks at your normal markup, you increase your turnover and profit for that period enormously. In Chapter 8, you will learn how some buyers attempt to achieve a desired rate of stock turnover, which is made by limiting beginning-of-the-month stock to a predetermined stock-sales ratio.

PLANNING MARKDOWNS. Now that you have planned monthly sales and beginning-of-the-month inventories, you are ready to plan one of your most important

			PLAN (This Year)	ACTUAL (Last Year)
	Initial markup (%)		48.5	47.5
	Gross margin (%)		42.3	41.8
	Cash discount (% cost purch.)		8.0	7.8
	Season stock turnover (rate)		2.8	2.6
	Shortage reserve (%) *ND*		1.5	1.8
	Advertising expense (%)		2.8	3.0
	Selling salaries (%)		8.0	8.5

Dept. Name __Junior Sportswear__ Dept. No. __145__

SIX MONTH MERCHANDISING PLAN

SPRING 198— ~~FALL 198—~~		FEB. AUG.	MAR. SEP.	APR. OCT.	MAY NOV.	JUNE DEC.	JULY JAN.	SEASON TOTAL
SALES	Last Year	24,200	28,400	34,600	31,000	28,200	21,600	168,000
	Plan	25,400	35,400	33,000	34,000	31,000	23,200	182,000
	Percent of Increase	4.95	24.6	−4.6	9.7	9.9	7.4	8.3
	Revised							
	Actual							
RETAIL STOCK (BOM)	Last Year	69,000	71,000	78,000	70,000	68,000	58,000	42,000 *
	Plan	65,000	79,000	74,000	72,000	68,000	52,000	42,000 *
	Revised							
	Actual							
MARKDOWNS	Last Year	4,000	5,000	5,600	4,400	4,400	4,200	27,600
	Plan (dollars)	3,800	4,000	5,000	4,000	4,000	4,200	25,400
	Plan (percent)	15.0	11.3	15.0	11.8	12.9	18.1	14.0%
	Revised							
	Actual							
RETAIL PURCHASES	Last Year	30,200	40,400	32,200	33,400	22,600	9,800	168,600
	Plan							
	Revised							
	Actual							

Comments

*Represents stock end of period.

Merchandise Manager _____ Buyer _____

Controller _____

Form 5-4. The six month merchandising plan showing the plan for markdowns.

tools for realizing a profit—markdowns. **Markdowns** are reductions in the selling price of merchandise. Some buyers regard markdowns as a curse to be avoided whenever possible. But a wise buyer will plan markdowns and "spend" them to recapture money that has been invested and, at the same time, earn a profit.

A buyer in the better dress department of a small department store was reluctant to spend his markdown money. He bought a "great little dress" that he was sure would "blow right out of the store" and placed it on a t-stand at $189. When it was still there at the end of four weeks, he marked it down to $170. At that price it was tried on by 10 women but still not sold. The buyer then took it down to $140 and it saw a lot more try-on action. After 12 more women tried it on, it had a ripped hem and lipstick on the sleeve. Unfortunately, the "great little dress" never sold. If the buyer had taken at least a 20 to 25 percent markdown when his dress was still fresh, it might have sold immediately and given the buyer back his initial cost plus a smaller-than-planned profit. Even if all he got back was his original cost dollars, he would be able to take that money and buy a new style that would be a better seller.

One experienced buyer explains the importance of using markdowns this way: "The first markdown is the cheapest—and it should also be the deepest. Money you have laid out for merchandise is very important because it is your company's money. It can't be tied up in goods that won't move. If you spend $79.75 for a dress, it's very important that you get your investment money back as fast as possible so that you can buy more goods."

Markdowns are an efficient way of meeting price competition, adjusting retail prices to declining market values, and speeding the sale of slow-moving, damaged, and out-of-season goods to make room for new merchandise. Because of rapidly changing consumer demand, markdowns are generally larger and of greater importance in fashion goods departments than in departments in which the merchandise is not affected as much by seasonal fashion changes, such as housewares or linens.

Markdown can be expressed as both a dollar amount and a percent. The dollar amount refers to the difference between the previous selling price of an item and the reduced selling price. **Markdown percentage** is the amount of dollar markdowns taken during a given period expressed as a percentage of the net sales.

For example, Form 5–4 shows that February markdowns are planned at $3,800 and February sales at $25,400. Expressed as a formula, markdown percentage is calculated as follows:

$$\text{markdown \%} = \frac{\$\text{ markdown}}{\$\text{ net sales}}$$

$$= \frac{\$3,800}{\$25,400}$$

$$= 14.96\%$$

Factors in Planning Markdowns. A certain percentage of any retail store's stock will always have to be marked down before it can be sold. Some stock may have to be marked down more than once. Since markdowns result in lowered gross margin (the difference between the cost of the merchandise and the price at which it is finally sold), you must plan and control them carefully. Markdowns of fashion goods are more important than they are for staple goods that have a steady but slower sales record. Buyers of fashion goods must be ready to take deep markdowns while goods are still salable or lose their profit and sometimes even their jobs.

Markdowns are usually planned as a percentage of each season's planned sales. They may then be allotted to individual months, according to the buyer's estimates of when and to what extent monthly markdowns are going to be needed to sell the goods. The chief factors to be considered in establishing seasonal markdown goals are:

☐ The past experience of the store or department.
☐ Trends in wholesale prices. (Markdowns tend to increase during periods of falling wholesale prices and decrease when wholesale prices are rising.)
☐ Comparative figures of similar stores.
☐ Amount of old stock on hand at the beginning of a new season.

In allocating a season's markdown estimate to individual months, you should consider not only dates throughout the season when changes in customer demand are expected to occur, but also store policy in taking markdowns. Large stores tend to take markdowns while there is still sufficient customer demand to move the goods quickly at minimum price reductions. Small stores tend to postpone taking markdowns, preferring to clear their stocks only at the end of a selling season.

PLANNING PURCHASES. Now that you have entered monthly sales, beginning-of-the-month stocks, and monthly markdown figures on the planning form, you are ready to calculate the value of the purchases that should be made each month if stocks and sales are to be kept in balance. **Planned purchases** is the term used to indicate the amount of money you can spend on merchandise during a given period without exceeding the value of the inventory planned to be on hand at the end of that period.

In most large stores, purchases are planned on a monthly basis. However, some smaller fashion merchants, particularly those who make infrequent market trips, budget purchases on a seasonal or market-trip basis. In either case, the procedure for planning purchases is the same. Planned purchases are derived from planned sales, stocks, and, markdowns, by a simple mathematical formula.

The formula for calculating planned purchases is as follows:

> planned EOM (end-of-month) stock
>
> + planned sales
>
> + planned markdowns
>
> = total needs for the month
>
> − BOM stock
>
> = planned purchases

The EOM stock figure that you begin this calculation with is the same figure as the BOM stock for the following month. To that figure you will add planned sales, because you will have to replace the merchandise that your store or department sold during the month.

Then, because some of this merchandise is brought into the store at full retail price and later sold at a markdown price, you will add these planned markdowns into your calculations. The sum of these figures represents your total needs for the month. But you begin each month with some merchandise already in your possession. For that reason, you will subtract your BOM stock from your total needs for the month. The resulting figure will be the amount of money you can spend on planned purchases for the month.

Focus

Planning Open-to-Buy: A New Formula for Easy Preparation

Even when retailers use computers to help organize their merchandise planning, the most tedious portion—the initial prepartion of open-to-buy that must be entered into the computer—still must be done by hand. To make that open-to-buy preparation easier, Gilberg's Fabrics of Tallahassee, Florida, developed a computerized algorithm designed to eliminate difficulties and errors.

Among the specific objectives of the step-by-step solution to planning were to reduce the time necessary to produce a plan, create a process that would encourage updating as new information becomes available, develop a plan based on goals and objectives for the store, and include inventory plans that are technically achievable.

"Most retailers are familiar with the way in which operating results are calculated. For example, if merchandise initially priced at a 50 percent markup is sold at an overall 10 percent markdown, the maintained margin is 45 percent," explained Mitchell Gilberg, vice president of the company. "Many, however, do not recognize the mathematical relationship also holds in reverse. If you know the initial markup and the desired maintained margin, you can calculate the allowable markdowns. It is also possible to take desired operating results, such as GMROI [gross margin return on investment], turn ratios, sales projections, etc., and calculate 'in reverse' the action required at the store level to meet those goals."[1]

According to Gilberg, the principal use of an open-to-buy plan is to be able to monitor actual sales performance and take actions to bring operations closer to the plan. Factors such as the emergence of a new fashion trend or a new store opening can require changes be made to the initial plan—which with his system on computer becomes a simple task.

"Suppose, after a few weeks of selling, a buyer realizes her initial estimate of a classification's sales was too low," says Gilberg. "Because it [has traditionally] been difficult to calculate a new OTB plan, and she knows the old plan is incorrect, she begins to operate without any plan at all. No plan, combined with the unquantified feeling that sales will be higher, is a sure formula for overbuying."[2]

Now let's apply the formula for planned purchases to the February figures in your dollar merchandise plan.

Planned EOM stock	$79,000
+ Planned sales	25,400
+ Planned markdowns	3,800
= Stock needed for the month	108,200
− BOM stock	65,000
= planned purchases	43,200

Form 5–5 shows planned retail purchases for the six-month period.

What Supplemental Elements Relate to Dollar Merchandise Planning?

Many retail stores, particularly large departmentalized stores, expand budgeting procedures beyond the four basic elements you have just completed for your dollar merchandise plan. They frequently include goal figures for several additional elements that directly relate to the profit of the operation. Important among these elements are initial markup, gross margin, cash discounts earned as percentage of purchases or sales, rate of stock turnover desired, shortage reserves, and operating expenses as a percentage of net sales.

In most cases, only seasonal goal figures for these supplemental elements are planned. In fewer cases, additional seasonal dollar and percentage-to-sales goal figures are worked out. Goal figures of each of these supplementary elements of the dollar merchandise plan, together with the figures representing the previous year's actual performance, are supplied by the store's controller or fiscal division. (See the top right section of the Six-Month Merchandising Plan shown in Form 5–5.) Since such goal figures reflect the financial objectives of the store as determined by top management, they are rarely left to the discretion of departmental planners.

Guidelines in budgeting these additional elements of the dollar merchandise plan are obtained from the store's own experience, from the *Merchandising and Operating Reports* (MOR) of the National Retail Merchants Association, and frequently from figures supplied by the store's resident buying office.

Dept. Name __Junior Sportswear__   Dept. No. __145__

SIX MONTH MERCHANDISING PLAN

	PLAN (This Year)	ACTUAL (Last Year)
Initial markup (%)	48.5	47.5
Gross margin (%)	42.3	41.8
Cash discount (% cost purch.)	8.0	7.8
Season stock turnover (rate)	2.8	2.6
Shortage reserve (%)	1.5	1.8
Advertising expense (%)	2.8	3.0
Selling salaries (%)	8.0	8.5

SPRING 198—		FEB.	MAR.	APR.	MAY	JUNE	JULY	SEASON TOTAL
~~FALL 198—~~		~~AUG.~~	~~SEP.~~	~~OCT.~~	~~NOV.~~	~~DEC.~~	~~JAN.~~	
SALES	Last Year	24,200	28,400	34,600	31,000	28,200	21,600	168,000
	Plan	25,400	35,400	33,000	34,000	31,000	23,200	182,000
	Percent of Increase	4.95	24.6	−4.6	9.7	9.9	7.4	8.3
	Revised							
	Actual							
RETAIL STOCK (BOM)	Last Year	69,000	71,000	78,000	70,000	68,000	58,000	42,000 *
	Plan	65,000	79,000	74,000	72,000	68,000	52,000	42,000 *
	Revised							
	Actual							
MARKDOWNS	Last Year	4,000	5,000	5,600	4,400	4,400	4,200	27,600
	Plan (dollars)	3,800	4,000	5,000	4,000	4,000	4,200	25,400
	Plan (percent)	15.0	11.3	15.0	11.8	12.9	18.1	14.0%
	Revised							
	Actual							
RETAIL PURCHASES	Last Year	30,200	40,400	32,200	33,400	22,600	9,800	168,600
	Plan	43,200	34,400	36,000	34,000	19,000	17,400	184,000
	Revised							
	Actual							

Comments

*Represents stock end of period.

Merchandise Manager _____   Buyer _____

Controller _____

Form 5-5. The six month merchandising plan showing the plan for retail purchases. The plan is now completed.

Markup

Markup is the difference between the cost price and the retail price of merchandise. Most stores express markup as a percentage of retail value, thus:

$$\text{retail markup \%} = \frac{\$ \text{ retail} - \$ \text{ cost}}{\$ \text{ retail}}$$

Some smaller stores and most manufacturers, however, calculate markup percentages on the basis of cost, or:

$$\text{cost markup \%} = \frac{\$ \text{ retail} - \$ \text{ cost}}{\$ \text{ cost}}$$

If an item cost $60 and is retailed at $100, you can calculate the markup percentage at retail by plugging these dollar amounts into the formula as follows:

$$\text{retail markup \%} = \frac{\$100 - \$60}{\$100}$$

$$= \frac{\$40}{\$100}$$

$$= 40\%$$

You can calculate the markup percent at cost by plugging the same figures into your cost markup formula:

$$\text{cost markup \%} = \frac{\$100 - \$60}{\$60}$$

$$= \frac{\$40}{\$60}$$

$$= 66\tfrac{2}{3}\%$$

Although as a fashion buyer you will almost always use the retail markup formula, you should be familiar with the cost markup formula as well, since it may be used in discussions with suppliers and other retailers. In Chapter 6 you will work again with markup formulas as you decide how to price your merchandise assortment.

The dollar difference between the delivered cost of merchandise and the retail price placed on it when it is first brought into stock is called the **initial markup.** Retail stores plan initial markup percentages to ensure that the income derived from sales (the difference between the cost of goods and the retail prices at which they are first marked) will be adequate to cover:

☐ all expenses incurred in the operation of the business
☐ anticipated reductions in the retail value of the inventory, such as markdowns, stock shortages, and employee discounts
☐ a reasonable margin of profit for the store

Some purchases may yield a higher or lower percentage of markup than is planned. But your aim throughout the season should be to *maintain an average markup* on purchases that is no less than the goal figure indicated on the dollar merchandise plan. This predetermined average figure is intended as a guide, not a figure that you must apply to all purchases.

Gross Margin

In addition to initial markup percentage, some stores plan a desired percent of gross margin. As you learned earlier in this chapter, gross margin is the dollar difference between net sales for a period and the net cost of merchandise sold during that period:

$$\begin{array}{r} \$ \text{ net sales} \\ - \ \$ \text{ net cost of mdse. sold} \\ \hline = \ \$ \text{ gross margin} \end{array}$$

Gross margin percentage is calculated by dividing the dollars of gross margin by the net sales for the period:

$$\frac{\$ \text{ gross margin}}{\$ \text{ net sales}} = \% \text{ gross margin}$$

Gross margin is a very important figure in dollar merchandise planning. It represents the amount of money left from sales income after deducting the total cost of merchandise sold during a given period. The gross margin represents the amount of money available to pay all operating expenses and taxes with a reasonable profit left over.

Cash Discounts

Cash discounts are the percentages or premiums allowed by manufacturers off their invoices if payment of the invoice is made within a certain specified period of time. Such discounts are allowed to encourage the prompt payment of invoices.

Cash discounts earned are an important source of additional income for a store or department. For that reason they are included in most dollar merchandise plans, representing either a percentage of net sales or a percentage of the cost of purchases. Cash discounts increase gross margin, because they reduce the actual cost of merchandise purchases. These are discussed further in Chapter 12.

TERMS OF SALE. The combination of allowable discounts on purchases and the time allowed for taking such discounts is referred to as **terms of sale.** The percentage of cash discount allowed and the length of time allowed for the taking of that discount are fairly standardized within each industry. However, they vary widely from industry to industry. See Chapter 12 for further discussion of terms of sale.

ANTICIPATION. An additional discount granted by some vendors for the payment of their invoices before the end of the cash discount period is called **anticipation.** This is an accounting transaction determined by the Accounts Payable department. Because anticipation further reduces the cost of purchases, retail stores can make profitable use of their capital by taking anticipation whenever bills are paid before the cash discount period ex-

pires. Chapter 12 covers this in greater detail.

Stock Shortages and Overages

Stock shortages or overages represent the dollar difference between the **book inventory** (the value of inventory on hand as indicated by the store's accounting records) and the **physical inventory** (the value determined by taking a physical count). When the book inventory is greater than the physical inventory there is said to be a **stock shortage.** When the physical inventory is greater than the book inventory there is said to be a **stock overage.** Stock shortages are experienced with consistent regularity by retail stores. Stock overages occur rather seldom. Both are discussed in detail in Chapter 8.

Stock shortages or overages can be determined only when a complete physical inventory is taken, which is usually only once or twice a year. But most stores set up interim monthly reserves for tolerable, or anticipated, shortages. This means that a certain percentage of monthly net sales is set aside in a special reserve account. The accumulated reserve fund is then applied as an offset to any actual difference between the book inventory and the actual physical inventory when the latter is taken.

Shortage reserve percentages are usually based upon past experience. The maximum allowable percentage is determined by store management at the beginning of a season or year and does not change from month to month. Actual differences between the value of the book inventory and the value of the physical inventory, as determined from an actual count, are compared with the accumulated shortage reserve when the physical inventory is taken. If the actual shortage is less than the reserve, gross margin is increased by the amount of the difference. If the actual shortage is greater than the reserve, gross margin is thereby reduced by an equivalent amount.

Stock shortages decrease a department's gross margin and ultimate profit and are essentially the responsibility of the buyer. For these reasons, many stores include seasonal shortage reserve figures in their dollar merchandise plans.

Operating Expenses

Two kinds of expenses are incurred in the operation of a selling department: direct and indirect.

Direct expenses are those that occur as a direct result of the operation of a specific department. These are the types of expenses that would cease if the department itself was closed. Examples of such direct expenses are salespeople's salaries, buyer's and assistant's compensation, expenses incurred in connection with buying trips, advertising expenses, and delivery charges.

Indirect expenses are those that do not directly result from the operation of an individual department but are shared by all departments of the store. Examples are compensation of top management executives, utilities, maintenance, insurance, and receiving and marking expenses.

Many stores that include operating expenses as an element of the dollar merchandise budget make it a practice to plan advertising expenses and selling salaries separately. They are planned as seasonal or monthly percentages of planned sales, since these expenses are most intimately related to the actual production of sales. The six-month plan in most stores does not include a budget for indirect expenses, but they are included in the planning of initial markup.

Buying Vocabulary

Define or briefly explain the following terms:

Anticipation	Initial markup
Book inventory	Markdown
Cash discounts	Markdown percentage
Cost of goods sold	Markup
Customer returns and allowances	Monthly stock-sales ratio
Direct expenses	MOR
Dollar merchandise plan	Net sales
Expenses	Open-to-buy
Gross margin	Physical inventory
Income statement	Planned purchases
Indirect expenses	Profit

Profit and loss statement   Stock shortage

Retail method of inventory   Stock turnover

Stock overage   Terms of sale

Buying Review

1. What are your two major objectives when buying stock for resale? How does planning help you realize these objectives?
2. What are the four major goals of financial planning in retail merchandising?
3. Briefly describe the usual procedure for preparing a dollar merchandise plan for one department of a large multiunit store. How would the same procedure be handled if you were buying for a small store?
4. Explain how your dollar merchandise plan can be used by your store management to measure your performance as a buyer.
5. What specific factors or conditions should be carefully considered in estimating the sales potential of a department or a store in a given future period? How may each of these factors or conditions actually influence sales potential?
6. Why do fashion trends frequently have a more important bearing on a - fashion department's sales potential than do economic conditions? Give examples to illustrate your answers.
7. Why is the use of percentages important in planning monthly sales goals?
8. Explain how seasonal and monthly variations affect different departments. When should stocks for these departments be increased or decreased?
9. Describe the two different types of stock-sales relationships. Explain briefly how each is calculated.
10. What are the factors to be considered in planning markdowns? How do you "spend" markdowns to buy additional stock?
11. Why is it important to be able to calculate markup on the basis of both retail value and cost?
12. Explain the difference between direct and indirect expenses. Give examples of both.

Buying Case

You are the buyer in the moderate-priced dress department of a large department store. You are responsible for preparing a six-month dollar merchandise plan, based on both the information discussed in this chapter and a copy of the six-month merchandise plan from last year, which is shown on page 97.

SIX MONTH MERCHANDISING PLAN

Dept. Name __Dresses__   Dept. No. __172__

		PLAN (This Year)	ACTUAL (Last Year)
	Workroom cost		
	Cash discount %		
	Season stock turnover	3.5	3.8
	Shortage %		
	Average stock		380,000
	Markdown %	15	15

SPRING 198—		FEB.	MAR.	APR.	MAY	JUNE	JULY	SEASON TOTAL
FALL 198—		AUG.	SEP.	OCT.	NOV.	DEC.	JAN.	
SALES $	Last Year	135,000	125,000	100,000	125,000	210,000	100,000	825,000
	Plan							985,000
	Percent of Increase							
	Revised							
	Actual							
RETAIL STOCK (BOM) $	Last Year	400,000	380,000	300,000	450,000	400,000	350,000	
	Plan							
	Revised							
	Actual							
MARKDOWNS $	Last Year							123,750
	Plan (dollars)							147,750
	Plan (percent)							15%
	Revised							
	Actual							
RETAIL PURCHASES	Last Year	115,000	45,000	250,000	105,000	160,000	130,000	
	Plan							
	Revised							
	Actual							
PERCENT OF INITIAL MARKON	Last Year							
	Plan							
	Revised							
	Actual							
ENDING STOCK July 31 Jan. 31	Last Year	380,000						
	Plan							
	Revised							
	Actual							

Comments

Merchandise Manager _____   Buyer _____

Controller _____

Your merchandise manager informs you that the store is planning on a small sales increase this year over last year and she expects you to plan accordingly. When you ask for clarification of the word "small," you learn that the planned store increase is to be "somewhere between 2 and 3 percent." Dresses this season have become a more popular fashion item, and you feel that a small increase in sales will not be too difficult to attain.

Calculate sales figures for each month to total your six-month sales plan. Also calculate BOM stock necessary to obtain planned sales, monthly markdowns within the prescribed limit, and the retail value of purchases that can be made within each of the six months being planned. From your planned stock turnover for the period, determine what will be your average stock for this season. Calculate the stock-sales ratio for each of the months being planned and enter these figures under Comments.

Chapter 6

The Fashion Merchandise Assortment Plan

In Chapter 5 you completed a dollar merchandise plan in which you estimated the dollar amount of sales, stock, markdowns, and retail purchases for each of the six months in your next buying season. Now, as you select the actual merchandise that you will offer to your customers, you are responsible for spending the money you have budgeted.

To be successful in your selection, you will have to accomplish an impressive set of goals that are similar to those of dollar merchandise planning:

☐ Estimate, with reasonable accuracy, the peaks and valleys in customer demand that will occur during the season being planned.

☐ Buy and maintain an inventory of those sizes, colors, and price lines that accurately reflect the demands of your customers.

☐ Time your deliveries so that each individual component of the inventory is available for sale neither too early nor too late for customer demand.

☐ Detect and respond to any and all signs of change in your customer's preferences.

☐ Keep your purchases in line with your ability to stock, display, promote, and pay for them.

☐ Keep funds available at all times for the purchase of new or additional goods as they are needed.

☐ Relate the demand for each type of fashion goods you select to the demand for all other types of goods in inventory, so that similar fashion influences and price levels will be reflected throughout your entire merchandise assortment.

☐ Continually evaluate your assortment in terms of newly developing trends in both the wholesale market and customer demand.

The term **merchandise assortment** refers to a collection of varied types of related merchandise that are intended for the same general use. A merchandise assortment is usually grouped together in one selling area of the store. Your **assortment plan** is a comprehensive and detailed listing of all the merchandise you will carry in stock during a given period, classified by size, type, and price line—for example, 48 machine-washable wool pullovers in sizes small, medium, and large, in assorted colors, at $45.

The Keys to Assortment Planning

Needless to say, this important job of assortment planning and merchandise selection cannot be left to chance. Your success will, to a large extent, depend on your ability to utilize the essentials of merchandising you studied in Unit 1 and stay within the budget you studied in Chapter 5, while maintaining a **balanced assortment.** This is an assortment in which the types, quantities, and price lines of merchandise in your inventory closely match the demand of your target customers.

There are six keys to assortment planning, as shown on the right. Each unlocks one important aspect of the fashion picture so that you will have a clear view of the fashion assortment decisions that must be made and the facts on which to base those decisions. These keys include:

1. A clear understanding of your store's merchandising policies.
2. Facts and figures detailing the past experiences of the department you are buying for. This should include buying decisions, sales records, and customer wants.
3. Current information about external factors, internal factors, and fashion trends that will affect your buying decisions.
4. A tailor-made classification system that reflects the specific needs of your customers and department.

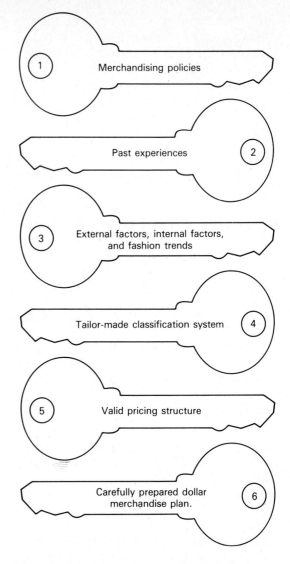

These six keys unlock the door to effective assortment planning.

5. A pricing structure that will allow you to comply with the store's merchandising policies and attract the store's target customers while making a profit.
6. A carefully prepared dollar merchandise plan.

In this chapter you will have the opportunity to examine each of these keys to assortment planning. Then you will have an opportunity to examine the ways in which your assortment planning responsibilities might be different for a single-unit store, a branch-operating department or specialty store or for a chain organization.

Understanding Your Store's Merchandising Policies

The owners or senior executives of your store are responsible for establishing and specifying your store's merchandising policies. You learned in Chapter 3 that these policies are clearly defined methods of doing business. No store can be all things to all people or supply all the needs of all people in a given trading area. As a result, each store must select one or more specific segments of the area's total population that it wants to serve. Then it must establish merchandising policies that best serve the interests and preferences of those target customers.

The merchandising policies of your store should serve as guidelines for you to follow as you develop and maintain merchandising assortments. As you learned in Chapter 3, these policies guide you in the following areas:

- ☐ Price range offerings—high, moderate, low, or very lowest.
- ☐ Quality standards—finest available, serviceable, unspecified quality, or imperfect.
- ☐ Breadth and depth of an assortment—narrow and deep or broad and shallow.
- ☐ Brand offerings—private, national, or unbranded.
- ☐ Exclusivity—emphasized or not emphasized.
- ☐ Fashion leadership—fashion leader, middle-of-the-road, or fashion follower.
- ☐ Maintenance of basic assortments—always in stock, usually in stock, or basic stock unimportant.

Gathering Facts and Figures on Past Experience

After you have determined what the store's merchandising policies are, you will want to gather information about the past buying decisions that were made for the department. This type of information is as important for a buyer who has been in the department for years as it is for a buyer who is new to the department.

You will want to study records of what was bought, sold, and marked down in corresponding past seasons. You will want to determine the best-selling items, the slowest-selling items, and the most (and least) popular styles, fabrics, prices, classifications, kinds, colors, and sizes of merchandise.

In any department where the merchandise is sized, size is often the key selection factor, taking precedence over color, price, styling, or any other fashion variable. A woman who requires a size 14 dress can scarcely be expected to buy a size 10, even if that is the only size available in the style that attracts her. Neither can a man whose foot requires an 11-D shoe be satisfied with the fit of a size 10-C, even if the style pleases him.

Not all sizes enjoy the same rate of sale. Nor is any one color or color combination equally popular in every size in which it is made. You should be sure that all sizes are well represented in your stock at all times in proportion to the needs of your target customers. According to a saying among retailers, "If you're out of a size, you're out of stock."

Some buyers have found they can bolster their store's fashion image and acquire faithful customers by including in their assortments a well-rounded variety of styles, fabrics, and colors in less popular sizes or in size ranges largely overlooked by competitors in the trading area.

Table 6-1

Foundation for Assortment Planning Review of Sportswear Sales for Previous Year

	The Fashion Place		Aurora Fashions	
	Units	Dollars	Units	Dollars
Skirts at $40 each	30	$ 1,200	35	$ 1,400
Skirts at $60 each	50	3,000	40	2,400
Total skirts	80	4,200	75	3,800
Sweaters at $50 each	28	1,400	26	1,300
Sweaters at $70 each	40	2,800	70	4,900
Total sweaters	68	4,200	96	6,200
Pants at $40 each	50	2,000	32	1,280
Pants at $60 each	60	3,600	80	4,800
Total pants	110	5,600	112	6,080
Jackets at $100 each	50	5,000	18	1,800
Jackets at $160 each	9	1,440	16	4,360
Total jackets	59	6,440	34	4,360
Grand total	317	$20,440	317	$20,440

You will also want to track the success that the department had in selling the merchandise supplied by various vendors. In Chapters 7 and 8 you will learn about the various records that will be available to you for gathering this information.

All of the facts and figures you obtain about past experience should be a reliable indicator of recurring demand. But you will want to study them very carefully. Identical sales figures from two different stores, for example, could indicate a significantly different demand.

For a highly simplified example, let's look at some sportswear sales figures for The Fashion Place and for another store, Aurora Fashions, catering to similar groups of customers in a similar geographical area. Each store had identical sales of $20,440 in skirts, sweaters, pants, and jackets last year. Table 6-1 shows two of the many ways in which that $20,440 could have been distributed among the four categories. This is assuming, again in the interest of simplicity, that there were only two price lines carried in each category.

The Fashion Place's customers showed considerable interest in jackets last year. Aurora Fashions' customers had little interest in these garments but showed appreciably more interest in sweaters than did their customers. The Fashion Place's customers showed noticeable interest in lower-priced goods, while the customers at Aurora Fashions had a pronounced interest in higher-priced goods.

In developing assortment plans for a six-month period, you must always carefully consider the important selling seasons that will occur during that period. You can gauge the effect of each on the demand for your department's merchandise. Seasonal variation in demand is one of your primary considerations when planning departmental assortments.

You will also want to consider consumer wants that are not being satisfied. For this information you should talk with salespeople and review want slips. You may also want to survey customers concerning their opinion of the store. Does it meet their expectations? Have they been able to find what they are looking for? If they were to change something about the assortment, what would it be?

Researching Factors and Trends That Influence Assortment Planning

The third key to planning assortments is researching the probable impact of external factors, internal factors, and fashion trends. As you learned in Chapter 5 these factors and trends affect how much customers may be expected to spend in an upcoming season and the types of goods they will buy.

EXTERNAL FACTORS. The economic condition of both the country in general and the local community have a marked effect on your planning. If these conditions indicate that there will be greater affluence in the trading area or a larger proportion of affluent customers than previously served, your store should include more high-priced goods in the assortment than before. You should also include a larger proportion of new and relatively untried fashions and probably a more generous representation of strictly "fun" apparel.

On the other hand, if the community has suffered financial setbacks, there may

be a generally pessimistic attitude toward the future of the economy. Perhaps the unemployment rate is increasing, or taxes, interest rates, and prices are escalating. If this were true, you would feature styles in the assortment that are versatile enough to make a limited wardrobe adequate for many, varied occasions. In this case, the most expensive goods in your assortment should involve minimum fashion risk.

You must also take the local competitive situation into account. Changes in that area may have a direct bearing on the makeup of your fashion assortment. For example, supermarkets and drugstores in a local trading area may be prominently featuring limited styles of low-priced hosiery on self-service racks. If you were hosiery buyer for a local quality department or specialty store, you might decide to play down utility items and increase the offerings of finer quality and newer styles.

INTERNAL FACTORS. Internal factors also affect the assortment plans for any or all parts of a store's inventory. If your selling department's floor space has been enlarged and remodeled, you will probably want to plan for deeper and broader assortments than you had previously. If related departments have been relocated so that they are next to each other, you may want to confer with buyers in these nearby departments and plan larger assortments of matching colors and patterns.

The extent and type of promotional activities your store intends to engage in during the period for which your fashion assortment is being planned is another factor that has a direct bearing on the makeup of your assortment. For example, if the store intends to increase its use of television presentations during that period, your fashion assortments should carry generous quantities of the merchandise that is to be featured. If your store's management has decided to initiate an advertising campaign stressing the values to be found in its merchandise offerings, then value must be a prime consideration when planning your department's assortment.

FASHION TRENDS. Fashion trends, of course, exert a powerful influence on assortment planning for fashion departments. Fashion makes the difference between what was the right assortment yesterday and what can be expected to be the right assortment tomorrow. This is true of both apparel and accessory assortments for men, women, and children. Whatever the trend, fashion rarely affects one department in the apparel or accessories groups without influencing the assortments in all the others.

As a fashion buyer, you should be aware of the fact that customers tend to purchase fashions at a certain stage of their fashion cycle. The degree to which your store's customers show a marked preference for fashions in the introductory, rise, culmination, or decline phases of their cycles is becoming a prime factor in planning assortments for fashion departments. (See Chapter 3 for a discussion of the fashion cycle.)

You must carefully analyze the fashion trends observed in market offerings and decide when, and to what extent, your customers will be ready to accept new fashions. If your customers want only newly introduced fashions, they will not be satisfied with fashions once they are rapidly rising in popular acceptance. But if your customers will not consider purchasing fashion goods until the goods have won widespread acceptance, they will look at, but not buy, fashions in earlier stages of the fashion cycle.

However, it is good merchandising policy for you to include in your fashion department's assortment some merchandise that is in earlier stages of fashion development. As a first step, you might list all the fashion trends you have observed or learned about. List them in what you believe to be their order of importance for your store's customers in the approaching season. Next, you can rank each fashion variable offered in the market—new styles, fabrics, colors, price lines, and any other significant characteristic—according to what you believe to be their prospective sales potential. The newer fashions may be just what the few fashion leaders or influentials among the store's customers are looking for. These leaders can thus give impetus to those fashions on the local scene. Too, a small percentage of merchandise that is more advanced in styling, color, and fabric than that which appeals to most customers lends an aura of fashion leadership to the store's image. Moreover, it helps to adjust customers' eyes to new fashions and prepares them to accept them earlier than otherwise.

Your decisions about fashion assortments should be made easier by your understanding of the fact that fashions are largely evolutionary rather than revolutionary in their movements. Fashion change tends to be fairly gradual. While change may occur in one or more fashion elements (silhouette, detail of design, texture, or color) from one season to another, rarely does change occur in all four elements. Actually, such change is readily predictable once the elements of fashion are isolated and examined in detail.

At the start of each season, you should include in your fashion stocks small test quantities of newly introduced styles, colors, and fabrics. At this time, much of the speculative risk involved in merchandising fashions can be reduced by using only a conservative portion of open-to-buy until customer preferences can be established more definitely. These preferences are established by customer acceptance or rejection of the choices offered in the opening assortments. Once you can see which styles, colors, and fabrics are most popular, then you can reorder these items in depth and promote them aggressively. At the same time, you can narrow down or eliminate from stock other items in the starting assortments in which customers have shown little interest.

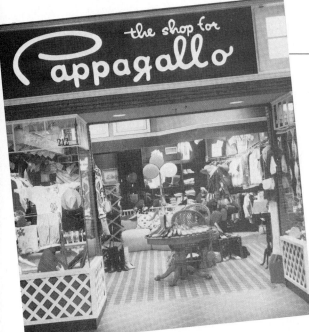

five subclassifications: high-heel dress shoes, 30 percent of the line; low heel, 10 percent; tailored dress shoes, 10 to 15 percent; flats and boots, 10 to 15 percent each.

In addition, Pappagallo moved into "total wardrobing" by complementing its shoes and bags with ready-to-wear, belts, legwear, and hats. Its total assortment is designed to coordinate in colors and styling; for instance, for a recent fall collection, a group of turtleneck shirts and sweaters, priced at $34 to $96, were bought in jewel tones such as emerald, sapphire, and ruby—to set off a range of skirts and pants, priced from $64 to $84, in winter white, navy, black, and charcoal gray. Some multicolored sweaters and monotone jacquard silk blouses featured patterns of paisley, plaid, and florals, which were echoed on legwear and embossed on some leather handbags.

Colors and patterns on the store's packaged hosiery also matched the ready-to-wear for the store's presentation. With hosiery being recognized as a fashion accessory by customers, Pappagallo had expanded its selection in that area as well, dividing it into classifications of casual legwear (socks and sport knee-highs) priced at $4 to $8, and packaged hosiery (pantyhose and textured knee-highs) at $3 to $6.

Rounding out and reinforcing its fashion message was a full assortment of jewelry, including enameled paisley pins, crests and stones on gold chains, and earrings. The jewelry, in fact, turned out to be a real winner for Pappagallo. Originally, the store carried only earrings, selling about 100,000 pairs in a recent year. But when it tested a full line of pins, necklaces, and earrings for the following fall, the merchandise sold so well that the retailer doubled its commitment to manufacturers for the next season.

This Focus is based on information from the following source:
Dorothy Kellett, "How Pappagallo Preens with Updated RTW, Accessories," *Stores*, August 1985, pp. 50–51.

Developing a Tailor-Made Classification System

The fourth key to assortment planning is developing a tailor-made classification system. As a buyer in a store that is currently doing business, you will almost certainly inherit an existing classification system. It will be your responsibility to determine whether this system meets the needs of both you and your customers and change it if it is not appropriate for your needs. In this section we will discuss the purpose of classification, then explain how you would set up classifications for a department in which there is no existing system. Next we will examine the ways in which classification of a fashion department is unique. Once you understand these basics, you will learn how to evaluate the classification system in your department in terms of your needs and the needs of your customers.

PURPOSES OF CLASSIFICATION. As stated in the NRMA *Standard Classification of*

Merchandise, a **classification** is "an assortment of units or items of merchandise which are all reasonably substitutable for each other, regardless of who made the item, the material of which it is made, or the part of the store in which it is offered for sale."[1]

There are two major reasons for subdividing merchandise into classifications. First, it allows you to more precisely define the nature and extent of customer demand so that merchandise is readily available to satisfy that demand. Second, it provides you with a means for better planning and control of the merchandising operation.

To achieve these aims, you must understand that your department is composed of many different types of merchandise. Each different type, although generally related, is intended for a somewhat different use. For example, a Men's Furnishings department is usually made up of such diversified types of merchandise as dress shirts, sport shirts, underwear, hosiery, robes, hats, and accessories. In terms of end use, none of these types of merchandise can be substituted for any other. Each type, therefore, should be designated as a separate classification for assortment planning and control purposes.

ESTABLISHING CLASSIFICATIONS AND SUBCLASSIFICATIONS. If there were no classification system in your department, you would begin the process of setting one up by listing every item at every price line that is currently in stock. The list should include items not currently in stock but which have been included in the department's assortment during the preceding 12-month period. The next step is to sort out the listed items by classification, or end use. Form 6-1, on page 108, shows some of the classifications that might be set up in your rainwear department. After you have established broad classifications on the basis of end use and nonsubstitutability, you continue, in most cases, to set up **subclassifications.** These identify the merchandise within each classification according to various product characteristics. In this way, specific areas of customer demand within the broad classification can be identified. It also may be necessary to indicate the seasons or months each classification and subclassification is carried, since many items, especially fashion goods, are seasonal in nature.

For merchandise planning and control purposes, each classification and subclassification is assigned a permanent identification code, usually a number. In most cases, the code for a classification consists of a fixed range of consecutive numbers. Each subclassification is assigned a specific range of numbers within the wider range assigned to the broad classification.

Next, you will want to study the price lines at which each classification and subclassification will be offered. This will ensure that (1) all price lines within your department's price range are represented in the assortment plan; (2) the best-selling price lines are appropriately represented with the widest variety of types, colors, materials, and sizes; and (3) duplication of merchandise has been minimized, if not prevented. Prices will be discussed more fully when the next key to assortment planning is presented.

CLASSIFYING A FASHION DEPARTMENT. You can apply the principles of classifying and subclassifying items to develop balanced merchandise assortments both to fashion goods and to merchandise that varies less dramatically in type, styling, or color from one season to the next. However, the techniques that you will use in applying

STORE

	ALL CLS	CLASS 1	CLASS 2	CLASS 3	CLASS 4	CLASS 5	CLASS 6	CLASS 7	CLASS 8	CLASS 9	CLASS 0
BRIDGEPO											
WEEK	311	201		110		150					42-
PTD	600	271		379							
SEASON	1682	355		969		400					
TR% CURR	526.31*										
TR%-1 MO	109.97*										
TR%-2 MO	112.64*										
STOCK	7277										
% SALES	3.65*	33.87		47.37		18.75					100.00
% STOCK	3.51*										
BAY SHORE											
WEEK	190			150		40	50				134
PTD	938	154		560		40	50				116
SEASON	1612	238		968		240					
TR% CURR	107.07*										
TR%-1 MO	223.17*										
TR%-2 MO	154.47*										
STOCK	6494										
% SALES	4.28*	16.41		59.70		4.26	5.33				14.28
% STOCK	3.13*										100.00
STAMFORD											
WEEK	412	75		337		50		126			
PTD	1043	145		744							
SEASON	2519	153		1775		209		378			
TR% CURR	195.68*										
TR%-1 MO	103.72*										
TR%-2 MO	114.41*										
STOCK	9294										
% SALES	4.76*	13.90		71.33		4.79		12.08			100.00
% STOCK	4.48*										
COMMACK											
WEEK	100			100		80		42			
PTD	511	154		235				42			
SEASON	1609	154		1245		130					
TR% CURR	56.33*										
TR%-1 MO	113.90*										
TR%-2 MO	65.65*										
STOCK	6232										
% SALES	2.33*	30.13		45.98		15.65		8.21			100.00
% STOCK	3.00*										
COMBINED											
WEEK	8034	2871	126-	4072		947	50	144			112
PTD	21897	4570	126-	14034		2229	50	1028			116
SEASON	63644	5866		47321		8000		2417			
TR% CURR	74.19*										
TR%-1 MO	116.32*										
TR%-2 MO	113.06*										
STOCK	207060										
% SALES	3.00*	20.87		64.09		10.17	.22	4.69			.51
% STOCK											100.00

**** CLASS LEGEND ****

1-BASIC LONG
2-BASIC SHORT
3-STORM LONG
4-STORM SHORT
5-ZIPOUT LONG
6-ZIPOUT SHORT
7-NOVELTIES
8-UNASSIGNED
9-UNASSIGNED

Form 6-1. This printout shows rainwear classified into seven different groups.

these principles, as you actually select the merchandise you will stock, make it a more creative job in a fashion department for several reasons:

First, customer preferences for product characteristics such as styling, color, and fabric usually vary from one season to the next and always vary from one year to the next. As a fashion buyer, you can therefore use past sales experience only as a rough guide in planning assortments for a coming season. Your planning must be based more on the recognition of major fashion trends and on an evaluation of those trends with respect to your store's target groups of customers. This sharply contrasts with the development of seasonal assortment for departments handling more staple goods. Products carried in these assortments have longer demand cycles, and style changes are far less frequent. In departments handling more staple goods, the rate of sale of most items can be plotted with reasonable accuracy. Thus the availability of merchandise remains fairly constant throughout a season and often from one season to the next.

Second, the demand for certain fashion classifications and subclassifications is highly seasonal; so, too, is the availability of this type of merchandise. To be effective, your classification systems for fashion goods must clearly indicate the season or seasons of the year that each classification or subclassification should be included in your assortment.

Third, fashion assortments are often geared to, and effective for, a specific period of time. As a result, you should establish the length of time that each item should be allowed to remain in stock (before being marked down). You can then code the day of receipt and age limit of each item on its price ticket for easy reference. For example, the age code for a

dress, received on April 25, and for which a six-week time limit has been set, might read "4256W." For most other types of assortments, a regular **season code,** indicating the month and season of receipt of the merchandise, is usually considered sufficient. An example would be X13, with X indicating the 1987 spring season and 13 indicating the thirteenth week of that season.

Finally, price-line planning by classification and subclassification is as important for fashion assortments as it is for other types of merchandise. And in many cases it may be more important. The financial risks involved in acquiring merchandise that is so highly seasonal, fragile, and vulnerable to loss in value are great. You cannot afford duplications in your stock or limited assortments in your most popular price lines. As one authority puts it:

Developing a classification plan for a fashion department involves the exercise of considerable imaginative effort prior to the start of each season, yet its creation is essential. It becomes, in effect, the foundation stone upon which the entire structure of assortments and a store's "level of service" must perforce rest.[2]

TAILORING YOUR CLASSIFICATION SYSTEM. Whether you inherit a classification system that has been set up by someone else or set one up yourself, you should evaluate your system in terms of your customers' needs. The question to ask is "Does the system reflect the way in which my customers buy merchandise?"

If the majority of your customers ask for fashions by color, fabric, and size, you can put the store brand merchandise together with that of a number of different designers within the same subclassifications. For example, if a typical customer

MERCHANDISE ASSORTMENT PLAN					PLANNING PERIOD AND YEAR Feb. 198—		PLAN MU % 53.9	DEPARTMENT NO. & NAME 270-Lingerie			PAGE NO. 1	
CLASS NO.	ITEM DESCRIPTION	STYLE NO.	VENDOR	COLORS	SIZE RANGE	COST	RETAIL	MU %	MINIMUM INVESTMENT — UNITS PER STORE				TOTAL UNITS
									A	B	C	D E	
812	C DIOR CAMI	8531	042	WHT, PINK	P-L	10.00	21.00		20	21	15	15	18	89
212	C DIOR PETTI	6531	042	WHT, PINK	P-L	10.50	22.00		20	21	15	15	18	89
615	C DIOR TAPPANT	5531	042	WHT, PINK	4-7	7.25	15.00		16	16	10	10	14	66
514	HENSON HIPSTER	2566	010	WHT, MOCHA	5-7	30.64	5.25		108	132	96	96	108	540
512	HENSON BRIEF	2666	010	WHT, ASSTD	5-7	33.12	5.75		216	252	180	144	144	1008
XXX	JOCKEY BRIEF	1500	069	BGE & WHT	5-8	25.00	4.25		144	144	96	96	144	1680
XXX	JOCKEY HIPSTER	1503	069	BGE & WHT	5-7	23.50	4.00		72	72	—	72	72	576
XXX	JOCKEY BIKINI	1505	069	BGE, WHT	5-7	22.00	3.75		240	180	180	180	240	2940

Form 6-2. This merchandise assortment plan is used by a buyer who is responsible for all the lingerie buying in a multi-unit organization. The buyer must plan the colors and sizes of each style from each vendor and then determine individual store needs for each item.

in your store asks for "blue wool pants in size 10," you can classify all pants together. Then you can make a subclassification for all wool pants. This means that you might have Anne Klein, Donna Karan, Calvin Klein, and your store's private label pants all together within the same subclassification. This is because customers who are looking for blue wool pants will probably consider those from one manufacturer a suitable substitute for those from another manufacturer.

However, if your typical customer asks for pants by name—"Anne Klein pants in size 10"—you will want to put all Anne Klein pants into one subclassification, all Donna Karan pants into another, all private label pants into another, and so forth.

When your classification system is tailored in this manner, you will be able to buy into these classifications and trace your unit control and inventory needs according to the specific needs of your customers.

Setting Your Pricing Structure

The fifth key to assortment planning is setting a pricing structure that will allow you to comply with the store's merchandising policies and attract the store's target customers while making a profit. As you already know, the store's pricing policy is set by management as a part of the established merchandising policies. In this section you will learn some important price-related terminology. Then you will learn three basic tools for pricing your assortment: establishing price lines, pricing the items you buy, and identifying best-selling price lines.

PRICE-RELATED TERMINOLOGY. For a clearer understanding of retail pricing and its importance in assortment planning, you should understand the meaning of several price-related terms and their relevance in assortment planning.

Price-Lining. The term **price-lining** refers to the practice of determining the various but limited number of retail prices at which your department's assortments will be offered.

Price Line. The term **price line** refers to a specific price point at which an assortment of merchandise is *regularly* offered for sale. For example, if the Misses' Dress Department at The Fashion Place regularly offers a selection of dresses in a variety of styles, colors, and sizes at $39, $49, $69, $89, $129 and $159, each specific price is known as a price line.

Price Range. The term **price range** refers to the spread between the lowest and the highest price line carried. The price range in the Misses' Dress Department mentioned above is $39 to $159.

Price Zone. The term **price zone** refers to a series of price lines that are relatively close to each other and that are likely to appeal to one particular segment of a store's or a department's customers.

The three most widely accepted retail price zones are:

☐ Promotional (lowest price lines carried)
☐ Volume (middle price lines, where the largest volume of sales occur)
☐ Prestige (highest price lines carried, usually to lend importance to the assortment as a whole)

All three price zones are normally found within any departmental price range, regardless of what or how many price lines may be included. They apply to the price structures of basement or budget departments, to prestige or high-fashion departments, as well as to moderate-priced departments.

For example, within the price range of the Misses' Dress Department at The Fashion Place the price lines included in the three typical price zones might be:

☐ Promotional (or lowest): $39–$49
☐ Volume (or medium): $69–$89
☐ Prestige (or highest): $129–$159

The number of units sold in each price zone, as a percentage of total department sales, will vary, however, from one department to another, from one store to another, and from one selling season to another. For instance, a department store tends to do 50 to 60 percent of its business in the volume price zone, 35 percent in the promotional price zone, and 5 to 15 percent in the prestige price zone. But in a high-fashion specialty store, the largest volume of business would be done in the prestige price zone, a moderate amount in the medium price zone, and almost none in the lower price zone.

TOOLS FOR PRICING. As a departmental buyer you are responsible for establishing specific price lines within the range assigned to your particular department. You are also responsible for the pricing and repricing of individual items included in the assortment.

Establishing Price Lines. In establishing retail price lines, you should be careful to establish significant dollar differences between price lines. Customers should be able to readily distinguish differences in quality that exist, or should exist, in your merchandise at various price lines.

While it is advantageous from the standpoint of customer goodwill for you to maintain the same price lines on a continuing basis, this is not always possible. Higher wholesale prices inevitably result in higher retail prices. Higher costs of doing business at the retail level inevitably result in a wider spread between an item's wholesale and retail prices.

Pricing the Items You Buy. Once you have established price lines, you will "buy into" those price lines. This means that you will price merchandise at the established price line that comes closest to covering the wholesale price of an item plus the initial markup. For example, if the wholesale price of an item is $30.00 and the initial markup required is 48 percent, you can calculate the item's retail price to be $57.62.

$$\text{Retail price} = \frac{\$ \text{ Cost}}{100\% - \text{Markup } \%}$$

$$\text{Retail price} = \frac{\$30.00}{100\% - 48\%}$$

$$\text{Retail price} = \frac{\$30.00}{52\%}$$

$$\text{Retail price} = \$57.62$$

Although $57.62 is not one of your established price lines, it is close enough to $58 so that you can easily price the item at $58. If your calculated retail price turned out to be between two price lines, you would consider the item's sales potential at one of these prices. If you thought the quality of the item was comparable to other items in stock priced at the higher price, you could select the higher of the two prices. If it was not, you would select the lower price.

In addition to wholesale cost and quality, other factors influence your retail pricing practices. These factors include:

☐ Competitors' prices for the same or similar merchandise
☐ Manufacturers' "suggested" retail price (for example, those of nationally advertised brands)
☐ Your store's pricing policies (low, medium, or high) and the required correlation of prices between its departments
☐ Nature of the goods (exclusive, high markdown risk, fragile)
☐ Demand and supply

Best-Selling Price Lines. Among your department's price lines, there will always be a limited number that account for the greater share of your department's dollar and unit sales volume. These are referred to as **best-selling price lines.** These lines are usually concentrated in the middle of your department's price range and this is where customer preference usually is targeted.

You should make an attempt to identify these best-selling price lines. Then you should plan your assortments so that the greatest number of units in the greatest variety of types, colors, materials, and sizes are offered at these price lines. You should then plan other price lines on the basis of the relative sales importance of each price line to your department's total volume.

Working with a Carefully Prepared Budget

The sixth and final key to assortment planning is your dollar merchandise plan. In Chapter 5, you learned how to prepare a dollar merchandise plan. And in this chapter you have learned how to plan your merchandise assortment. As you already know, when you plan your assortment, you must stay within the figures you have developed in your dollar merchandise plan. There are two methods of planning your budget. The first, known as dollar merchandise planning, was discussed in Chapter 5 and will be reviewed here briefly. The second method, known as unit planning, is discussed in detail in this chapter.

DOLLAR MERCHANDISE PLANNING. For purposes of review, the six-month merchandise plan is based on the dollar value of anticipated sales, optimum stock levels, necessary markdowns, and allowable purchases. The dollar plan is an essential part of merchandise assortment planning for the following reasons:

- ☐ It indicates the minimum sales objectives of the store or department.
- ☐ It serves to guide management in planning for and controlling the capital needed for inventory investment throughout the period.
- ☐ It serves as a guide in making purchases.
- ☐ It provides a base against which sales-related operating expenses can be measured.
- ☐ It serves as a guide in planning promotional expenditures.
- ☐ It provides management with a means of measuring the results of merchandising efforts by establishing seasonal goal figures such as planned sales, rate of stock turnover, and gross margin.[3]

Under the dollar method of planning, it becomes your responsibility to provide, within dollar limitations, a merchandise assortment that is at all times balanced to customer demand in terms of classification and price line.

UNIT PLANNING. However, dollar planning does not ensure that your assortment will be well-balanced to demand. This is because it does not pinpoint the nature and extent of customer demand at specific times within the planning period. As a result, an increasing number of buyers are now combining dollar merchandise planning with unit planning, especially in fashion departments. Under **unit planning,** you plan your sales and beginning-of-the-month inventories in terms of units of merchandise by classifications and price lines. When you multiply these units by their respective price lines, your outcome is dollar classification figures for planned sales and stock. You then plan unit purchases in the same way you plan dollar purchases.

The advantages of planning by units rather than dollars are:

- ☐ It is more consistent with the way sales are actually made, since customer purchases are made in units of merchandise.
- ☐ It serves as a guide to the types and quantities of stock needed to achieve unit sales goals for each price line in each class.
- ☐ It helps reduce inventory investment in slow-moving merchandise.
- ☐ It provides a base for developing monthly open-to-buy figures so that active classifications and price lines are not penalized because of the more sluggish ones.
- ☐ It helps to minimize departmental overbuying.

Table 6-2 illustrates how a casual dress department with two major classifications might construct its sales plan for February using unit planning.

First, you determine the number of unit sales anticipated at each price line within each classification. Next, you compute the dollar value of the unit sales planned at each price line within each classification by multiplying the price line by the number of units. Finally you total both the units of planned sales and their dollar equivalents to produce the overall, departmental planned sales for February.

Table 6-2

Dept.: 40
Name: Casual Dresses

Season: Spring 198_
Month: February

Class	Price Line	Description	Planned Sales Units	Planned Sales Dollars
12301	$ 39	Dresses, misses'	30	$ 1170
12302	49	Dresses, misses'	36	1764
12303	69	Dresses, misses'	40	2760
12304	89	Dresses, misses'	38	3382
12305	129	Dresses, misses'	15	1935
12306	159	Dresses, misses'	12	1908
12300		Total, dresses, misses'	171	12919
12801	$ 39	Dresses, juniors	25	975
12802	49	Dresses, juniors	32	1568
12803	69	Dresses, juniors	36	2484
12804	89	Dresses, juniors	30	2670
12805	129	Dresses, juniors	18	2322
12806	159	Dresses, juniors	10	1590
12800		Total, dresses, juniors	151	11609
		Total, Casual Dresses	322	24528

The unit sales plan will also help you in planning the stock needed at the beginning of each month or season. Stock-sales ratios may be applied to the unit sales planned at each price line. You can derive totals in both units and dollars, as in sales planning. Finally, you calculate planned purchases in both units and dollars for each price line in each classification, and for the department as a whole. The procedure described in the explanation of dollar purchase planning in Chapter 5 is used for these calculations.

Using the Keys to Assortment Planning

Planning, establishing, and maintaining a complete fashion assortment should be an ongoing program, not just one that is undertaken only when sales are down and inventories up. Formal, end-of-season reviews of departmental assortment plans serve a very beneficial purpose for future planning. Less formal reviews conducted on a regular basis throughout each six-month season are also essential in fashion departments.

Fashion is rarely static, and your fashion assortment plan must reflect the dynamics of the fashion industry. Fads come and go. Fashion trends follow a fairly normal pattern of development or fade quickly into obscurity. "Hot items" appear unexpectedly. These and other changes in customer preference often take place after a planned season is already under way.

To be successful, you must be constantly on the alert for, and receptive to, such changes. When you use the six keys to assortment planning, you will develop a successful assortment plan that satisfies the goals listed at the beginning of this chapter.

Fashion Assortment Planning in Multiunit Retail Organizations

The six keys to assortment planning are as valid for a multiunit retail organization as they are for a small independent department store such as The Fashion Place. However, the process for "accomplishing" some of these keys may differ. In this section we will discuss some of those differences.

Multiunit retail organizations are of two types: (1) branch-operating department and specialty stores and (2) chain organizations. Each of these two types of organizations has traditionally used merchandising and operating methods that are almost completely different from those of the other. Each is gradually adopting some of the other's methods, however, and while still distinct, these organizations are not as different today as they once were.

Branch-Operating Department and Specialty Stores

In branch-operating department and specialty stores, assortment planning and control are essentially as they have been described in this chapter. Planning techniques, however, may vary from one retail organization to another, depending upon the number, size, and location of branches.

ASSORTMENT PLANNING. In smaller retail organizations with only a few, relatively small branches in nearby locations, responsibility for merchandising all stores in the group is vested in the parent store executives. Branches are considered "outposts" and concentrate solely on selling. Buyers and other executives of the organization are headquartered in the parent store. Communication with branches is maintained mainly by telephone and periodic visits by parent store executives. All merchandising records are kept in the parent store for the convenience of buyers and other store executives. Buyers are ultimately responsible for transmitting merchandising information to all sales personnel, wherever located, and for departmental sales results.

In operations of this size, seasonal departmental merchandise budgets are prepared by the parent store buyers and include figures for branches as well as the parent store. There is little formal planning of assortments for each of the branches, since branch and parent store stocks are usually considered as one.

In developing a preliminary seasonal assortment plan for all stores in the group, fashion buyers use the keys to assortment planning described in this chapter. They study records and reports on sales, stock, markdowns, and promotions in the corresponding season of the previous year. They carefully shop the market. They consider the different preferences of customers of each store in the group, through personal observation and discussions with store personnel at the branches. Guided by these considerations, they develop a preliminary assortment plan for their departments, regardless of where the merchandise will be located.

In retail operations of this size, fashion merchandise is usually tested only in the parent store at the start of a new season. Once the season has gotten under way, buyers rarely place merchandise orders for specific branches. Instead, they simply select from newly received shipments those styles, colors, sizes, and price lines most suitable for each branch, and the merchandise is transferred to that branch.

In larger retail organizations with larger, more numerous, and often more distantly located branches, planning is much more formal. Usually, separate merchandise budgets are prepared, separate assortments are planned, and separate unit controls are maintained for each branch. Customer preference may vary widely from branch to branch, especially in the case of fashion goods. Therefore, branch store managers, merchandise managers, and department managers are usually consulted when seasonal assortment plans are being developed.

To attract its target market, a branch-operating organization, no matter how widely dispersed its branches are, should maintain a distinctive fashion image. To do this, it must always have in stock certain fashion assortments and price lines in keeping with that fashion image. However, this merchandise need not make up the total fashion assortments of any one branch. Basic fashion assortments can be provided to all stores by the parent store's departmental buyer. But other items in a branch store's assortments should be more directly related to specific local demand at that branch.

TRENDS. Large branch organizations today are allowing their individual branches greater autonomy in developing their own fashion merchandise budgets and in developing and maintaining their own assortment plans. This has come about for one or more of the following reasons:

□ Many branches today are as large as, or even larger than, the parent store.

□ Sales volume of branches now far exceeds that of most parent stores.
□ Many branches are located at considerable distance from the parent store, thus complicating communication. The Chicago-based firm of Marshall Field, for example, has branches in Texas.
□ Patterns of demand and competitive practices vary from branch to branch according to the trading area in which each branch is located.

In general, therefore, the more numerous a store's branches, or the larger their size, or the greater their distance from the parent store, the greater the need for fashion assortments that are precisely tailored to the needs of the customers of each branch.

Chain Organizations

A chain organization has previously been defined as a group of retail stores that are centrally owned, all handling similar goods and merchandised from a national or regional headquarters office. (See Chapter 4.)

Chain operation is chiefly characterized by central buying and merchandising. Individual units of the chain are engaged only in selling. Central buyers, located in major market areas or a headquarters office, are responsible for providing merchandise for all units of the chain. Centrally purchased fashion merchandise is usually sent to a distribution center, where merchandise is allocated and distributed to the various units of the chain.

Methods of planning fashion assortments for each unit vary from one chain to another. This is particularly true with respect to the amount of autonomy granted individual units in determining the composition of their assortments. For example, in one chain, assortment planning for all units may be the responsibility of the national or regional headquarters office. In another chain, all regular assortments may be planned by the headquarters' merchandising staff, with store units only permitted to make decisions relating to the timing, type, and extent of promotions in which they may wish to engage. In yet another chain, what is considered a basic, seasonal fashion assortment is detailed by the headquarters staff. Suggestions for additional items, classifications, subclassifications, and price lines that are available through the buying office, to round out and complete the seasonal assortments of each unit, are offered in the form of a listing prepared and distributed by the chain's headquarters or regional merchandise office. In this case, complete descriptions, costs, and retail prices of suggested merchandise are provided to assist the unit management in making selections best suited to that particular store's customers. In such cases, the chain's district manager usually works with the store manager, the fashion (or soft-goods) merchandise manager, and the appropriate department manager in finalizing a seasonal fashion assortment plan.

Individual store merchandise budgets, seasonal assortment plans carefully detailed by classifications and price lines, and weekly or biweekly sales and stock-on-hand reports provide the framework within which fashion merchandise is distributed to each store unit. The success of a chain operation depends on the continuous flow of accurate sales and stock information from its store units to its headquarters office. Only in this way can inventories be properly balanced with demand.

Chain organizations were pioneers in the use of computerized systems to control retail inventories. Only computers can handle the tremendous flow of merchandising data generated in a chain's operation. And only such systems can rapidly convert those data into accurate and timely reports for use by chain executives in decision making.

CATALOG OPERATION. In chain organizations, the planning of fashion assortments to be offered in catalog issues is the responsibility of a separate catalog buying and merchandising staff, located in the headquarters office. The reason for maintaining separate staffs for store sales and catalog sales is the timing of the offerings. However, the two staffs work closely with each other. Catalog assortments have to be decided upon many months before those that are offered in the chain's retail stores. This is because of the amount of time involved in the assessment of trends, the selection of individual items, the printing of the catalog, and the delivery of that catalog into the hands of the customers. All of this must take place before the peak of demand for the merchandise offered in the catalog. Fashion merchandise offered in catalogs thus has to be planned and priced far in advance of its actual availability in the wholesale market. For this reason, its planners not only have to excel in accurate prediction of fashion trends but in most cases have to buy fabrics and have them made up to the chain's specifications. In addition, the catalog buying and merchandising staff has to make sure that stock of each item in the catalog will be available upon demand.

Conventional retail organizations are adopting many chain store techniques for more profitable merchandising results. For example, a buyer working in the flagship store unit may be responsible for selecting goods for all the branches of a department store. Such a buyer is typically relieved of the selling floor responsibilities traditionally associated with the position. At the same time, chain organizations have begun to adopt, to an increasing extent, some of the more successful techniques of traditional retail merchandising. In particular, many chain organizations are now allowing executives of store units more autonomy in merchandising and operating decisions.

Chain organizations are also becoming increasingly fashion-minded. They are devoting considerably more space in their stores and in their catalogs to apparel and home furnishings. They are expanding and upgrading their fashion assortments. They are emphasizing fashion coordination more in their advertisements and displays. Their newer stores are bright, spacious, and colorful, with attractive fixtures, fitting rooms, and carpeting. Many have beauty salons and a variety of other fashion services. All indications point to a continuation of this trend.

References

1 NRMA, *Standard Classification of Merchandise*, p. 15.
2 Charles G. Taylor, *Merchandise Assortment Planning*, Merchandising Division, NRMA, New York, 1970, p. 15.
3 Taylor, op. cit., p. 25.

Buying Vocabulary

Define or briefly explain the following terms:

Assortment plan	Price-lining
Balanced assortment	Price range
Best-selling price lines	Price zone
Classification	Season code
Merchandise assortment	Subclassification
Price line	Unit planning

Buying Review

1. What are the major goals of assortment planning?
2. Name the six keys to assortment planning and briefly explain or define each.
3. Name and briefly discuss five major areas of merchandising policy that influence the composition of a store's or a department's fashion assortment.
4. Describe at least three internal and three external factors that might affect your assortment planning.

5. Discuss the importance of fashion trends in assortment planning. How does the degree to which your store's customers show a preference for fashions in the four phases of the fashion cycle affect your buying choice?
6. Describe how fashion stock is tested by including newly introduced styles in your fashion assortment at the beginning of each season.
7. Briefly explain how you would go about altering an already established classification system to better suit your needs. Under what circumstances is it advisable to consider adding additional subclassifications?
8. Why is the price structure of your store and/or your department an important consideration in planning assortments? Who is usually responsible for determining price structure? What factors should you consider when pricing goods?
9. Why do stores use price lines and what are some considerations in establishing price lines? As a buyer, how do you "buy into" price lines?
10. Name and briefly describe the two major methods of planning merchandise budgets and assortments. Which method is considered best for planning fashion assortments, and why?
11. Compare and contrast fashion assortment planning in: (a) smaller, branch-operating department or specialty stores, (b) large, branch-operating department or specialty stores, and (c) chain stores.

Buying Case

You are an assistant buyer in a large branch-operating menswear store, Frank Stewart, Ltd., which carries a medium-to-high-priced line of dress and sportswear for men.

You have been asked to price a new shipment of dress shirts that your buyer has purchased. The store has established price lines for dress shirts at $25, $28, $34, $38, and $42. Given the following information on the wholesale prices, set the retail price for each shirt.

Wholesale prices: (1)$11.50, (2)$14.25, (3)$26.50, (4)$15.50, (5)$15.75, (6)$17.50, (7)$16.20. The initial markup is 49 percent. Show all of your calculations on your answer sheet. If it is not possible to fit these retail prices into your established price lines from the information presented, describe the problem as you would if you were talking with your buyer.

Chapter 7

Unit Control

"I must have total control of my business at all times," explained a bright young fashion buyer from the Chicago-based buying offices of Marshall Field. "My selling card [record of sales figures] is very important," she continued. "I have to know how many weeks' supply [of stock] I have on hand at any one time based on my sales figures." She had to know both what was selling well and what was *not* selling.

As a successful buyer, you too will need to keep tight control on the fashion assortment. By identifying developing trends in customer demand, you will be able to adjust your assortment as the season progresses and plan for upcoming seasons. Your control decisions will be based on current detailed reports, stock on hand, and stock on order.

The system for obtaining these records is called **unit control.** Unit control records tell you the total history of a particular merchandise item or style; show the number of units purchased, sold, ordered, returned, and in stock; and help you to gauge and predict buying trends. Buyers who learn how to analyze these records are able to tell which items are "hot" and which are rapidly becoming outdated.

There is no standard unit control system. Systems differ in format from store to store and from one type of merchandise to another. They also vary widely in terms of the methods used for collecting and reporting data and in the amount of detail collected.

In a single small store, unit control may be relatively simple and informal. Because the amount of stock is limited, a buyer can often use "visual inspection" to see what is selling rapidly, slowly, or not at all. As stores grow in physical size and sales volume, however, the need for a formal unit control system becomes increasingly important. And as branches are opened, the need for a good unit control system that provides sales and stock information about all store units—regardless of their number, size, or location—becomes absolutely essential. An increasing number of stores now have computerized unit control systems that instantly tabulate current information and issue daily reports. These are discussed later in this chapter.

In learning about unit control, it is helpful to remember that the word "control" is somewhat misleading. A better term might be "unit records," since the various systems are set up to collect data which buyers use in their analyses. The systems themselves do not provide controls, only information to help you control your inventory and determine how closely your assortments meet customer demand.

Type of Information Recorded

Regardless of the type of system used or the type of merchandise involved, a unit control system may be set up to show:

- ☐ net sales in number of units
- ☐ stock on hand and on order in number of units
- ☐ additional breakdown of this sales and stock information in whatever detail is considered relevant, such as cost, price line and/or price range, style number, size, color, vendor, classification and subclassification, season code, and, in multiunit stores, the store unit involved.

The kind of sales and stock information and the extent of details collected depend upon the type of merchandise involved. They also depend on what the buyer needs to know in order to properly gauge changes in customer demand. Changes in styling or rate of acceptance for staple goods, for instance, are relatively slow. For this reason, unit control systems used for staple goods may be set up to collect only general information which may be quite adequate for their purpose.

Even in a highly volatile department, such as women's sportswear, there are some fashion items that are slow to change, such as crew neck sweaters or polo shirts. This type of item may require only the recording of unit sales and stock figures by size, price line, and color.

For fashion sportswear in the same department, however, you will need a system to collect more detailed information. For example the consumer who is shopping for a better blouse is more likely to be looking for one particular style. And the demand for this type of fashion merchandise is subject to rapid change. The unit control information should include sizes, colors, classification, vendor, retail price, style number, and season code. The unit control system that is right for any individual department or business is one that provides current and accurate facts about what its customers are or are not buying, and at the same time does not collect unnecessary details.

Types of Systems

There are two basic types of unit control systems used to record fashion assortment data: perpetual (running or continuous) control and periodic stock-count control. The types of merchandise for which each is best suited and the procedures involved in maintaining each are discussed in the following sections.

Perpetual Control

In a **perpetual control** system, purchase orders, receipts of merchandise, and sales are recorded, as they occur, by individual style numbers. From these figures, you can compute stock on hand. This system eliminates the need for actual stock counts except for regular physical inventories.

The information provided by perpetual controls can help you keep track of any of the merchandise that is subject to frequent style change. If you put a new-look, two-piece wool suit with a pleated skirt on the floor on September 9, you will want to know how it is selling on a day-by-day basis. If you thought you had a three-week supply and it sells out in 10 days, you will want to identify this as a "hot" item and adjust your plans to take advantage of the demand.

THE LOGIC OF PERPETUAL CONTROL. Perpetual control begins when you decide on the merchandise that will be carried in your assortment. At that time you record (either manually or by computer) each style that has been selected in each classification. You note specific identifying information such as classification, style number, a brief description of the merchandise, vendor, cost price, and retail price. Each time you place an order for that merchandise, you record the number of pieces ordered and the date of the order.

When the goods are received, you make an entry to show the total number of pieces received and their date of receipt. At the same time, you reduce the number of pieces noted as "on order."

When you record sales in units (either manually or by computer), the date of sale is noted, and the number of units "on hand" is reduced accordingly. You also record by units both returns-to-vendor, which decrease the stock on hand, and returns from customers, which increase the stock on hand.

Most perpetual inventory systems also provide for a breakdown of each style by size and color. Thus, at any time you can tell from looking at the perpetual control records how many units of an individual style, color, and size were purchased, have been sold to date, are on order, and remain in stock by store location.

Stores with only one or a few branches, and with a central unit control system, usually tally by size and by color the number of units in each style that are transferred to each branch. The parent store then records branch store sales by style, size, and color from the sales records received from the individual branches. Larger department stores with numerous branches usually use a unit control system that permits them to keep sales and stock-on-hand information for each branch as well as for the parent store. This enables the buyer at the parent store to calculate sales and stock data by style, size, and color for each store and for all stores combined.

FORMS. Although manual perpetual control systems are being replaced by computerized systems in the majority of stores, we will look briefly at the forms that are used with a manual system. Then we will look at the same information as it is recorded in a computerized system.

Manual. Form 7-1 shows how a manually kept perpetual control record of an individual style might look after the buyer has received into stock 86 pieces of that style. On August 15, 86 pieces were ordered, and at that time strokes were made in pencil in the applicable color and size block for each unit ordered. When the merchandise was received on September 5, the "on order" entry was circled to indicate that it had been received in full. An entry was also made to this effect in the

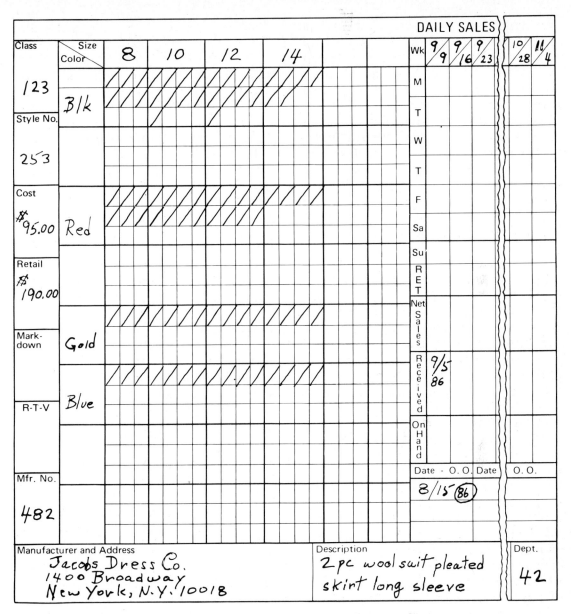

Class	Size / Color	8	10	12	14				Wk	9/9	9/16	9/23		10/28	11/4
123	Blk	////	////	////	////				M						
Style No.			////	////	////				T						
253									W						
									T						
Cost $95.00	Red	////	////	////	////				F						
									Sa						
Retail $190.00									Su						
									RET						
									Net Sales						
Mark-down	Gold	////	////	////	////				Received	9/5 86					
R-T-V	Blue	////	////	////	////				On Hand						
Mfr. No.									Date - O.O.	8/15 86		Date	O.O.		
482															

DAILY SALES

Manufacturer and Address
Jacobs Dress Co.
1400 Broadway
New York, N.Y. 10018

Description
2 pc wool suit pleated skirt long sleeve

Dept. 42

Form 7-1. A perpetual inventory control record. This is how the form was filled in manually when the order was received.

"received" block. Penciled tallies of the units of sizes and colors ordered were then inked over with a diagonal line to indicate the exact number of pieces received by color and size.

Form 7-2 shows how the control card for the same style number might look after the style had been on sale for two weeks. Sales have been recorded daily, noting the total number of units sold each

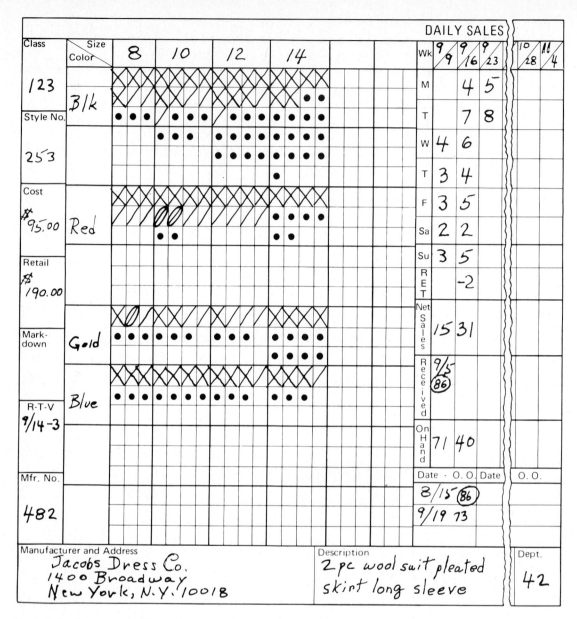

Form 7-2. The perpetual inventory control record as it was filled in after the merchandise had been selling for two weeks.

day as well as their size and color distribution. Customer returns have also been noted and reentered into stock on hand by size and color. Net sales for each week have then been totaled. Any return-to-vendor has also been noted, indicating date of return and the number of pieces involved. Lines corresponding to each size and color returned have been circled to indicate this action.

In this case, the buyer could see that the demand for larger sizes and for the color black was underestimated. When reordering the style, the buyer will note the date and the number of pieces in the "on order" section of the form. Appropriate dots in pencil will serve to indicate the number of units reordered in each color and size.

One buyer's experience illustrates how practical these records are. Early-season information showed that black coats were selling unusually fast. This was further confirmed by sales personnel. The buyer immediately shifted all his new coat purchases exclusively to black. When the major selling season started, this buyer's department was the only one in the area with an assortment of black coats in the depth needed in wanted styles and sizes. Customers passed the word of the place to buy the black coats, and sales zoomed.

Automated. An automated unit control system is simply a computerized version of a manual unit control system. The sales and stock records kept in the system's memory banks may be updated weekly, daily, or as transactions occur. At any point the system can be instructed to print out periodic reports in as much depth as needed on a department's sales and stock by classification, vendor, style, and price line.

Today a number of large retail organizations have computerized systems that handle, among many other jobs, the automatic collection and processing of merchandise information. An increasing number of medium-size and smaller stores are also benefiting from electronic technology by using the services of independent computer service centers. These centers provide computer knowledge, standardized data-processing programs (including unit control programs), and

computer time to participating companies. Still other companies are purchasing their own microcomputers or small business computers together with the software they need to handle their own computerized perpetual inventory systems. Form 7-3 shows a computerized perpetual inventory report. On this report you will notice the same kinds of information as shown on the manually prepared report, Form 7-2. (A more detailed description of automated unit control systems and procedures will be given later in this chapter.)

Whatever the exact method, a perpetual control system enables a merchant to compare the total number of units sold of each style or group of styles from day to day and week to week. It also shows the total number of units sold thus far in the season.

The importance of this knowledge becomes apparent if one considers the sample of two styles, each of which has had sales of 60 pieces during a 10-week period. If weekly sales reports are available, a situation such as that shown in Table 7-1 becomes obvious: One style is dwindling in acceptance, while the other is increasing in popularity. Without such weekly reports, this very important difference could be missed.

Periodic Stock-Count Control

A unit control system in which stock is counted and recorded at regular intervals and the results used to compute sales for the intervening period is known as **periodic stock-count control.** This type of unit control system is best suited for merchandise that is moderate to moderately low in price and less subject to fashion change than ready-to-wear. It is also suitable for merchandise that does not lend itself to easy tagging by multipart or print-punch

Elston's
COLOR AND SIZE UNIT CONTROL REPORT

Dept. 42   **Three Days Ending 12/08/8-**   Page 3   01

SELLING PRICE	CLASS	VENDOR	STYLE	STORE NO.	NET STORE TOTALS	COLOR CODE	06	08	10	12	14	16
48.00	40	012	0555	2	−1	01				−1		
				13	2	01					2	
58.00	40	018	0699	4	1	01				1		
64.00	40	018	0753	3	1	01				1		
32.00	40	020	0401	1	3	01				1	1	1
				45	1	01					1	
32.00	40	020	0406	1	1	22				1		
				23	1	22						1
26.00	90	020	0422	3	1	50					1	
26.00	90	020	0424	4	1	50					1	
				23	1	50						1
32.00	40	020	0458	1	1	01				1		
32.00	90	020	1120	1	−1	00						−1
				4	3	01			1	1		1
					1	47					1	
					3	01				1	2	
				53	−1	40			−1			
44.00	43	020	1206	1	1	15				1		
				10	−1	34				−1		
44.00	43	020	1217	1	1	01				1		
40.00	90	020	1401	4	2	34		2				
40.00	90	020	1403	4	1	01				1		
					4	34				2	2	
				3	1	00				1		
				7	1	01			1	1	−1	

Form 7-3. Part of a computer-generated color and size unit control report. Much of the information on the manually prepared perpetual inventory control record is reported here.

Table 7-1

Sales of Two Separate Styles

	Units Sold	
	Style 142	Style 256
Week 1	10	2
Week 2	10	2
Week 3	10	2
Week 4	8	3
Week 5	7	5
Week 6	6	7
Week 7	3	8
Week 8	2	8
Week 9	2	10
Week 10	2	13
Total, 10 weeks	60	60

tickets. Examples of this kind of merchandise are children's socks, cosmetics, hosiery, and notions. This type of stock control is considerably easier for you to maintain than a perpetual control system and consequently less expensive for the store.

PROCEDURE. In periodic stock-count control, you do not need to record sales as they occur. You can simply calculate stock on hand, stock on order, and sales from the inventory changes that have taken place between counts. The results of this calculation are not as accurate or detailed as the results provided by a perpetual control system. However, they are sufficiently detailed and accurate to indicate trends in demand and the level of demand for less volatile merchandise. They also enable you to maintain stock levels consistent with the sales rate of individual items or groups of items.

In a manual periodic stock-count control system you are responsible for seeing that stock is counted at designated time intervals. The number of units on hand and on order—by classification, price, style number, size, and color (if applicable)—is recorded. You must also see that there is an accurate record of the orders placed and merchandise received since the previous count was taken. You can then compute unit sales during the intervening period (daily, weekly, monthly) as follows:

Unit sales during the intervening period =

units of stock at previous count

+ units received since previous count

− units on hand at present count

The common procedure for periodic counts is for the buyer to divide the stock into sections and specify the dates on which counts of these sections are to be made. Responsibility for making these counts is divided among various salespeople and assistants. By assigning different dates and different personnel to this job, you can be sure that no one person or one day is devoted entirely to stock counts. Some vendors send representatives to stores to take these counts. The vendor assumes responsibility for informing the buyer of the results and works with the buyer to plan what has to be ordered.

FORMS. The most convenient form for keeping such records manually is a loose-leaf notebook with a pair of facing pages assigned to each style or group of items. (See Form 7-4R and 7-4L.) On the left-hand page (7-4L) are listed style numbers, classification codes, descriptions, vendor's name and address, cost and retail prices, and other information needed for writing up an order. Such information may include the minimum packaging for each item. This is an important factor to

Department No. 15

Vendor Ricci Glove Company
Gloversville, New York 12078

Ship via Lee Transport

Manufacturer No. 102

Terms 6/10/E.O.M.

Class	Style	Cost	Unit Retail	Description	Color	Min. Pack	Coverage	
							Weeks	Units
268	140	41.50dz.	7.00	Driving glove	White	1 dz.	6	36
268	140	41.50dz.	7.00	Driving glove	Black	1 dz.	6	24
268	140	41.50dz.	7.00	Driving glove	Beige	1 dz.	6	24

Form 7-4 (left-hand page). *Periodic stock count control record: identifying and reorder information.*

consider in reordering, because an item may be retailed individually but purchased by the half dozen, the dozen, or the gross. Vendors may ship small quantities but the cost of ordering and the shipping charges on small orders make it wiser to order in larger lots.

Also noted on the left-hand page are maximum quantities of each item that should be in stock and on order at all times during the item's selling season. Your careful analysis of sales in previous corresponding seasons, plus specialized knowledge of current production and market conditions can serve as a guide in determining "coverage" of each item needed throughout a selling season. The term **coverage** refers to the maximum quantity to which each item's stock should be built after each regular stock count. It is expressed either as the number of weeks' supply or as the number of units or both.

To determine coverage needed for each item under periodic stock-count control, first estimate the weekly rate of sale of an

item during a given selling season. Then note the number of weeks established between scheduled stock counts. Next you estimate, in terms of weeks, the normal delivery period from the date of reorder to the date of actual receipt of the merchandise. You must also estimate, in terms of weeks, the safety or reserve stock needed at all times to allow for an unexpected increase in sales or an unexpected delay in delivery.

To calculate the weeks' supply needed, you add the number of weeks between counts, the number of weeks required for delivery of reorders, and the number of weeks' supply estimated as a necessary safety or reserve factor. The number of units required is then determined by multiplying the estimated weeks' coverage by the estimated weekly rate of sale of each item.

Assume, for example, that in Form 7-4 the weekly rate of sale of style 140, white, is estimated at six pairs. If the delivery period is estimated at two weeks, the interval between counts at two weeks, and the

Department	15
Manufacturer No.	102

Class	Style	Date 5/3 OH	O.O. 5/6	Rec. 5/14	Sold	Date 5/17 OH	O.O. 5/20	Rec. 5/28	Sold	Date 5/31 OH	O.O. 6/2	Rec. 6/10	Sold
268	140 White	20	(12)	12	10	22	(12)	12	12	22	(12)	12	
268	140 Black	20			8	12	(12)	12	4	20			
268	140 Beige	30			10	20			8	12	(12)	12	

Form 7-4 (right-hand page). Periodic stock count control record: on hand, on order, received, and sales information.

safety or reserve period at two weeks' supply, then the coverage needed is a six-week supply, or:

$$\text{coverage} = \text{estimated weekly rate of sale} \times (\text{delivery period} + \text{interval between counts} + \text{safety period})$$

$$\text{coverage} = 6 \times (2 + 2 + 2)$$

$$= 6 \times 6$$

$$= 36 \text{ pairs}$$

You should check stock counts immediately after they are taken and place reorders promptly to bring the stock of each item up to its designated coverage figure. At all times during a selling period, the quantity of an item on hand and on order should equal the coverage established for that item. If this is done, you will be certain stocks are maintained in direct relation to anticipated demand.

The right-hand page of the stock-count control form (see the form on the right) is usually columnar, with blocks of columns available for successive counts. There is a space above each block for the date on which the count was made. The columns are usually headed:

OH   Quantities *on hand* when count is made

OR   Date and quantity *ordered* since previous count was made

REC   Date and quantity of merchandise *received* since previous count was made

SOLD   *Sales* made between counts, a figure calculated by adding receipts to previous count and then subtracting present count

On the basis of these figures, sales are calculated for the period between counts. The right-hand page of this form is often punched in both margins so that it can be turned and used on the second side. This page carries only the briefest identification of each item—often only a page number—since all necessary details are on the facing page.

Focus

Taking Stock of Hosiery: Getting a Leg Up on Inventory

Hosiery, with its wide range of styles, sizes, and colors, is one of the most difficult items for which department and other stores must maintain unit control. And that difficulty has become more pronounced in recent years, with more and more women joining the work force and swelling the market for these products. Besides, as hosiery has come to be considered more and more a fashion accessory, there has been a tremendous growth in the number of new patterns, fashion colors, and even designer products being introduced to retailers' shelves.

This situation has made tracking inventory more difficult for stores to handle accurately. Traditionally, retailers have depended on manufacturers' sales representatives or in-store personnel to manually count SKUs. But with larger assortments being carried, that system seemed to be failing. Said Ron Baltruzak, divisional merchandise manager at Houston-based Foley's department store, commenting that the number of SKUs had gotten out of hand: "The tried and true method of vendors' counting items does not seem to hold up anymore. And the key to healthy hosiery sales is being in stock."[1]

Of course, being in stock can be accomplished only with an accurate knowledge of inventory. But because of the expanding number of styles and the growing number of vendors of hosiery, buyers risked being unable to stay attuned to their inventory—and as a result, some stores found themselves out of stock by as much as 25 percent in certain best-selling items in any two-week period.

One solution to the problem was recently tested by Kayser-Roth, supplier of pantyhose under the Liz Claiborne, Calvin Klein, and Leg Looks names. The company established a supplementary force, which it called its Sales Service Organization, specifically to help its customer stores maintain an accurate inventory count on hosiery.

Said Sam Meyer, director of sales services for Kayser-Roth, of this new team: "They have been hired and trained to count branded hosiery, not to sell."[2] Their findings, to be reported back to the store executives as well as the K-R sales reps, would help identify each retailer's needs quickly, and fill in necessary stock just as quickly, he noted.

The new program was tested in Florida stores in the fall of 1985 and, if proven successful, was to be expanded to other Southeastern states, and eventually nationwide. As a model for other stores and suppliers, it could be one way to help retailers keep a better handle on what they've sold and what they have to sell—which in turn will help them better meet and improve their goals for sales and profits.

1 Jil Curry, "Changing Patterns," *Stores*, June 1985, p. 15.
2 Ibid., p. 20.

RESERVE REQUISITION CONTROL. For fast-selling, low-priced items, particularly those that are prepackaged, reserve requisition control is often used. **Reserve requisition control** is a form of periodic stock count in which the stock on the selling floor is considered sold and only the reserve stock is counted. A reasonable amount of stock is kept on the selling floor, but the main supply is kept in a stockroom. As the forward (selling-floor) stock runs low, more is requisitioned from the reserve.

Under this system, sales are calculated by adding up the requisitions since the last count and by considering as sold everything that has reached the selling floor. Periodic stock counts are made, but only the reserve stock is counted and considered "on hand."

The reserve requisition control system is especially useful in high-volume, small-unit sales departments, such as hosiery or notions. It is much faster, for example, to count one carton of 144 pairs of pantyhose in the reserve stock than to make a count on the selling floor of 48 boxes, each containing from 1 to 3 pairs. And it is much easier to record requisitions for 36 pairs of one style and 24 of another than to record possibly 30 individual sales transactions involving the same 60 pairs.

VISUAL CONTROL. In "eyeball" or **visual control,** a rack, shelf, drawer, or bin is assigned to each style, size, or classification. You would make a periodic check to see whether each of these *looks* too empty or too full. With experience, you can make an on-the-spot judgment about action to be taken when the bins, shelves, drawers, and racks are checked.

Fashion merchandise does not usually lend itself well to visual control. An exception might be a very small store in which the proprietor's memory serves as the record. Another might be a boutique or specialty shop that carries one-of-a-kind items or the newest and most unusual styles. Still another exception might involve the stock of special-purpose, lower-volume merchandise, such as packaged T-shirts. In these cases, visual control, rather than more formal and detailed controls, might prove satisfactory for determining sales and stock-on-hand information.

Sources of Information for Maintaining Unit Control

The primary responsibility for unit control rests with the buyer. As a buyer, you may have a unit control clerk or another assistant to help maintain these records. You, or this assistant, must make sure you have access to certain store records or the system cannot be properly maintained. The principal sources of such information are purchase orders, receiving records, sales records, merchandise transfers, merchandise returns (to vendors and from customers), cancellations of orders, and price changes.

Purchase Orders

A **purchase order** is a contract between a store and a vendor to purchase certain specified merchandise under explicitly detailed conditions. When signed by an authorized store executive such as the buyer or, in a larger store, a division merchandise manager or a financial officer, and accepted by the vendor, it becomes a legally binding document.

When a purchase order is placed, the original copy is given to the vendor and one or more carbon copies are given to the store's accounting department. The buyer who places the order retains a carbon copy for future reference and for making appropriate entries in the unit control records. (See Form 7-5.) The amount of information about each order that you enter in the unit control records depends on the type of system used. In general, however, the purchase order is the source of such important control information as the following:

☐ The date of the order.
☐ The vendor's name and address, together with the shipping point, if different from the showroom address. (A vendor may maintain a sales office in New York City but produce and ship from elsewhere.)
☐ Shipping instructions, including the date by which all shipments should be completed or the order can be legally canceled, the route by which shipments should be sent, and all arrangements relating to shipping costs.
☐ The terms of sale (how soon after shipment the invoice must be paid, and with what discount).
☐ The department for which the goods are purchased.
☐ The address of the store unit to which shipment should be made (if store wishes deliveries to be made to other than the main store or distribution center).
☐ Any special directions about packing and shipping. (For example, a store with several branches may request each branch's goods to be separately packed and labeled, even though all merchandise is to be received at a central location.)
☐ Details of styles purchased, including classification, number, description, and cost price. Descriptions, depending on the article, should specify color, fabric, size, or other relevant points. There should be enough information to make it easy for the store's receiving department, as well as for the vendor's shipping room, to know exactly what the order specifies. Failure to include this information on an order leaves the vendor free to ship anything.
☐ The retail price (*shown only on the store's copies of the order, not on the vendor's copy*). The buyer indicates the unit retail price intended for each style number. Thus the total retail as well as the total cost value of each order can be calculated, and the initial markup percentage can be worked out. On copies of the order that are intended for the marking room, the column of cost figures is blacked out, and only the retail prices, needed for making up price tickets, are visible.
☐ Any special arrangements concerning the purchase. (For example, the vendor may agree to contribute a specified amount,

Elston's

STORE NAME	DEPT. NO.	ORDER NO.
ELSTON'S #1	42	M 184925

BILLING, PACKING, AND SHIPPING REQUIREMENTS

1. INVOICE MUST BE ENCLOSED WITH SHIPMENT, AND CARTON CONTAINING INVOICE MUST BE SO MARKED ON THE OUTSIDE
2. MERCHANDISE FOR TWO OR MORE DEPARTMENTS SHIPPED AT THE SAME TIME, MUST BE BILLED AND PACKED SEPARATELY, AND INVOICES AND CARTONS PLAINLY MARKED FOR THE SEPARATE DEPARTMENTS. HOWEVER, ALL SUCH SHIPMENTS MUST BE COMBINED UNDER ONE BILL OF LADING.
3. DEPARTMENT ORDER NUMBER AND WEIGHT MUST BE SHOWN ON THE INDIVIDUAL CONTAINERS
4. ALL GARMENT PACKAGES MUST CONTAIN COLOR AND SIZE LISTS BY STYLE NUMBER

NAME _Aiken Dress Co._
ADDRESS _1400 Broadway_
CITY AND STATE _New York, N.Y. 10018_

TERMS _8/10 EOM_

WITH ANTICIPATION FOR PREPAYMENT

DATE OF ORDER	DUE DATE AT STORE	CANCEL BY	HOUSE NUMBER
8/15/8-	9/10/8- Complete	9/10/8- (will be cancelled or shipment returned at vendor's expense)	482

SHIP TO: _Main Store Cincinnati, Ohio_

STYLE NUMBER	CODE OR CLASS	DIS LETTER	DESCRIPTION	SIZES 8	10	12	14		TOTAL QUANTITY	UNIT COST	TOTAL COST	UNIT RETAIL
253	123		2 pc wool suit									
			pleated skirt									
			long sleeve									
			Black	6	9	9	6		30			
			Red	6	8	8	4		26			
			Gold	3	4	4	4		15			
			Blue	3	4	4	4		15			
									86	95 00	8170 00	

ROUTING INSTRUCTIONS

FOLLOW OUR ROUTING · WE CHARGE BACK ANY EXCESS TRANSPORTATION COSTS TO YOU

☒ F.O.B. STORE NAMED OR WAREHOUSE
☐ 1 TO 20 LBS. - PARCEL POST DIRECT TO STORE · DO NOT INSURE
☐ 21 TO 50 LBS. - REA EXPRESS DIRECT TO STORE · MINIMUM VALUE (SPECIFY COMMODITY TARIFF ON WAYBILL)

OVER 50 LBS. (TRUCK ROUTING) _IOU Service_

SPECIAL ROUTING INSTRUCTIONS _Hangers_

VALUATION EXCEPTION: NO DECLARATION OF VALUE IS TO BE MADE BY THE VENDOR EXCEPT ON FURS AND JEWELRY, IN WHICH CASE ACTUAL VALUE UP TO $1000 SHOULD BE DECLARED.

FORM 312 REV. 12-63

This order subject to conditions of purchase appearing on the reverse side and is a contract only when confirmed by merchandise office signature.

GRAND TOTAL COST	8170	00
GRAND TOTAL	RETAIL	
% MARK UP		

Jane Dean DEPT. MGR.

T. J. Evans DIV. MDSE. MGR.

Form 7-5. A purchase order.

under specified conditions, toward the advertising of a purchase; or as is sometimes the case, particularly in orders for such merchandise as furs and high-ticket jewelry items, the buyer may have the privilege of returning unsold goods by a specified date. This is known as **buying on consignment.**)

☐ Standard trade practices. Established many years ago by the National Retail Merchants Association in cooperation with the associations representing the apparel trades, these practices are usually printed on the back of each store's order blank. The provisions spell out the obligations of buyer and seller to one another and define what constitutes fair or unfair practice in relation to an order.

Multiunit stores, such as department and specialty stores with several branches, usually prepare order forms with separate columns for each store unit for which merchandise is purchased. In this way, a single order can cover purchases made on behalf of as many store locations as need to be served. On orders placed for distribution to specific branches, quantities and applicable details of color and size distribution are specified for each location. The more stores to be served, the wider the form becomes. With such a form, however, you can see if the order results in a balanced assortment of styles, sizes, and colors for each store unit. Merchandise for specific branches may be sent directly to those stores. Or, the order may specify that all merchandise be delivered to a central receiving place from where it will be distributed to all the stores. The order form also is used to confirm agreed-upon shipping arrangements, cancellation dates, special delivery dates, and any unusual agreements made regarding the merchandise specifications. Terms and dating of the sale are also specified in the spaces allotted to that information on the order form.

PRE-RETAILING ORDERS. Buyers may determine retail prices at the time the order is placed rather than wait until goods arrive with the invoice at the store. When you **pre-retail** your orders, the retail value of each invoice can be calculated and goods can be marked and placed on sale even if you are away from the store. Pre-retailed orders can also be processed quickly so that the store can take advantage of the cash discounts offered by vendors for prompt payment. However, pre-retailed orders do not give the buyer a chance to analyze the goods to determine if the retail price is too high or too low in respect to other goods in stock.

Receiving Records

Good retail practice requires that a record be made of each unit of merchandise received by a store. (See Form 7-6.) When a copy of this record is turned over to you, you can then update the "on order" entry by indicating the number of units received and the date of receipt. If the total order is received, in some systems the "on order" entry is circled.

The many purposes served by receiving records can be seen in Form 7-6. This form is in two parts: one above and one below the horizontal, perforated line. In the upper right-hand corner of both parts is a number—one of a consecutive series—that is assigned to an incoming shipment. This number is used for all future identification of that shipment. The right-hand corner also has space for recording the number of cartons or packages in the shipment, the name of the carrier, and the date of delivery.

The upper left-hand section of the form provides space for a variety of information that will be needed by the accounting department in processing the invoice for payment. When the upper part of the receiving form is detached from the bottom part and attached to an invoice, it is called a "receiving apron." A **receiving apron** is a sequentially numbered form for incoming information about each shipment.

The bottom part of the receiving form has space for the receiving clerk to indicate how many pieces of each size and color have been counted in the shipment. From this information, the purchase order can be checked, and the work of making price tickets and affixing them to the merchandise can proceed. This lower section, or a copy of it, should then be passed to you. It supplies the details needed to keep the unit control style records up to date.

RECEIVING RECORD

No. 16181

Received From _Jacobs Dress Company_
Address _1400 Broadway_ City _New York, N.Y. 10018_

Date Received
_9/5/8-_

Department	Order No.	Transportation Charges		Buyers Approval or Remarks	Received Via
		Total Paid	Charge Shipper		
42	M184925	48.00		Jane Dean 9/16	IOU Service

Invoice Date	Terms	Invoice Passed	Discount		Amt. of Invoice	Retail Value	Pkg's.	Pieces	Cartons
			Date	Amount					
9/5/8-	8/10 EOM	9/12/8-	10/10	189.89	8170.00	16,340.00	86 (hangers)		

ATTACH INVOICE HERE

Received From _____

No. 16181

Vendor No.	Unit Cost	Color	Description	Size				Quantity		Class	Unit Price
				8	10	12	14	Amt.	Unit		
482	95.00	Blk	Style 253, 2 pc.	6	9	9	6	30	ea.	123	190.00
482	95.00	Red	Style 253, 2 pc.	6	8	8	4	26	ea.	123	190.00
482	95.00	Gold	Style 253, 2 pc.	3	4	4	4	15	ea.	123	190.00
482	95.00	Blue	Style 253, 2 pc.	3	4	4	4	15	ea.	123	190.00

Order Checked	Date	Mdse. Checked	Date	Price Tickets	Date	Mdse. Marked	Date	Cost Extension	Retail Extension	Merchandise Received/Date	
										Stock Room	Department
HLC	9/6	FBJ	9/6	NPR	9/6	mng	9/9	8170.00	16,340.00	a.J.L.9/10	

Form 7-6. A receiving record.

Sales Records

In manual perpetual control systems, you or an assistant receives for every sale either a sales check or a price-ticket stub identifying the specific article sold. This information is then recorded on the appropriate style record. In periodic stock-count control systems, you need to record sales only for a specific period by calculating the difference between one stock count and the next.

Because the majority of sales registers are now computerized, sales records are frequently obtained automatically, as a by-product of the sales transaction. See the section on computerized unit control later in this chapter for a more detailed description of computerized sales records.

Merchandise Transfers

Departmentalized stores frequently transfer merchandise from one department to another or from one store or branch to another. Special forms are used to report such transactions, and these must be meticulously maintained to avoid losses in one unit and overages in the other. For unit control purposes, transfers are equivalent to sales for the department or branch releasing the goods; transfers are

```
                                    No.E54165

              BRANCH STORE TRANSFER

From_____ Main _____ To___ # 6-42
Dept._____ 42 _____ Date___ 9/9/8-

| Class | Style | Description     | Qty. | Retail Unit | Retail Extension |
| 123   | 253   | 2 pc. polyester | 16   | 190 00      | 3040 00          |
|       |       |          8 10  12  14            |       |                  |
|       |       |    Black  1 1    1   1          |       |                  |
|       |       |    Red    1 1    1   1          |       |                  |
|       |       |    Gold   1 1    1   1          |       |                  |
|       |       |    Blue   1 1    1   1          |       |                  |
|       |       |                                |       |                  |
|       |       | Vendor: 482                    |       |                  |

Written by____ Janet Bauer
Checked by____ P. Anders ___ Container 38
```

Form 7-7. A form for reporting the transfer of merchandise from one branch to another.

equivalent to purchases for the department or branch receiving the goods. The stock on hand of the former is reduced, and the stock on hand of the latter is increased.

Form 7-7 illustrates a report of the movement of merchandise between various branches. An appropriate entry for all such transfers is made on the style's unit control record.

Merchandise Returns

When merchandise is returned by a store to a vendor, a form known as a "return-to-vendor" or "charge-back" is issued. (See Form 7-8.) A **return-to-vendor** is a store's invoice covering merchandise returned for cause to its vendor. A **charge-back** or **claim** is a store's invoice for claims against and allowances made by a vendor. In most stores, the same form is used for either returns-to-vendors or

charge-backs. Copies of these return forms go to the buyer so that stock on hand of individual styles may be appropriately decreased on the unit control records.

Should a customer make a merchandise return to the store, a charge credit or cash refund is issued. A copy of these forms goes to the buyer, who adds the returned article to the record of the total number of that style currently in stock.

Both customer returns and returns-to-vendor should be automatically recorded on the forms used in perpetual control. If periodic stock count is the control method used, however, small adjustments like these can be ignored. Only a transaction of major proportions, such as the return of a vendor's entire shipment needs to be entered on the periodic stock-count control form.

Order Cancellations

A buyer may cancel an order for justifiable reasons, such as a vendor not shipping the designated merchandise by the shipping date specified, or a vendor eliminating a style from an order. This cancellation date is specified on the order form to avoid late shipments. When an order is canceled in whole or in part, this change must be made promptly on the appropriate unit control form. This ensures that whoever studies the control records will not mistakenly think that an additional supply of merchandise is still on order.

Price Changes

Unit control records should indicate the retail prices at which merchandise is placed in stock, as well as any price changes that occur later. In most stores, a special form is required for reporting all upward or downward revisions in retail

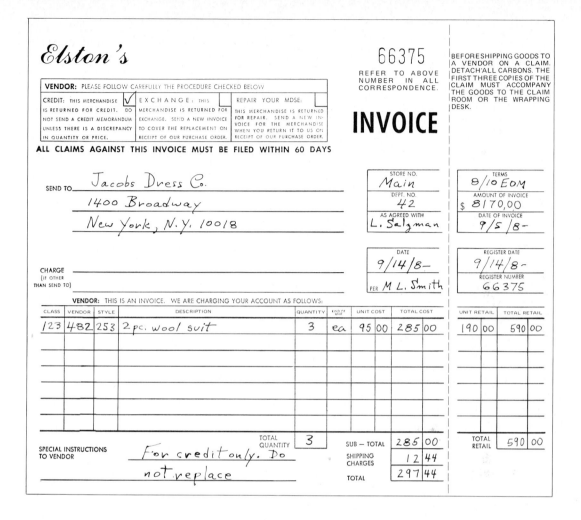

Form 7-8. A return-to-vendor.

prices so that the retail value of the inventory may be adjusted accordingly. (See Form 7-9.) Price changes are usually initiated by the buyer, but the required forms may be completed by a salesperson or stock clerk. Copies of these forms are routed to the buyer's office as well as to the inventory control office for appropriate action. Most stores use a single **price-change form** for recording markdowns, markdown cancellations, or additional markups. A few stores provide a separate form for each type of price change.

Computer-Assisted Unit Control

The computer has done a great deal to improve unit control systems. These improvements include speed, accuracy, and efficiency. However, before a computerized

PRICE CHANGE

(X) TO SHOW TYPE
- [X] MARK-DOWN
- [ ] CANCELLATION OF MARK-DOWN
- [ ] ADDITIONAL MARK-UP

DEPT. NO. 42

B 29001

DATE Aug. 10, 198-

ISSUE SEPARATE SHEETS FOR MARK-DOWN CANCELLATION, MARK-UP, STOLEN, AND SALVAGE ITEMS

SHOW REASON BY LETTER		ORIGINAL MARK-DOWN NUMBER	CLASS	ITEM DESCRIPTION VENDOR — STYLE	QUANTITY	SEA. LET.	VERIFIED QUANTITY	OLD RETAIL	NEW RETAIL	DIFFERENCE	AMOUNT
A PROMOTIONAL PURCHASE REMAINDERS	E	—	172	Cotton lace, 385 #1120	4	M5	4	46 00	32 00	14 00	56 00
	F	—	126	Sleeveless print, 482#401	3	M6	3	42 00	29 00	13 00	39 00
B SLOW MOVING OR INACTIVE STOCK											
C SPECIAL SALES FROM STOCK											
D PRICE ADJUSTMENTS											
E BROKEN ASSORTMENTS AND REMNANTS											
F SHOPWORN, SOILED OR DAMAGED											
G ALLOWANCE TO CUSTOMER											
H STOLEN											
J SALVAGE											

DO NOT ENTER ANY PRICE CHANGES BELOW THIS LINE

DEPT. MGR'S SIGNATURE	DATE	MDSE V. OR MGR'S SIGNATURE	DATE	MARKER'S SIGNATURE	DATE		TOTAL
Jane Dean	8/10/8-	T.J. Evans	8/10/8-	Ann Hogan	8/12/8-		95 00

Form 7-9. A price change form.

system can be used, merchandise must be coded and an input system must be selected.

Coding

A computer-assisted unit control system collects exactly the same kind of sales and stock information that a manual system does, although it is often programmed to collect more detail than is feasible in a manual system. The major difference, then, is that a manual system uses people and forms to record and process data, while an automated system uses people and machines.

However, before merchandise information can be used in an automated system, the information must be coded. This code usually consists of numbers, since automated equipment works mainly with numbers. Although no two retail organizations use exactly the same coding system, most fashion merchandise is coded for unit control purposes to identify department, classification, vendor, style, color, size, price, and season in which received.

Take another look at the sample receiving record, Form 7-6. It shows the receipt by department 42 of six black suits in size 8, classification number 123, style number 253, at $190 retail, from the Jacobs Dress Company, which is vendor number 482. Classification, style, size, price, and vendor already are expressed in numbers. Suppose the color black is assigned the number 4, and the season code is 33. Then the code numbers appearing on the price ticket of each of those six black suits received into stock would be:

Department	42	Color	4
Classification	123	Size	8
Vendor	482	Season	33
Style	253	Price	$190

A growing number of large retailers today identify their merchandise with SKU numbers. A **stockkeeping unit,** or **SKU,** is either a single item of merchandise or a group of items within a classification. An identifying number is assigned to this group of items for the purpose of keeping separate sales and stock records. An SKU is the minimum level of merchandise identification and takes the form of a two- to four-digit number. Under this type of control system, an identifying SKU number is assigned within each merchandising classification to each item or group of items of merchandise on order or in stock that has specific characteristics (size and color, for example) which distinguish it from all other merchandise.

After you have worked with a computerized system for a while, you will find that the code or SKU number assigned to a unit of merchandise is as descriptive as a handwritten or verbal description.

Selection of an Input System

The information you have coded is of no use if it is not entered, or input, into the unit control system so that it can be summarized in useful reports. There are a number of different ways of entering this coded information into the system. Some of the more basic methods of input have been in use for many years, and some of the more complex have come into widespread use relatively recently. Three examples of computerized input systems are described below.

PRINT-PUNCH PRICE TICKETS. In one of the oldest systems of inputting coded information, printed price tickets are coded with a series of punch holes. These holes correspond to the printed information on the price ticket and can be read and interpreted by an electronically controlled machine. (See Form 7-10.) These tickets are often referred to as "Kimball tickets" after the company that first introduced this type of price ticket or tag. Each price ticket consists of two to four perforated sections, all of which contain identical printed-punched information. When an item is sold, the end section of the ticket is removed. This removed section is then fed into a machine that "reads" and sorts out the coded information punched on it. This makes it possible to obtain a detailed unit control report in which all of the precoded information from the punched tickets is listed for all of the items that have been sold that day.

COMPUTERIZED REGISTERS. Another system involves the indexing of SKU numbers into the computerized register. The information captured by the SKU coding cannot be as detailed as that coded into individual price tickets, because the number can only extend to four digits. But the unit control information entered into a computerized register is an up-to-the-minute source of sales trends.

HAND-HELD WANDS. In this system of inputting unit control information, each item's price ticket is coded with a magnetic strip or a series of magnetic bars. This coding can be "read" by a hand-held wand that is "hooked into" the computerized register. As the wand is passed over the magnetic coding on the price ticket, the coded information is transferred into the register. (See the illustrations accompanying Form 7-10.) The register records

Form 7-10. A price ticket recording detailed information about the merchandise. The number codes can be input into the point-of-sale computer terminal (as shown in the photograph to the immediate right) to update the store's inventory records. In some stores, hand-held wands "read" the codes embedded in a magnetic strip on the price ticket (as shown at the far right). The wand transmits the information into the store's system via the point-of-sale terminal.

the transaction and relays the information to the company's computer system.

This type of electronic system has several advantages. First, there is little chance of salespeople making errors as they record sales, because all of the sales information, including the price, is automatically entered into the register by means of the wand. When all items for a particular sale have been recorded, the computerized register automatically computes the total. Second, the detailed information on each price ticket provides the store with a detailed and up-to-the-minute system of perpetual inventory control. Third, the store's computer can be programmed with an economic ordering quantity for each item of merchandise.

When the stock for an item reaches a predetermined level, or **economic ordering quantity (EOQ),** a notice to reorder is automatically triggered. When enough units of an item have been transferred from the "on hand" record to the "sold" record, the buyer is notified so that a reorder can be processed immediately if one is needed.

Value of Automated Systems

The automation of unit control systems offers buyers the same benefits as the automation of other data-collecting and data-processing chores in retailing. First, automated systems in general, and electronic computer systems in particular, are infinitely faster than manual systems. Second, automated systems are almost infallibly accurate, as long as the right information is fed into them. Third, automated systems can collect and process more detailed information than typical manual systems can. This means that more useful reports for evaluating merchandise assortments can be produced.

However, there are also problems related to automated systems. First, if inaccurate information is fed into the system—and this can happen, in spite of the elaborate controls of such systems—errors can be very hard to track down. Second, because of the tremendous capabilities of these systems, store managements sometimes program the systems to turn out reports containing far more detail than buyers need or can use. Too much information can be as confusing and misleading as too little, and buyers for departments of a large store may be inundated with information and details that have no relevance for their departments. The key to a good automated unit control system is accuracy in recording data and a program that produces useful reports.

How the Buyer Utilizes Unit Control

Unit control records give you detailed information about both sales and inventory. The records that are produced show departmentalized sales by classification, price line, vendor, size, color, and other helpful merchandise characteristics. These records can serve as fact-based decision guides as you go to market. The information from these records is also the basis for keeping total control of your budget through open-to-buy calculations.

Fact-Based Decision Guides

Facts are a much more reliable guide than memory about the nature of consumer demand, even for the immediate past. With facts obtained through unit control, you can go into the market armed with such data as the following: Most of vendor A's styles were reordered, while vendor B's had to be marked down before they were sold. You might also see that more size 12s were sold this season than in the previous season, learn that the department sold more higher-priced separates this year than last year. Facts, not guesses, are essential in keeping track of consumer demand. And the correct interpretation of these facts will enable you to meet the needs and wants of your customers.

Properly used, unit control systems contain built-in reminders that encourage you to take immediate action when conditions require it. The reminder should prompt you to check the assortment for completeness and balance in terms of current indications of consumer demand. Unit control records and reports provide the means for regularly checking previously planned sales and stock projections against actual results.

Basis for Open-to-Buy

Open-to-buy, defined in Chapter 5, refers to the available amount of money that a buyer can spend at any *particular* time. By calculating your open-to-buy, you can keep your merchandise investments in line with your merchandise dollars.

For each month, you have alloted in your six-month plan a certain amount of money for retail purchases. Each time you place an order, you decrease the total amount of money that is available for more purchases. But because most merchandise orders are not received in the same month they are placed, you have to keep close track of the money you have spent and the money that is still available to spend. The information you obtain from unit control can help you to calculate your open-to-buy.

Basically, your open-to-buy is the amount of planned purchases that have been budgeted for a given period of time, minus the actual orders (on order) that have already been placed for delivery during that same period but have not yet arrived. Open-to-buy may be expressed in dollars or units, or both.

The following is an example of how open-to-buy is calculated at any point during a month.

Planned sales for balance of month	$1,000*
Planned end-of-month stock (EOM)	+ 2,000*
Total stock requirements for balance of month	= $3,000
Stock now on hand or (BOM)	− 1,500
Purchases for balance of month	= $1,500
Orders previously placed for delivery this month (on order)	− 1,000
Open-to-buy for balance of month	= $ 500 OTB

*From Dollar Merchandise Plan.

In department stores, open-to-buy reports are usually issued weekly to departmental buyers and may cover future periods as well as the current period. In small stores, buyers are responsible for calculating their own open-to-buy figures. See Form 7-11.

From the viewpoint of top management, the open-to-buy report reflects the buyer's competence and efficiency. The overly optimistic buyer tends to buy too heavily and to be chronically overbought, even when the selections are excellent. Another type of buyer who overstocks is the one whose selections tend to fall just short of being right and therefore sell more slowly than planned. Some buyers tend to underbuy, even though they have a gift for anticipating what customers will want and for presenting it to them temptingly. They may have too little confidence in their own judgment or too much confidence in the ability of resources to deliver additional stock in a rush. Accuracy in planning and skill in merchandising to the plan reveal themselves in a department that has adequate stocks yet always has some open-to-buy available for unexpected developments.

Problems Related to Unit Control

Unit control systems are not always properly run or properly used. Moreover, they cannot be expected to do some jobs.

In working with unit controls, carelessness can result in inaccurate and misleading figures. This is true even with electronic systems, since a computer can digest only the information fed into it. An expression familiar to computer users is "GIGO," an acronym for "Garbage in, garbage out."

Manual systems are slow, and sometimes the clerks handling them are so far behind in their work that their reports are of little use by the time buyers receive them. Electronic systems, on the other hand, are sometimes programmed to give so much detail, and so rapidly, that buyers are unable to digest it all and are therefore unable to make effective use of it.

UNIT OPEN TO BUY REPORT

Dept. 42 Casual Dresses   WEEK ENDING FEB. 21,198–

CODE	PRICE RANGE	E.O.M. INV. 1/31/8-	FEB. ON ORDER	AVAILABLE FOR SALE	PLANNED SALES	ANTICIPATED MARK DOWNS	PLANNED 2/28/8- INV.	OPEN TO RECEIVE FEB.	MAR.	APR.	MAY	JUNE-JULY	OPEN TO BUY MAR-JULY
700	28.00	771	100	871	500	40	750	419	300	800	1000	100	2885
702	32.00	621	85	706	425	30	900	649	500	1000	250	0	2625
704	36.00	1412	210	1622	800	70	1500	748	200	1400	1400	50	3410
706	42.00	3201	610	3811	1600	120	3000	909	800	800	0	0	4310
707	48.00	2120	350	2470	1000	80	2500	1110	1000	750	500	0	4820
708	56.00	1409	300	1709	600	50	1200	141	150	150	100	100	2530
TOTAL MISSY		9534	1655	11189	4925	390	8850	3976	2950	4900	3250	250	20580
710	28.00	494	500	994	700	50	1050	806	1000	1000	500	500	3405
712	36.00	1464	1000	2464	1000	80	1500	116	850	850	550	550	4460
714	48.00	2026	800	2826	1100	100	1700	74	1500	1200	700	0	4795
716	56.00	2251	100	2351	850	70	1500	69	1000	200	100	0	3620
TOTAL JUNIOR		6235	2400	8635	3650	300	5750	1065	4350	3250	1850	1050	17280
TOTAL CASUAL		15769	4055	19824	8575	690	15600	5041	7300	8150	5100	1300	37860

Form 7-11. A unit open-to-buy report.

Another problem is that it is difficult to estimate the true costs of unit control systems. A number of people are involved in some aspect of the unit control job—clerical workers, technicians, supervisors, buyers, assistant buyers, and sales and stock people—however, not any part of their salaries is charged to the unit control expense.

Cost, however, is a relative factor. In general, a merchant weighs the costs of maintaining a unit control system against the benefits derived from the system. If a store provides its buyers with accurate and correct information and the buyers use that information to good advantage, then the cost is likely to be considered worthwhile. However, if the buyers do not use that information, the store has a costly system. On the other hand, if a buyer is deprived of useful information, the store is probably practicing a costly economy.

One problem of all unit control systems is that they cannot reveal one very important facet of consumer demand: what items, colors, and sizes customers wanted to buy but could not because they were not present in the assortments. Unit control records may show unfilled demand by showing that a certain style, size, or color enjoyed brisk sales for a period, then was out of stock for a week or two, and then, when restocked, resumed its brisk sales. But unit control systems cannot be set up to show the requests made by customers for merchandise that was never part of the assortment. The only means by which buyers can find out about unfilled wants of customers is through want slips, customer surveys, and comparison shopping (as discussed in Chapter 2), and these methods of determining customers' wants and needs must be taken into account along with the facts reported by the unit control system.

Buying Vocabulary

Define or briefly explain the following terms:

Buying on consignment	Price-change form
Charge-back	Purchase order
Claim	Receiving apron
Coverage	Reserve requisition control
Economic ordering quantity (EOQ)	Return-to-vendor
Periodic stock-count control	Stockkeeping unit (SKU)
Perpetual control	Unit control
Pre-retail	Visual control

Buying Review

1. What are the two basic types of information any unit control system is set up to provide? What additional types of merchandise information can it also provide? Why do you usually need more information about higher-priced items?
2. Name the two basic types of unit control systems used for the recording of fashion data. How do they differ in method of operation?
3. For which specific types of merchandise is each of the above systems best suited, and why?
4. In what ways do manual forms used for periodic stock-count control differ from those used for perpetual control? How are sales determined in a periodic stock-count control system?
5. Identify and discuss the kinds of unit control information that can be obtained from the following store records: (a) purchase orders, (b) receiving records, (c) sales tickets, (d) merchandise transfers, (e) returns-to-vendor, (f) charge-backs, (g) customer charge credits and cash refunds, (h) order cancellations, and (i) price changes.
6. What is meant by the term "SKU"? Discuss its use and advantages in automated or electronic data-processing systems.
7. Name and briefly describe three examples of automated input systems.
8. Discuss the use of EOQ in an automated control system.
9. Discuss the major advantages and disadvantages of computerized unit control systems.
10. Explain how store management can use an open-to-buy report to check on your performance as a buyer.
11. Discuss the importance of accurate records for a unit control system.

Buying Case

You are the buyer in the girls preteen department of a large department store. You are aware, from your own experience and from checking sales records, that opaque white tights and dressy dresses are big sellers during the month of December.

You currently have coverage of 60 pairs of white tights and $750 open-to-buy for dressy dresses.

Given the following facts, determine if you have enough coverage in tights and enough open-to-buy for the dresses. Show how you arrived at your answers.

Opaque White Tights:
Weekly rate of sale:	18 pairs
Delivery period:	2 weeks
Interval between counts:	2 weeks
Safety or reserve:	3 weeks

Dressy Dresses:
Planned sales for balance of December:	$1,200
Planned end-of-month stock:	$1,500
Stock now on hand	$1,200
Orders previously placed for delivery in December	$ 750

Chapter 8

Dollar Control

To be an effective buyer, you must control your fashion assortments to reflect as accurately as possible the demands of your customers. This means observing the "five rights" of effective merchandising: having the right merchandise in the right place at the right time in the right quantities at the right price. At the same time, you must control the money that you invest in inventory so that the store makes a profit.

All stores use similar procedures for inventory control, whether this function is accomplished with or without the help of computers. The appeal of fashion merchandise, however, is highly unpredictable compared with the appeal for other consumer products, such as furniture and housewares. As a result, the risks and rewards involved in merchandising fashion goods and services are correspondingly greater than those involved in merchandising more staple products.

Close inventory controls and the ongoing evaluation of stock on hand are essential to profitable fashion merchandising. As a buyer of apparel and accessories, you have a special need to become thoroughly familiar with the inventory control procedures and various management tools discussed in this chapter.

Dollar Inventory Control

As you learned in Chapter 5, you plan your dollar investment in fashion assortments well in advance of each selling season. The dollar merchandise plan then becomes the base for evaluating actual results. Once a selling season gets under way, purchases of additional inventory are controlled by comparing actual dollar sales with planned dollar sales and by comparing the value of stock on hand with the planned dollar value of stock on hand.

Retail Method of Inventory Control

Most retail organizations today use an accounting system known as the retail method of inventory. Stores operating under this method not only plan their merchandise budgets and assortments entirely on the basis of retail values but they record all transactions affecting the inventory of the store using retail values. This means that all sales, purchases, markdowns, transfers, and returns-to-vendor are recorded at retail value. In keeping with this practice, all values referred to in this chapter are retail values, unless otherwise indicated.

The Book Inventory

The term "book inventory" refers to the dollar amount of inventory that should be in stock at any given time, as indicated by each department's accounting records. The figures used to compute the book inventory are derived from various records submitted to the accounting department. These records report additions to, and subtractions from, the inventory as they occur.

Systems for computing book inventories may be manual or electronic. Under either method, figures relating to inventory value are usually shown as separate monthly and cumulative year-to-date totals. Form 8-1 shows how a computerized master inventory ledger for a department might appear for the final month of an inventory period. As a buyer, you are responsible for initiating all records used by the accounting department to maintain a book inventory for your department. You are responsible for guaranteeing the accuracy of these records. This responsibility represents a very important part of your job. Inventory records are one of the ways in which your performance as a buyer can be measured by management.

Entries are made in the book inventory as changes are reported to the accounting department. Management can thus have a current evaluation of the retail value of its inventory investment at any time—monthly, weekly, or whenever wanted—either for the store as a whole or for any accounting subdivision. Although an increasing number of stores are using computerized inventory control systems, the buyer is responsible for initiating the records or procedures that will keep the system up-to-date.

BEGINNING INVENTORY. Under the retail method, a physical count of each department's merchandise is taken at least annually. Sometimes it is taken more frequently, particularly in fashion departments. From this count of each item in the inventory and the listing of each by the retail price at which it is marked, the total retail value of the inventory is calculated. If the retail value derived from the physical count differs from the book inventory figure as of the same date, the physical count figure is accepted as correct, and the book inventory figure is adjusted. The procedures for taking a physical inventory are discussed later in this chapter.

INVENTORY TRANSACTIONS. Once a beginning inventory has been established, all subsequent transactions affecting the value of that inventory are entered in a department's book inventory as they are reported to the accounting department.

Accuracy in recording inventory transactions is extremely important because a mistake will result in shortages or overages for your department.

In Table 8-1 you can see how different transactions can either increase or decrease your inventory.

STOCK LEDGER PERIOD ENDING 12/29/8

DIV: 044   DEPT: 020

	THIS MONTH				SEASON-TO-DATE				SIX MONTH PLAN
** INVENTORY ANALYSIS **	COST	RETAIL	TY%	LY%	COST	RETAIL	TY%	LY%	
BEGINNING INVENTORY *1*	676,873	1,337,167	49.38	0.00	626,334	1,180,426	46.94	0.00	
RECEIPTS									
PURCHASES *2*	175,594	322,320	44.28	0.00	597,703	1,218,276	50.93	0.00	
INBOUND FREIGHT	834				6,807				
LINE HAUL					1,744				
MARKUPS						948			
INTERSTORE TRANSFERS						1,154			
ADVERTISING LOAD									
MAS LOAD									
IMPORT LOAD									
MISC ADJUSTMENTS	205-				2,183-	3,833-			
NET RECEIPTS	180,223	322,320	44.08	0.00	604,071	1,216,545	50.34	0.00	
A. BEGIN INVENTORY + NET RECEIPTS	857,096	1,659,487	48.35	0.00	1,230,405	2,396,971	48.67	0.00	
INVENTORY REDUCTIONS		314,725	48.67	0.00		1,052,209	48.67	0.00	
B. ENDING INVENTORY - AUDITED *3*	690,266	1,344,762	48.67	0.00	690,266	1,344,762	48.67	0.00	
ADD: IN-TRANSIT	25,307	56,023	54.82	0.00	25,307	56,023	54.82	0.00	
TOTAL ENDING INVENTORY	715,574	1,400,785	48.91	0.00	715,574	1,400,785	48.91	0.00	
RETAIL REDUCTIONS									
MDSE: MARKDOWNS	PCT SALES	9,806	2.89			39,923	3.86		
EMPLOYEE DISCOUNTS	PCT SALES	2,131	0.62			5,097	0.49		
ADJUSTMENT CHECKS	PCT SALES	27	0.00			495	0.04		
TOTAL MARKDOWNS	PCT SALES	11,964	3.52			45,515	4.40		
SHORTAGE PROV (EST/ACT)	PCT SALES	36,235-	10.68-			25,436-	2.46		
C. NET SALES	PCT CHANGED	338,996	0.00			1,032,130	0.00		
NET RETAIL REDUCTIONS		314,725				1,052,209			
** GROSS MARGIN COMPUTATION **									
D. MDSE COST OF SALES (A-B)	166,830	PCT SALES	49.21		540,139	PCT SALES	52.33		
E. MDSE GROSS PROFIT (C-D)	172,166	PCT SALES	50.78		491,991	PCT SALES	47.66		
F. OTHER COST OF SALES									
PRIOR YEAR ADJUSTMENT	759-	PCT SALES	0.22-		759-		0.07-		
WORKROOM		PCT SALES	0.00				0.00		
MISC OTHER COST OF SALES		PCT SALES	0.00				0.00		
TOTAL OTHER COST OF SALES	759-	PCT SALES	0.22-		759-		0.07-		
G. EARNED DISC. CALC.									
DISCOUNT RESERVE (BOM)	25,788	PCT *1*	3.80		23,988		3.82		
CASH DISCOUNT TAKEN	6,745	PCT *2*	3.75		22,603		3.78		
DISCOUNT RESERVE (EOM)	6,230	PCT *3*	3.79		26,230		3.79		
DISCOUNT EARNED	6,303	PCT SALES	1.85		20,361		1.97		
H. GROSS MARGIN (G)	179,228	PCT SALES	52.87		513,111		49.71		

Form 8-1. A department's inventory ledger.

Impact of Inventory Transactions

	Information recorded	Form(s) used
Incoming merchandise (increases inventory) (INS)	Purchases	Purchase order/receiving record
	Customer returns	Merchandise returns/credit slips
	Transfers from other depts./branches	Merchandise transfers
	Markups Markdown cancellations	Retail price change forms
Outgoing merchandise (decreases inventory) (OUTS)	Sales	Sales slips/SKU info. from sales register/price ticket stubs
	Transfers to other depts./branches	Merchandise transfers
	Returns-to-vendors	Returns-to-vendor/charge-backs/claims
	Markdowns/Employee discounts	Retail price change forms

Transactions that Increase Inventory (INS). Purchases, customer returns, and transfers from other departments or branches all result in incoming merchandise that increases inventory. Purchases are recorded in inventory at both cost and retail. To facilitate the recording of your purchases in inventory, you will probably be asked to pre-retail your orders, that is, to indicate the intended retail price of all items on each purchase order. For example, a dozen pairs of children's socks purchased at a cost of $1.25 a pair might be assigned a retail price of $2.50 a pair. The addition of a dozen pairs of socks to a department's book inventory would be entered at a cost value of $15 and a retail value of $30.

Customer returns also increase the value of your inventory. When returns are made by customers, they are recorded on merchandise return forms or credit slips. These figures are totaled daily and entered into inventory as an increase in the retail value of your book inventory.

The third transaction that increases inventory is the transfer of merchandise into your department from another department or branch. Some stores, for example, transfer sale merchandise into a "last stop" department or to one special branch. Whenever merchandise is transferred into your department, the transfer is reported on a form similar to Form 7-7, and your book inventory is increased by the retail value of the merchandise.

When you change the price on merchandise after you have placed it in stock, a record of each change must be made on price change forms. (See Form 7-9.) These forms are forwarded to the accounting department, which then increases or decreases the value of the book inventory by an appropriate amount. Price changes may take any of the following forms:

☐ Additional markups or increases in retail prices above those at which the goods were marked when first received into stock.
☐ Markdown cancellations, or increases in price to offset all or any part of previously taken markdowns. (Such cancellations may occur, for instance, after a special sale for which goods from regular stock were briefly reduced.)

Net additional markups (total additional markups minus total cancellations of additional markups) increase the retail value of a book inventory.

Transactions that Decrease Inventory (OUTS). Sales, transfers of merchandise to other departments or branches, returns-to-vendor, cancellations of additional markups, markdowns, and employee discounts are all transactions that decrease inventory.

Sales are recorded from SKU information (see page 139), from sales slips, or from price-ticket stubs. The retail amount of the merchandise sold is subtracted from the total amount of book inventory.

Just as transfers of merchandise into your department will increase your inventory, transfers out of your department will decrease your inventory. If you transfer merchandise out of your department, it is particularly important that you report the transfer on a form similar to Form 7-7. Remember, if the transfer isn't reported, your book inventory will show a shortage.

The third type of transaction that decreases your book inventory is the return-to-vendor. When you return merchandise to vendors for credit, it is reported to the accounting department on a return-to-vendor or charge-back form. (See Form 7-8.) A description of the merchandise being returned and the quantities are listed on this form at both unit and total cost and at retail prices. The total cost value of each return-to-vendor decreases the cost value of the book inventory. The total retail value of the return decreases the retail value of the book inventory. It is important to understand, however, that most vendors will refuse to accept returns unless their permission is first granted.

Some charge-backs are not concerned with actual return of merchandise but with claims or allowances. For example, a vendor may agree to a lump-sum allowance toward transportation costs if goods arrived at the store later than the promised delivery date. In this case, the amount of the allowance reduces the transportation cost of purchases by a corresponding amount. There is no change in the retail value of the book inventory.

Book inventory may also be decreased in the following ways:

☐ Cancellations of additional markups previously taken and recorded reduce inventory.
☐ Markdowns or reductions in the retail price of goods currently in stock also reduce inventory.

Net markdowns (total markdowns minus total markdown cancellations) decrease the retail value of an inventory. In the case of any price change, only the retail value of the inventory is affected. There is no change in the cost value. Accuracy in recording price changes is very important because mistakes can result in stock shortages or overages.

The Limited and Lerners: Regaining Lost Control over Inventory

When The Limited, the Columbus, Ohio-based chain of 577 specialty women's clothing stores, purchased the 800-unit Lerner Stores in April 1985, one of the first tasks at hand was a complete and drastic overhaul of Lerner's inventory system. And the actions taken to improve the system caused shock waves throughout the garment industry.

Lerner had somehow gotten itself into a tremendous inventory backlog, complicated by an inadequate record-keeping system. The situation was so bad, according to Leslie H. Wexner, The Limited's chairman, that "They were still getting Shetland sweaters! We'd dropped them two years ago!"[1] Part of the problem was Lerner's use of an outdated computer system, which meant that buyers could not determine whether they needed to order more of a hot-selling item, or whether a branch store had a huge surplus of an item that was out of stock in another branch.

Much of the merchandise in Lerner's inventory was outdated in the eyes of the new management. Of even greater concern was stock that wasn't even carried on the retailer's books. Said Robert H. Morosky, vice chairman of The Limited and Lerner: "They weren't even using purchase orders. We weren't aware of the extent of the problems."[2]

One of the first steps The Limited took after the Lerner purchase, and one which sparked furor in the market, was to cancel some $200 million in clothing orders made by Lerner before its acquisition. Most of the manufacturers affected by the cancellations were furious, and some even initiated lawsuits against The Limited. Of the action, Morosky said: "The vendors who are upset haven't been dealing properly with Lerner."[3] Some of them, he claimed, were taking advantage of the poor inventory control to sell to Lerner at above-market prices. But within a matter of months, after being able to take stock of its true inventory and open-to-buy situation, the retailer turned around and either accepted the canceled merchandise or placed orders for newer, better goods from the suppliers.

Merchandise on Order

Most stores keep computerized records of the cost and retail values of outstanding orders for both current and future delivery. Form 8-2 is an example of a typical computer printout of a department's outstanding orders. It indicates the date of each order, the order number, the vendor, the total cost and total retail values of the order, and the months in which delivery of merchandise is intended. These on-order reports are usually processed on a weekly basis. Stores that depend on manually prepared reports also issue a report of each department's outstanding orders, but it may be issued on a less frequent basis.

WEEKLY REPORT OF OUTSTANDING ORDERS

Department __42__ Date __3/17/8-__ Sheet No. __1__

Order No.	Order Date	Vendor	Total Retail	March Cost	March Retail	April Cost	April Retail	May Cost	May Retail
91428	3/4	Jacobs Dress Co.	550	252	550				
91478	3/11	Supreme Dress Co.	1,800			896	1,800		
91464	3/8	Lane Dress Co.	1,180	322	590	322	590		
91514	3/15	Casualaire	3,500					1,856	3,500
		Total Small Purchases	130	70	130				
		Total on Order	24,668	876	1,611	9,361	18,140	2,678	4,917
		Open to Buy					29,700		43,100

Form 8-2. A record of a department's outstanding orders.

Merchandise on order does not affect the book inventory because it represents merchandise that has not yet been received in stock. But you should keep all outstanding orders on file and watch them carefully since they represent future upward revisions in inventory value as well as future financial obligations. If an order is cancelled either by you or by the vendor, equivalent cost and retail amounts are deducted from the on-order figure for the month in which delivery originally was expected.

The Physical Inventory

Errors inevitably creep into records, even those maintained by computers. Sales may be rung up at the wrong prices, price changes and transfers may be made for more or fewer pieces than were actually involved, and transactions may be incorrectly identified as to department or classification. Real shortages also occur through pilferage (employee theft) and shoplifting.

With the wide variety of items and transactions involved, the book inventory is never exactly the same as the true, marked retail value of all goods currently in stock. This is the reason for taking a physical count of all merchandise in a department at the end of each fiscal year. The count is sometimes taken more often if a special situation, such as excessive shortage, warrants it or if the goods are fashion merchandise that changes seasonally.

INVENTORY PROCEDURE. Taking a physical count of all merchandise on hand in a store or department requires a precise cutoff date on the handling of records affecting inventory. Every merchandise shipment received by that date must be counted, marked, and entered in the book

In the physical inventory, all the department's stock is counted, including stock on display and in under-the-counter bins on the selling floor.

inventory before an actual count takes place. Every sale, every return, and every price change up to that date must also be entered. This assures that the book inventory is updated to the exact time of the physical inventory.

In a physical inventory, every piece of merchandise belonging to a department must be accounted for. This includes merchandise on the selling floor, in the department's stockrooms, on loan to the advertising or display department, in "will call," and in other selling departments. Furthermore, all items of merchandise should be examined and carefully identified as to classification, season code, and current retail price before the counting and listing starts. You should be sure that all items of stock are easily accessible for counting and listing. Guesswork is not compatible with a thorough physical inventory of stock. Merchandise that has just arrived from vendors but has not yet been entered into department records must be kept in a separate area and not included in this inventory.

The acutal count is best made after store closing hours or on a holiday when the store is not open for business. In this way, selling does not confuse the inventory count. However, to expedite inventory taking, reserve stockroom areas may be counted before final inventory taking begins and sealed off from use until all other counting has been completed. Ideally, the count should be made by crews who do not normally work with the merchandise they are assigned to count and list. These crews are made up of teams of two persons—a caller and a writer. Such crews have no preconceived ideas about the amount of merchandise in stock, and therefore their report must be based solely on the actual count. After the count has been completed, spot checks should be made by a member of the financial office to verify the original counts.

INVENTORY FORMS. Sheets or cards on which the counts are recorded are provided by each store's accounting office. These are usually sequentially numbered, and you, as a department buyer, are responsible for seeing that each issued sheet or card is accounted for at the conclusion of the inventory period. (See Form 8-3.)

In most cases, only one classification of merchandise is listed on each sheet or card. The sample inventory form in Form 8-3 shows an identifying style number for each item listed. To the right of the description are columns in which the writer from the inventory team enters the exact number of pieces of each specific item by the retail price and season code indicated on each item's price ticket. Each inventory sheet is also carefully identified as to department, classification, or other requested subdivision.

When the counts have been completed, the forms are returned to the accounting office. There, totals are calculated and compared with book inventory figures. If the two do not agree, the book figure is adjusted to the physical inventory figure, resulting in either a stock shortage or a stock overage.

Stock Shortages and Overages

In the normal course of business, the physical inventory rarely tallies precisely with the book inventory figure. If the physical inventory figure is less than that of the book inventory figure, the discrepancy is a stock shortage. If it is greater than the book figure, the difference is a stock overage.

Overages are rare; they are found most commonly among stores with several branches. For example, a stock overage is created by transferring merchandise to one branch while charging that merchandise to the inventory of another branch.

Shortages are common and are on the increase. In the past, stock shortages might have averaged 1 to 2 percent of net sales. Today this figure has more than doubled in many cases and is still rising.

The major causes of stock shortages are merchandise losses due to theft, damage, and spoilage. Some departments, of course, have higher shortage percentages than others, mainly because of the nature of the merchandise handled and the selling techniques employed. Open selling and self-service tend to increase departmental shortages because they permit greater opportunities for undetected theft.

Stock shortages are an important factor influencing retail pricing. The initial retail price of merchandise must be set high enough to compensate for loss of income due to stock shortages.

Stores constantly strive to reduce shortage figures by stressing greater accuracy and more care in recording purchase,

INVENTORY SHEET

FLOOR ☑
STOCK ROOM ☐
WAREHOUSE ☐

No. 59987

FIXTURE No. | SHELF No.
10 | A

DEPT. No. | CLASS.
201 | B

	Description	Number of Units	Kind of Unit (ea., pr., dz., etc.)	Selling Price per Unit Dollars	Cents	Season Letter	Check in Pencil	Inventory Signatures
1	Velour shirts STYLE 951	20	ea	48	00	M5	✓	Listed By N. Jones
2	Velour shirts STYLE 821	16	ea	36	00	M4	✓	Counted By
3	~~Knit shirts STYLE 785~~	~~15~~	~~ea~~	~~26~~	~~00~~	~~M3~~		J. Costello
4	Knit shirts STYLE 640	10	ea	24	00	M5	✓	Merchandise Recounted By
5	Knit shirts STYLE 689	13	ea	26	00	M4	✓	M. Murphy
6	Sweaters STYLE 942	18	ea	32	00	M4	✓	Listing Checked By
7	Sweaters STYLE 865	19	ea	36	00	M3	✓	L. Pappas
8	Knit shirts STYLE 785	17	ea	26	00	M3	✓	Last Line Used Was Number → 8
9								FOR OFFICE USE ONLY
10								AGE ANALYSIS
11								Age in Months / Dollars / Cents
12								
13								Current
14								7 thru 12
15								Over 12
16								
17								
								GRAND TOTAL

Form 8-3. An inventory sheet. Notice how corrections are recorded.

price change, and sales data. Greater precautions against theft, such as the use of sensitized price tags and increased security staff, are also being taken. It is an old saying in the department store business that although shortages may not be directly the fault of the buyer in whose department they occur, more buyers have been fired for high shortages than for any other reason. Shortages reduce profits, and a profitable operation is the buyer's responsibility.

The Purchase Journal

As a buyer, you will be issued by the accounting office a monthly or semimonthly report known as a **purchase** or **merchandise journal.** On this report are listed all of your invoices for purchases, transfers of merchandise in and out, and returns to or claims against vendors that have been charged or credited to your department's book inventory during that period. (See Form 8-4.)

Dept. 320 Fashion Accessories   **Division 2**   Page No. _1_____

Vendor No.	Vendor Name	Type Trans.	Apron/KeyRec No.	Apron/KeyRec Date	Invoice No.	Invoice Date	Invoice Amount	Freight Costs	Discount	Net Cost	Total Retail	M%
1140-1	Baar & Beards	Inv.	55504	01/06	7132	01/04	243.00		19.44	223.56	504.00	
	Vendor Total						243.00		19.44	223.56	504.00	55.6
1192-4	Ben Goodman	Inv.	54707	12/29	9211	12/27	360.00		28.80	331.20	720.00	
		Dum.	55155	12/28		12/28	3.00			3.00	6.00	
		Inv.	22823	01/10	9697	01/08	135.00		10.80	124.20	288.00	
	Vendor Total						498.00		39.60	458.40	1,014.00	54.8
1822-8	Glentex	RTV			3441	01/18	−183.31		−14.40	−168.91	−336.00	
		Inv.	52852	12/14	8761	12/12	360.00		28.80	331.20	672.00	
		Inv.	52852	12/14	8708	12/04	945.00	9.22	75.60	869.40	1,764.00	
	Vendor Total						1,121.69	9.22	90.00	1,031.69	2,100.00	50.4
2795-2	Regina Products	RTV			3439	01/18	−32.70		−.65	−31.05	−55.00	
		RTV			3438	01/18	−422.90		−8.46	−414.44	−706.00	
	Vendor Total						−455.60		−9.11	−446.49	−761.00	41.3
3013-9	Society Mills	RTV			3442	01/18	−72.49		−5.70	−66.79	−133.00	
	Vendor Total						−72.49		−5.70	−66.79	−133.00	49.8
				DEPARTMENT TOTAL			1,334.60	9.22	134.23	1,200.37	2,724.00	55.6

Form 8-4. A purchase journal.

The journal contains the following types of entries for each incoming invoice:

☐ Department name and number
☐ Vendor name and number
☐ Shipment receiving number and date
☐ Invoice number, date, and amount
☐ Freight costs
☐ Discounts earned
☐ Total cost
☐ Total retail
☐ Markup percentage

The journal also contains the following types of information for merchandise transfers and returns to or claims against vendors:

☐ Issuing department number
☐ Name and number of department or vendor to which issued
☐ Document number and date
☐ Details of transaction
☐ Total cost and total retail value of each document
☐ Transportation costs

You should carefully check each item on the purchases journal against your own copies of receiving aprons, transfers, and return-to-vendor forms. Any errors should be reported immediately to the accounting office. Any undetected or unreported error on these reports represents a potential stock shortage or overage. For example, an invoice for merchandise received by the misses' sportswear department, but incorrectly charged to the junior separates department, represents a stock overage for misses' sportswear and a stock shortage for junior separates.

Periodic Financial Reports

Buyers receive a number of periodic reports on the actual results of their departments' merchandising operation. The purpose of these periodic reports is to guide the buyers in operating their departments more profitably. The same reports go to top management and, in large stores, to appropriate divisional merchandise managers as well. Thus the figures are available to both buying and management levels for study and for decisions on the actions that should be taken to improve results, if necessary.

Although these reports vary widely from store to store in both format and extent of information presented, the periodic reports usually include sales reports, sales and stock reports, departmental operating statements, and open-to-buy reports.

Sales Reports

As you learned in Chapter 5, sales are the basis of all merchandise planning and control. So you must study actual sales results very carefully to evaluate their effect on other elements of the merchandise budget. A number of sales reports are usually available to buyers for this purpose.

FLASH SALES. Daily reports of sales, by department, are routinely developed from the unaudited sales checks and cash-register tapes for the previous day. They usually include the dollar sales of the corresponding selling day in the previous year. These reports are circulated early the following business day to all buyers and merchandise executives and are generally referred to as **flash sales reports.** If a store has branches, sales of each branch are usually shown separately from those of the main store, plus a total sales figure for all locations.

PERIODIC SALES REPORTS. More detailed sales reports are prepared on a one-day, three-day, weekly, or semimonthly basis. In large stores that have several branches, this review shows sales of both the main store and individual branch stores. It also shows customer returns in units or dollars or both, by classification, price line, style number, and vendor. (See Form 8-5.) In smaller stores, departmental sales may be reported simply in units and dollars by classification.

Detailed weekly reports can give you a quick, on-the-spot review of sales at all locations. With this information you can take prompt action when adjustments to your merchandising plans are necessary. Computer-generated reports often show cumulative sales for the month or season to date and sales for the previous year. They can also be designed to show any other detailed information that is of particular interest to you and your department. If, for example, you wanted to test the popularity of similar fashion jewelry from two different manufacturers, you could design your sales report to give you a breakdown of sales from each manufacturer.

BEAT-LAST-YEAR BOOK. The simplest form of daily sales record you will keep is the **Beat-Last-Year book.** This may be a single-sheet, monthly record of daily sales, or a three-year or five-year diary. Sales figures are entered day to day, and subtotals are inserted to show sales to date during the month and compared to those of the previous year. The big advantage of using this daily journal is that you can make a note of special conditions affecting sales, such as bad weather, transit strikes, and ads or other promotional efforts. But in order to become a valuable reference, this information must be entered every day.

BUYERS' SALES REPORT

Dept. 42   3 Days Ending 12/18/8-

SELLING PRICE	CLASS	VENDOR	STYLE	STORE NO.	LAST 3 DAYS	THIS WEEK	ONE WEEK AGO	2 WEEKS AGO	TOTAL LAST 4 WEEKS	TOTAL TO DATE	ON HAND	INITIAL DATE OF RECEIPT	TOTAL CUSTOMER RETURNS	ACTIVITY INDICATOR
40.00	51	001	8527	1	1	2	5	4	23	26	31	11138-		
				6			1	3	1	1	1	11248-		
				5	−	1	−				1	11178-		
				7		3		4	7	10	8	11138-		
				2			1	1	3	4		11138-		
				3			1	4	5	6	12	11178-		
				T		5	8	11	39	47	52		7	SLOW 1
44.00	51	001	8533	1	2	2	1	3	9	35	8	10068-		
				5						3		10168-		
				7				4	3	9	9	10068-		
				2						5		10068-		
				3	1	1	1	3	7	13	12	10068-		
				T	3	3	2	10	19	65	29		8	
44.00	51	001	8537	1	3	4	2	3	10	19	20	10168-		
				6		1			1	1	13	11138-		
				5							6	11178-		
				7			1	1	2	3	7	10168-		
				2	−	1	1	1	2	9	15	10168-		
				3		1			1	3	6	10168-		
				T	2	5	5	5	16	34	67		1	
40.00	51	001	8539	1	3	5	4	4	16	16	8	11248-		
				2		1			1	1	5	12118-		
				3			1	1	2	2	8	11248-		
				T	3	6	5	5	19	19	21		2	
44.00	51	001	8540	1	2	5	4		11	14	1	11138-		
				6					2	3	15	11138-		
				5	1	2	1		3	3	3	11178-		
				7	1	2	1		4	5	6	11138-		
				2	2	3	3	1	7	7	4	11138-		
				3	2	2			4	5	7	11178-		
				T	8	14	9	1	31	37	36		1	
40.00	51	001	8541	1	1	2	1		2	13	15	10068-		
				6						5		10068-		

Form 8-5. A buyers' sales report for a multi-unit store.

SALES AND STOCK REPORTS. Sales alone tell only half the merchandising story. The other half concerns stocks. Weekly, semimonthly, or monthly, you will receive a sales and stock report. This report shows sales for the period, inventory on hand and on order, planned sales and stocks, and the sales and stocks for the corresponding period of the previous year. In addition, some reports may show cumulative figures for the year to date. Others may show dollar purchases and markdowns for the current period and year or season to date.

If computerized reports are used, they may show not only departmental totals but also classification and subclassification totals. (See Form 8-6.)

With this type of detailed report available, you will be able to track classifications that are far enough above or below plan to require appropriate action. Similarly, where there are branches, a separate set of figures for each location may reveal a need for action at one or more sites, whereas overall figures for all stores combined would mask such a need.

OPEN-TO-BUY-REPORTS. For buyers and store management, the open-to-buy report is the most important merchandising tool in keeping the inventory investment in line with plans and a desired ratio to actual sales. When a promising new item or trend appears, the buyer who wishes to exploit it must move promptly, particularly if it is a fashion item. If the buyer does not have enough open-to-buy, purchase plans may be rearranged to allow for the new item or management may be asked for extra purchasing funds.

DEPARTMENTAL OPERATING STATEMENTS. Another very detailed report that you and your managers will receive on a regular basis from the accounting office is the departmental operating statement. It is a summary of the financial aspects of your department's total merchandising operation. (See Form 8-7.) The format of this

WEEKLY SALES AND STOCK REPORT

DIV 1   DEPT. NO. 15   DEPT NAME Handbags   WEEK ENDED 01/07/8–   PAGE 6

CODE	CODE DESCRIPTION — PRICE GROUP	PRICE	SEASON TO DATE SALES — PLAN	SEASON TO DATE SALES — THIS YEAR	TREND	BEGINNING ON HAND	ADJUSTED PHYSICAL INVENTORY	SALES	RECEIPTS	ADJUSTMENTS PLUS	ADJUSTMENTS MINUS	ENDING ON HAND	INTRANSIT	COVERAGE PERIOD	SALES FOR COVERAGE PERIOD PLAN	BALANCE OF SALES FOR SEASON PLAN
241	DRESS PLASTIC															
	1	23.00 25.00	32	16	50–	15		4				11	24	9	29	6
	3	26.00 28.00	85	36	58–	13						13	36	5	11	1
	5	29.00 31.00	20	9	55–	32						32		8	6	
	7	32.00 999.00		1		1–						1–		8		
	9	14.97												7		
241	TOTAL UNITS		137	62	55–	59		4				55	60		46	7
	TOTAL DOLLARS*		3663	1696				96				1575	1548		1173	171
242	CASUAL PLASTIC															
	1	23.00 25.00	8	11	38	20						20		9	13	1
	3	26.00 28.00	199	72	64–	24		3				21	24	5	11	2
	5	29.00 31.00	56	25	55–	25		1				24		8	6	
	7	32.00 999.00		6		6						6		8	6	
	9	13.97 14.97	49	10	80–	6–						6–		7		
242	TOTAL UNITS		312	124		69		4				65	24		36	3
	TOTAL DOLLARS*		7931	330	58–			111				1977	648		1000	78
352	FRENCH PURSES															
	2	12.00 13.00	22	3	86–	14						14		6	5	1
	3	13.50 UP	6	3	50–	21		1				20		7	5	
	9	6.97		7		19		2				17		6		
352	TOTAL UNITS		28	13		54		3				51			10	1
	TOTAL DOLLARS*		365	132	69–			29				594			135	12
	DIVISION TOTAL															
	TOTAL UNITS		1191	536		92		46	48			94			193	1929
	TOTAL DOLLARS*		14807	7365				598				1597			1867	20409
	* CENTS OMITTED IN DOLLAR FIGURES															

Form 8-6. A weekly sales and stock report.

STATEMENT OF DEPARTMENTAL OPERATING PROFIT

Dept. No. _____ Dept. Name _____   _____ Weeks Ended _____

	This Year %		Last Year %		This Year %		Last Year %	
1. Net Sales & % Change				XX				XX
2. Cost of Goods Sold		XX		XX		XX		XX
3. Gross Merchandising Profit								

DEPARTMENT MERCHANDISE STATISTICS

	This Year %		Last Year %		This Year %		Last Year %	
4. Markup	XXX		XXX		XXX		XXX	
5. Markdowns (at Retail)								
6. Shortage (est.) (at Retail)								
7. Total (5 & 6)								
8. Markdowns & Shortages (at Cost)	XXX		XXX		XXX		XXX	
9. Special Discount								
10. Gross Profit (4−8+9)	XXX		XXX		XXX		XXX	
11. Regular Discount Earned (Memo)		XX		XX		XX		XX

DEPARTMENT DIRECT EXPENSES

	This Year %		Last Year %		This Year %		Last Year %	
12. Departmental Salaries								
13. Dept. Advertising (Space used in Mailers & Newspapers)								
14. Less: Co-op Advertising (Allowances from Vendors)								
15. Net Advertising Cost (13−14)								
16. Interest on Average Inventory Investment								
17. Total Direct Expense (12+15+16)								
18. Dept. Oper. Profit (3−17)								
19. Cost of Store Expenses								
20. Expressage and Warehouse Cost								
21. Other Home Office Expense								
22. Net Profit or (Loss) (18−19−20−21)								

Form 8-7. A departmental operating statement.

report varies from store to store, but it will probably include actual and planned dollar figures for all phases of the merchandising operation, such as gross sales, customer returns, net sales, markdowns, purchases, gross margin of profit, operating expenses, and cash discounts earned. Departmental operating statements are usually issued monthly, but in some large stores a midmonth report is also provided. Figures are usually stated both in dollars and as percentages of net sales. Some stores also include the retail value of all merchandise on order; others include the number of transactions and the average gross sale for the month.

Devices for Evaluating Your Merchandising Operation

Buyers use many devices to measure the success of their departments' merchandising operation and to guide it toward greater accuracy in meeting consumer demand. And because buyers are held accountable for their buying decisions, these devices are also used by management to evaluate the performance of buyers. Because they may, at some time, be used to evaluate your performance, you should become familiar with the following evaluation devices: basic stock lists, prior stock reports, markdown analyses, customer returns, vendor analyses, stock turnover, sales transactions and gross sales reports, and sales per square foot.

Each of these devices is a way of tracking one facet of your merchandising operation that affects that operation's overall profitability.

Basic Stock Lists

An item of merchandise is described by buyers as **basic stock** if it enjoys such consistent demand that it should be in stock in a complete range of sizes and colors at best-selling price lines throughout a year or season. A basic may be a specific item or a group of substitutable items, such as women's pantyhose in neutral shades, nurses' oxfords, or men's dress shirts or pullover sweaters.

If you run short of an item that enjoys consistent demand, both customer goodwill and sales are at stake. To prevent this problem, you should list any items in your department that might be considered basic each season. You should then set up periodic stock counts or similar ways of making sure there is always an adequate supply of these goods. Many stores require that a list of such items be retained in the merchandise manager's office. At unannounced intervals, the merchandise manager sends someone into a department to check the basic stock and report any listed items that are not on hand or are in low supply. A buyer whose department repeatedly makes poor showings on such checks is subject to criticism.

To ensure adequate stocks of basic merchandise, some stores draw up two separate budgets for each department or classification: one for basics and one for fashion merchandise. Executives of such stores believe that an overstock elsewhere in a department should not deprive the buyer of needed open-to-buy for basics. Other stores have a policy of permitting basics to be reordered regardless of the state of the departmental open-to-buy. Still others leave the entire matter in the buyer's hands, expecting them to reserve part of their budget and enough of their open-to-buy for basics.

Prior Stock Reports

Retail stores usually place a code for the season on each price ticket. The season

The computer generates valuable information for buyers, but they will need the ability to analyze and interpret the data that this tool provides.

code is a figure indicating the month of the year in which the merchandise was received into stock. In fast-moving fashion categories, the season code may also include a numeral to indicate the week, in addition to the month, in which the article arrived in stock. Some stores put the complete coded date of receipt on the price ticket of each piece of fashion merchandise.

By flipping through the tickets on a rack of garments, you can quickly see which ones have been in stock for a while and should be given prompt attention. In some stores, and for some merchandise, a week is considered a long time. In other cases, a month may not be considered long.

Prior stock reports are reports that summarize information about the amount of stock still on hand in each of a number of earlier seasons. The report is in units as well as dollars, and information is gathered from the season code on each price ticket. Such reports may be prepared by the accounting office from data listed on inventory sheets or from special inventories taken of all or part of a department's stock for age-record purposes. The reports are created by dividing the listing of stock into age groups, totaling each group, and then showing what percentage of the total inventory each age group constitutes. You will probably be required to recheck these reports periodically, indicating what steps have been taken to dispose of prior season stock. (See Form 8-8.) Some stores, particularly those using computerized equipment, run off actual lists of the specific items of merchandise

PRIOR STOCK

Department No. 42
Sheet No. 1

Class.	Style No.	Article (List each classification separately)	Season Letter	Inventory Date 1/31/8-		First Month Date 2/28/8		Second Month Date 3/31/8-		Third Month Date 4/30/8-	
				Qty.	Price	Qty.	Price	Qty.	Price	Qty.	Price
12301	1234	Dress	H4	5	28.00	2	18.88	0	—	—	—
	789	Dress	H5	7	28.00	4	18.88	1	12.88	0	—
	1401	Dress	H5	3	28.00	3	18.88	1	12.88	0	—
12302	239	Dress	H4	6	35.00	4	26.88	2	18.88	1	12.88
	141	Dress	H5	8	35.00	4	26.88	1	18.88	0	—
	984	Dress	H5	1	35.00	0	—	—	—	—	—
12308	957	Dress	H3	1	56.00	1	39.88	1	26.88	0	—
	245	Dress	H4	2	56.00	1	39.88	1	26.88	0	—
	698	Dress	H5	2	56.00	1	39.88	0	—	—	—
	Season		H3	27	862.00	14	558.00	3	72.00	—	—
	Season		H4	41	1625.00	22	868.00	7	120.00	3	48.00
	Season		H5	64	2959.00	31	1440.00	11	228.00	3	84.00
	Total			132	5446.00	67	2866.00	21	420.00	6	132.00

NOTE: *These sheets must be returned to the Merchandise Office on the 5th of each month with all data shown complete.*

Form 8-8. A prior stock report.

that are "old." These lists are presented to the appropriate buyers for action.

Women's apparel departments rarely have inventory that is more than six months old. One large chain organization requires that all women's apparel remaining in stock 10 weeks after its receipt must be marked down.

Markdown Analyses

Downward revisions in retail prices are reported to the accounting office whenever they are made. To provide data for further study, stores issue price change analyses on which reasons for taking the markdowns are indicated. You should study both your markdowns and reasons for taking them. Management may also use your markdowns as an indication of your proficiency in both gauging customer demand and supervising your department.

MARKDOWN CAUSES. Markdowns may be taken in the following circumstances:

- ☐ Planned markdowns
- ☐ Promotional purchase remainders
- ☐ Poor assortment of sizes
- ☐ Quantities (including overstock conditions as well as excessive quantities of specific styles)
- ☐ Special sales from stock
- ☐ Broken assortments, remnants, shopworn goods; unattractive fabrics, styles, or colors
- ☐ Price adjustments to meet competition, because of generally falling prices, or to consolidate or eliminate price lines
- ☐ Allowances to customers on adjustment claims

BUYER RESPONSIBILITY FOR MARKDOWNS.

Hardest to recognize but most in need of correction are markdowns due to poor timing. These stem from offering merchandise too soon or too late for its normal selling season or for that stage of the fashion cycle to which the store's customers are attuned. Such markdowns may be reported under almost any of the headings above. But the discerning eye of an experienced merchandise manager will usually recognize them for what they are and search out the roots of the buyer's problem.

Errors in timing the presentation of merchandise to the customer are not always solely the fault of the buyer. There are occasions when tardy deliveries or uncertain weather conditions are to blame. Since late deliveries frequently represent potential markdowns, buyers are expected to weigh the advisability of accepting overdue shipments against the possibility of slackening customer demand. If overdue shipments are accepted, cost adjustments should be obtained whenever possible from vendors who shipped late.

Delay in taking markdowns or failure to take adequate markdowns, however, is definitely the fault of the buyer. Fashion merchandise loses sales appeal so rapidly that stores caution their buyers against postponing markdowns or making only timid reductions once they recognize that goods are not readily salable. Yet buyers often engage in wishful thinking; they postpone the inevitable and then have to slash prices drastically in the end when the season is past and merchandise is unwanted. The markdown book records it all, and management finds in that book an index to the buyer's competence.

Customer Returns

The extent to which goods are returned in your department can be considered an important index of your competence. If a large proportion of the goods sold is brought back for credit, there is something obviously wrong with the assortment, the merchandise, the selling techniques used, or a combination of all three. Sometimes a persuasive salesperson or a low price may encourage a customer to purchase a dress. If the dress is unflattering, unfashionable, or poorly made, however, the customer is likely to have second thoughts about it after getting it home, and back it goes to the store.

The nature of the merchandise also affects the ratio of returns to sales. In departments devoted to women's and misses' apparel, the rate of returns to gross sales normally exceeds 10 percent. In departments devoted to menswear and boys' wear, the rate of returns is well below 10 percent.

Stock Turnover

The more rapidly its retail stock is sold, the more profitably a store operates. Good turnover is the result of a combination of your careful planning and management's effective control procedures.

As explained in Chapter 5, stock turnover is calculated by dividing net sales (for a year or season) by the average retail value of the monthly stock inventory. Stock turnover represents actual performance and is used as a means of measuring your proficiency as a buyer.

IMPROVING TURNOVER.

The best way to improve turnover is first to examine the details of the assortment and identify the slow-selling classifications or items. These items must then be disposed of through better display, better selling techniques, or markdowns. You should then use the funds released through the disposal of slow sellers to build up stocks of fast sellers.

Turnover cannot be improved merely by slashing the buying appropriation. And elaborate classification and unit control data can do no more than point out those parts of the stock with the best and the worst turnover. The merchandise itself must be inspected. When the extremely slow-selling numbers are gathered on one rack and the very fast-selling ones on another, the differences between them generally stand out sharply. You can see that your clientele is accepting certain lines, colors, and prices and rejecting others. Better assortment planning then becomes possible, and better turnover results.

Not all causes of slow turnover are correctable, however. Some imports must be bought and paid for long before they reach the selling floor. Domestic merchandise in irregular supply must also often be bought well in advance to ensure timely delivery. Turnover in these cases necessarily suffers. This deliberate sacrifice of turnover in order to secure desirable merchandise is not considered an error of the same magnitude as is the slowing of turnover through inept management of the fashion assortment.

IMPORTANCE OF GOOD TURNOVER. In explaining the value of good turnover, more than one merchant has compared fashion merchandise to fresh fish: both deteriorate rapidly!

The advantages of a good turnover rate include:

☐ Fresh, appealing merchandise that will interest customers.
☐ Fewer incidents of merchandise soiled or damaged by excessive handling.
☐ Increased open-to-buy, which creates the opportunity to freshen assortments with new goods.

☐ Renewed interest on the part of salespeople who might become bored with stock on hand too long.
☐ Reduced inventory investment, which in turn means a reduction in interest costs, the need for borrowed capital, insurance rates, and opportunities for pilferage.
☐ Increased profit, which is the most important reason to strive for good turnover.

EXCESSIVELY HIGH TURNOVER. A good turnover rate, however, is not always the highest rate possible. There are disadvantages to an excessively high rate of turnover. If your rate is too high, you will constantly have inadequate stocks for your needs, and your assortments will be unbalanced. This will result in unhappy customers who cannot find the styles, colors, and sizes they want. And if your high turnover is caused by placing many small orders rather than a few larger ones, you will be incurring unnecessarily high handling and billing costs. This added expense will reduce operating profit.

Other Measuring Devices

You should also be familiar with a few other devices that are used by retail management to evaluate your effectiveness. These include the number of sales transactions, the average gross sale, and the dollar sales per square foot in your department. Each of these devices sheds light in its own way on one or more aspects of your competence as a buyer and the efficiency of your merchandising operation.

TRANSACTIONS. The more transactions a department rings up in a year, the more customers it is assumed to have served. If the number falls off from one year to another, this is a possible indication of failure to attract or sell customers. The transaction figure itself is not an index of major importance, but increases or decreases are useful guides when hunting for the strengths or weaknesses of a department.

AVERAGE GROSS SALE. On an annual or sometimes a seasonal basis, stores divide the net sales of a department by the number of its sales transactions. The result is known as the **average gross sale.** If your average gross sale has risen, this may indicate rising prices, successful efforts to sell higher-quality goods, successful efforts to sell more than one item to a customer, or all three. An average gross sale that is higher than the previous year's figure can indicate a better merchandising operation or simply rising prices. When combined with a rising transaction figure, however, it usually means that a department really is pleasing its customers.

SALES PER SQUARE FOOT. Store management annually calculates the number of square feet of selling space assigned to a department and divides that number into the department's total net sales for the year. The resulting figure, in dollar **sales per square foot,** is an index to how well the department has paid its "rent" to management. This figure is becoming increasingly important as store operating costs continue to escalate. The goal of every department is to have an increasing number of sales per square foot over the preceding year.

As a means of combatting increasing operating costs new display fixtures are being used to make use of every inch of selling space. Your suggestions for rearranging your departments or installing new fixtures will meet with little resistance from management if the changes are likely to increase sales per square foot. In departmentalized stores, management may even agree to expand the selling area of a department or classification that shows exceptionally high sales per square foot. On the other hand, management may condense those departments that do poorly in this respect.

Buying Vocabulary

Define or briefly explain the following terms:

Average gross sale	Merchandise journal
Basic stock	Prior stock reports
Beat-Last-Year book	Purchase journal
Flash sales reports	Sales per square foot

Buying Review

1. What store department is responsible for keeping the book inventory? What general types of records are used in maintaining book inventory?
2. Name the seven basic inventory transactions. Briefly explain the effect each type of transaction has on a department's book inventory.
3. Discuss the advantages to you as a buyer of pre-retailing merchandise.

4. As a buyer, what is your responsibility with regard to stock shortages and overages? What are the two major causes of shortages and overages? Give examples of each cause.
5. What is involved in checking a purchase or merchandise journal? Why should it be carefully checked by you or an assistant buyer?
6. Explain why the use of computers has improved the quality of flash sales reports and periodic sales reports. Why is a Beat-Last-Year book still a useful tool for a buyer?
7. What is the primary purpose served by a departmental operating statement? How often is it usually issued? What specific information does it contain?
8. Discuss markdowns with regard to poor timing. Why is age of stock a very important consideration for you as a buyer?
9. Discuss stock turnover with respect to (a) how you can achieve a higher rate, (b) benefits you will gain from an improved rate, and (c) disadvantages of an excessively high rate.
10. Explain how store management might make use of information on transactions and average gross sales to evaluate your performance as a buyer.
11. Why are sales per square foot becoming an increasingly important measure of success for individual departments within a store? What are stores doing to increase sales per square foot?

Buying Case

You are the assistant buyer in a children's clothing store named Kids Klothes that has opened a branch store within the year. You have just learned that this year you will be responsible for the physical inventory in the newly opened branch store. You have just 20 calendar days to make all of the preparations. Inventory is scheduled to be taken on a Sunday. The regular store hours for Sunday are 12:00 noon until 5:00 p.m. On the day of inventory, the store will be open only from 12:00 noon until 3:00. Inventory is scheduled to be taken from 3:00 until it is completed. Describe in detail what you would do in order to be ready to supervise the taking of inventory. Divide your work into the following time segments: early preparation (20 days to 7 days before inventory), week-of-inventory preparation (6 days before inventory through Friday evening before inventory), Saturday (the day before inventory), and Sunday (the morning of inventory). To the best of your ability, organize your planning in the order in which you would actually accomplish it within each time segment.

Case For Unit 2

You have just been promoted from assistant store manager to store manager and buyer of Fran's Fashions, a small women's specialty shop located in a town of 14,000 in upstate New York. The store is owned as an investment by the Fisher family from Danbury, Connecticut, and you will have complete control of the budget and will be expected to make all of the buying decisions. For your first year, however, you will report your decisions and progress on a regular monthly basis to an appointed representative from the Fisher family.

You have been assistant store manager for the past two years, and you have accompanied the previous manager-buyer on some of the buying trips, but until this time you have only observed the buying process. You have been given this opportunity because your predecessor accepted an excellent offer from a firm in San Francisco. This is your first actual week on the job, and your predecessor is already in San Francisco.

Fran's Fashions carries an assortment that is very strong in better sportswear and better "dressy" dresses. The clientele is made up primarily of upper-middle-class women in the 30 to 55 age bracket, from a radius of five miles from the store. The majority of the current customers do not work outside of the home.

There is no store within the town limits that is in direct competition with Fran's Fashions, and each year for the past eight years the store has shown a small but steady increase in sales. Last year, however, a new 150-store shopping mall opened within three miles of the store. The mall has one department store and a small, privately owned specialty store that are in direct competition with your store. The impact of the mall has been a 3.5 percent decrease in your sales for the first six months it was open and a 3.3 percent decrease in sales for the past six months.

Next month, however, a major corporation will open its new corporate headquarters complex at a location that is only two miles from your store down a new four-lane highway, but five miles from the new shopping mall via an old, winding two-lane road.

You are currently gathering information so that you can prepare the six-month merchandising plan and apply that plan to your fashion assortment.

1. What information would you like to obtain for the preparation of your first six-month plan?

2. At this time do you anticipate an increase, a leveling off, or a decrease in sales for the next six months? Explain your answer.

3. How might you adjust your fashion assortment? Explain the reasons for these adjustments.

4. You have just taken an inventory and found that you currently have about 12 percent of your stock tied up in old merchandise. This merchandise consists primarily of sweaters, fashion pants, and blouses. What plans do you have for decreasing this stock of old merchandise?

5. What are your goals for your first year as manager-buyer of Fran's Fashion?

Unit 3

Buyer/Market/Vendor Relationship

"I'm going to the market." These are exciting words for any buyer, and a trip always presents a new and different challenge. The "market" can be any one of many places in or near your hometown or anywhere in the world. It is in the market that your talents as a selector of goods, director of specifications, and negotiator of terms are recognized. When these talents are combined with the correct planning and controlling of your dollars and merchandise, your success as a buyer is assured. The smooth balancing of all these factors enables you to give your customers the five rights of merchandising: the right merchandise, at the right price, at the right time, in the right quantities, in the right place.

After determining what and how much to buy for your target customer, you must find the right sources of supply. Chapter 9, "Analyzing and Selecting Resources," explains how to determine which resources are best for your company. You will learn to recognize vendors that appreciate the factors involved in the business of satisfying your customer.

Chapter 10, "Buying in the Domestic Market," addresses all the decisions that are made before and during your market trips. This chapter shows how a buying plan is implemented in the domestic market and explains the procedures followed in the market during your visits. Techniques for budgeting your time, working the various segments of your market, and following showroom etiquette are covered.

Since fashion merchandise for your customers can be found anywhere in the world, you must be aware of how to buy foreign-made merchandise. In Chapter 11, "Buying Foreign Merchandise," the advantages and disadvantages of foreign merchandise and buying methods that apply to foreign merchandise are discussed.

The computation of landed cost, as well as the retail pricing of imports, is explained in detail. All these factors are essential to help you determine the true profit of direct imports.

After visiting domestic and foreign market centers and choosing the right resources, you must next determine the best buying techniques to use in placing your orders. Chapter 12 explains the different techniques and terms of sale that can be used to buy merchandise most advantageously for both you and your customers.

Chapter 9

Analyzing and Selecting Resources

After determining what merchandise to buy, and how much of it to buy to meet the needs of the target customer, the buyer must find sources of supply—merchandise **resources,** as they are known in the retail business. There are many different types of merchandise resources and each type offers a unique blend of goods and services to its customers. Resources are also referred to as **vendors, suppliers,** and, if they actually make the products that the retailers sell, **manufacturers.**

Sources of Information on Where to Buy

Each category of fashion merchandise has hundreds and, in many cases, thousands of individual merchandise resources in each market, and it is an important part of a buyer's job to determine which re-

source will best suit the needs and wants of his or her customers. To aid in making contacts with possible resources, the buyers have many sources of information available to them. Sources of information about resource location, what they manufacture, and the level of their success and cooperation can be found through many different methods and areas. Both internal and external sources offer information to help the buyer decide on the criteria for resource selection.

Past Experience

Every retail buyer keeps records, and these records can supply material for judging the success or failure of the resources that have been used in the past. Even new buyers have access to these unit-control and accounts-payable records. Past experience, recorded over a period of time, can provide a solid basis on which to judge the expansion or contraction of business with resources already working with the buyer. Past experience can indicate how important a certain resource has been in the success and profitability of a department. Past sales records will help the buyer determine whether the department's resources are making merchandise that is consistent with the wants of the customers. Naturally, sales by themselves tell only part of the story. Past experience in resource reliability, quality standards, and other important factors helps the buyer make decisions about the **resource structure,** or list of vendors from which all merchandise is selected, in the store or department.

Trade Publications

Trade publications are a major part of the communication system of fashion merchandising. These publications are a source of professional news about industry developments. All fashion buyers read several trade publications to keep up with current events that relate to style developments, new breakthroughs in technology affecting fashion merchandise, trends in color and silhouette, and resource information—who's hot, who's not, who's new, who's left the business. These trade periodicals constantly try to keep their readers up-to-date on everything happening in the fashion business, and discovering and analyzing new merchandise re-

Trade publications keep the buyer up to date on the activities of resources. Some report on all facets of the fashion industry; others specialize in particular merchandise categories. Buyers also read fashion publications for consumers to observe which manufacturers' names and merchandise are in the public eye.

sources is a priority with many of them. These papers and magazines review the seasonal lines of resources, keeping buyers aware of what each resource is doing for the coming season. Two of the major trade publications in the fashion industry are *Womens Wear Daily* and *Daily News Record*.

Resources Themselves

Many resources spend a great deal of time and money keeping in touch with buyers and telling them what they are planning, producing, and selling. Resources rate stores, too. A new resource may want to be part of the resource structure of your department because of information it has gained about you and your store's fashion image and reliability. Representatives of various resources will contact you and will most often want to put their best foot forward in terms of delivery and advertising—after *you* have determined that their merchandise is right for your customers.

Comparison Shopping—Other Buyers

Comparison shopping can reveal many new resources to buyers. Just walking through the selling floors of stores in their own city, in other cities, or in New York City, astute and aware buyers can determine what is selling well, and what resource it came from. If the resource's name is not on the merchandise, a helpful salesperson may assist buyers in discovering the name of the resource.

Buyers often openly discuss trends with other buyers of noncompeting stores. During market weeks in New York, California, Texas, or Florida, buyers from stores in various cities frequent the market at the same time. They meet in vendors' showrooms, at fashion markets or marts, resident buying offices, fashion shows, and restaurants, and if they are not in direct competition, they exchange information about resources very freely.

Trade Shows and Market Centers

A visit to a market center, a regional mart, or a trade show can be a quick and easy method of discovering and learning about new resources. Within a single building buyers can make quick evaluations of the potential of new resources by viewing the lines shown and talking to the sales executives in charge. In these concentrated areas buyers can easily compare and contrast many resources so that their customers' wants can best be satisfied. Also, many resources will be aware of noncompeting resources at a trade show, and then are usually quick to let their customers know about them also.

Resident Buying Offices

Market representatives are always shopping the market for new and innovative resources and merchandise. It is an important part of their responsibility and helps make their offices more useful to their member stores. The usual practice is for the stores' buyers to receive printed bulletins from the RBO. Many of these bulletins will recommend new resources, new trends, price levels, and merchandise availability. The buying office may also suggest test quantity orders to the buyers, from newly formed or discovered resources. In this way buyers can find out quickly if a new resource's merchandise is what their customers find appealing.

Reporting Services

Services such as the Retail News Bureau report on important new resources, as well as on advertised merchandise that is selling well in various other retail stores

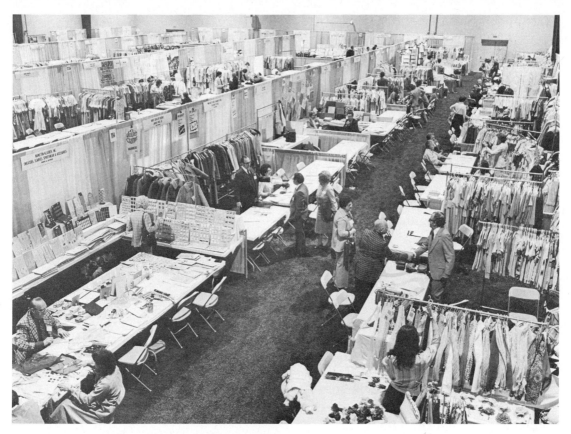

The Exhibition Hall of the Kansas City Market Center houses the temporary displays of many resources during market weeks. Buyers visiting this regional mart can compare and contrast the resources' offerings.

and on the manufacturers supplying this merchandise. The Tobé Report is another service that digests the trends of the fashion markets and recommends resources, styles, and promotional points of view. Stores subscribe to these services. They can provide invaluable help to buyers and act as corroboration for other information the buyer has compiled.

Selection Factors in Choosing Resources

Buyers and vendors are vital partners in the business of satisfying the customer and are therefore dependent on one another for success. They agree that buyer-vendor communications are indispensable so that each will understand the capability and fashion direction of the other. There must be mutual appreciation of each other's contribution and problems. It is mutual profitability that makes a buyer-vendor relationship successful. A vendor should be judged and evaluated in the following five key areas: (1) merchandise suitability, (2) meeting store merchandising policies, (3) production capacity, (4) distribution policies, and (5) production to specification.

Suitability of Merchandise

This is a primary consideration. The merchandise must be compatible with the needs and wants of your customer. No matter how good the delivery, how sharp the price, or how much advertising money is available from a vendor, if the merchandise it produces is not right for your target customer, this vendor should not be considered for your store. Remember, your selling areas are very valuable real estate and you should never give this space to merchandise that is not suitable for your customers.

Meeting Store Merchandising Policies

As discussed in Chapter 3, the store's merchandising policies are the basis for the image of the store. Since these are usually determined by top management, it is part of a buyer's job to ensure that all vendors meet the criteria of the store's policies.

EXCLUSIVES. As explained in Chapter 3, vendors can be an important partner in your ability to provide your customers with merchandise that is "exclusive." Resources may make your store the only store in your trading area to carry their merchandise. They may manufacture specialized versions of their merchandise containing exclusive features that will be for your store alone. Resources may also work with you to produce merchandise of your private design and specification. No matter how you attempt to offer your customers exclusive merchandise, you must always work with resources that are ready, willing, and, of course, able to produce such exclusive merchandise for you.

NATIONAL/PRIVATE BRANDS. Buying from a resource whose merchandise has ultimate customer recognition is helpful to a buyer. Nationally advertised brands have become well known and accepted by customers because of the time and effort spent by the resource in targeting its merchandise to a certain customer. Stocking this type of merchandise ensures that many of the buyer's customers are presold on the styling, quality, and pricing of this national brand. However, working with national brand resources restricts a bit of the buyer's freedom in choices of stock levels, delivery dates, advertising formats, and pricing. In any case, making the decision to carry national brands remains with top management. Once these decisions have been made, a buyer cannot change them.

In contrast to the national brand resource, there are many resources that will work with buyers to provide merchandise with the store's private label, which may be created to the buyer's own specifications. Again, be sure that the resource is one that can work with specifications and will not produce identical goods for use by other, competing stores with *their* private labels. **Specification buying** is buying done by the store's representatives (buyers and merchandisers) by designating particulars about the selected item to be manufactured. In specification buying, the buyer and the manufacturer agree on the details of the individual product, which is not a duplicate of any other item that manufacturer makes. The buyer selects or develops the style and type of fabric or other material, and stipulates the size notations, coloration, ornamentation, and/or other detail. For such merchandise, the vendor agrees not to manufacture that item, as specified, for any other retailer for an agreed-upon period of time. If the store chooses to give a special label to these goods, they may be listed among that store's private brands.

Liz Claiborne: Right on Target to the Working Woman

Interpreting and projecting consumer demand are as important for suppliers as for retailers. And while we know that in reality, no one possesses a crystal ball in which future trends can be seen, it almost seems that designer Liz Claiborne does have such a tool.

When Claiborne started her own firm in 1976, there were certainly women in the work force—although not nearly in the numbers or at the executive levels that they are today. Yet "working women" was the market she went after, and her company sold more than $2 million worth of clothing in the first year. By 1985, with over 50 percent of women working outside the home, Claiborne's sales had grown to over $550 million.

What magic key does Liz Claiborne hold that could account for such a rousing success? A good portion surely comes from her "first commandment"—namely, "Satisfy Thy Consumer."[1] And exactly who is that consumer? She is identified by Jerome A. Chazen, Claiborne's executive vice president-marketing, as the "executive and professional career woman who is a little more updated in her taste level, as opposed to a very traditional customer who might wear structured suits and blouses with ties."[2] Others have elaborated on the description, calling the customers for Liz Claiborne creations women who "lack the time to shop for appropriate clothes and the individual wealth to pay *haute couture* prices."[3]

With that target customer in mind, Liz Claiborne, Inc., developed a full line of clothing (excluding formal evening wear, coats, nightwear, and bathing suits) designed to take a woman "from the office to dinner to a casual setting to a very casual weekend."[4] Selling in the "better" price range but below traditional "designer" prices, Claiborne clothes may range from about $40 to $60 for a casual skirt or blouse, up to $150 for a jacket, or $170 for a dress. Marketing studies by the company show that American women think of Liz Claiborne as a personal friend, one whose taste they can trust.[5]

And to make sure that new and existing styles continue to meet consumer needs and wants, Claiborne works closely with retailers, helping them to present the merchandise in its best light, and also tracking sales to the end customer. Weekly reports, dubbed the Systematic Updated Retail Feedback

(SURF), are gathered from 16 stores representing a cross section of geographic location and store size, and the results give the firm a clear picture of exactly how consumers are reacting to the merchandise being shipped.

It is all a part of Liz Claiborne's continuing strategy to identify customer needs and then satisfy them—a tactic her retail customers appreciate. Said Carol Greer, senior vice president and general merchandise manager, ready-to-wear and shoes, for Rich's, Atlanta: "What Claiborne does best is thoroughly understand the customer, her lifestyle, and the price she's willing to pay."[6]

1 Rayna Skolnick, "Liz the Wiz," *Sales & Marketing Management*, September 9, 1985, p. 50.
2 Ibid.
3 Vartanig G. Vartan, "Liz Claiborne's Many Fans," *New York Times*, July 11, 1985, p. D8.
4 Skolnick, op. cit., p. 50
5 Lisa Belkin, "Redesigning the Empire that Liz Built," *New York Times*, May 4, 1986, p. 29.
6 Skolnick, op. cit., p. 50 .

PRICING. The price structure of a resource can be a major factor in your selection of it for your department. If your store carries goods in only certain price points, a resource with a price structure above or below your established price policy should not be considered, no matter how exciting, innovative, or interesting that resource's merchandise may be.

Another pricing policy to investigate is how the resource prices its merchandise for clearance, either after or, in some cases, during the peak selling season. At some resources, buying the regular line may be a condition for getting an ample share of specially priced merchandise. Some resources sell such goods to a few large or preferred accounts, while others sell off-price and clearance goods to price-promotional outlets that are not regular customers. It is important for the buyer to fully understand the pricing policies of a resource before a relationship is built.

FASHION LEADERSHIP. As we have already learned, timing in the introduction of new fashions is a vital element of a store's merchandising policy. Choosing resources that help reinforce this fashion image is of prime importance. No matter when in the fashion cycle your store chooses to sell its goods, purchasing merchandise from resources that plan and produce for the same point in the fashion cycle is essential. Having goods when your customers want them—whether on the introduction or early rise, on the late rise and early peak, or on the peak into the decline stage of the fashion cycle—means that you must deal with resources that consistently produce for that same point in the fashion cycle.

QUALITY STANDARDS. The buyer is the person most responsible for quality standards. It is the buyer who, working within the store's merchandising policy, must set the standards for quality of merchandise. The buyer must also follow through and check constantly that merchandise received from resources is consistent with agreed-upon quality standards. The buyer is responsible for the quality check of merchandise, making sure that the merchandise delivered is identical to merchandise selected in the market, that it agrees with samples on which the order was based, and that it incorporates all of the quality specifications drawn up and agreed upon between the buyer and the resource.

Production Capacity

Many resources may have production capacities either too small or, in some cases, too large to suit your particular needs. A small resource might be perfect for small groups of exclusive styles but not right for a large "special promotion" order. Conversely, a large production resource may demand too large a minimum order for each style and be unable to fill your needs on small orders.

Some resources refuse to put anything into production until firm orders are received. In many cases, buyers feel that resources should share the inventory burden, at least in staples and fashion merchandise that has the potential to become reorder styles. Prompt replenishment of retail inventories is a prerequisite for good buyer-resource relationships. The ability of the resource to control and maneuver its production capacity is of mutual advantage to both buyer and resource.

Distribution Policies

Having a line "confined" to your store in an area is a plus for you as a buyer. However, most resources, especially those that

Before goods reach the selling floor, the buyer should be sure that the merchandise delivered to the store is identical with the merchandise ordered.

produce national brand merchandise, will have a policy of wide distribution. If you need this merchandise, you have little choice but to buy from these resources. Some resources sell to more than one retailer in a trading area—but only to retailers of a price and fashion level that coincide with your own. This is called **selective distribution.**

However, the distribution policy of a resource may be very loose. Such resources sell to anyone and everyone who comes into the showroom and writes a confirmed order. This may include your direct competitor and also indirect competitors, such as mass merchandisers, discount or off-price retailers, and full-line department and specialty stores. It is the legal right of the resource to sell to whom it wishes and it is also the legal right of any retailer to buy and expect delivery on a confirmed order. Therefore, investigate the distribution policy of a resource before you use one—it is your legal right to determine that it is not for your store.

Production to Specification

If you are using a resource for specification buying, you must be certain that the resource is not only willing but able to follow directives. The manufacturer must have trained and qualified specification specialists who can understand and interpret your detailed notations as to fabric, pattern, grading, sewing techniques, and finishing methods. Many giant retailers help resources with the purchase of required raw materials and equipment and with the industrial techniques for producing the specified merchandise at a designated price. In these cases, the merchandise is ordered in huge quantities and the specifications are involved in quality, manufacture, and price. However, sometimes a buyer will only want a detail changed or removed so that the merchandise is not in direct competition with other retailers. A buyer may also change details in order to bring the merchandise down in price, or add details to build it up to a more profitable, higher price line. Either way, it is imperative that the resource understand and be able to perform in the required manner. Usually manufacturers will make merchandise to specification only for retailers who can place substantial quantity orders. Some small retailers may buy such goods with other retailers through their common resident buying office. For large retailers, specification buying is frequently used with foreign market resources. Sometimes small retailers get unique products by asking a manufacturer to modify an article from the regular line by changing or adding special ornamentation. This, however, is not truly specification buying. (Specification buying is discussed further in Chapters 11 and 12.)

Concentration of Resources

The primary goal of any buyer is to do business with the most suitable company resources. To reach this goal, buyers must systematically evaluate what each resource has done—and what it can do in the future—to improve department or store operations. Obviously, a long-term resource relationship can be extremely beneficial. Although having a broad coverage of market resources is important, many stores consider that a large part of the buyer's purchases should be concentrated with a few resources in order to ensure the buyer's importance to these vendors. By investing the open-to-buy with just a few resources, the store buyer has greater buying power with each of these resources.

Key or Preferred Resources

These selected resources are then known as **key** or **preferred resources**—the ones the buyer uses repeatedly. They are important to a buyer in terms of sales volume, exclusivity, service, and store image. There is a mutual feeling of partnership between the store and its key resources. Each plans to maintain an ongoing relationship, season after season and year after year. A key resource does not "belong" to a buyer. The relationship is usually built at the top management level of both retailer and resource, and even when new buyers come in, the key resource remains and continues to service the store as before.

Focus

Leslie Fay, Leading Manufacturer

Leslie Fay, founded in 1943, claims that its success is based on its appeal to a broad spectrum of American women in terms of age, styling, and price. And successful it is. This manufacturing group is made up of eight divisions with annual sales of over $200 million at wholesale value.

Each year Leslie Fay merchandises in excess of 2,400 styles—not numbers or sizes or colors, but complete, individual styles. The major product is dresses, and over 90 percent are manufactured in the United States and targeted for the moderate and better markets. Recently Leslie Fay has entered the sportswear market with emphasis on the same target market as its dress business.

Leslie Fay is run as a series of separate companies, and their main objective in business is to put out the best-made product they can. John Pomerantz, president of the company and son of the founder, says, "If we continue to do that, we'll continue to be respected by retailers, and that's what matters."[1]

Because Leslie Fay and its many divisions are important as "key" vendors or "preferred" resources, they must constantly work to update and modernize their operations so that they can be better partners in a vendor-retailer relationship. Although Leslie Fay is in the fashion business, fashion is not the only important factor behind its success. A reputation for good personnel in key positions and constant striving to meet retailers' demands have allowed the Leslie Fay companies to build their relationship with retailers throughout the country.

One of the new methods they are employing to meet the retailers' demands is Quick Response. It is well known that one of the biggest negative impacts upon gross profit in a fashion business is excessive markdowns. Therefore, the closer one can operate to the market need, the less risk of excessive markdowns. As a manufacturer, Leslie Fay must cater to the needs and wants of its customers, the retailers, as the retailers do to their customers. With Quick Response, Leslie Fay can improve its reliability in meeting retailers' delivery dates, thus reducing the threat of cancellations. The system allows the manufacturer to deliver more product with fewer shipments, and to get its product to the proper markets at lower handling costs in its distribution centers.

Leslie Fay is a giant in the women's apparel market, but because each year retail buyers analyze and select the resources they consider right for their customers on the basis of changing factors, Leslie Fay continues to cultivate its reputation for quality and service. In this way its companies can continue to enjoy successful vendor relations with their accounts.

1. Mark Sullivan, "Manufacturer Profile", *New York Apparel News,* Spring 1982, Part I, p. 93
This Focus is based on the above article and on Jean E. Palmieri, "Kogan Is Keen on Kathryn Conover—A Division of Leslie Fay," *Apparel News South,* Spring ed. October 1984, p. 54.
Sanford Mazer, "Steering Faster Turns," *Bobbin,* January 1985, pp. 29–30, 32.

Although concentration of resources is considered to be a sound and profitable arrangement with many advantages for both retailers and resources, there can also be some disadvantages to this method. Advantages and disadvantages include the following:

ADVANTAGES

☐ Preferential deliveries are made for large opening orders and reorders.
☐ Cooperative advertising money may be forthcoming.
☐ Advertising and display aids and materials are provided.
☐ Markdown money is given for slow-selling styles.
☐ Returns are allowed for poor-selling styles.
☐ Sales training and premium inducements for sales help are offered.
☐ Cancellations are allowed.

DISADVANTAGES

☐ Using only key resources can limit stock assortment.
☐ Little opportunity is given to new resources.
☐ There is limited freedom of choice.
☐ Risk exists of key resource's merchandise not meeting customer's wants every season.

☐ Risk exists of key resources not having the desired fashion image season after season.

Resource Services

Many times the negotiations of purchases include matters other than the merchandise and the price. The resource is often willing and able to provide services to the buyer that make the resource a valuable partner in the business of satisfying the needs of the retailer's customers.

The variety of services that may be available vary with the classification of the merchandise, the type of store, and the importance of the resource to the buyer— and of the buyer to the resource, as determined by the volume of goods ordered. In most cases it should be the buyer who decides whether the service available is in the best interests of the store and its customers. A checklist of usual vendor services appears in Table 9-1.

However, before accepting the services offered by a resource, a buyer should ask the following questions:

☐ Will the service increase the sales and profits of my entire department or simply take sales away from other merchandise?
☐ Is the resource better equipped to develop

Table 9-1

Services Vendors Provide to Retailer

Personal selling

Sales training for store's salespeople

Awards program for salespeople for selling the vendor's product

Vendor-employed demonstrators assigned to the store

Servicing the merchandise and providing warranties

Advertising

Layouts for print ads to which the retailer can add its own logo and store information and then submit to print media

Radio and TV scripts

Copies of manufacturer-prepared ads for use in direct mail and package inserts

Cooperative advertising allowances

Visual merchandising

Sample merchandise and packaging for display

Display fixtures and signs

Videotapes and sound/slide programs for in-store customer viewing

Inventory

Vendor-prepared price tickets

Warehousing of purchased goods

Assistance with inventory control

Financing

Extending credit

Consignment selling

Return privileges

---

more effective promotional aids than my store?

☐ Does the service offered reduce the opportunity for other merchandise to be sold?

☐ Will resource-sponsored advertising allowances have a negative effect on my store's fashion image?

Vendor Analysis

On the basis of the factors we have already learned, buyers find it helpful to analyze the resources they have done business with during the previous selling period. They use this analysis to eliminate unsuccessful resources and to try to concentrate their business with the better ones. Those resources that are found to be the most satisfactory usually become key or preferred resources.

You will want to rate your suppliers in terms of how accurately their merchandise meets the needs of customers. Sometimes there is an affinity between one vendor's merchandise and the preferences of a store's customers that persists for seasons and even years. Sometimes the affinity is fleeting.

To help evaluate your department's resources, you may, with the help of the store's accounting office, maintain records of dealings with each vendor. Typical evaluations include vendor name and address, purchases at cost and retail, and the year's or season's total purchases. Vendor returns and claims, as well as markdowns, are also reported by season or year. This type of evaluation will help you see if a resource has added to the past season's profits or to its problems. (See Form 9–1.)

Many buyers rank their resources according to amounts purchased, initial markup, percentage of markdowns, or other criteria. This list serves another purpose. Top management of the store can see who the principal resources are for each department, and they will contact them at least once a year to thank them for participation in a profitable operation. Often such contact between heads of stores and heads of resources leads to better understanding and to long-range planning that benefits the resource, the store (including its buyers), and the customer.

Dept. 444 CHILDRENS UNDERWEAR **Division** 1 **Period Ending** 01/31/8- **Page** 17

VENDOR NUMBER	NAME	MARK UP %	YEAR-TO-DATE NET PURCHASES RETAIL	COST	FREIGHT	DISCOUNT	YEAR-TO-DATE MARK DOWNS $	%	YEAR-TO-DATE RETURNS-TO-VENDOR RETAIL	COST	FREIGHT	DISCOUNT
3529-7	TRALEE								4000	2175	174	
3006-6	SMITH DISTRIBUTORS INC	34.2	1400	921								
2499-6	MODERN GLOBE INC	37.9	24600	14664	1173	613						
4484-9	BAGS BY MR ROBERTS	38.3	48600	30000	600					3000	60	
4439-3	CASSIE COTILLION	41.4	35880	20580	1646	433	360	10.0	1500	825	66	
2184-9	KID DUDS	43.1	38880	21760	17408	3596	423	10.9				
3776-1	METRO NOVELTY CO	43.5	6000	3461	68		10	16.7				
4264-1	CHERRI LYNN	43.5	52500	29660	23732		420	8.0		640		
2142-3	K M T CO	44.4	51380	29128	5649		649	12.6	31000	19463	390	
3352-9	WILLIAM CARTER CO	44.4	57400	31857	6346	7039	341	5.9	49700	26710	535	
1002-2	A D SUTTON & SONS	44.6	129600	69450	1389	2319			3800	1320	26	
2140-7	K GIMBEL ACCESSORIES INC	44.7	34800	18730	370	512	52	15.0				
4274-9	SOFTSKIN TOYS	44.8	52200	27360	547	1431						
3187-9	TOM FIELDS INC	45.1	119500	66273	657		137	11.5	800	445	04	
1045-6	ALEX LEE WALLAU INC	45.5	143600	81157	3558	639	87	6.1	3300	2761	36	
2244-6	LE ROI HOSIERY CO	45.7	32920	18020	3603	2260	265	8.1	300	146	03	
4062-2	JUST ACCESSORIES	46.0	-36000	-18000		-1438						
4981-6	EARL BERNARD INC	46.1	12000	6600	132		30	25.1				
4272-2	PILLOW PLAYMATES	46.7	105000	52860	349	3098	120	11.4				
1622-5	EASTERN ISLES	47.4	784000	414076	32999	4838	975	13.3				
1557-1	DETERMINED PRODUCTIONS	48.6	99000	49950		924	259	26.2				
1931-3	HER MAJESTY IND INC	48.6	1390700	779030	65743	868	1529	11.0	70400	42403	3194	
1756-6	FREDERICK WHOLESALE CORP	49.9	945400	494158	31733	11692	756	3.0	87500	43958	879	
1618-7	E K WERTHEIMER & SON INC	50.0	36000	18000	540							
4207-2	GIANT UMBRELLA CO INC	50.0	72000	36000	1080		40	6.0				
2741-3	PYRAMID LEATHER GOODS CO	50.1	34800	17935	2044	1490	39	11.2				
3654-4	GAYSTONE PRODUCTS	50.4	14400	7355	216							
1862-7	GUILD LINGERIE OF CALIF	51.2	100800	53467	4296		187	18.6				
2759-6	R G BARRY CORP	51.4	24880	12134	2588	-379	278	11.1				
1755-8	FREDERICK ATKINS INTERNTL	51.7	40000	19340								
4233-1	A M A EXPENSE TRANSFER	51.7	-40000	-19340								
3531-9	VELVA SHEEN	53.5	143900	66975			156	10.8				
4920-4	HOLLYWOOD CHILDRENS DRESS	54.0	87600	43800	3504		98	11.2				
	DEPARTMENT TOTAL	47.7	7283300	3955628	226793	43895	7258	10.4	252300	143846	5367	

Form 9-1. A vendor analysis form.

Profitable Resource Relations

Good resource relations are characterized by cooperation rather than by conflict. However, many buyer-resource discussions tend to focus on differences and complaints.

Resource relations are largely determined by the buyer's sense of loyalty, the loyalty that a buyer feels to the store versus the loyalty to a resource. Experts in the fashion field recognize three distinct types of buyers: (1) buyers who feel no obligation to the resource, only to themselves and the store; (2) buyers who have more loyalty to key resources which treat them like VIPs and which can be relied upon in a search for a new buying position elsewhere; (3) professional buyers who recognize their obligations both to the store and to the resource. However, the buyer's loyalty first and foremost must be to the customers. The greatest gift that a buyer can receive from a resource is well-made merchandise that sells! Developing too close a relationship with resources can sometimes affect objectivity and make it hard to be impartial in seeking the best merchandise at the best possible price. Here are some points to keep in mind to ensure profitable resource relations.

☐ Constantly review your resource mix, classification by classification. Allow each resource the opportunity to reach its potential.

☐ Do not overdo the concept of key resources. Always be open for new exciting items from new or off beat sources.

☐ Confirm in writing as quickly as possible all agreements with resources. In this way misunderstandings can be avoided.

☐ Set and keep schedules for seeing resources' salespeople. Even if you can't buy, there is always something new to see and something new to learn.

- ☐ Be a goodwill ambassador for your store on visits to the market and in resource showrooms. Avoid making appointments you cannot keep.
- ☐ Avoid snap judgments in eliminating or changing resources. It is the performance of a resource over the long period that counts.
- ☐ Remember, resources rate *you* and analyze the profitability of doing business with your store. They rate your store on how well it does with their merchandise and also on the fairness with which you treat them.

Buying Vocabulary

Define or briefly explain the following terms:

Key resources	Selective distribution
Manufacturers	Specification buying
Resources	Suppliers
Resource structure	

Buying Review

1. What part does past experience play as a source of information in selecting resources for buying?
2. How can comparison shopping be helpful in selecting new resources?
3. What trade periodicals are available to guide you with current fashion events?
4. Explain how resident buying offices work to target the resources for your use.
5. How is a vendor's suitability for a successful buyer-vendor relationship judged?
6. Why are production capacity and timely delivery factors in vendor selection?
7. Discuss the vendor requirements for meeting your store policies?
8. What factors should you take into account when evaluating vendors? What is the main purpose of such an evaluation?
9. List any advantages in concentration of resources.
10. Do the disadvantages of concentrating on key resources weaken this buying approach?
11. List the benefits of concentrated buying from a key vendor.
12. What are the personal advantages to a buyer of a close relationship with an important preferred resource?

Buying Case

You will be going to New York City early in November to shop the market and place orders for spring coats and suits for your department in a large department store in Washington, D.C. You have been the buyer for this department of moderate-priced coats and suits for four years and have shown successful results over this period.

Explain in detail which of your vendors you will visit on this trip. Would you take time on this trip to shop any new vendors? If so, why? How would you make the final decision on the resources used for this spring buy? Explain how you reached your final decisions.

Chapter 10

Buying in the Domestic Market

The most exciting and rewarding moments in a retail fashion buyer's life are when customers buy the merchandise that the buyer has selected. At these moments all the hours of research, all the pressure of decision making, and all the experience of the buyer come together to provide the customers with what they want! Fashion buyers shop the market for hundreds of customers, rather than for themselves. And although they may find themselves caught up in the heady and hectic environment of the fashion market, they must always keep the needs and wants of their customers uppermost in their minds.

Sometimes it seems that there is never enough time, space, money or information to make the process of decision making easy. Selecting the actual merchandise to implement the buying plans is a constant and never-ending process. The pro-

cess takes place at your desk, in manufacturers' showrooms, in resident buying offices, in comparison shopping, and in regional and foreign market centers. Decisions must be made—constantly, quickly, and firmly. During your trips to the market you make decisions that are vital to the profitability of your department and to your store. Maximizing the productivity of your market visit is becoming more and more imperative.

When and how often a buyer goes to market are determined by the size of the store or department, the fashion-cycle stage, the turnover of the merchandise carried, and the policy of top management. A store that wants to build or maintain a strong fashion image may send its buyers to market several times during a year or a season. Retailers who feature promotional prices may also send their

A fashion show is one of the exciting activities during a buying trip, but the buyer must be able to separate the glamour of the event from the appeal of the merchandise itself.

buyers to the market frequently in constant search of special buys. Extra market trips are usually required when there are special promotions planned, fashion innovations, and newly emerging categories of merchandise to be bought for the store. Also, more frequent trips with smaller dollar purchases help to increase inventory turnover.

The Buying Plan

A buyer on a trip to the wholesale market leaves the store prepared to spend a considerable amount of money. To make sure this money is not spent haphazardly, and to show that there is need for the trip, most stores require that a written buying plan be drawn up and approved prior to departure. A **buying plan** is a general description of the types and quantities of merchandise a buyer expects to purchase for delivery within a specific period of time. It also sets a limit on the amount of money to be spent, so that purchases will be kept in line with planned sales and desired inventory levels.

The more enthusiastic a retail buyer is about fashion merchandise, the more the stabilizing influence of a written buying plan is needed. It is a constant reminder to avoid spending too much on the first new and exciting goods encountered while neglecting other sectors of the assortment.

A buying plan makes all the difference, for example, between going to market to see what is offered in dresses and going to market to find dresses at specific retail price lines, in specific quantities, with specific delivery dates—all in accordance with budget limitations, assortment plan, present inventory, present commitments, and sales potential of the coat department. Until a buyer or store owner actually inspects producers' lines, the buying plan cannot be completely explicit. To be without one, however, invites unplanned assortments that are poorly related to customer demand.

The buying plan is part of the homework that every buyer undertakes before making any major commitment of funds to buy fashion merchandise. Department and chain stores generally do not release travel funds to their buyers until a plan has been made and has been approved by the merchandise manager or senior store executive. Form 10-1 illustrates a simple buying plan that might be used in a moderate- or large-volume store.

Information Required for a Buying Plan

In addition to identifying data such as department number and name, date of trip, destination, and length of stay, a typical buying plan requires detailed information about a number of other points. These include various projections in either dollars or units of merchandise, or both, based on the department's merchandise budget as well as the merchandise assortment plan.

When you have supplied all the information required in a buying plan, the merchandise manager or senior store executive is in a position to evaluate the need for the trip and also to bring greater experience and judgment to bear upon the tentative decisions that a buying plan represents.

BUYING PLAN   Page 1

Dept. 42, Misses Dresses Date Feb. 20, 198-
Planned MU% 48.5
Buying trip to: New York
From: Feb. 24 To: Feb. 27
Reason for trip: Additional Easter Mdse; Review Mar. – Apr. O.O., New Mdse for early Apr. delivery

Mo. of Delivery	O.T.B. 2/20/8-	Planned Purchases	O.T.B. Balance	Actual Purchases Cost	Retail
March	$9,300	$7,900	$1,400		
April	13,600	6,700	6,900		

APPROVED: GMM ABD Date 2/22/8- DMM TJC Date 2/21/8-

(1) Class	(2) Unit Retail	(3) Description	(4) Actual Sales L.Y.	(5) Planned Sales T.Y.	(6) Planned Stock 4/15/8-	(7) Total (5+6)	(8) O.H. 2/20/8-	(9) O.O. 2/20/8-	(10) Total (8+9)	(11) O.T.B. (7-10)	(12) Plan to buy	(13) Purchases No.	Cost	Retail
123	22		141	150	250	400	176	90	266	134	Mar 60/Apr 60			
	26	Street, business and general occasion wear dresses	163	175	300	475	202	100	302	173	Mar 90/Apr 80			
	30		155	160	225	385	162	80	242	143	Mar 80/Apr 60			
	35		94	100	180	280	112	60	172	108	Mar 60/Apr 42			
140	30	Dressy and after-5 dresses	42	45	80	125	94	36	130	—				
	35		30	35	65	100	80	18	98	—				
	40		19	25	50	75	60	18	78	—				

Form 10-1. A buying plan.

REASON FOR TRIP. The purpose of a buying trip may be to attend regular seasonal openings of vendors' lines, to seek out special values for a forthcoming promotion, or to bolster a section of the assortment that is enjoying an unexpected burst of demand. The reason given for making the trip, as well as some of the other data in the buying plan, also shows management whether the trip is urgent or routine.

OPEN-TO-BUY. Open-to-buy, as discussed in Chapters 5 and 7, is the amount of merchandise that can be purchased for delivery during a given period minus outstanding orders scheduled for delivery during that same period. To review, the formula for calculating open-to-buy is as follows:

planned sales for period

+ planned markdowns

+ planned closing stock

= total requirement for period

− stock on hand

− merchandise on order for delivery this period

= open-to-buy for period

Example: planned sales	100,000
planned markdowns	+8,000
closing stock	+125,000
total required for period	233,000
stock on hand	−85,000
	148,000
on order	−50,000
OTB	98,000

Open-to-buy can be calculated and shown on a buying plan either in dollars or in units of merchandise, or both. It is usually shown by classification and price lines or price ranges within each classification. The total dollar figure on the buying plan automatically shows management whether or not the proposed purchases are within the dollar limits established in that season's merchandise budget. The unit figures are based on the season's unit assortment plan. In some cases, open-to-buy figures may be shown for one or more months into the future. This is a useful guide when the buyer is authorized to make commitments for delivery of goods beyond the current period for which buying is then being done. Today many stores order merchandise three to six months ahead of delivery and selling periods. This is usually done to ensure delivery of wanted goods at the proper time. More and more manufacturers are requiring longer lead time for production timing.

STOCK ON HAND AND ON ORDER. For each classification of merchandise to be purchased, current merchandise on hand and on order for delivery during the period for which purchases are being planned are indicated on a buying plan. Usually each price line in each classification at which purchases are planned is entered separately, with the **stock on hand** and **on order** indicated in units or dollars or both. In moderate- and large-volume stores, unit price and total amounts to be purchased are shown at retail values, while smaller stores sometimes use cost figures. By comparing these figures on the buying plan with those in the merchandise budget and the assortment plan, management can determine whether or not the intended purchases are within the budgetary limits set for the department or classification and are in line with its assortment plan.

SALES FOR THE PERIOD. The buying plan, prepared just before a market trip, includes the most recent sales estimates and reports available. These may be shown in units or dollars or both. If the buying trip is made before the start of a season, the sales figures in the plan will be those projected on the dollar merchandise budget and the merchandise assortment plan, modified according to current trends for fashion sales. If the selling season has already begun, these figures will have been adjusted to reflect anticipated sales for the balance of the period for which buying is to be done. If the merchandise budget and the assortment plan have been revised to meet current conditions, the revised figures are used. The important point is that the buying plan includes the most up-to-date sales, stock-on-hand, and stock-on-order figures available at the time it is prepared. The market condition, active or quiet, is also observed. Sometimes not all the open-to-buy money is spent. Other times, when delivery is tight, you may have to get permission to "overbuy" in order to obtain the quantities that are needed.

PLANNED STOCK AT END OF PERIOD. The planned end-of-period inventory figures, in both dollars and units, are very important in planning the buying of fashion goods. Because demand rises rapidly to a peak in fashion goods and falls off even more sharply after the peak has been passed, it is essential to keep the inventory within the established limits. If a buyer brings in too much stock and has more than planned at the close of a selling period, it is likely that heavy markdowns will be needed to get rid of that excess stock.

If the buyer plans to make purchases for more than a month or two, the **planned stock** for the end of that period is entered in the buying plan. If buying is short term, only the current month's closing stock estimate may be needed.

QUANTITIES TO BE PURCHASED. Buyers indicate on their buying plans, in terms of both units and retail dollars, how much of each type of merchandise they want to purchase on this trip in order to maintain an assortment that will meet anticipated customer demand. These figures are based on buyers' judgment of sales potential, availability of merchandise, market conditions, and other factors. Quantities to be purchased vary with the timing of a market trip, the store's merchandising policies, the type of merchandise, and delivery conditions. At the start of a selling season, perhaps only trial quantities are ordered, while larger quantities may be purchased with more assurance as the season advances. Most stores establish loosely defined percentages of the seasonal open-to-buy that may be purchased early. The experienced buyer saves a good part of both the unit and dollar open-to-buy for later in the season, for unexpected and opportune purchases, for reorders, and for purchases required by changing customer demands.

ADDITIONAL DATA. Some plans provide space in which the buyer enters the amount of actual purchases after shopping the market. As illustrated in Form 10-1, these entries are usually placed alongside the approved, planned figures. A number of stores require the buyer to submit, at the conclusion of each trip, a detailed reconciliation of all orders placed, by classification and price line, with quantities approved on the original buying plan. Either of these procedures underscores the importance of adhering to planned figures unless there is good reason to do otherwise.

A few store managements require a list of resources the buyer intends to visit on the market trip. Such a list is usually expected to include the names of one or more resources with which the store has not yet had dealings, but whose potential the buyer will explore. It also includes resources with which the department has already dealt, sometimes for years.

This requirement serves a double purpose. It stimulates the buyer to make realistic plans as to which and how many producers to visit in the time available. In addition, it is a reminder to inspect the lines of resources that have proved successful in customer acceptance and yet avoid the danger of going only to regular resources. Just as any business constantly seeks new customers, so an alert store seeks new and gifted resources to add fresh and interesting items to its assortments.

How a Buyer Plans

Before actually drawing up a buying plan, fashion merchants or buyers review the stock in several respects. They check their basic stock requirements. They study any overstock conditions. They note any items that are winning strong acceptance. They take upcoming sales events into consideration. This overall review is intended to give a good idea of exactly what is needed and what should be sought in the market.

OVERSTOCK. Any section of the assortment on hand that exceeds its planned size requires analysis. The adjustments needed to reduce such overstocked conditions may affect buying plans for categories in which sales are proceeding according to plan. For example, slow sellers in higher-priced lines may have to be marked down into lower-priced lines. In such cases, buying plans for the lower-priced line may have to be adjusted to take such additions to the existing stock into account. There also may be some common factor among a department's slow sellers which can be regarded as a warning against further purchases of a disappointing price line, color, fabric, detail, or other features customers have not favored. These make the buyer aware of what the customer does not want.

"HOT" ITEMS. Items, new or otherwise, that have demonstrated greater customer acceptance than was anticipated receive thoughtful consideration from the buyer. Even though they may not have been prominent in the original assortment plan for the season, it may be necessary to make an important place for these **hot items.** To do that, buying plans for other items may have to be cut back.

If the hot item is one the buyer has heard about but has not yet actually had in stock, judgment on its sales potential may be reserved until it has been studied in the market. Then approved buying plans for the more predictable and familiar items may be adjusted, and the buyer may decide to add the hot item to the assortment. Color is very important. By careful observation, the buyer can spot the best-selling colors and give color direction to the new stock.

SPECIAL EVENTS. If the buying trip for which the plan is drawn involves preparation for a promotional event, special sale, catalog distribution, advertisements, or similar activity, the buyer is fortified with details on what was offered to, and bought by, the store's customers on similar occasions in the past. If a buyer is about to purchase handbags for the annual storewide sale, it is important to know how many handbags were sold in last year's sale, the best-selling price point, and whether styling in handbags has had a significant change. This information then has to be weighed against what is available in the market this year. Open-to-buy money must be allocated for these special events.

IMPORTANCE OF COMPLETE DATA. When drawing up a buying plan, the buyer is still in the store. Here all the sources of information on present conditions and past experience, described in Chapters 5 and 6, are available. Once the buyer is in the market, however, only the condensed data of the buying plan itself can be consulted. The more thoroughly the buyer checks while still at the store, the more valuable the capsulized data on the buying plan will be.

Timing of Your Trip

Every minute you spend in the market is valuable. It is impossible to replace. Since most fashion-oriented merchandise is influenced by seasonal changes in demand, manufacturers of these lines often set opening dates for the showing of their new seasonal lines. Most apparel and accessories firms sponsor two major market periods: October/November for Spring/Summer and April/May for Fall/Winter. During these market periods, buyers from all over the country, and from all over the world, come into the major market areas to view manufacturers' lines. This creates an exciting and stimulating atmosphere for the visiting buyers. These market periods are used to exhibit new styles in the greatest variety and with a maximum of showmanship. Fashion shows, press meetings, resident office clinics, cocktail parties are all part of the excitement and hype of the major market periods.

Changes in Market Dates and Period

Recently, earlier market openings with longer spread between showings and de-

During market weeks in major markets, suppliers present many programs to bring buyers up to date on current trends. Here a textile manufacturer introduces new fabrics to buyers visiting its New York office.

livery dates have been the trend. Manufacturers claim that longer lead time is now necessary to have the merchandise produced and into the stores for early testing purposes. However, reorders, the lifeblood of the fashion business in the past, have become very difficult to obtain and to successfully merchandise, even with the longer lead time.

The trend is toward having new styles constantly available throughout the year. The most successful fashion buyers are the ones that maintain a continuous flow of new merchandise. The arrival of new styles every week is more interesting to customer demand than are two or three market openings throughout the year with in-between delivery of stock largely confined to reorders. Who of us has never asked, "What's new?" when we shop our favorite store? The store whose stock rarely has something new slowly but surely loses its customers.

Informing the Market of Your Visit

Before you leave for any market trip it is important to notify the people you intend to work with that you are coming. Announcing your coming and needs in advance to the key people you expect to see will alleviate much confusion and make your time in the market more productive. The following are some of the people who should be alerted to your impending visit:

☐ Your resident buying office
☐ Your major resources
☐ Fiber, fabric, leather, or other primary producers from whom you may be able to obtain information on fashion trends and resources in your merchandise lines
☐ Magazines from which you might accept editorial credit

Once you have notified your resident buying office (RBO) of the date of your arrival, they will have it published in *Womens Wear Daily* under the Buyer's Arrival listing. This listing will notify the market of your arrival dates, and people interested in seeing you will call your RBO and make an appointment to see you.

The Resident Buying Office

Advise your buying office as far in advance as possible of your buying trip dates to assure that time is reserved for you. Phone or write to tell your market representative about your merchandise needs, what is currently selling well in your store, and why you are coming to market to shop.

If you are looking for sale or promotional merchandise, be sure to give the resident office ample time to check the market to see what is available, so that when you arrive they will have screened special purchase opportunities for your review and selection.

Ask the opinion of your market representatives on the market in general, as well as categories or items that are developing. Ask them to list for you the strongest lines in each category you are planning to buy, and to be prepared to discuss them with you on your arrival. This will save you valuable time and permit you to start shopping the market at the earliest possible moment.

Working the Market

If you do your planning and paperwork thoroughly and conscientiously before you leave your store, you will arrive at the market with all the facts and guidelines you need. Shorter and more frequent trips are becoming increasingly important to fashion buyers. During these shorter time periods buyers make decisions that are vital to the success and profit of their departments. Maximizing your productivity on these short trips to the market is imperative. Exploring the market and evaluating the merchandise you see must be the focus of your attention.

Budget Your Time

In the market your first stop should be your buying office to review both your source list and your buying plan and check best-selling items and lines that your market representative tells you are selling. Be sure to ask about new items, new resources, and special offerings available for promotions as well as for extra markup. Participate in the merchandise presentation clinics arranged by your office. These clinics will be informative about fashion trends, new markets, and unique or best-selling merchandise. The visit to your resident buying office offers

Elston's **MARKET TRIP ITINERARY**

DEPT. NO 275/291   NUMBER OF DAYS IN MARKET 5   NAME *L. Silverman*

	MONDAY 5/14	TUESDAY 5/15	WEDNESDAY 5/16	THURSDAY 5/17	FRIDAY 5/18
8:30					Corporate Office
9:00 / 9:30	* Miss Elaine 39th Fl. 261 Madison 555-1666 M. Selden Tom Hogan	Corporate Office Meeting 13th Fl.	*Barad 180 Madison M. Barad Sid Wilner 555-3150	* Olga Park & 37th Ave. Shelly Berger 555-7343	*Vanity Fair 640 5th Ave. 555-6767 George Monahan 6th Fl.
10:00 / 10:30		* Wilker Bros. Empire State 555-7690 Murray Larkin J. Wilker		* Cinema Etoile 392 5th Ave. E. Kahn Regina Gould 555-3000 7th Fl.	* Kayser 640 5th Ave. Willy Zaltman M. Glatt 555-9600
11:00 / 11:30	*Barad 180 Madison M. Barad Sid Wilner 555-3150	*Gilligan & O'Malley 135 Madison 555-3200 B. Cohen J. Cohen Bill Hamilton 17th Fl.	* Bianche 136 Madison 555-1810 E. Hamwi		

Form 10-2. A buyer's market trip itinerary. Copies of this schedule are kept in the RBO or corporate office in the market (in New York, in this example) and at the store so that the buyer can be reached at all times.

the opportunity to exchange opinions with other buyers. Those you meet at the buying office will be from noncompeting stores whose fashion policies are similar to those of your store.

Schedule calls on resources in the order that you think will be most helpful to you.

Allow time for nonmarket activities. When you are not in the showrooms, the resident office, a fashion show, a magazine office, or other market-related location, take time to "people-watch." See what is being worn in the streets and restaurants, visit an art museum, or see a new play. All this will help you determine emerging fashion trends.

Comparison-shop and window-shop throughout your market trip. See store windows and displays of stores featuring fashion at various stages of the fashion cycle and at various price points. This can be done while walking to appointments or traveling to and from your hotel.

Order of Seeing Lines

Before setting out each morning, a buyer should have a tentative itinerary set up for calls to be made that day. The schedule cannot be too rigid, since delays are bound to occur. Nevertheless, some sort of itinerary helps a buyer to make sure that each day in the market produces its quota of calls. Shop the higher-priced markets first for fashion leads. The information can then be used in making selections in the lower-priced markets.

GEOGRAPHICAL. Some buyers, keenly aware of time limitations, visit showrooms in what might be called geographical order: one building at a time. With dozens of vendors' showrooms in each skyscraper in the Garment Center (as the area in which apparel and accessories showrooms are located is usually called),

New York's Garment Center, around Seventh Avenue, is a beehive of activity. Movable garment racks crowd the busy streets.

the calls made in one building alone can often make up a good day's work for the buyer. On the other hand, the building-by-building technique may fail to produce an overall impression of trends, because each building tends to draw tenants dealing in the same type and price range of goods. To get a more general view, several buildings must be visited.

BY TYPE AND PRICE LINES. Other buyers, at some cost to themselves in terms of effort, ignore geography. They instead concentrate their efforts on shopping as much of the market as possible for the specific types and price lines of merchandise in which they are interested. The advantage of this type of shopping is that buyers can compare one vendor's merchandise with that of others while impressions are fresh in their minds.

BY KEY RESOURCES. A third approach is to first visit key resources, those from which their departments have consistently bought a substantial amount of merchandise in past seasons. (See Chapter 9.) Under normal circumstances, buyers can expect to continue to purchase an important share of their goods from these resources as long as the merchandise continues to meet the customer demand and quality standards of their stores.

Rapport between buyers and such resources is usually excellent, and the exchange of ideas and information fairly rapid. The buyers hope to find much of the merchandise for which they are shopping in the showrooms of their prime resources so that they can proceed to complete their market tour in a more relaxed frame of mind. Also, when they know what their prime resources are showing, buyers are in a better position to evaluate the styles they see later in other showrooms.

BY PRICE LINES. Still another approach is by price line, or visiting the showrooms of higher-priced resources in each class of merchandise first and then continuing the visits through successively lower-priced markets. Although this approach has obvious disadvantages, buyers usually find more fashion news, more original styling, and more fashion information among the higher-priced vendors than among those in the lower-priced brackets. Buyers who prefer this method point out that it gives them a quick overview of fashion trends as an important base for evaluation of all other lines to be seen during the remainder of the trip.

The choice of method is usually left to the buyer, unless the store has established a preferred method. In a store that strives for fashion leadership, buyers may be re-

After seeing a key resource's new line, the buyer may schedule a meeting with his regular sales rep to reevaluate styles that seem especially promising.

quired to see the showrooms of the fashion leaders among their resources first. They then meet with the store's other fashion buyers to evaluate what they have seen and to decide which fashions or looks appear right for their store. Only then are buyers free to go on with the rest of their market work.

Showroom Procedures

When important resources first show or "open" a new seasonal line for retail buyers' inspection, most buyers review the line in its entirety, usually taking notes on styles of special interest. Buyers of stores that are regular customers of individual vendors then usually make an appointment for a return showroom visit. At that time, they work with their regular sales representative in reviewing the vendor's line. Styles that originally impressed the buyer are again evaluated, as well as any others that the sales rep believes, because of past experience, would be of special interest to the customers of the buyer's store. Such showroom visits usually are quite time-consuming, and buyers have to plan accordingly.

As each season advances, buyers may make additional market trips for reasons previously discussed. They may visit vendors' showrooms to check on orders placed when the new line was opened, portions of which have not yet been delivered. The purpose of such a visit may be to revise undelivered orders in light of actual store sales experience. Or they may wish to reorder styles that have sold well. Or they may be searching the market for specific merchandise in line with their buying plans. Such showroom visits must be brief. Wise buyers see to it that they do not permit eager sales representatives to take up more valuable time on this type of market trip than the buyer can afford. In the interest of maintaining good vendor relations, however, the buyer should never appear curt, impatient, or rude with either vendors or their sales staff.

Managements urge buyers to listen to the sales staff's comments and suggestions and to avoid cutting off what might prove a source of useful information. They instruct them, also, to tell their resources about the success they have had with the line and to express appreciation of business courtesies extended—if only to prepare for some possible future day when they have to request a favor from the resource. Business, and especially the exchange of information about the fashion business, proceeds best in an atmosphere of mutual respect. And respect is what store managements expect their buyers to establish in the market.

Taking Numbers

Normally buyers do not write up orders when they are looking at lines in vendors' showrooms. Instead, they take numbers for styles they may want to buy. **Taking numbers** means writing an adequate description of each style the buyer is considering for possible purchase, including style number (as specified by the manufacturer), size range, available colors, fabric, wholesale price, and any other details the buyer considers relevant to the style.

It is important to note here that when buyers are viewing a vendor's line, they are mentally converting the quoted wholesale price into an established retail price line at which that merchandise should be marked if they are to maintain the average departmental markup required by their merchandising plans. They must also evaluate whether the item under consideration compares favorably in quality with the merchandise they now own or have on order at the same retail

During their showroom visits, buyers take numbers so that they can review what they have seen before committing their stores to an order.

Elston's	MARKET MEMO														

DATE: _7/30/8—_ RESOURCE: _Jacobs Dress Co._

CLASS NO.	STYLE NO.	ITEM DESCRIPTION	COLOR RANGE	SIZE RANGE	AVAIL. DATE	COST	RETAIL	OPENING ORDER QUANTITIES					TOTAL	
								1	2	3	4	5	UNITS	$
123	253	2 pc. wool suit, pl. skirt	Blk. Red	8-14	9/1	95	170	86	65	67	53	70		
		long sleeve	Gold blue											

Form 10-3. A market memo can be used to record preliminary decisions about what to order.

price line. Furthermore, they must consider whether the new item has a limited or excellent sales potential in their stores. Should the new item fail to meet any of the above requirements, the buyer would be well advised to postpone the decision about purchasing the item or perhaps even eliminate the item from further consideration.

In some classifications, such as scarfs, gloves, hosiery, and costume jewelry, the lines buyers view may be very extensive, and they may find it difficult to write a sufficient description of each number for later recall. For such merchandise, a buyer separates the samples into three groups: desirable, less desirable, and least desirable. Later, when the entire line has been examined, the buyer takes the numbers of those styles of greatest interest.

At the end of their trips, buyers compare descriptions of similar merchandise they have seen during their market trip,

eliminate duplications and less desirable styles, and make their decisions as to exactly which styles they wish to purchase. If such restraint is not exercised, a buyer may order too lavishly from the first few resources, leaving no funds for more desirable merchandise seen later. Buyers retain for future references, however, those numbers they have taken but decided not to order at the time. These may serve a valuable purpose should the style the buyer did order be canceled or should customers request merchandise that was seen but not ordered.

After eliminating the less desirable styles and developing what they believe to be the best possible list of numbers from those they have seen, some buyers work again with the buying office's market representative. They call on the latter's intimate knowledge of a specific market for further guidance before actually writing up their orders.

Focus

A Moral Dilemma or Hands in the Cookie Jar

"On the take," "in their pocket," "open palms," and "kickbacks" are all euphemisms for taking bribes! It is an age-old practice, but it is as immoral and wrong today as it was in times gone by. Until recently, retailers thought such chicanery was a thing of the past, left over from a flamboyant time when vendors sought buyers' favor by dazzling them with cash and lavish gifts. But industry officials say bribery is back with a vengeance, triggered by overseas sourcing, more competition among vendors, and just plain greed.

As a result, more retailers are closely scrutinizing their buyers with extensive background checks and polygraph (lie detector) tests. In fact, retailers are so concerned that many of them are taking suspected buyers to court, a practice previously considered too costly and time-consuming.

Buyers take bribes for many reasons, officials say. Many who do are disgruntled employees. Others suffer from drug dependency or gambling debts. But no matter the reason, the basic underlying cause is always the same—greed!

While it is the vendors and buyers who profit from bribery and kickback arrangements, retailers and consumers ultimately pay for it. Many retailers are forced into costly markdowns on unsalable merchandise purchased by a corrupt buyer. Also, many dishonest buyers do not demand discounts and other allowances that are provided to honest buyers. In many instances buyers fail to use the negotiation skills that will allow them to buy at a competitive price. Because goods bought at a price 50 cents too high are typically retailed at a dollar more than they should be, those goods are as a result noncompetitive with those of retailers whose buyers are not "on the take." Honest manufacturers are also hurt by these bribery schemes. A crooked buyer will not carry their goods, thereby hurting the manufacturer and ultimately limiting the choice of goods to the consumer.

Uncovering corruption is difficult, but today retailers are using sophisticated methods to ferret it out. Professional investigators are hired to follow up corruption rumors, to check into the lifestyles of buyers, and sometimes to work with the Internal Revenue Service. Many states have commercial-bribery laws that prohibit suppliers from giving anything of value to a buyer without the

Writing the Order

Until an order has actually been placed, buyers are free to change their mind about what they want to order. Once they have placed an order, however, it is considered a contract between the store and the vendor, and buyers have committed their stores to take the merchandise. Any change of mind at some later date requires the written permission of the vendor with whom the order has been placed.

To ensure that an order covers all required points and to avoid committing the store to unacceptable conditions, buyers should write up orders only on the forms provided by their own stores (or, in some instances, on the forms of their resident buying offices) and not on the vendor's form. The common practice is to write up orders after leaving the market and to have them countersigned by the merchandise manager or other responsible store official.

Buyers should always determine from the vendor exactly when the latter expects to ship each style of merchandise that is being ordered. This is of utmost importance for two reasons. First, the buyer's open-to-buy is reduced by the retail value of all merchandise ordered for delivery each month. Second, the buyer needs this information in planning ads and other promotional activities.

The typical store order form requires the buyer to specify all the information previously noted in Chapter 7.

Merchandising Notes

At the time they write up their orders, buyers also should write up brief notes about the merchandise ordered, the reasons for choosing it, and the overall impression gained from the market trip. From these notes they later prepare training talks for their salespeople about incoming merchandise and fashion trends. These notes also may serve as memos about the selling points of the goods for salespeople as well as for the advertising and display departments. If they do this work while the merchandise is fresh in their minds and while enthusiasm for it is strong, some of the excitement of the market trip will spread to everyone else at the store who will eventually be concerned with the sale of the merchandise. Ad dates for goods to be advertised should also be noted. Buyers should note expensive items bought for special customers and items that will be used in special events.

10 Rules for a Market Trip[1]

1. Identification. Who are you? Does anyone know or care? They will if you will have a business card to give to people.

2. Review. Review what you did in the past. It is your best guide for the future.

3. Make Appointments. Timing is everything. Set up the time for appointments. Line up your work. Work your lines.

4. Bring Your Own Order Sheets. Make sure your order is right before you write your order.

5. Decide on a Story and Follow a Theme. The store that tells a story has a happy ending.

6. Have Lunch in a Department Store. Increase your store of knowledge by visiting a knowledgeable store.

7. Meet Other Buyers. Talk to other buyers. Every time two people meet a sale is made.

8. See New Lines. Make a rule: "I must see at least one new line today." The shortest distance between two lines is the point of sale.

9. Bring a Business Attitude. Successful businesses begin with successful attitudes.

10. Bring Enthusiasm. The reason is simple. Enthusiasm sells merchandise because it is contagious.

Reference

1 Based on Murray Raphel, "Planning a Buying Trip?" *Earnshaw's,* March 19, 1979, pp. 54–88.

Buying Vocabulary

Define or briefly explain the following terms:

Buying plan	Stock on Hand (OH)
Hot items	Stock on order (OO)
Overstock	Taking numbers
Planned stock	Working the market
Special events	

Buying Review

1. What preparatory steps are required to plan a successful buying trip?
2. Explain briefly the value of the stock-in-sight (stock on hand + stock on order) figures for your open-to-buy.

3. How do you convert a dollar open-to-buy into units to be purchased on your buying trip? Why is this advisable?
4. What part do promotional plans and special events play in your purchases?
5. Explain how you determine what percentage of your open-to-buy is to be spent on a buying trip. What facts affect that percentage?
6. Explain how and why your buying plans can be changed when you have shopped the market.
7. What is meant by the continuous flow of new merchandise? How is that accomplished? Why is it advisable?
8. Explain how you can accomplish substantial purchases in a short buying trip.
9. Describe how the resident buying office can be vital in a market trip. How can you be certain of maximum assistance from the buying office?
10. What order of seeing lines would be most effective in working the market? Explain why.
11. Is taking numbers in the showrooms the best procedure to follow? Discuss the reasons for your answer.
12. What benefits can you see from merchandising notes?

Buying Case

You are the designer sportswear buyer for a large department store in the Far West. You are scheduled for a June buying trip to the New York sportswear market. Your trip is planned to coincide with your resident buying office's June meeting. Your market representative will be conducting her seasonal product review and development meeting as well as issuing a market coverage report on trends, hot items, and new vendors.

What steps must you take to prepare for this trip while you are still in your store? Whom must you contact to aid you in obtaining the maximum benefit from your market trip? How would you plan to "work the market" so that you could accomplish the most work possible while there?

Chapter 11

Buying Foreign Merchandise

American fashion buyers are constantly shopping for creative, innovative styles to offer their customers. The concept of foreign fashions merchandised with domestic fashions is practiced by many buyers who seek to make their assortments exciting and appealing.

Now that fashion merchandise can be found anywhere in the world, buyers should be aware of the advantages and disadvantages of buying and selling foreign merchandise. Buyers also need to understand the reasons for having foreign merchandise in their stores and to learn what the best methods are for obtaining this kind of merchandise.

Foreign merchandise often adds a special look and feeling to the merchandise mix of a store. Different parts of the world offer different things—Europe, style and elegance; Asia, value and workmanship; South America, uniqueness and color.

Objectives of Foreign Buying

Whenever possible, buyers will try to obtain foreign merchandise that will make their departments and stores appear unique and special, different and better than competitors. The major reasons most stores buy foreign merchandise include creating an image of prestige, obtaining unique items, obtaining higher quality or lower prices for certain items than are available domestically, following a fashion trend, and buying to specification.

Prestige-Store Image

Limited quantity, "exquisitely designed," "expensive," all add up to an image of prestigious merchandise. Wishing to satisfy customers who want prestigious goods, many buyers find it easier to work with foreign manufacturers and designers.

Prestige does not always depend upon price. Many customers are impressed with merchandise just because it was made in a foreign country. For many, the label featuring "Made in ————" conjures up visions of exotic lands and peoples that the customer can only dream about visiting, although this factor is less important than it once was. The level of prestige importance can be determined by the store image that management presents to the customer.

Uniqueness

Fashion buyers are constantly on the lookout for a special advantage over their competitors and the opportunity to pass this advantage on to their customers. The astute buyer looks for new and different merchandise selections that can bring a uniqueness and an individuality to their merchandise assortments.

Some foreign markets are known for their creativity and constant flow of new items and ideas. The fashion buyer shops foreign markets very carefully for these items and categories. Distinctive styling, unavailable domestically, can be a major image-builder for a department or store. The cultures of foreign lands, such as India, China, and Brazil, provide varied and intriguing design elements. This type of merchandise is costly to duplicate in the United States, and there is always the danger of losing the character of the original item. It is easier to find unique merchandise in foreign countries because craftsmen and small producers abound, and the production of one-of-a-kind or ethnic-oriented merchandise is easy and natural for them. The United States does not produce articles comparable to Scottish cashmere sweaters, Spanish leather shoes, Chinese silk blouses, and Indian hand-woven fabrics.

Better Quality

Quality comes at all levels of fashion and price. The quality that can be put into a high-priced item will be at a totally different level from that of merchandise at medium or low prices. However, products at all price levels should have a quality element inherent in their manufacture. Although American-made merchandise is produced with a stated standard based upon cost of production, there is a different kind of quality that can be found in foreign countries. The reasons for better quality are many.

In some cases, the natural resources of a country might contribute to the quality of the merchandise. Both Belgium and Ireland have the finest linen produced in the world, Germany and Austria the finest cut glass and crystal for jewelry manufacture, Italy the finest leather for clothing,

An appeal of this merchandise imported from South America is its distinctive folk designs. The craft objects in the display highlight this feature.

China the finest silks, and India some of the finest cotton. Craftsmanship also accounts for the better quality of merchandise available in foreign countries. Centuries of training in slow, painstaking craftsmanship have given many countries a rich supply of labor that pridefully and carefully practices the skills and crafts of their ancestors. Unlike those in the United States, where limiting the time of production is important, the workers in foreign countries take all the time needed to produce goods of uncommon quality.

Lower Cost

Many of the developing nations of the world are using the exportation of labor-intensive merchandise as a means of building their economies. The low cost of labor in most foreign countries permits the buyer to purchase goods at prices below those available domestically. Also contributing to these lower costs is the fact that these countries provide their own raw materials for the items they make.

Although foreign merchandise might be lower in cost, it is important that it be comparable to American-made goods in terms of quality, variety, and style. If buyers can buy items that their customers want and can pay lower prices for them, then importing goods is the best way to satisfy the customer. For example, much of the current stock of fashionable, well-made ladies' shoes is imported from Brazil and Spain; the expensive, highly styled leather and suede shoes come from Spain, while the less expensive but equally high-styled leathers are from Brazil. In both cases, these shoes cost the buyers less than comparable shoes manufactured in the United States. Therefore, buyers are able to sell fashion-oriented shoes, both high-priced and lower-priced, meeting their individual fashion image policies and features prices that are lower than those of shoes made in the United States.

Fashion Trends

Today all customers, fashion leaders and fashion followers alike, are more sophisticated in their fashion taste than ever before. Because of the speed of communications, fashion news and newness is presented to everyone at the same time. The fashion buyer goes to foreign countries not only to buy but also for direction—to discover new trends in fashion and in the presentation of merchandise, as well as display ideas, color newness, and innovative design elements.

Europe is still considered to be the great influencer of fashion and the place where originality starts. The famous fashion showings in Paris and Milan are covered

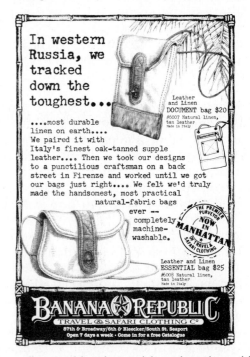

According to this ad materials and workmanship from several countries contribute to the value of the merchandise.

by the world fashion press, and trends discovered on the runways are soon flashed to consumers worldwide. However, Hong Kong and Tokyo are fast becoming fashion trend-setters, and one of fashion's most innovative and successful materials, Ultrasuede, came from Japan.

Buying trips abroad call to buyers' attention the fashion trends and directions for upcoming seasons. The trips also provide information that is relevant to the promotion of such merchandise. Store import promotions are proliferating in all parts of the country. Whether it is a salute to Italy, Japan, Israel, Great Britain, India, China, or France, these import promotions afford the store and the buyer an opportunity to present to their customers what is new, exciting, fashion-forward, and exclusive to them.

Specification Buying

Specification buying (see Chapter 9) in its simplest form means a minor change in merchandise already manufactured; in its most complete form it means that the buyer provides directions and specifics for manufacture, from the type of raw material to the final production and packaging.

Buyers may direct specifications that enhance the quality of materials and workmanship, or they may direct the elimination of certain factors in a way that serves to bring the price down without greatly altering the quality and workmanship. A prime requisite for specification buying in the United States is a volume of sales that allows large enough orders to be placed to make production runs economically viable. Because of the mass production practiced in the United States, even a minor change alters the flow of operations and will add to the cost of the merchandise. All this does not present quite the same problems when buying overseas. Because most of the resources in foreign countries are small, they are willing—and, more important, able—to change pattern and production methods to meet the buyer's requirement. Buyers who develop large specification orders typically work out these specifications in conjunction with manufacturers, usually ones they have worked with before. However skilled and experienced a buyer may be, a competent manufacturer can make valuable suggestions about the features and manufacturing processes involved.

Specification buying is usually practiced by very large stores and chains. However, smaller stores, using their buying offices, can become part of "group purchase" specification buying and enjoy the same exclusivity of merchandise.

Foreign Buying Problems

As we have seen, there are many important and money-making reasons for buying foreign merchandise. But the problems involved with buying foreign merchandise can be numerous and must be studied and evaluated before buyers involve themselves with such purchases. A good buyer weighs these problems against the advantages and determines whether or not to buy foreign merchandise.

Variations of Quality Standards

The buyer who purchases merchandise from many countries must always be aware of variations in product quality among countries. What is considered to be the highest quality standard in one part of the world may be considered low in another. A further problem is that inspection of imported merchandise prior to shipment is often impossible, as is the return of poor-quality merchandise. Not only is this type of return difficult because of the time and distance involved, but loss of customer satisfaction as a result of "short" inventories can be very damaging to image and to sales volume. Quality can vary from manufacturer to manufacturer in the United States, but this kind of situation is more easily remedied here than it is when dealing with foreign suppliers.

Deliveries and Reorders

Delays in delivery can be one of the most unpredictable problems in buying foreign merchandise because most of the reasons for delivery delay cannot be predetermined or guarded against. "Acts of God" such as monsoons, ocean gales, fire, and floods can make deliveries late. Also, dock strikes, labor strikes, or nondelivery of raw materials to manufacturers cannot be guarded against. While some of these occurrences can affect the delivery for domestic merchandise, the problem is compounded in the purchase of imported goods. How distressing it is for stores and buyers to produce a planned circular ad or Import Fair promotion only to have to inform customers that the merchandise has not been delivered.

Reorders are another problem facing the import buyer. Lead time to guarantee delivery of reorders is virtually impossible. If an item is a staple that continues to be in demand over a long period of time, reorders can be planned to allow for long delivery periods. In the case of seasonal and fashion merchandise, reorders are virtually impossible. For example, beautiful handmade Italian knits might be fashion-right and fast-selling but may require a delivery date of three months for a reorder. In that case, the selling season could be over before the reorder arrives in stock.

Size Discrepancy

Size measurements and designations differ worldwide. American sizing tends to be larger than that of anywhere else in the world. Hence, European or Asian sizing specifications are too small to fit the American body properly. This is true not only for ready-to-wear but in shoes and gloves and in the proportion and sizing of furniture.

Not only are the size specifications different, the designations for sizing differ. European and Asian styling use women's sizes 38–40–42–44 to coincide with American women's sizes 6–8–10–12. Also, S-M-L means different sizing in different parts of the world. An S from Taiwan may fit an American 4–6, while an S from Sweden may fit an American size 8–10. Another problem can be encountered in the translation of American sizes into foreign sizing. Unless buyers can supply foreign manufacturers with exact measurements or patterns, there is always a risk of size discrepancy and the problems this presents. Increasingly, foreign manufacturers use United States patterns and size specifications for goods intended for shipment to this country.

Money Allocation

One of the biggest problems today for retailers is the cost of money, that is, the cost of high interest rates charged by lenders to stores when they borrow money for operating capital. The largest retailers do not always have an even cash flow. They have to pay for merchandise in stock before they can sell it, necessitating the borrowing of money. All this adds at least 10 percent to the cost of doing business. Fluctuations in the value of the U.S. dollar compared to foreign currency also poses difficulties in the purchase of foreign goods.

When buying from domestic manufacturers, retailers rarely pay for the goods in advance of shipment. However, manufacturers abroad insist upon payments being made by letter of credit. A **letter of credit** is issued to a foreign producer by an American bank at the request of the U.S. store that is the producer's customer. The letter of credit is delivered to the foreign producer, and when the merchandise is ready for delivery to the United States, the foreign producer presents the letter of credit to a bank in that foreign country. If all instructions set by the U.S. store have been met, the foreign producer is paid by the foreign bank, which charges the account of the American bank representing the store. In other words, the U.S. buyer is paying for the goods before the merchandise arrives in the store. Not only that, but the American bank has "frozen" the money set aside to cover the letter of credit, making this money unavailable for use. Retailers might find such arrangements unprofitable.

Early Selection and Decisions

Successful buyers anticipate their needs and make certain that their open-to-buy is kept as fluid and available as possible. Import buying forces the buyer to make very early selection of colors, silhouettes, and fabrics. It also forces early decision making on quantities, stock content, and promotional planning. It makes the buyer set aside or tie up purchasing dollars for merchandise that will not be sold for sometimes as long as one year after the buying decision has been made.

Information is available to help buyers make these early selections and decisions. Trade papers and reporting services have become instrumental in keeping the buyers aware of very forward trends. IM International, Nigel French, and Here and There are some of the fashion reporting services covering the worldwide fashion markets. In addition, *Women's Wear Daily* and *Daily News Record* also report on trends and happenings in the far-flung world of fashion.

During the research and planning of early selection and decision making, buyers have to be certain about their customers' wants and needs and be prepared to make the most of early successes and recognize and remedy the failures.

Time Involved

Buying trips that involve too long or too short a time can create problems. Visits to foreign markets usually require more time than it would take to cover the American markets. Covering the American market may take a matter of days because of the geographic and conveniently vertical way resources are grouped. Foreign markets are so spread out that it is sometimes difficult and time-consuming to move from one to the next.

To ensure that foreign markets are sufficiently covered, a buyer must spend a great deal of time away from the department or store. In many instances this can prove to be a problem and can adversely affect the smooth functioning of the operation. Inexperienced assistants, large advertising promotions, six-month planning, or domestic market weeks may need a buyer's attention at home, and being away on a foreign trip will delay these activities. Conversely, many buyers make trips that are too short, and they are forced into "rush" buying methods, pressured decision making, and superficial coverage of the foreign market. If a fashion buyer wishes to shop markets in both Europe and the Orient, a trip of less than three weeks would not be worthwhile.

Many buyers who do a great deal of specification buying will spend three weeks in either area, or in some cases in one specific country. Many stores are finding it easier to send buyers for shorter periods of time but to send them more often, adding considerably to the cost of buying foreign goods.

Actual Cost

Many factors have to be considered in determining how much the actual cost will be for foreign merchandise on its delivery to the United States. (This is explained in more detail later in the chapter.) A variety of international rules and regulations have a great impact upon the actual cost of foreign-produced merchandise.

Foreign merchandise is subject to an import duty unless it is specifically exempted. The United States federal government has developed a **Generalized System of Preferences (GSP),** which permits items bought from and produced in developing countries to be imported into the United States without a duty. A **duty** is a charge added on to the declared dollar value of foreign merchandise. Duties, when required, are levied in one of three ways: (1) **ad valorem,** a precentage of the dutiable value, (2) **specific,** a specific amount per unit of weight or other measure of quantity, and (3) **compound,** a combination of ad valorem and specific, such as 25 cents a pound and 20 percent of value.

Methods of Buying Foreign-Made Merchandise

Foreign-made merchandise can be purchased in a number of ways. The retailer may choose a method on the basis of such factors as the size of the store, the planned proportion of foreign goods to domestic goods, the time permitted for a buyer to be away from the store, the cost involved in buying the merchandise, and the degree of exclusivity and specification buying required.

Domestic Sources

Many buyers want the special flavor of foreign merchandise in their stores but cannot make overseas trips to buy these goods directly. For these buyers and the stores they represent, there are many domestic sources that will sell them foreign merchandise. The merchandise bought from these sources will cost more than if it were bought abroad, but the sources will absorb many of the problems and disadvantages of direct importing.

AMERICAN IMPORTERS. These are American companies that stock foreign-made merchandise and sell it to buyers in much the same way an American manufacturer sells goods to a buyer. The goods available from American importers cost the buyer more than if the merchandise were acquired through a direct visit. However, this extra cost is more appealing to a small store than the expense and problems incurred by direct importing. Another advantage of buying from American importers is that the buyer can buy goods much closer to the time of need. The open-to-buy dollars can be current and not preplanned months and months in advance. Still another advantage is that buyers can reorder fast-selling styles from an importer. It is the importer who takes the risks involved in buying foreign merchandise and stocking it for reorders. Importers can also demand specification and sizing requirements because of their large purchasing power. However, when buyers buy from importers, they give up the ability to demand exclusive styling or goods made up especially for them. Stores all over the country will be able to buy the same fashion merchandise. Another disadvantage is that importers rarely provide advertising dollars or other concessions in price.

RESIDENT BUYING OFFICES. Taking advantage of the foreign purchasing available through their RBO is another method buyers use to obtain foreign goods from a domestic source. The biggest advantage is that the RBO will be placing orders for foreign merchandise that are planned and produced with the target customer of member stores in mind. Also, individual stores or buyers can place orders as large or as small as they can absorb. Being part of group purchasing usually means a lower cost price to participants in the group purchase. Sometimes if goods are not as ordered, the RBO will arrange a rebate or other corrective action when they deal with the foreign producer in a new season. However, even in the case of RBO group purchases, commitments must be made far in advance of the selling season.

FOREIGN SELLING AGENTS. Foreign selling agents represent a group of foreign manufacturers who may or may not carry stock here in the United States. These agents make periodic trips abroad and keep buyers up-to-date with foreign market developments. The advantages of buying at these sources is that the buyer can view the actual foreign merchandise with the styling and uniqueness of the foreign design and manufacture. Another advantage is that the size of the order does not have to be large because the agent compiles many orders before sending the order overseas. However, there is no guarantee that quality standard, size discrepancies,

This buyer is examining merchandise in the New York showroom of an importer of Latin American goods.

or other problems of direct importing will not occur.

IMPORT TRADE FAIRS. Many foreign producers, recognizing that not all American buyers can or want to make buying trips overseas, have organized trade fairs in the United States. Some of the fairs feature fashion merchandise from only one country, such as the Japan Fashion Fair or the Italian Donna Moda. Other trade fairs feature merchandise from countries worldwide. Many manufacturers and export selling agents rent space to display and sell merchandise to visiting buyers. One of the largest and most successful is the New York Pret, held in the Jacob Javits Convention Center in Manhattan. Here over 1,200 manufactueres show their goods and an American buyer can see foreign goods from all parts of the world in one visit. Although there is an advantage in being able to view so many lines in one place, because of space limitations, most manufacturers can only show a small portion of what they manufacture. However, this type of foreign buying and selling is growing and these fairs are becoming larger and larger.

Foreign Sources

To buy directly from foreign sources usually requires a trip abroad by the buyer. As we have mentioned, there are both advantages and disadvantages to this method. In the minds of most retailers, however, the advantages appear to outweigh the disadvantages, and more and more buyers are being sent around the world to work directly with foreign sources.

In making contact with any foreign resource, the buyer usually requires the assistance of a foreign resident buying office. This may be an office owned and operated by the corporate owners of the store or by the resident buying office in the United States that represents the store. Often, it is a foreign independent buying office, called a **commissionaire.** The commissionaire usually charges the buyer a commission for its services.

BUYER TRIPS ABROAD. Usually this method of buying foreign merchandise is practiced by the very large retail organizations. Buyers who represent department store and chain organizations in the United States shop foreign markets on a regular basis and at regular intervals. Large retail organizations may send teams of key merchandising executives, such as merchandise managers, buyers, fashion directors, and marketing and promotion directors, on foreign buying trips. This is because very often a significant expenditure of purchasing dollars is involved, and careful planning and expertise are needed to ensure the success of such a purchase. Team efforts are now being used by most stores who buy foreign merchandise directly from the producer in a foreign country.

There are certain advantages to a buyer making a trip and buying directly from a foreign resource.

1. The prices quoted are often much lower than can be quoted by domestic sources offering imports.
2. Specifications can be developed by the buyer with the foreign manufacturers to ensure quality, style, and fit.
3. The buyer can buy exclusive merchandise that will not be available to competitors, therefore allowing the possibility of a higher markup.
4. Foreign fashion trends can be spotted quickly and acted upon immediately by the buyers.
5. A continuing relationship with foreign manufacturers can be developed; this rapport can lead to long-range planning and development of certain suppliers as key resources (much as we do with domestic resources).

There are, of course, certain disadvantages to direct buying of foreign merchandise.

1. The cost of the buyer's trip is usually very high and has a direct bearing on the profit of the department.
2. There is danger of overbuying, because the merchandise tends to appear more exciting

and salable in its foreign surroundings than it will back in the store.

3. The buyer's time away from the store or direction of the operation can create problems with sales and promotions of goods already in the store.

4. The buying organization must assume all the costs of importing that would be assumed by American importers or foreign selling agents were the store to buy imports from them.

5. Foreign orders placed on a direct trip are placed far in advance of delivery dates and selling seasons, and payments must be made upon delivery to the foreign shipping port, therefore tying up store funds that could be better used to purchase current stock to produce current sales.

Foreign Buying Offices

Because of the many intricate steps in foreign buying, all buyers make use of foreign buying offices. The short time most buyers spend in each foreign market makes it imperative for the store and buyer to have constant representation in foreign fashion markets. As noted, these offices may be owned and operated by a store or by the independent resident buying office in the United States that represents them. Often, smaller stores and small American buying offices use the services of a commissionaire.

AMERICAN-OWNED FOREIGN BUYING OFFICES. These offices are in the major fashion centers of the world. They work year-round advising buyers about new trends, resources, and items. They also accompany American buyers on their market visits, acting as interpreters and planning travel and market itineraries. Because of their daily contact with the market, the market representatives in these offices are able to direct their American buyers to the best resources for their needs. They also function as a follow-up service to ensure prompt delivery and quality control of the foreign merchandise bought in each country. Most large stores and chains maintain a foreign buying office in each of the large fashion capitals of the world, such as Paris, London, Rome and Milan, Hong Kong, and Tokyo. Examples of the type of store that maintain foreign buying offices are (a) large department store organization such as Macy's, Allied Stores Corporation, May Company, and Batus; (b) the giant general-merchandise chains such as Sears, J. C. Penney, and Montgomery Ward; (c) large U.S. resident buying offices such as Frederick Atkins and the Associated Merchandising Corporation.

FOREIGN COMMISSIONAIRES. The foreign-owned resident buying offices are used by retailers in much the same manner that they use a resident buying office in America. The commissionaire is usually located in a major city of a foreign market area. It is staffed by market representatives who constantly keep abreast of market developments. Commissionaires' representatives travel with the American buyers and help them locate specific types of merchandise or simply help them "see" the market. The commissionaire does not make purchases for its store clients, however, unless authorized to do so by the client. The store pays the commissionaire a fee that is usually a percentage of the **first cost,** the wholesale cost, of any purchase made. The commissionaire then follows up to make certain that the deliveries of ordered merchandise are made, and made on time. Commissionaire offices are foreign-owned and the staff are all usually from the local area. However, they must all be at least bilingual, and some offices have representatives that speak three or more languages.

Focus

Hong Kong: American Retailers Look to the East for Rising Fashion

It used to be that the words "Made in Hong Kong" conjured up images of cheap imitations and inexpensive mass-produced merchandise. But that has changed. Hong Kong in recent years has been nurturing an upscale fashion image—and it is doing all it can to get that message across to American retailers.

Instrumental in spreading the word is the Hong Kong Trade Development Council, which in January 1984 organized a lavishly staged fashion show for retail executives attending the National Retail Merchants Association annual convention in New York. Titled "The Return of the Fashionable Five-Toed Dragon," the show presented a spectacular array of trend-setting sportswear, luxurious evening wear, and inspired daywear from some of Hong Kong's top fashion designers.

Carrying the fashion message further, a Women's Sportswear Show was mounted for buyers in Hong Kong that fall, which observers said "should leave little doubt about [Hong Kong's] growing talent and capabilities to produce quality fashion merchandise geared to American tastes."[1] And retailers ranging from upscale May Department Stores to discounter K mart seem to agree.

The ways in which different retailers work the Hong Kong market may differ greatly, however. For May Department Stores, for instance, Hong Kong has been the primary source for private label sportswear and other apparel, according to David Cohen, managing director-Asia. May designers in New York provide specifications and designs for the merchandise which are then taken to the Hong Kong factories the company knows can best execute them.

Both knits and wovens are part of May's Hong Kong program in women's sportswear, although Cohen pointed out that the long lead time—around five months—in getting yarn-dyed fabric from Japan makes the wovens trickier to work with than knits. In addition, the wovens involve a minimum of seven months from the time of placing the order to shipping, while sweaters and other knits can be turned around in as short a time as three or four months.

K mart, the nation's leading discount chain, also sources private label apparel in Hong Kong, but instead of providing designs and specifications, the chain's buyers give their manufacturers actual samples to reproduce. Especially important are areas such as misses' blouses and tops—like May's, in both knits and wovens.

And although K mart does not carry merchandise of the high-fashion type of May and other department stores, its executives do shop Hong Kong with a wide-open eye toward fashion trends. Said the store's Keith Lam, merchandise manager, after a showing at a Hong Kong high-fashion house: "We are here looking at the styling and the colors, which really impressed us. . . . We will also advise our buyers of the colors and styles we saw here, and we will compare them with the color cards our fashion coordinators get from Europe."[2]

1 Joan Bergmann, "Hong Kong . . . Better," *Stores,* December 1984, p. 22.
2 Ibid., p. 28.
This Focus is based on information from the article cited above.
See also Steve Weiner, "Asian Bargains: K mart Apparel Buyers Hopscotch the Orient to Find Quality Goods," *The Wall Street Journal,* March 19, 1985, pp. 1, 24.
Joan Bergmann, "Sourcing: Far East Style," *Stores,* April 1986, pp. 13–23, 67.

Determining the Profit of Direct Imports

Stores send buyers abroad to ensure that their stocks will reflect innovation, creativity, prestige, and competitive pricing. Your trip may seek all these objectives, but the major reason that most stores send buyers to the overseas market is to produce a good profit performance—not only a profit to match what can be produced with goods bought domestically, but a better one! So before you plan your foreign trip itinerary, define your major objectives so that you can allocate your time and energy wisely and can do and see all that is necessary to get a profitable return on your foreign travel investment.

Stores do not measure the success of a buyer's trip abroad only by how much money the buyer spends. You must remember that your buying plan is simply a guide; if what you want and planned for is not available in the foreign markets, do not spend your money just for the sake of using up all that was allocated to you. It is an old axiom in the business that it takes three overseas trips before a buyer is experienced enough in these markets. On their first foreign buying trip new fashion buyers tend to overbuy because everything looks new and exciting (including the foreign surroundings). Then their stocks are overloaded and excessive markdowns have to be taken. On their second trip, because of the markdowns, they tend to underbuy to guarantee no markdowns! It is only by the third trip that the merchandise and the buy, like Goldilocks's porridge, chair, and bed, are "just right." In relating the cost or purchase price of foreign goods to your retail prices you have many factors to consider. These will all affect the determination of the planned profit to be realized on your foreign purchases.

Customs Regulations

Importing from foreign countries into the United States is governed by U.S. customs laws and regulations that are administered by the U.S. Customs Service in the Department of the Treasury. This service governs what may be imported, outlines the labeling and invoicing requirements, and determines the duty, if any, that must be charged. Much of the fashion merchandise imported is subject to one or more of our laws and regulations that govern the labeling and/or material content and construction of the merchandise. Two of the major factors that buyers must be aware of are quotas and duties.

QUOTAS. A **quota** is a predetermined limit put upon articles entering the United States. Quotas can be changed, but only by the government and only after much investigation and litigation. An example is the quota set by the United States limiting the quantity of jeans that may be imported from each foreign country. Once this quota has been filled, no more jeans from that country will be allowed to enter the United States during that fiscal period. Other countries have quotas also. Japan has a very strict quota governing the number of American cars that can be imported into Japan from the United States. Most fashion buyers check with the foreign manufacturer to be sure that their shipment will be within the allowable quota for that product from that country. It is the responsibility of the foreign producer to obtain the quota for the merchandise. All foreign buying offices and commissionaires check this factor before they place your order.

DUTIES. In principle, the value of the merchandise for duty purposes is the dutiable value at the time of exportation to the United States; in practice, the invoice cost is commonly accepted by the customs service. Before placing an order, buyers should obtain from their store's import manager, RBO, foreign buying office, or commissionaire the correct applicable rate of duty for the merchandise they plan to buy.

Computation of Landed Cost

There are two different types of cost used by buyers of foreign goods. One, mentioned earlier, is the first cost (the invoice cost of the goods at the foreign vendor) and the second is the landed cost. The **landed cost** is the cost at the store after importation from abroad; it is comparable to the delivered billed cost of domestic goods. The landed cost is the cost upon which you determine your retail price. Form 11-1 is a reproduction of a form used by a large group of stores to figure the landed cost. If, for example, you bought a hand-knit wool dress in Florence, Italy, for the ex-factory cost of $120.00 each (American dollars; the Italian *lira* rate would be furnished by your foreign office or commissionaire), you would have to add all the other factors to this first cost of $120.00 before you could determine the landed cost in the United States. If the inland shipping cost is 50 cents (to the port of exportation), the buying commission 10 percent, the duty a 20 percent ad valorem rate, the ocean freight $1.50, the insurance rate 2 percent, the brokers' fees 1 percent, wharfage and handling $1.00, and cartage 50 cents, the landed cost would be $163.10. This is the cost upon which the retail price is determined. Remember, all the percentages are based upon the first cost of $120.00.

However, when buyers are overseas, they do not have the time or, sometimes, the exact figures to compute the landed

ELSTON'S

BUYING QUOTATION WORKSHEET

Vendor _Aldo Bruccicelli_

Street _Via Torina 16_

City & State _Florence, Italy_

Commodity _Hand-Knit Wool Dress_

Mfrs. Item No. _Style # 108_

Tot. Quantity Ordered _144 pieces_

Ex-factory cost, per _$120.00 each_

Inland shipping cost _50¢_

FOB dock origin _Genoa_

Commission (10%) _$12.00_

Duty _20%_ _24.00_

Ocean freight _1.50 each_

Insurance rate _2%_ _2.40_

Brokers' fees _1%_ _1.20_

Wharfage and handling _1.00 each_

Cartage _50¢ each_

U.S. port landed cost _$163.10_

Inland freight _not applicable_

GENERAL INFORMATION

Is ELSTON'S label or other identification
of mdse. required:

yes - 100% Wool
Hand-Knit in Italy
Expressly for - Elston's

Preticketed: YES   NO ✓

PACKING

1. Unit pack _1_

2. Units per inner pack _12_

3. No. of cartons to master pack _12_

4. Weight per master pack ___

5. Dimensions ___

6. Cube ___

7. Ocean freight rate:
   (a) Conference contract ___
   (b) Conference noncontract ___
   (c) Nonconference rate ___

MARKS

Dept. No. _100_
Order No. _92324_
Code No. _010_
U.S. Port _N.Y._
Numbers 1/up

8. Latest shipping date _6/15/--_

9. Cancellation date _6/30/--_

10. Approximate U.S. arrival date at:

    N.Y. _7/15_ Phila. ___ JAX. ___

11. Quantity:

    _144_ ___ ___

12. RN Number: _12345_

Form 11-1. A buying quotation worksheet.

cost of everything bought. Yet, a determination of an approximate retail price must be placed on the landed cost of each item bought. In order to allow the buyer to form an idea of the possible future retail price of goods at the time they are buying those goods, a multiplier factor can be used with the first cost. Most stores use a 3x or 4x multiplier to gauge a probable retail; some exclusive expensive stores sometime use a 5x multiplier. Using the first cost of $120.00 of the Italian hand-knit wool dress, a 3x would mean a $360.00 retail, a 4x a $480.00 retail, and a 5x a $600.00 retail. Using the actual landed cost of $163.10, a $360.00 retail would produce a 54.7 percent markup, a $480.00 retail would produce a 66 percent markup, and a $600.00 retail would produce a 72.8 percent markup.

Retail Pricing of Imports

In addition to all the varying elements of costs, both first cost and landed cost, you, as a buyer who buys foreign merchandise, must also consider other factors. When you buy imports there are usually no advertising allowances, no supportive national advertising, and no opportunity to return goods or request adjustments for merchandise that is damaged or otherwise unsalable.

When import buyers review the factors that affect the costs, they must realize that the initial markup from landed cost to retail has to cover the cost and risks involved, and yet show a better than normal profit! Usually an initial markup of at least 10 to 20 percent higher than the initial markup on domestic goods is normal. Remember that the advertising and promotion costs of imports have to be borne by the department alone unless they are part of a storewide promotion. Also, because of all the other risks and disadvantages already discussed, there has to be an extra margin for error.

Since imported merchandise, especially goods made specifically for you, is not easily compared to goods in other stores, this type of merchandise can have a much larger than normal markup. If there is no comparable merchandise, the retail on this merchandise can be whatever your target customer will pay. If, however, some of this merchandise has to be reduced, the reductions can be much greater and still produce a better profit. In order to clear the stocks, most stores take deeper markdowns on merchandise purchased overseas.

However, imports are not always used for extra markup dollars. There are exceptions to taking high initial markup on imports. Many stores prefer to use imports at lower markup to enhance their fashion image, or to participate actively in price-competitive promotions with other stores.

Promoting Imports

At the very moment you buy foreign merchandise the excitement, uniqueness, quality, or price advantage of the merchandise should translate itself into selling points and promotional ideas. Why bother to go through all the planning, time and money allocation, and added risks if you do not expect to have this merchandise do something extra for your department and store? Write it all down while it is fresh in your mind. Make notes for yourself, for the fashion director, the advertising department, the display department, and the selling staff—all the people who will play a part in selling the goods.

These notes could include special and interesting features about the merchandise that add romance, attraction, and salability. Such features are hand work such

For J. C. Penney's Salute to Italy the buyers selected merchandise that conformed to storewide policy for this special promotion. In return, each department benefitted from the advertising for the event.

as knitting and beading, regional age-old skills, traditional and ethnic patterns and styles, and some history and color about the area where the merchandise is made.

These are the kinds of detail and information that inspire the display and advertising staffs to make special efforts to present the imported merchandise in an exciting and different manner. You can make a real impact on the buying mood of your customer in choosing between "a knit dress" and a "100 percent wool hand-knit dress from Italy featuring the classic colors and patterns of the Tuscany region interpreted just for you."

Import buying is an integral part of the buyer's job in departments and stores across the country. It is the type of buying that demonstrates to top management that you are a capable professional. Each import purchase must be planned and measured as to its compatibility with existing and planned domestic merchandise assortments and how the imports can enrich that assortment. All this requires sound planning with an understanding of foreign markets and the ability to find facts quickly about the quality and performance of many, many foreign producers. If you can function successfully far from home base, in strange surroundings, working with unfamiliar resources, then you can rate yourself an experienced, capable buyer!

Buying Vocabulary

Define or briefly explain the following terms:

Ad valorem duty	First cost	Letter of credit
Commissionaire	Generalized System of	Quota
Compound duty	Preferences (GSP)	Specific duty
Duty	Landed cost	

Buying Review

1. Explain the advantages of foreign buying.
2. How are size and fit problems solved when purchasing fashion merchandise in the Far East countries?
3. Explain why short-lived high-fashion items are not bought in Asian countries.
4. What merchandising decisions are necessary when buying foreign goods?
5. Why is a large commitment required for foreign buying?
6. Describe briefly how you can buy import merchandise from domestic sources. Which method do you think is best and why?
7. What advantages are there in buying imports from domestic sources? What disadvantages?
8. How often do buyers generally go abroad each year?
9. What disadvantages are there in direct foreign buying?
10. Describe the role of the foreign buying office?
11. What purposes does the commissionaire serve?
12. How profitable can direct imports be?

Buying Case

You are leaving for the Orient soon and will be buying moderate-priced handbags, small leather goods, and luggage for your store, which is a multiunit apparel specialty store in the state of Florida.

One of your buying objectives is to buy a large assortment of better genuine leather handbags for a planned sale promotion of $29.99 retail. The store expects this $29.99 handbag promotion to be a big part of their fall promotional effort.

Your trip is planned for February. The goods you buy will be for sale in September, October, November, and December. What preparatory steps would you take before leaving the store on this trip? Explain in detail to whom and where you would go for guidance and help for this trip. What landed cost could you pay in order to obtain your sale price of $29.99 at a 42 percent markup?

Chapter 12

Buying Techniques
and Placing the Order

After all the assortment and dollar planning is completed, buyers must visit the different markets implementing these plans. Visiting domestic and foreign market centers and choosing resources are the next considerations in obtaining the right merchandise for your customer. Determining the best buying techniques to use and then placing the orders are the essential steps in satisfying your customers' wants and needs. The buying techniques that can be used and the negotiations employed in placing the orders are discussed in this chapter.

Buying Techniques

Effective buying techniques, from the planning through the reorder, must be learned by the buyer who wants to be a success. Attention to the techniques of effective buying brings with it the most efficient use of a buyer's time and, ultimately, success to the department and store.

Astute buyers avoid taking too many chances in deciding which fashion will be accepted by their customers. There is risk in letting yourself be carried away by enthusiasm for merchandise that you have seen in the market. The same risk is present when you assume that your own ideas of the right color, line, or texture are identical with those of your customers. You, the buyer, risk your fashion reputation in the community, as well as store dollars, every time you select merchandise for stock. Your job is further complicated by the numerous methods and techniques that can be used to purchase merchandise.

However, your buying plan (as discussed in Unit 2) will help you determine which method or technique of buying will work best for you.

Regular Buying

Buying merchandise to sell at regular, established price lines in your merchandise assortment is generally known as **regular buying.** This is the method used by most buyers of fashion merchandise at the start of each new season. The usual practice is for you to view a manufacturer's sample line and then place an order by style number, color, and size at the cost price quoted by the manufacturer. While viewing a line you will shop each major classification separately. For example, if you are buying blouses by tailored, dressy, and shirt styles, you then work within each subclassification—solid color, print, long or short sleeves. Because of the multitude of new items continually being offered in the wholesale market, you must be very selective.

In regular buying, the first order of a new fashion is for a small quantity. If this sample sells well, the buyer will reorder in larger quantities.

SAMPLE-TEST-REORDER TECHNIQUE. In regular buying most buyers greet a new fashion with the **sample-test-reorder-technique.** They buy in small quantities in a wide range of possible acceptable styles (a broad and shallow selection) to observe customer reaction. Then they reorder in substantial quantity those styles and colors that appear to have won an initial favorable reception (a narrow and deep selection). The rest are quickly marked down and cleared out.

For example, suppose that every indication points to a growing popularity of deep jewel-tone shades in wool dresses. A buyer may feel very strongly that ruby red will be the season's preferred jewel-tone shade and that shirtwaist types will be the preferred styles. Instead of buying ruby red shirtwaists alone, however, the buyer will perhaps try deep garnet, ruby, and amethyst and will purchase each color sparingly in several styles. When the goods arrive at the store, customer comments as well as actual sales will determine which colors and styles are best received. The buyer may find that deep garnet is as well received as ruby red; therefore, ample quantities of both colors should be ordered. At this point, the buyer places additional orders for the most acceptable styles. These may or may not be the same styles originally thought to have the greatest sales potential. Actual experience now gives the buyer more confidence to purchase in larger quantities at regular prices.

PROBLEMS WITH REORDERS. An increasingly difficult problem facing all retailers today is that producers of fashion merchandise are becoming reluctant to accept reorders for any but the most classic of their styles. Instead, they prefer to offer newer styles throughout a selling season.

Customers are making it plain that they want to see new styles each time they shop a fashion department.

The testing procedure is not entirely without risk. In offering customers a wide range of styles at the start of the season, a buyer inevitably stocks certain numbers that will have to be marked down because they are hard to sell. In general, however, the losses that occur in testing are offset by the success of the good sellers.

Specification Buying

For many years much of the buying for major department store and specialty store chain companies has been specification buying. Recently, smaller department stores, specialty stores, and other types of retail outlets have gone into this type of buying. As we have already learned, much of today's foreign buying is also specification buying.

Buyers who develop extensive specification projects usually work out the program with one or more selected or preferred key resources. These buyers may plan and suggest specifications that upgrade the quality of materials, workmanship, or styling, thereby building a better product with which to enhance their image and exclusiveness. Or, they may suggest specifications that do not upgrade the quality or value but simply make the merchandise different from relatively similar merchandise carried by other retailers. Still other buyers may work with specifications that keep cost uppermost in the mind of the manufacturer so that the merchandise can be manufactured within a predetermined lower cost. Then the buyer can determine whether to use this lower cost to obtain goods to retail at a very competitive sale price, or to use the lower cost to achieve higher markup.

DEVELOPING SPECIFICATIONS. No matter how skilled you may be as a buyer, during the planning stages of specification purchases you should have joint discussions with associates and several manufacturers. A competent, experienced manufacturer can often make valuable suggestions as to the specification and manufacturing processes involved. Many large retail companies have a **specification manager** or **product development manager** attached to buying departments. These people are usually familiar with, and trained in, government and industry standards for products and therefore are able to assist you on acceptable size measurements, material, and workmanship. You alone, however, are ultimately responsible for the final overall balance of elements in the finished product. When specification buying is done by groups through buying offices or other associative arrangements, the project may be carried out by a committee of buyers from several member stores.

Careful buyers make sure that their products do not fall below the standards of specification originally set. Where necessary, the retailer's own testing bureau or a public testing bureau is used to aid in the setting of specifications and in the maintenance of quality control.

PRODUCTION REQUIREMENTS FOR SPECIFICATION BUYING. In order to make manufacturing and production economically feasible for the vendor, specification buying must be conducted in a volume large enough to allow this to happen. It is very costly for mass producers to make even minor changes to their flow of operations. Therefore, before a manufacturer will agree to make changes, or to produce merchandise specifically tailored to your specifications and standards, you must be able to guarantee a quantity of merchandise

SIZE:	Spec Requested		Sample Measures		Difference	
M-1 Waistband: Rigid						
M-2 Waistband: Elastic: Relaxed (measure along top edge)						
: Ultimate Stretch						
M-3 Waistband Depth:						
R-1 High Hip: 3" below waistband seam						
R-2 Hip: 7" below waistband seam						
T-1 Dart Length:						
T-2a Dart Start:						
T-2b Dart Finish:						
V- Fly or Zipper Opening: Below waistband to bar tack.						
W-1 Pocket Depth:						
W-2 Pocket Width :						
W-3a Pocket: From center front						
W-3b Pocket: From bottom of waistband						
W-1 Pocket Depth:						
W-2 Pocket Width:						
W-3a Pocket: From center back						
W-3b Pocket: From bottom of waistband						
X-1 Elasticized panels:						
X-2 Belt:						
Y-1 Skirt Length: Below waistband seam						
Y-2 Bottom Sweep: measured along curve						
Y-3 Side Seam Length: Below waistband seam						
Pleats:						
Slits:						

Vendor: *ALDO BRUCCICELLI* Country: *ITALY* Style: *#108*

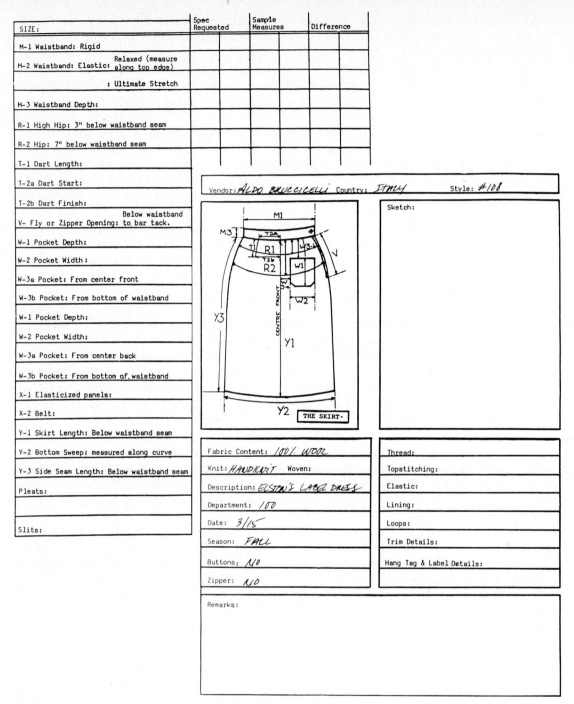

Sketch:

THE SKIRT-

Fabric Content: *100% WOOL*

Knit: *HANDKNIT* Woven:

Description: *ELSTON'S LABEL DRESS*

Department: *100*

Date: *3/15*

Season: *FALL*

Buttons: *NO*

Zipper: *NO*

Thread:

Topstitching:

Elastic:

Lining:

Loops:

Trim Details:

Hang Tag & Label Details:

Remarks:

Form 12-1. A buyer's specification instructions. Completing this form will enable the buyer to communicate to the manufacturer the exact measurements and details desired.

that is large enough to make your special cutting profitable to the manufacturer. Most manufacturers require a minimum **cutting ticket,** an order based upon the minimum quantity it can profitably produce. For large mass-merchandise chains, department and specialty chains, and group purchases by large resident buying offices, these quantity requirements rarely prove to be a problem. For the medium- or smaller-size chains or stores, however, this is sometimes a deterrent for specification buying. Because of the usually smaller minimum quantities required by producers in Europe and the Near and Far East, more and more specification buying is being done in these foreign areas.

Many manufacturers find specification buying advantageous because it offers an opportunity for year-round production, since large specification orders are usually placed well in advance of normal production requests. If manufacturers can keep their plants and workers functioning on a steady year-round basis, there are many opportunities for greater profit. Producing only during peak seasonal times slows down the steady flow and momentum of both workers and production, as well as adversely affecting the manufacturer's cash flow.

Private Label Buying

In many retail organizations, buyers are urged to do specification buying instead of buying nationally branded items. Although the national brand merchandise does have customer acceptance and a good quality image that is fostered by the advertising and promotion done by the manufacturer of the brand, it does not carry any exclusivity. Since national brands can be carried by many stores, these brands will not give your store a distinctive look or image. Because of this, **private label buying** has become one of the most important parts of a store's specification buying program.

Private label development and buying play an important role in a retailer's merchandising strategy. The producers of national brand merchandise seek repeat sales of their brand, regardless of the retail outlet, while the buyers want repeat sales for their particular retail outlet. Therefore, many buyers, with direction from their top management, have decided to decrease or give up the pulling power of a national brand's promotional program and try to buy the identical merchandise under the store's own private label. Or, as explained in specification buying, buyers alter the standards and specifications sufficiently to give the store's own branded lines truly individual characteristics.

Like specification buying, private label buying presupposes a certain amount of purchasing power. It also requires time and money to build up customer confidence and demand. Slow-turning inventories and excessive markdowns may have to be planned until the demand for the store's private label has grown. Quality must be controlled very carefully, because when a customer buys a store's own private label, the image of the merchandise must be the same image that the store has spent time and money building. Besides the gain of repeat sales, private label buying should provide many other advantages, among which are:

☐ Lack of direct price competition
☐ Possibility of higher markup
☐ Exclusive merchandise
☐ Better quality than market offerings
☐ Consumer patronage influence

Focus

Designer Licensing: The Ultimate Private Label for Retailers

As department and specialty stores intensify their search for unique, exclusive merchandise to set themselves apart from their competition, private label programs have increasingly become the answer to their needs. Merchandise bearing the stores' own name not only offers them a different look and selection but generally provides a better markup than traditional national brands.

The problem with private labels—albeit a solvable one—is that retailers need to involve themselves in the details of total design and manufacturing of goods, along with the standard merchandising of them. That is why some are looking to the direct licensing of designer names as a fashionable and profitable alternative.

Among the retail groups that have jumped into the concept are J. C. Penney (with Halston), The Limited (with Kenzo), K mart (with Gloria Vanderbilt), Federated Department Stores (with Cacharel and Allen Solly), and Frederick Atkins (with Christian Aujard). In each of these cases, the designers have agreed to create a particular line of merchandise exclusively for the licensing retailer, and the retailer in turn pays a licensing fee to the designer.

This type of specialized buying provides advantages to both sides. For the designers, there is a presold market for their goods in the stores. And for the retailers, there is new merchandise not found in the competition—plus a designer's name to add to the store fashion image. Said Ferd Lawson, president and chief executive officer of Frederick Atkins: "Signing with the Christian Aujard name enables us to provide merchandise with image and status, but also with quality and value. It is a private label, yes, but it also is a license—and an established, designer, prestige label."[1]

The idea of a retailer licensing a name for an exclusive merchandise program is not new and is not confined to designer names. Sears's Cheryl Tiegs sportswear and K mart's Jaclyn Smith apparel are examples of retailers' licensing a nondesigner name to give recognition, impact, and exclusivity to their merchandise. Licensing designers, however, provides that extra cachet for stores that want to maintain a high fashion profile.

As stated by Stan Schwartz, president and chief executive officer of Guy Laroche North America, which owns the Christian Aujard name: "The days of standard private label programs in fashion for department stores are over. It is difficult to impossible for a store's product managers to design a fashion line; so what usually has ended up happening is that they study the season's fashions, find things they like, and then have them knocked off. On the other hand, working with a designer on an exclusive licensing basis gives the store access to a true design house. Then the store is free to concentrate on details of coordination and marketing those designs."[2]

1 Penny Gill, "Retailers Press Direct Designer Licensing," *Stores,* February 1985, p. 12.
2 Ibid.

One of the problems of private label buying is that the retailer, through the buyer, is put into the role of a manufacturer. The responsibilities usually attributed to the manufacturer, such as styling, availability of reorders, advertising, and control of production inventory, are now borne by the retailer as represented by the buyer.

Promotional Buying

Retail organizations usually feature special events and sale-price promotions, and because of this buyers are always looking for special promotional buys. Buyers must consider all of these events when they work on their buying plans and promotional calendars.

When you are buying new items as part of your regular seasonal buying plan, you should think through a promotional plan for the item before making the buy. At this time advertising allowances may be available from the manufacturer, who will assist in your promotional plans, and if you decide quickly you can arrange for this promotional tie-in before other retail-

ers in your area do. Promotionally minded buyers are always on the lookout for items that can give excitement to the department and store and special value to the customer. Another consideration is that some manufacturers of branded sportswear lines will offer advance goods at one-third off for substantial orders.

SPECIAL PRICE SALE EVENTS. For the special-price sale events, such as Anniversary Sales, pre- and postholiday sales, or end-of-season sales, you are responsible for buying goods that can be offered to the customer at a price that is lower than the regular selling price. These goods should be part of an overall plan and not bought on a spur-of-the-moment impulse. The merchandise should offer the customer a good value and also afford you an opportunity to produce an increase in sales or a possibility for added gross margin. You must be careful in calculating the amount of merchandise required for these promotional type sales in order that the remainder of the promotion will not have an adverse effect on your stock content or

Picture this at the prom...
a white flash of flounces and lace.
A glimmering glow of red and white.
Both gowns from Gunne Sax.
12A. Red satin bustier with
white bow accent, 3-13, 100.00.
12B. On or off the shoulder,
ruffled bodice gown trimmed
with lace and bows, 3-13, 132.00.
Juniors' Dresses (D. 376), all stores
except Downtown, Severance,
Midway, Randall, Euclid.

A fabulous finishing touch to the big
night...lace pantyhose from Maya.
12C. White cut and sewn lace
fashion-minded pantyhose. One size
fits all. 15.00. Hosiery (D. 251), all stores.

Marvelous Marvella...the look
of seed pearls that's oh-so versatile.
12D. From a collection including
a five-row choker, 10.00; or 30" length
necklace, 17.50; to wear twisted or draped.
Clip or pierced earrings, 12.50.
Jewelry (D. 142), all stores.

12D

Pearl perfection...

This page from a Higbee's catalog advertises special-promotion merchandise for prom night.

become a reason for excessive mark-downs. The best merchandise for a sale is the merchandise that is regularly carried in your stocks. When this merchandise is sold at a sale price, the customer can easily recognize the value, and the reputation and image of the department are enhanced. Another plus is that this type of sale merchandise does not create a problem in either an overstock situation or excessive markdowns. In the parlance of the business, "the best sales goods are regular goods."

Because you know when these sales events are planned, you do your buying with them in mind. Buying your regular-priced seasonal merchandise, you plan the flow of goods so that regular goods are available for these sales. It is now, when you place your opening orders, that advertising allowances, lower cost prices, and special promotional aids should be worked out with your vendors. Of course, when you are involved in specification and private label buying, your promotional buying needs must also be planned into the project.

THEME PROMOTIONS. Another kind of promotional buying involves storewide events such as foreign country import promotions, color promotions, or other theme promotions. This type of promotional buying may involve sale prices, but in most cases the merchandise you buy must be part of the overall promotion and should be oriented more toward prestige and image building than toward price: a Daffodil Yellow promotion in February, an Italian or Chinese promotion in the spring, or a theme promotion tying in with a new movie, book, or local event. For these events the merchandise purchased brings the impact of the storewide promotion into your department and makes a total storewide impression upon the customer. Many times, goods purchased for these types of promotions are attention-getters and are bought with the knowledge that they may be subject to markdowns. But if the items purchased for a promotional event really serve their purpose, the added interest and customer traffic they generate far outweigh any markdowns they may cause.

Off-Price Buying

Discount stores have been common since the end of World War II, when they emerged primarily in the hard goods field. In the late 1970s and 1980s, a new kind of discount store, known as the off-price store, came to the fore in the fashion field. These stores offer name-brand fashion items at deep discounts from the regular prices. Stores such as Cohoes Specialty Stores, Burlington Mills, Marshall's, Hit or Miss, and T. J. Maxx are well known for their extensive range of famous-brand merchandise at far below regular retail prices. Buyers for such stores seek manufacturers' overproduction at deep discounts. These low prices are then passed on to the customers with lower than usual markups for super bargains. When buyers for off-price stores buy name-brand merchandise at regular prices, they mark it up about 20 percent less than a buyer for a regular price store would do. This is necessary to maintain the bargain image that is the main attraction of off-price stores. Some manufacturers have outlet stores that offer equivalent values, and some shopping centers feature off-price stores and discount stores.

Job Lot Buying

Although job lot buying is done by many buyers for many different merchandising reasons, the most important point to remember about job lots is that they are usually made up of leftover stock. A **job lot** is an assortment of merchandise that a vendor has been unable to sell at regular prices and therefore offers at a reduced price, usually a flat price. A buyer must not buy a job lot unless the price is low enough to guarantee that the entire lot will be sold quickly and at a good markup.

Because the job lot is an assortment of vendor leftovers of various styles, sizes, and colors, the buyer must be careful in determining how these items will fit into the regular stock. Although many buyers use the job lot method of buying, they must be careful that the job lots they buy will not lead to increased markdowns, lower the store's image of quality merchandise, or detract from goods already in stock. The best type of job lots are those consisting of merchandise that has already been bought for regular stock. Then the job lot can be brought in either to round out sizes and colors or to help make a better assortment when the regular goods are marked down for special sales. The worst kind of job lot to buy is an unseasonable one, even though this kind is usually the best bargain in price. This type of goods is usually too late in the season for even the most bargain-conscious customer to buy, and the price that the goods must sell for will not give the buyer a good markup, no matter how low the cost price.

The buyer who buys job lots must also consider the effect of the job lot's retail price on regular merchandise in the department. For example, a buyer may have a large stock of dresses on hand at $39.99 and may be offered a job lot of identical or similar dresses that can be retailed at $29.00. However, buying the $29.00 job lot would force a markdown of the $39.99 dresses, possibly before they would need to be marked down. A better way would be to sell out a large portion of the regular stock before introducing the job lot, thus controlling the size of the markdown.

Buying Irregulars and Seconds

Very often sale advertisements will read: "Slight imperfections, will not affect wear or durability" or "Slightly irregular $15, if perfect $29.99." Because the very nature of manufacturing results in a certain amount of imperfect and damaged goods, vendors make these available to buyers at reduced prices. These "IRs," as they are called in the trade, and seconds are found during the inspection or quality control procedure at the manufacturers. The proportion of this type of goods depends on what the manufacturer has set as the standard for "perfect."

Irregulars are items that contain slight imperfections or repairs not visible to the naked eye. Seconds are items that contain more obvious or extensive imperfections or repairs. Many buyers are able to buy these substandard products at such low prices that they are able to offer enormous savings to the customer. Generally the values can be greater than those of less expensive perfect goods manufactured to lower quality standards. White sales are the popular place for seconds of high-quality sheets and pillowcases that are offered at prices equal to or below those for perfects of poorer-quality goods. Hosiery is a department where irregulars are featured; usually the irregularities are only a difference in shade or an uneven seam or closing on pantyhose where it cannot be seen.

However, some buyers and retailers believe that their quality image is tarnished by such purchases and do not stock them. The merchandising policies top management has set will guide a buyer as to whether or not to buy irregulars.

Consignment Buying

In **consignment buying,** the buyer and the vendor agree that within a stipulated period of time the buyer may return unsold merchandise to the vendor. This return privilege is usually what makes consignment buying attractive to a buyer. Buyers of such luxury merchandise as furs and diamonds may find it worthwhile to use this technique to enable them to offer several choices to special customers. After the customer has made a selection, the remaining items can easily be returned to the vendor. However, although there are many advantages to consignment buying, the disadvantages should be carefully studied.

Remember that the most valuable asset you have is the floor and counter space in your department, or the layout space in a catalog. This "real estate" is where your customer sees and, one hopes, buys your merchandise. By giving up some of this valuable space to consignment buys, you may take space away from merchandise that is more salable and more closely meets the needs of your customers.

Consignment merchandise is usually merchandise that has some selling risk connected with it. The merchandise may be very new, *avant-garde,* or simply more fashion-forward than you would normally carry in your stocks. It might be a higher price than you would normally mark an item, or the merchandise might be from a vendor who is new in the market and therefore has no history of selling success. In all these cases, it would benefit the vendor to be able to deliver the merchandise into your stocks, where it could be seen by your customers, but you may not gain the same benefits. Although you know that unsold merchandise is returnable, the amount of time, energy, and space it consumes usually does not translate into more sales or better gross margin.

Consignment buying is justified at times, even though there are frequently many abuses connected with it. It is in the interest of both buyers and vendors to establish definite policies concerning the conditions under which they agree to consignment buying.

Special-Order Buying

This type of buying is most used by full-service specialty stores and by smaller stores whose reputation is based on individualized service to the customer. It also enables stores that have limited selections

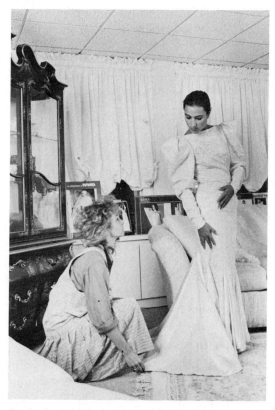

Typically, bridal gowns are special ordered.

in color, size, and style to offer larger merchandise selections. In **special-order buying** a buyer will place an order with a vendor for a particular style in a specific color and size. Even though this type of buying is time-consuming, the overall savings in small inventories will often make up for the extra time and sometimes the extra cost charged by the vendor for handling small orders.

A small store, or a specific department within a large store, will use this buying method to offer a special service to its customers. Such a store may also use it to meet competition. Although there are some classifications that are traditionally bought by this method, such as bridal gowns, bridesmaid gowns, mother-of-the-bride gowns, or merchandise for a specific designer boutique or department, any fashion-oriented department in a store may elect to offer this service to special customers. Stores usually require substantial down payments from customers for special orders. This necessitates added recordkeeping.

Placing the Order

After a buyer has made a decision about what type of merchandise to buy and which vendor to buy it from, the next step is negotiating the price and other conditions of purchase. Before the order is actually written, thought must be given and plans must be formulated regulating these negotiations.

Negotiating the Price

The **negotiation processs** involves the exchange of ideas between buyers and sellers for the purpose of coming to a mutually satisfying agreement. In a good negotiation process both parties recognize that each has needs and wants that must be taken into consideration by the other. This process is really the same bargaining activity that has been going on for centuries in bazaars and stores all over the world. One of the most important negotiations between buyer and vendor is the price negotiation. The Robinson-Patman Act of 1936 requires manufacturers to offer services and prices to all retailers on a proportionately equal basis.

Alert buyers are always pressing for advantages in price and terms. Although most vendors' prices and terms are usually predetermined, there is always an opportunity to negotiate. Price negotiation is sometimes the best method for arriving at the price of new goods or new versions of goods. The vendor's price usually depends upon quantity expectations, the average size of reorders, and the methods of packing and delivery requested by the buyer. Buyers, in their attempts to negotiate advantageous prices, usually make use of the following knowledge and techniques.

Most important is a thorough knowledge of the market. This is accomplished through frequent visits to various types of resources, conversations with salespeople, checking competition, and studying the catalog and price lists of vendors. With this information you will bring to a negotiation session an awareness of the prices and availability being offered by competitors of the vendor, and the probable salability of the merchandise at a certain price. Another power base for you as a buyer is to understand the vendor's costs. Of course, this is difficult and it is only through experience that you will become adept at it. The more you know, however, the better your estimate will be about price. Therefore, you should always try to learn more about vendors' merchandise

Negotiations are most successful in an atmosphere of mutual professional respect.

and gain as much product knowledge as possible. Estimating the retail value of merchandise is another technique of price negotiation. If you consistently practice determining what the normal retail price should be on an item and learn to evaluate the pricing elements, in time you will become a good judge of retail values, which by subtracting markups can be translated into cost prices against which to measure cost prices quoted by a vendor.

Negotiating Terms of Sale

Another part of the negotiation process when placing orders is securing discounts and allowances and determining the mode and cost of transportation. Together these two factors are known as **terms of sale.**

DISCOUNTS. Reductions in the list or quoted price given to a buyer by a vendor are called **discounts** or allowances. There are various kinds of discounts and allowances available to a buyer.

Quantity Discounts. A **quantity discount** is one that is predicated upon a number of units to be ordered or an amount of money to be spent, stipulated by the vendor. An example would be a vendor telling you that on an order of over 100 dozen of an item you can take an extra $1 off the price of each dozen. Buyers should be careful of the advisability of quantity discounts. Remember, taking a quantity discount may require purchasing more goods than you can sell. **Cumulative discounts** are a type of quantity discount based on volume over a certain period. Usually quantity discounts are on a one-order basis; cumulative discounts are concerned with the total business done with a resource during a certain period. Cumulative discounts encourage buyers to place the bulk of their orders with one resource. You must keep in mind that the added chance for a few percentage points off an order should never outweigh considerations about the salability of the merchandise to the customer.

Trade Discounts. A **trade discount** is a single discount or series of discounts from the "list price," which is the manufacturer's published catalog price. Discounts can vary as much as the manufacturer desires. Thus the "net price," or the price after the discounts have been subtracted, can be considered the cost price. The "list price" is often the same as the "suggested retail price." In this case, the trade discounts are in reality the markup achieved for them. Very little fashion merchandise is sold with a trade discount; this discount applies more to hard goods.

Trade discounts are usually listed as three numbers. The first number is the percentage of the regular discount, the second shows the extra percentage for a quantity order, and the third is a percentage for early purchase. The three percentages do not get added together, but each discount is taken off after the previous one has been deducted. Thus a $100 list price item with a 45-10-5 discount would be figured as follows:

$100.00 (list price)
−45.00 (regular discount: 45 percent of $100)
$ 55.00
−5.50 (discount for quantity order: 10 percent of $55)
$ 49.50
−2.48 (discount for early purchase: 5 percent of $49.50)
$ 47.02 due to vendor (totaling 52.98 percent discount)

Seasonal Discounts. A **seasonal discount** is offered to a buyer for purchasing merchandise out of season. For example, a bathing suit manufacturer might give a seasonal discount on a large order placed after the summer season is over, or very early before the season starts. Manufacturers who deal in seasonal goods allow such discounts because they help them even out production schedules and reduce problems involved with seasonal help. Retailers should be wary, however, of buying goods out of season, particularly if there is any chance of big fashion changes.

Cash Discounts. A **cash discount** is a deduction from the cost price for paying the invoice within a specified period of time. In reality, cash discounts are a reward vendors give buyers for paying their bills on time. Other discounts can be deducted in conjunction with a cash discount. Buyers may take quantity, trade, and seasonal discounts and also a cash discount if they pay on time. Standard cash discounts are common in some industries. For example, in the women's ready-to-wear market, an 8 percent cash discount is usually allowed for bills paid within the time period specified. For accessories such as handbags, the usual cash discount is 3 percent, and for men's clothing, it is 7 percent. The firm that pays its bills promptly gains many price advantages on the cost of goods.

Dating. **Dating** refers to the length of time that the vendor gives the buyer to pay for goods purchased. There are many variations in dating and in cash discounts for paying earlier. They are the following:

□ **Regular dating,** the most common form of dating, allows a buyer a discount if the bill is paid within the time period stipulated, for example, 30 days.

- **EOM dating** enables a buyer to take a cash discount if the invoice is paid within 10 days after the end of the month in which the invoice is dated. The notation "8/10 EOM" means the store gets an 8 percent discount 10 days after the end of the month.

- **Receipt of goods** (ROG) allows a buyer to take a cash discount if the invoice is paid within ten days after the receipt of goods into the store. An 8 percent discount for 10 days after the goods are received at the store is written "8/10 ROG."

- **Extra dating** gives a buyer a specified number of extra days in which to pay the bill and to earn the cash discount. In writing the terms, extra is usually written as an X, for example, 3/10-60X. This means a buyer will get a 3 percent cash discount if the bill is paid 70 days from the invoice date.

- **Advanced dating** means that the invoice is dated from a specified future date, not from the designated invoice date. For example, an invoice covering winter coats shipped on September 15 may have terms of 8/10 net 30 as of December 1. This arrangement will give the buyer until January 1 to pay the bill. This will allow the buyer to sell the goods before having to pay for them.

- **Cash on delivery** (COD) means that there will be payment in cash upon receipt of the merchandise. Only very small stores or stores with very bad credit ratings will buy goods on these terms.

- **Anticipation** allows an extra percentage discount to be taken for paying an invoice in advance of the cash discount date. This is usually only done by those buyers who have ready cash available. The actual computation of anticipation is performed by the Accounts Payable office and is not the responsibility of the buyer.

TRANSPORTATION. Transportation costs can be very high, so buyers always try to persuade vendors to assume all or some of the cost and liability of shipping merchandise. Transportation terms that can be negotiated may be one of the following:

- **FOB (Free on Board) Factory.** This means that the buyer will pay all the transportation charges and costs and will own the goods from the moment they are shipped.

- **FOB Destination.** This means that the vendor will pay all transportation charges and costs and will own the merchandise until it arrives at the place designated by the buyer. It can also be written as FOB Store, FOB Buyer's Warehouse.

- **FOB Shipping Point.** This means that the vendor pays any crating necessary for sending the goods to a place at which they are turned over to a transportation company. Can also be written as FOB Consolidation Point.

- **FOB Destination; Charges Reversed.** This means that the vendor will own the goods until they get to the buyer's designated point; however, the buyer agrees to pay the transportation charges.

- **FOB Destination; Freight Prepaid.** This means that the goods are to become the possession of the buyer as soon as they are shipped; however, the seller will pay the freight charges.

In addition to determining the form of FOB, you must determine the best method of shipment. Time and cost are two important elements you must consider when figuring out the methods of transportation and storage. The main methods are railroad freight, railway express, motor freight, parcel post, air express, air freight, and truck-rail. It is always wise to check with your operation manager to find out what kind of transportation may be preferred by management for speed and low cost.

Kinds of Orders

There are many different kinds of orders that a buyer may write during a single season. Each type of order serves a special situation and they fall into the following types:

- ☐ **Regular or Stock Orders.** These are placed by the buyer directly with the vendor. They give full specifications in regard to time, amount, and shipment. In the case of large chains, the distribution requirements for each store unit may be indicated.
- ☐ **Reorders.** These are orders for additional quantities of goods already ordered before.
- ☐ **Special Orders.** These are placed by the buyer, usually for single units, to satisfy the special demands of customers.
- ☐ **Advance Orders.** These are regular orders placed for delivery some time in the future, rather than for immediate delivery.
- ☐ **Open Orders.** These are placed by the resident buying office, and the name of the manufacturer is filled in by the resident buyer after it is determined what will be the best resource for this type of merchandise.
- ☐ **Blanket Orders.** These are orders that cover the delivery of merchandise for all or part of a season. The buyer will place a requisition against these orders as the merchandise is needed.
- ☐ **Back Orders.** These are orders placed by the buyer for shipments or parts of shipments that were not filled on time by the vendor.

Follow-Up

The follow-up on orders is as important as the initial placement of the order. This requires checking shipping dates on orders and noting invoice numbers, truckers' lading bills, and air freight confirmations. Prompt delivery is as important as a low price. Sales will be lost if goods do not arrive as planned, and fashion merchandise may become valueless if not received when the customer wants to buy.

In order to make sure that vendors ship on time and that a steady flow of goods is guaranteed for your stocks, it is important to set up a system to follow up orders. The need for such a system is particularly important during peak selling seasons when everyone is screaming for goods. Many buyers go themselves or send assistants or their RBO representatives to manufacturers' factories or shipping warehouses to make sure that their ordered goods will be delivered—as ordered, and on time! Even when the buyers' merchandise is not ready for shipment, they may induce the vendor to "steal" from another shipment so that they can have their order.

Follow-up sometimes involves contacting not only the shipper but also the transportation company. Delayed and lost shipments must be traced. It does not help to be told that "the merchandise is on the truck." You can't sell it from the truck! After merchandise has been received by the store, orders must be checked to make certain that the vendor shipped exactly what was ordered. Most problems occur because some buyers and some vendors may be careless about their responsibilities. Both parties need to remember that the good name and reputation of the store and the vendor are constantly in flux during negotiations. Both the buyer and the vendor should establish policies that will ensure good relationships and that will lead to successful business for everyone.

Buying Vocabulary

Define or briefly explain the following terms:

Advanced dating

Advance orders

Anticipation

Back orders

Blanket orders

Cash discounts

Cash on delivery (COD)

Consignment buying

Cumulative discounts

Cutting ticket

Dating: regular, EOM, ROG, extra dating

Discounts

FOB: factory, destination, shipping point, charges reversed, freight prepaid

Irregulars

Job lot

Negotiation process

Off-price buying

Open orders

Private label buying

Product development manager

Promotional buying

Quantity discounts

Receipt of goods

Regular buying

Regular orders

Reorders

Sample-test-reorder technique

Seasonal discounts

Seconds

Special-order buying

Special orders

Specification manager

Stock orders

Terms of sale

Trade discounts

Buying Review

1. Why are buying techniques important to the buyer? To the companies for whom they work?
2. Under what conditions would specification buying be appropriate? Would you recommend this form of buying to your employer?
3. Give some current company examples of private label purchases. Why do you think the retailer made these forms of purchases?
4. Describe briefly out-of-season buying. When might it be effective?

5. In an Appleton, Wisconsin, shopping center, there is a "Polo" Outlet Store. Here Ralph Lauren fine men's and ladies' clothing and substantial quantities of irregulars and seconds are available. Why is this appropriate?
6. Describe a typical consignment purchase arrangement. Could this be an advantage or a disadvantage to the store?
7. Can purchase prices be negotiated? When is negotiating prices most likely?
8. What other order conditions are negotiable?
9. When might telephone orders be placed? What is done after a verbal telephone order?
10. Why is expediting orders a part of the buying function?
11. Who can do order follow-ups? Why are these necessary?
12. How might knowledge of terms of sale save a buyer money when buying different types of merchandise?

Buying Case

Henry Isaacs was the new buyer of men's furnishings for Butler's, a smart men's specialty store located in one of the more affluent suburbs of Seattle. Butler's catered to an upper-middle-class clientele in the 25 to 44 and 45 to 64 age groups. The store does well in both sportswear and business apparel.

One of Henry's first decisions was to select the brand or brands of regular dress shirts upon which to place major emphasis. Regular dress shirts were his largest merchandise classification. He could continue to stock and promote the well-established, nationally branded Supreme shirts, which his predecessor had emphasized. The manufacturer's intensive year-round advertising program all but presold the average American customer. Emphasizing Supreme shirts virtually assured maintenance of the "historical" 50 percent markup on sales.

The alternative was to develop and emphasize a well-made shirt under a Butler's label. Henry was quite knowledgeable about the development of private brands and believed that the Butler's reputation for handling only good-quality merchandise would give the shirts a great deal of prestige. Because of specification buying and long-term commitments, Henry would be able to purchase a shirt equal to, and in some ways superior to, the Supreme shirt at a lower cost but to maintain the same retail price. This, of course, would give him a higher markup, in this case, 55 percent. Acceptance of the private label would be riskier than the proven acceptance of Supreme, however. Which of the two brands should Henry emphasize and why?

Case For Unit 3

You have been promoted to buyer of better sportswear at a large Texas department store. For three years you had been assistant to the buyer, and you were offered the position when the buyer was promoted to division merchandise manager.

The last year's volume in this area was $14,000,000 in all 10 stores. The store has been quite active promotionally in recent years and the volume is growing. Your budget is set up at an 8 percent increase to $15,110,000.

You are preparing for the first buying trip to New York in April for fall purchases. In October you will leave for Hong Kong to buy merchandise to be shipped for the following fall needs.

1. Outline and describe how you would decide on selecting resources for your New York trip; for your Far East market trip.

2. What steps would you take to have the information necessary to complete your buying plan? To alert both New York and foreign resident offices for your visits? With time an essential element, outline how you would work the market.

3. In Hong Kong, how would you overcome foreign buying problems, work with your foreign buying office, and determine the costs you could pay for imports?

4. What buying techniques will you use in New York? In Hong Kong?

5. How will you negotiate the various prices, discounts, and transportation costs in both domestic and foreign markets?

Unit 4

The Buyer and Sales Promotion

Planning to sell fashion goods to consumers without sales promotion is like planning a party without inviting the guests. Although everything may be ready, nobody comes. You cannot assume that customers will come to your store without encouragement or reminders. ''Goods well bought are half sold'' is a familiar saying among retailers. They know that half the job of selling to consumers consists of recognizing what they want and offering assortments geared to those wants. They also know that the other half of the selling effort is sales promotion—the business of arousing the consumers' buying impulses. This half requires just as much careful planning and execution as the other. Because the fashion industry is fast-moving and highly competitive, everyone from the designer with a new sketch to the merchant with new styles in stock is eager to talk about, show, and promote the sale of new goods.

There are almost as many different definitions of sales promotion as there are businesses engaged in it. For the purposes of this unit, we will define sales promotion as the coordinated effort of advertising, visual merchandising, publicity, and personal selling to obtain profitable sales.

Each of the four chapters in this unit will cover one aspect of sales promotion. Chapter 13 focuses on advertising, which is any paid form of nonpersonal presentation by an identified sponsor to promote ideas, goods, or services. Advertising appears in print media such as newspapers, magazines, and direct-mail pieces, in broadcast media such as radio and television, and in outdoor media such as outdoor signs and transit advertising.

Visual merchandising, which is the presentation of merchandise and services to their best selling advantage for maximum customer acceptance, is introduced in Chapter 14. Visual merchandising includes display, store layout, and store decor.

Publicity and public relations are covered in Chapter 15. Publicity is the free and voluntary mention of a firm, brand, product, or person in some form of the media. The purpose of publicity is to enhance the interest of potential customers. Public relations is the execution of a specially designed program by a business in order to earn public understanding and acceptance. Public relations programs sponsor such events as fashion shows, trunk shows, and storewide salutes to countries, and make use of advisory boards. Both publicity and public relations will be discussed in detail in Chapter 15.

The final chapter of this unit introduces personal selling. Advertising, visual merchandising, publicity, and public relations can help to create a potential customer who is ready to buy, but if there is no competent and knowledgeable salesperson available to sell, the sale may be lost. Chapter 16 will discuss the buyer's responsibilities in fashion selling.

Chapter 13

Advertising

Every time you open a newspaper, turn on the radio, or take a moment to watch television, you are exposed to advertising. By far the largest share of the sales promotion budget for most stores is allocated to advertising.

In this chapter we will explore the purpose of advertising, the two basic types of advertising, the requirements of a successful ad, the variety of advertising media available to retail buyers, and the advantages and disadvantages of cooperative advertising. Then we will take a look at the advertising responsibilities of a buyer and how they might vary in a chain store, major department store, small department store, specialty store, and small fashion shop.

Objectives of Advertising

The major objective of retail advertising is to make sales by attracting potential customers to the store. Another important objective is the building of a fashion image and the strengthening of store goodwill. While it is being used for these important purposes, advertising might also be used to introduce new fashions, teach customers new ways to wear existing fashions, help salespeople by "preselling" customers, and help assure that customers are happy with their purchases.

Types of Advertisements

There are two basic types of ads used by stores. One is designed to sell merchandise, the other to "sell" a store's image.

A **merchandise** or **promotional advertisement** is one that endeavors to create sales of specific products. Goodwill, store image, and enhancement of the store's fashion prestige are incidental, although these are nevertheless considered when any such ad is planned and prepared.

A **prestige** or **institutional advertisement** is one that "sells" the store rather than specific merchandise. It may discuss a new fashion trend. It may point out the store's value as a headquarters for fashion news, for bargains, or for clothes for the family. Perhaps it may publicize a community event. Any merchandise mentioned in the ad is usually considered incidental. The ad's value to the store is measured solely in terms of such intangibles as prestige, goodwill, and enhanced store image.

Requirements of a Successful Advertisement

To be successful, an ad must appeal to the buying motives of the potential customer who will see or hear it. In Chapter 2, you learned that customer buying motives can be described in many ways, one of which is to measure them along a continuum that runs from operational satisfactions to psychological satisfactions. Operational satisfactions are those derived from the physical performance of a product or the

Merchandise and institutional advertising for a store should present the same store image to the target market.

An ad may appeal to rational buying motives or to nonrational, emotional reasons such as elegant styling or luxurious fabric.

physical benefits provided by a service. Psychological satisfactions are those derived from the customer's social and psychological interpretations of the product's performance or service's benefits.

In selecting a winter coat, a woman may buy for the psychological satisfactions of style, elegance, and originality, but she might also buy for the operational satisfactions of warmth, durability, and practicality. On a continuum that runs from psychological satisfactions to operational satisfactions, the customer's mo-tives for purchasing an elegantly styled, excellent quality, classic black wool coat could be plotted approximately at the midpoint between psychological satisfactions and operational satisfactions.

A successful advertisement addresses the customers' psychological and operational buying motives and, at the same time, accomplishes four important tasks. These tasks are referred to as the **AIDA concept**—attracting ATTENTION, developing INTEREST, creating DESIRE, and securing ACTION.

Attracting Attention

An ad can be of no value unless your potential customer notices it. To attract and hold this person's attention, printed ads use such devices as eye-catching illustrations, vivid colors, strong headlines, and unusual type. Broadcast ads use such devices as attention-getting music, interesting dialog and video, the voices (and endorsements) of well-known people, and often-repeated jingles and slogans. Many people automatically recognize the music used in the Jordache commercials. In their minds, the viewers are hearing the words "the Jordache look," even if there are no words actually being sung to the music. This type of commercial accomplishes the first task by attracting the attention of the potential customer.

Developing Interest

The attention of customers can quickly be lost if there is nothing in the ad that they consider interesting. Attractive illustrations, well-written copy, dramatic layout, and well-chosen type are all vital to the success of a print advertisement. To develop this interest and direct it toward your product or service, you should try to direct your ad to the experiences or attitudes of the customer you are writing the ad for. You should try to speak the "language" of your customer in both pictures and words. The pictures and language for a hosiery ad directed toward teenagers may be different from what appears in one directed toward career women, even though the ads are for the same product.

Creating Desire

After the customer is interested in your product or service, the next task for advertising is stimulating a desire on the part of that customer to own your product or use your service. For this task the ad must address the buying motives that were discussed in the previous section of this chapter. For each product or service, it is important to decide what the potential buying motives of the customer are. If you believe that the product appeals to both the psychological and operational satisfactions of the customer, your ad may choose to address either the psychological satisfactions or the operational satisfactions, or both. In a recent issue of a popular fashion magazine, one ad for skin lotion created desire by appealing almost entirely to operational satisfactions. It asked readers to "face facts." Then it gave some basic facts about the superior quality of the product and closed with the words "The choice is yours!" An ad in the same magazine for body oil told readers to "Imagine how you would feel running your hands over your body and feeling silk. Pure silk." The ad went on to describe the pleasures of using the body oil and described it as an oil that feels even lighter than most lotions. This ad was based primarily on psychological satisfactions.

Securing Action

The real challenge of any ad is getting the customer to take action. That action may be to visit your store, mail in an order, fill out a coupon asking for information, or call in an order using a toll-free number. Although a large portion of the ads that appear in newspapers are designed to provide immediate buying action, others, such as those that frequently appear in magazines, are designed to persuade customers more gradually to buy a product or service. Each one of a series of ads is designed to play a role both in moving the customer toward the purchasing decision and in establishing store loyalty.

Selecting Advertising Media

A wide variety of advertising media is available to the retail fashion buyer. These media can roughly be categorized as print media and broadcast media.

Print Media

Print media includes newspapers, magazines, direct mail, catalogs, shopping guides, a variety of other printed publications, billboards, and transit advertising.

NEWSPAPERS. Retailers use local newspapers extensively in promoting fashion merchandise because their customers are mainly from within the areas served by such newspapers. Producers whose fashion goods have national or at least regional distribution tend to favor national magazines for their ads. Some may cooperate with their retail store customers, however, by helping the stores pay for ads of their merchandise in local newspapers. (See cooperative advertising in a later section of this chapter.)

Newspapers Offer Good Timing. Newspapers are the preferred advertising medium at the retail level because they provide immediate impact and broad local exposure. The time between preparation and insertion of an ad can be quite short, and last-minute changes can be handled readily. Compared with a monthly magazine whose ad pages "close" weeks before publication, a daily paper normally can accept changes almost up to the moment that its presses begin to roll. And this is only a matter of a few hours before the edition is on the streets.

Speed is vital in promoting fashion merchandise. A newspaper ad can be prepared for new fashion merchandise even before the goods are in stock, provided the resource has made a firm promise of delivery and can be relied upon. Should there be an unforeseen delay in the availability of the merchandise, the ad can be pulled at the eleventh hour. The importance of this last-minute flexibility is obvious in view of the many kinds of sudden changes that can require a change in advertising plans.

Newspapers Offer a Targeted Readership. In a community where several newspapers are published, each attracts a particular readership in terms of income, education, and interests. It is wise to advertise in the paper that appeals to the readers who are most similar to your store's clientele in fashion awareness and income level. In New York, for example, stores that feature fashions in the early stages of their cycles usually buy space in *The New York Times,* which reaches affluent, city-oriented, fashion-aware customers. Stores or departments that offer fashions at the peak and in the declining stages of their cycles have less reason to use the *Times* and therefore rely upon other city or suburban papers where they can place equally attractive and effective ads for a lower price. Occasionally an enterprising suburban or small-town store will advertise its newest fashions in a prestigious big-city paper that has circulation in its community. Although much of the paper's circulation is wasted as far as such a store is concerned, the use of a city newspaper dramatizes the store's fashion authority in the eyes of city-oriented members of its community.

MAGAZINES. Magazines offer advantages in the presentation of advertised products because they are printed on high-quality paper and are capable of reproducing both black-and-white and color illustrations with excellent quality. They also have a longer life than newspapers. They may be kept in waiting rooms, on coffee tables in readers' homes, or in special library collections for many months after their original publication.

However, merchandise chosen for magazine advertisements must be carefully selected because of the length of time that elapses between the magazine's closing date (when all copy and illustrations must be in the hands of the publication) and its date of issue (when the magazine reaches the newsstands or the mailboxes of its subscribers). Apparel and accessories that are advertised in such magazines are either timeless classics or styles typifying incoming trends.

For our purposes, we will discuss three basic categories of magazines—national, national with regional editions, and regional. National magazines can also be categorized as fashion-oriented or general. Placing ads in national fashion magazines such as *Mademoiselle, Glamour, Vogue, Gentlemen's Quarterly,* and *Bride's Magazine* can help to emphasize that a retailer's fashion image is sufficiently important to be carried in the pages of a publication whose fashion authority is nationally recognized. This prestige advertising is intended to emphasize the store's image—as a place to buy one-of-a-kind jewels, as a salon for the latest in high-fashion apparel, as a headquarters for travel clothes and accessories, or whatever the case may be. Such advertising implies that the shop or store, regardless of location, is on a par with the country's best in fashion authority and desirable fashion assortments.

Some national magazines such as *Good Housekeeping* have regional sections within the national magazine. Others have regional editions. These options can enable retail advertisers to direct their messages to specific geographic regions, rather than the nation as a whole.

Other magazines, such as *New York Magazine, Chicago Magazine,* and *San Francisco,* are distributed primarily in specific regional areas. These magazines can also offer the advantages of magazine-quality advertising together with the ability to direct the advertising message to a specific geographic region.

DIRECT MAIL. As the contents of our mailboxes clearly indicate, **direct mail,** which is any form of advertising issued directly to prospective customers and sent through the mail, continues to proliferate at a staggering rate, despite increases in mailing and printing costs. As a means of reaching a target customer, direct mail is outstanding. Direct mail also lends itself extremely well to fashion promotion, whether in the form of a single-item enclosure that arrives each month with the store's bill or an elaborate catalog showing a store's fashion assortments. These full-color illustrations of fashion items together with brief but explicit descriptions are geared to motivate immediate customer response.

Manufacturers and their cooperative dollars play a major part in a store's use of direct mail. Statement enclosures, often colorfully printed, are available from many garment and accessory makers to show items in their current assortments. These are produced by the hundreds of thousands, with blank spaces reserved for the addition of specific store information. These preprinted enclosures are a valuable means of advertising for smaller stores. Other stores prefer that any printed material going out with their names attached be produced within their own facilities. These stores reject any preprinted manufacturers' inserts but frequently develop the contents of such inserts in their own style and mail them out.

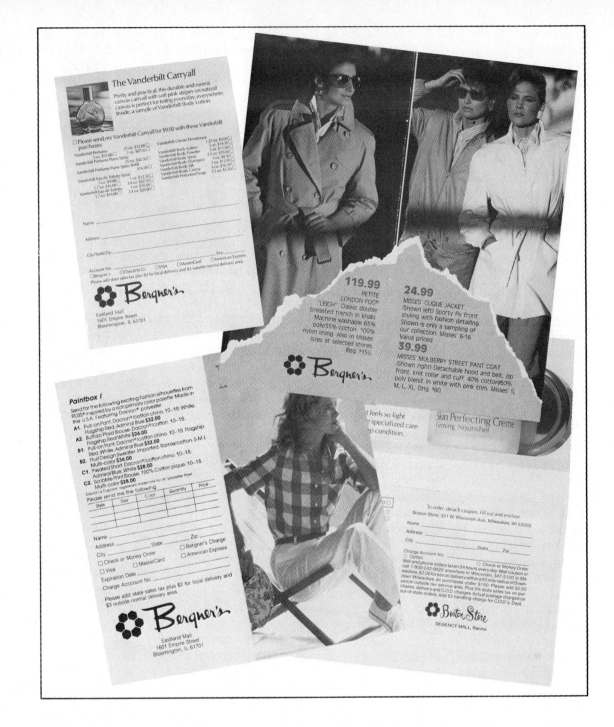

Direct advertising is an effective way of reaching the target market segment.

Postcards and Letters. Another form of direct mail used by stores is postcards or letters to inform valued charge customers in advance of upcoming events, including special sales and holiday offerings. Other forms include inserts that are tucked into a customer's package by salesclerks or in the packing room, and personal notes sent by salespeople to special customers, alerting them to new items in which they might be interested.

Direct mail has been a favorite medium for selling bridal fashions for many years. Notices are sent to engaged women, inviting them to attend a bridal show or to visit the store's bridal salon for advice on wedding plans and for selection of clothes for the wedding party.

Specialty Catalogs. By far the most startling development in direct-mail advertising has been the explosion of the specialty catalog. For many years stores produced one catalog each year, usually for a Christmas season mailing. Today catalogs play a major role in the direct-mail advertising of many fashion stores. Bloomingdale's and Neiman-Marcus, for example, have separate direct-mail departments that specialize in upscale retail catalogs. Bloomingdale's By Mail issues 16 beautifully executed catalogs each year directed toward those who live outside the trading area or would rather shop by mail. In addition, the store publishes 14 more catalogs designed to generate in-store sales.

At Sears, although there has been a "baby book" for years featuring maternity and baby goods, a recent innovative approach has had tremendous success. The new 32-page Sears baby book can be found in the obstetrician's office. The first 16 pages of the book are filled with helpful information about everything from morning sickness to feeding. The next 16 pages features their latest maternity wear and baby gear. Sears also has an array of other special-appeal catalogs, including those for people wearing petite sizes and large-size menswear.

Bullock's has created a 16-page, four-color 14 × 22-inch luxurious book with many full-page fashion photos and no advertisements, "to let fashion speak for itself through the drama and size of the vehicle."[1] Each quarter, 1.9 million copies of this publication, called *B,* are distributed to charge customers and used as newspaper inserts.

The trend toward creating exciting catalogs that are designed to go directly from the mailbox to the coffee table is one that is likely to continue. Retailers who have invested in these direct-mail pieces believe that they are worth the time and money required to turn out quality catalogs with fine graphics and visual design.

OUTDOOR ADVERTISING. A time-honored method of advertising that is still being used today, **outdoor advertising** includes a variety of signs.

Outdoor signs may be either standardized or nonstandardized. Standardized signs, which are often called billboards, measure 12 feet 3 inches high and 24 feet 6 inches long. These signs may be rented from outdoor advertising firms. When you buy a standardized outdoor sign, you use **gross rating points (GRP)** as a guide to the effectiveness of the advertising location. Very basically, a location's GRP indicates the percentage of the population in a particular area that can be expected to see the advertising message.

Nonstandardized signs can be any size or shape. They can be placed on the outside of the store itself, or they can be placed in locations away from the store that can be rented from the owner.

Focus

Department Store Fashion Magazines: Catalogs They're Not!

In an effort to appeal to the "armchair" shopper, retailers of all types have been churning out record numbers of catalogs, many of which concentrate on merchandise of one particular specialty. Apparel, for instance, was the focus of some 473 separate catalogs in 1984, compared to just 253 in 1981, according to the *Directory of Mail Order Catalogs.*

But now, some retailers are taking the catalog concept a step further and are presenting their up-to-the-minute fashion news and merchandise in slick, glossy, readable *magazines.* One of those retailers is Dallas-based Neiman-Marcus, long famous for its classy catalogs packed with innovative and exclusive merchandise. The retailer still publishes some 27 of those traditional advertising vehicles, but now it has added a publication called *NM* to its roster.

Unlike catalogs such as its Christmas Book, which is sent to all active Neiman-Marcus customers (almost 2 million in number), *NM* goes to a select list of just over 900,000 active charge customers in the store's 15 major trading areas. Originally designed by the store's vice president-fashion communications as a "workbook" to alert sales staff to new fashion trends and merchandise, the publication was transformed into a full-fledged fashion magazine, containing a mix of articles and advertising. Published quarterly starting in 1986, *NM* has even been sold on newsstands at a cover price of $2.50.

Similarly, Jordan Marsh, Boston, ventured into the magazine business in 1979 with a store publication called *Jack and Jill.* The title characters had been created in an effort to attract a younger, more fashion-oriented customer to the store, which was perceived then as being somewhat stodgy. The magazine itself failed, but it did attract the attention of the 22- to 35-year-old customers Jordan Marsh wanted. And in order to keep them, the retailer looked for a new vehicle that would reinforce its newly blossoming fashion image.

Rather than add another catalog to the more than 20 it was already sending out each year, Jordan Marsh devised a new publication called *JM Magazine.* Published twice a year, the magazine is distributed via the New England edition of *The New York Times,* and to a controlled circulation of about

Outdoor ads can be an effective way of reaching potential customers with an attractive illustration and a few well-chosen words about your store, products, or services. In some areas, however, they are becoming increasingly unpopular because environmentalists consider them to be a form of "sight pollution."

TRANSIT ADVERTISING. Included in the category of **transit advertising** is advertising that is placed on both the outside and the inside of transportation vehicles, and posters that are placed in subway stations, train stations, and bus terminals. These ads, when carried inside vehicles or in stations, can carry a sizable amount of copy because the average passenger is exposed to the ad for at least 30 minutes. The ads on the outside of vehicles, however, are similar to other outside advertising. They are seen for a very short period of time and should carry an attractive illustration with a minimum of copy. Transit advertising can be a relatively inexpensive way to reach customers when they are in the area of your store, and the repetitive nature of transit advertising can have a positive effect on potential customers who may automatically remember your store when they have a need for your type of product.

Broadcast Media

Another avenue for delivering the fashion advertising message is through the use of **broadcast media**—radio and television.

RADIO. By the early 1980s, the youth of the country had made its media preference known—radio. As stations playing the top 40 hit songs proliferated, so did teenagers' listening time increase. With transistor radios came round-the-clock involvement with the rock stars of the day. Retailers quickly realized that the newspaper was not the medium to use to attract youth; the radio was. Now, years later, radio advertising is recognized as a must by the retailers interested in reaching the youth group. The car radio is also used to reach the working adult. Morning and evening "drive-time" radio is accepted by retailers as the best means of reaching this group with their message.

There are no hard-and-fast rules indicating which means of communication retailers should use. Each store, each area, and each customer profile presents a different situation. Simply stated, when radio reaches customers more effectively than other media, stores are quick to use it.

TELEVISION. While a brief relationship between retailers and television existed years ago, most retailers have only recently embraced this medium as a means of conveying their fashion messages to consumers. This may seem surprising, considering the constant, daily impact that television has on our lives and the benefits that such an exciting and colorful medium can offer. After the close relationship of retailers to local television in the early years of the medium, however, several factors kept retailers away from television for almost two decades.

Early Retail TV Advertising. In the late 1940s and early 1950s when television stations were new and inexperienced, the costs of commercial and program time were very small. Television stations, needing to fill daytime hours with programming, turned to experienced retailers for help. The famous department store, Rich's in Atlanta, actually provided three hours of programming a day for a new Atlanta television station in 1950 and 1951. The station brought its cameras and lights to Rich's as a television studio. The store programmed the three hours with fashion shows, lectures, how-to demonstrations, autographing teas, cooking lessons, and many other activities, which involved showing the store's merchandise on camera.

But such an arrangement could not last. As television caught on and more and more sets were purchased, the cost of programming and advertising time began its upward climb. Within a relatively short time, the cost was beyond the range of practically all advertisers except giant national manufacturers. Retail stores, as always, had to spend their advertising dollars carefully to ensure the best results. They could not afford the astronomical cost of each 60-second or even 30-second commercial. In addition to their expense, such "one-time shots," unlike newspaper ads, could not be set aside for use again later. Thus retailers, who had at first embraced and supported the new medium, decided that it was too costly and its selling results too uncertain. This disassociation with television lasted, with few exceptions, until the 1970s.

Retailers' Use of TV in the '70s. By the 1970s, some of the nation's leading retailers were returning to TV advertising for several reasons. First, the medium had grown up and had achieved a commanding influence in the lives of the American people. Second, newspaper costs had risen alarmingly, to the point that, in some cases, television had become less expensive for the stores to use. Third, increasing numbers of firms now specialized in the production of TV shows and commercials for buyers of television time. Some of these firms were specifically geared to retailer's needs. Fourth, and probably most important, the broadcasting systems, desirous of a larger share of retailers' advertising dollars, were constantly demonstrating the pulling power of television to these retailers.

Stores in areas served only by weekly newspapers found television a means of reaching their customers more frequently. Stores located in large cities found that television enhanced the pulling power of their print advertising and helped them tell their fashion story more effectively.

By the mid-1970s, national chains, such as Sears and the J.C. Penney Company, were buying prime time on national shows to tell customers around the country about their merchandise offerings. In addition, many major department stores around the country were routinely using television spot advertising on a local basis, as well as sponsoring such programs as the local newscast or weather report. Not to be outdone, many small specialty shops found that constant exposure on a specific television station at a specific time of the day was a means of fixing their names firmly in the public's mind.

Cable TV and Retail Advertising. Then, in the early 1980s, the widespread acceptance of cable television introduced literally hundreds of new stations into the homes of consumers. And with these new stations came new advertising possibilities. Because cable television is still in its infancy in comparison to the more experienced traditional television stations, small cable stations are looking for programming in much the same way as the traditional stations of the late 1940s and early 1950s. Even the smallest retailer can advertise for a relatively modest investment, and in some cases, the retailer can contribute to the actual programming. Such offerings as the fashion shows, lectures, and how-to demonstrations of the early Atlanta stations are now being produced on cable television.

A new development in cable television advertising is interactive television. In 1977, Warner Cable Corporation launched its Qube system in Columbus, Ohio. Subscribers were equipped with a computer keypad that included five response buttons. At first these buttons were used for instant recording of the viewers' votes in opinion polls in response to presentations on the cable stations. The response buttons' potential as means of ordering merchandise was obvious, and soon there were stations whose programming consisted of televised catalogs. As cable shoppers indicated their selections on their keypads, the order could be transmitted immediately and verified before shipment by a confirmation phone call to the customer. Qube systems were set up in other cities, and cable shopping spread.

TELEPHONE AND VIDEO. Although the telephone has been used as a tool for communicating with potential fashion customers on an individual basis for years, it is now being used as a creative advertising tool by some firms. An increasing number of toll-free public service telephone numbers are available to consumers. They are invited to call a toll-free number in order to hear a prerecorded message about one of any number of consumer topics, or to respond to broadcast advertisements. Callers are invited to listen to messages about such topics as hair care, makeup and skin care, shoe selection, fur buying, and back-to-school clothing selection. Innovative fashion retailers have learned that if they sponsor toll-free messages, they are allowed to add a brief advertisement at the end of each message.

A similar type of advertising has recently been introduced into the video cassette market. Your store may sponsor an exercise video cassette, for example, that will carry a brief advertising message for your exercise fashions, or an aerobics cassette that will carry a message about your aerobic dance shoes.

INTERNAL ANNOUNCEMENTS. Some highly promotional stores use an internal communication system to announce specials over the loudspeaker. Customers are told about special buys and advised that only a limited time is allotted for the unusually low prices to be obtained. The customers are urged to hurry to a designated area to purchase these bargains. Accurate records of the sales of these items can be recorded daily.

Cooperative Advertising

Sometimes a manufacturer will absorb all or part of the cost of placing a retailer's advertising for the manufacturer's products in local media. This arrangement is called **cooperative advertising.**

Form 13-1 is an example of a notice of paid advertising that shows details of a store's cooperative advertising agreement with a manufacturer. Cooperative advertising offers advantages to both parties, but it also presents some problems or opportunities for abuse.

Advantages of Cooperative Advertising

Among the advantages that cooperative advertising offers to the fashion merchant is the added money for advertising. Cooperative money is usually considered to be in addition to whatever amount the store has budgeted from its own funds for promotion. Buyers should request such funds whenever their purchases are large enough to support such advertising. Additional advertising funds may enhance the impact of the store's advertising in two ways. First, the store may place larger or more frequent ads, thus increasing the impact of its name upon the public. Second, the additional space purchased with co-op money may help the store to qualify for a lower cost rate on all its advertising. This will enable the store to buy more space for the same cost. Newspapers usually give progressively lower rates as the total linage purchased for advertising increases.

Cooperation from producers in other respects is more certain once they have invested funds of their own in the store's advertising. Prompt deliveries, assistance in training the selling staff, and other services are more likely to be available. If the advertised brand, line, or item is new to the area, the producer shares introductory promotion costs with the store and thus shares the initial risk.

From the producer's point of view, the benefits include the fact that the producer's money buys more advertising space than if the ad was placed directly. The retailer, as a consistent buyer of space in local media, commands lower rates than does a producer with occasional advertising. The prestige of the store's name reinforces on a local basis the acceptance an item may enjoy on a regional or national basis. This is especially valuable when lines or brands are being introduced in a new area.

The retailer, having invested funds in advertising the merchandise, can be more readily counted upon to carry adequate stocks, provide window and departmental displays, and brief the salespeople on the selling points of the goods.

In large cities, where the manufacturer's line may be sold also through small neighborhood stores, the impact of a major store's advertising helps the sale of the line in the smaller stores as well.

Disadvantages of Cooperative Advertising

From the store's point of view, the major drawback in cooperative advertising is that buyers have been known to "buy" advertising rather than merchandise. Because of limited advertising funds and their own eagerness to see their departments promoted, some buyers pass up good merchandise for which there is little or no cooperative money available in order to buy what may turn out to be less desirable styles but for which there are cooperative advertising funds. This practice may result in poor assortments.

Elston's

VENDOR ADVERTISING AGREEMENT

Dept. No. __40__

Date __4/3/—__

(PLEASE PRINT)

__SLEEP DREAMS__

Vendor Name

__135 MADISON AVE.__

Billing Address

__NEW YORK, N.Y. 10000__

City, State, Zip Code

__CYNTHIA SYKES__

Attention

Trade Name

Date of Ad: __5/1/8—__

Does Vendor require tearsheets? Yes ☑ No ☐

Item to be advertised: __Sleepwear__

Mill, Mfg., etc. Contra Involved? Explain

NEWSPAPER

Please Check:	Total Inches Requested	Vendor Percent Paid	Vendor Dollars Paid	Vendor Color Dollars
✓ Herald		50		
News				
Post				
Sentinel				
Gazette				
Other:				

DIRECT MAIL / MAGAZINE

Date of Promotion: _____

Name of Mailing Piece: _____

Distribution: _____

No. Sample Copies _____

Bill Vendor:

$_____ Full Page
$_____ Half Page
$_____ One-fourth Page
$_____ Other _____

Sizes are approximate, due to exegencies of layout and design. No logotypes or boldface brand names are being used.

AUTHORIZATON

__CYNTHIA SYKES__

Name of Vendor Agent — Please Print

__Cynthia Sykes__

Signature of Vendor Agent

Comments: _____

__James Pierce__

Buyer's Signature

Divisional Merchandise Manager Signature

Method of Payment: (Please check one)

Deduct from Invoice ✓
Payment by check *
Vendor Allowance on Invoice
Do not deduct Basis
*Charges not paid witihn 30 days will be deducted

Form 13-1. A cooperative advertising agreement.

From the standpoint of the vendor, a major drawback of cooperative advertising is the danger of inadvertently discriminating against some customers in favor of others. Participation in the advertising of a well-known store that uses a big metropolitan daily may be worth much more to a vendor than participation in the advertising of a small shop that uses only a local suburban weekly. Yet, under the provisions of the Robinson-Patman Act (a section of the antitrust laws), a producer in such a situation might seem to be granting discriminatory allowances to the larger store. Rather than leave themselves open to charges of making offers for which only large stores can qualify, a number of apparel firms have simply abandoned cooperative advertising entirely. Others base their monetary assistance on a percentage of the total order placed. Thus, small orders do not generate enough money to pay for an advertisement.

The Buyer's Role in Advertising

The buyer's responsibility for advertising may vary widely from store to store. In a very small, owner-operated store, the buyer, owner, and advertising manager may be the same person. In a large department store, there may be a sales promotion manager, an advertising manager, artists, copywriters with whom the buyer must work in order to see that the merchandise is properly advertised.

In this section we will discuss seven basic tasks that must be accomplished in order to make fashion advertising a reality. Then we will give some generalized examples of the people who might be responsible for these tasks in different types of retail stores.

Basic Advertising Tasks

Before any fashion advertisement can appear in the media, the following series of basic tasks must be accomplished:

1. Establish goals for advertising.
2. Prepare an advertising plan and budget.
3. Select specific goods with proper assortment to be advertised.
4. Determine the media to be used and the exact dates or times the ad is to be run.
5. Prepare the ad in the form(s) required by the media.
6. Produce the ad.
7. Place the ad in the chosen media.

After a fashion advertisement has appeared in the media, the task of evaluating the results must be accomplished.

Preparing the Advertising Plan

Most stores, regardless of size, have some type of advertising plan based on the goals they have established. An **advertising plan** is a projection of the advertising that a store intends to use over a period of time, such as a season, quarter, month, or week, in order to attract business. In general, such a plan outlines the dates on which advertisements will be used, the departments and items to be advertised, the estimated sales expected to result from such ads, the media to be employed, the amount of space or time to be used in each medium, and the cost thereof. The cost is usually estimated both in dollars and as a percentage of the sales expected to be realized.

In a department store, the storewide advertising plan is a general guide to the timing and amount of advertising to be done by each department in the store during a specific season or other period of time. Exact dates, selection of media, decisions on ad sizes, writing of copy, and

Elston's

SALES PROMOTION PLAN

DATE	L. Y.	PLAN	ACTUAL	PROMOTIONS	GROSS	NET
Mon.				*Mother's Day Promotions*		
Tues.						
Wed.				*Sleepware – Famous Name*		
Thurs.				*½ pg. ad - ½ Vendor paid*		
Fri.					10,000	5,000
Sat.				*Daywear -Slips, Pants,Petts*		
Week Total	108,000	110,000		*½ pg. ad - ½ Vendor paid*		
Mon.				*Mother's Day Specials*		
Tues.				*Robe Special 18.99*		
Wed.						
Thurs.				*½ pg.*		
Fri.				*Nightgown Sale 19.99*	10,000	10,000
Sat.						
Week Total	125,000	125,000		*½ pg.*		
Mon.				*Bridal Promotions*		
Tues.						
Wed.				*Neglijee Sets / Peignoir Sets*		
Thurs.				*Nightgowns*		
Fri.					3,000	3,000
Sat.						
Week Total	85,000	85,000				
Mon.				*Bridal Promotions*		
Tues.				*Trousseau Sets*		
Wed.						
Thurs.						
Fri.					1,500	1,500
Sat.						
Week Total	80,000	85,000				
Mon.				*Bra and Girdle Sale*		
Tues.				*and Specials*		
Wed.				*All vendors participate*		
Thurs.				*Newspapers - Catalog*		
Fri.					25,000	5,000
Sat.						
Week Total	130,000	150,000		*Full page - vendor paid*		
Mon.				*Graduation Specials*		
Tues.				*Travel Robe Sets*		
Wed.					600	300
Thurs.						
Fri.						
Sat.						
Week Total	85,000	85,000				
TOTAL	613,000	640,000				
AUDITED						

	$	Sales Plan
ADVERTISING $ REQUESTED	60,100	640,000
MFG. CONTRA-CREDIT	25,300	
TOTAL	34,800	

Form 13-2. An advertising plan for a one-month period.

other details are worked out later, closer to publication time.

Both the budget and the schedule of the general plan for any store are prepared with the understanding that unforeseen developments may require sudden adjustments. These are the same kinds of adjustments that merchandise plans sometimes require. An advertisement that produces spectacular sales results may be repeated promptly, even if the original plan did not call for a second run. Conversely, a planned ad may be scrapped if the merchandise to back it up is not in stock or for some other sound reason.

After the storewide advertising plan has been prepared, it is broken down first into seasonal plans for each selling department and then into monthly plans for those departments. The monthly plans are drawn up about a month in advance. They specify the item or items to be advertised, the dates on which ads will appear, the size of each ad, and the medium in which it will appear.

INTERNAL SOURCES OF INFORMATION. Like the merchandise plan, the advertising plan is based on past experience, present conditions, and future expectations. In most stores, someone is responsible for keeping careful records in scrapbook form of what was advertised last year, how it was advertised, at what cost, and with what results. Such a scrapbook usually contains **tear sheets,** copies of the ads torn from the pages of the newspaper or magazine in which they were published, of all print advertising previously run. On each ad is noted the dollar cost of the ad and the sales that resulted from it, as reported by the department for which the ad was run. When drawing up an advertising plan for a new season, the planner goes through the scrapbooks for similar periods in pre-

vious years and studies both the ads run and their sales results. Each season's plans incorporate as many features as possible of successful advertising used in the past. They avoid the features of that advertising which did not produce desired sales results.

Neither institutional advertisements nor broadcast advertisements lend themselves to immediate sales that can easily be tracked. Therefore, criteria for judging them are rarely as dependable as they are for promotional ads. However, sales from merchandise sold for several days after such advertisements are run are recorded in the ad books, just as are sales from any other media, and compared to sales of the previous year. Attempts are made to analyze any results from such ads.

EXTERNAL SOURCES OF INFORMATION. The experience of other retailers is also used in planning. In addition to the store's own advertising scrapbook, the person who is responsible for planning advertising studies the advertising of other stores, particularly that of competitors whose advertising results have been observed. Also studied is the advertising of friendly noncompeting stores in other communities which are willing to exchange advertising information.

Through such sources as the store's resident buying office, the Retail News Bureau, the National Retail Merchants Association, and various trade publications, it is possible for those people who are responsible for advertising to keep track of the promotion experience of other stores. Reports of what is being sold in the country's top fashion stores are eagerly studied. So, too, are the advertising pages of consumer fashion magazines. Such reports are often a source of inspiration to advertising managers. They should always be evaluated, however, in terms of their own store's target group of customers. They know that the spectacular results from an ad placed by Saks Fifth Avenue, for example, might not be duplicated in their own stores if they placed an identical ad. Yet the approach used by another retail store may trigger an idea that can be used.

Finally, the people who have advertising responsibility constantly need information from the merchandising division in order to develop effective copy and illustrations. They expect buyers and merchandisers to give them specific details about fashion trends and to indicate noteworthy features of items to be advertised.

Selecting Goods or Services to be Advertised

Only the buyer can set in motion the complex process that begins with the arrival of a sample fashion and ends with an advertisement that motivates the public to purchase the fashion.

In a department store a buyer may verbally introduce a fashion item at the weekly advertising meeting of the advertising manager, copywriters, and art staff. The divisional merchandise manager and other buyers from that division may also be present. The buyer must then make a formal **advertising request.** A typical example of the form used for such a request is shown in Form 13-3. In a smaller store, the process is somewhat less formal.

The objective in selecting goods or services to be advertised is to promote the best-selling items in the store or department, not slow movers that will reflect poorly on the fashion image of the store. These can be evaluated separately, and, after being marked down as needed, can be considered for inclusion in storewide ads for a sale or clearance event.

Determining Media and Scheduling Advertising

Although the newspaper is still the favorite media selection of many fashion advertisers in large, medium, and small stores alike, it is important for buyers and advertising managers to research the available media on a continuing basis. There might be significant advertising advantages, for example, in being the first store in an area to sponsor a cable television fashion show, a promotion, or a particular item for sale.

Although the scheduling of ads is tentatively planned when the storewide advertising plan is prepared, this timing is seldom so firmly set that it cannot be changed. Ads must be scheduled for times when the advertised merchandise is available in large enough quantities to meet the customer demand and available in the right store locations.

Ads should also be scheduled to coincide with local or regional events as well as national holidays. Any advertising may help to increase the sale of the advertised fashions or services. Assume that a special newspaper and radio promotion for better dresses has been tentatively planned for March 25, and that you, as the better dress buyer, have recently learned that a big country club dance has been scheduled for the same day. Because your promotion will be too late to gain any business from the people who will be attending the dance, you will probably want to arrange for early delivery of the dresses and to reschedule your ad for March 18, at the latest.

Preparing, Producing, and Placing the Ad

Whether you, as the buyer, prepare the actual ad, as you might do in a small,

Elston's

ADVERTISED MERCHANDISE INFORMATION

Advertising information and the merchandise to be illustrated must be in the Advertising Department two weeks prior to the week in which the ad runs in the newspaper.

Department No.	74
Date Ad Runs:	June 1, 198–
Paper(s):	Tribune
Space:	7-col. full

Item	Regular Price	Sale Price
Cotton canvas tote bags Matching webbing belts	Bags $25-8 Belts $26	No

List features in order of importance

1. Spacious, weightless, cotton canvas totes for town or travel

2. Five featured styles, wide assortment of colors, darks, neutrals, high shades

3. Webbing trim in contrasting colors, belts in cotton webbing matching bag trim

Sizes Roll: 17×10, #27, Kangaroo pocket, 17×12-1/2, #27; Shoulder: 11-1/2 × 10-1/2, #26; Ring: 11-1/2 × 10, #25; Maxi: 16-1/2 × 13, #28

Colors Roll: red, navy, black, natural; Shoulder: natural, tan, navy, red; Kangaroo and Ring: natural, black, navy, red, kelly green, pink, tan; Maxi: red, navy, black, natural, tan

Art Instructions Sketch woman's torso showing belt, bags, cascading down length of page

At What Stores At all stores

Submitted by Dorothy Smith, buyer

Date Received in Advertising Department May 15, 198–

Does manufacturer share cost of ad? Yes   Is credit claim attached? Yes

Reason for Advertising:

- ☒ New Line
- ☒ Fashion News
- ☐ Sale
- ☐ Special Purchase
- ☐ Staple Stock
- ☐ Clearance

Quantity on Hand Date Ad Runs	Date Merchandise will be in Stock	Total Retail value of Merchandise	Use Trade Mark or Label	Is Manufacturer Paying for Ad?	Extra Delivery Charge?	Telephone Orders?	Mail Orders?	Mail Order Coupon?
250 pcs	5/26 complete	$3,750	Yes ☐ No ☒	Yes ☒ No ☐ 20 % of Payment	Yes ☐ No ☒ Amount? ___	Yes ☒ No ☐	Yes ☒ No ☐	Yes ☐ No ☒

Form 13-3. An advertising request.

owner-operated store, or have it prepared, which is by far the most common practice, someone must write the ad copy and prepare or select the illustrations. If the ad is for a broadcast medium, a script must be prepared, and, if there is video action, a "storyboard" must be created to describe this action in careful detail.

Frequently, the buyer serves as the product authority for the advertising copywriters who prepare the actual ad. Copywriters are constantly asking buyers to include more information in their advertising requests. Buyers, pressed by other duties, often urge the copywriters to make do with what they have. To write attention-getting copy, the copywriter must have, at the very least, a brief description of the item, together with a few words that describe its importance and why the customer will want to buy it.

For instance, a buyer may write: "Sleeveless, rayon crepe dress with surplice top. White, polyester linen jacket. Dress in red, blue, or beige print. Sizes 6 to 14. $100." The copywriter then translates this into: "Our jacket dress doesn't keep 9 to 5 hours . . . here are two pieces that will dance you right out of the office and into the evening ahead." The fashion artist who sketches the garment may choose to show the wearer obviously ready for an evening out, with the costume as fresh and elegant as when she arrived at the office in the morning.

Whether artwork or photography is used to illustrate fashions is usually a decision arrived at by the sales promotion director with the approval of the merchandise managers and, in some cases, top management. Many times the change from one form of illustration to another is made as much from a desire for "something different" as from any particular analysis. Manufacturers sometimes provide glossy photographs or sketches of their garments, along with suggested copy layouts, to assist in ad preparation. The decision to use a specific aid from the manufacturer is made by the advertising department. These advertising aids are almost never used by major retailers, however. They prefer that only their own particular style and quality of artwork and copy appear in newspapers.

Placing ads in the chosen local media is a routine trafficking task of the advertising department. It does not involve the buyer except in small firms where the buyer also performs other functions.

Evaluating the Results of the Ad

In addition to tracking the actual results of the ad, the buyer may have some responsibilities to coordinate other sales promotion activities on the day that the ad breaks.

Some stores post copies of each day's ads on walls in or near elevators, escalators, restrooms, and other areas of heavy customer traffic for additional exposure. Each department usually exhibits its current ads on its own selling floor where customers may see them. The buyers are responsible for making sure that their salespeople know what is advertised, where it is stocked, and what the selling points are, so that they can talk intelligently to customers about the merchandise.

In stores that do a considerable amount of telephone-order business, each day's ads are also posted in the order board area to aid the telephone operators. Today, many larger urban stores operate their telephone-order boards 24 hours a day, 7 days a week, for customers' convenience. To increase efficiency, some order boards are now answered automatically using a

Form 13-4. An instruction tag. The buyer provides sample merchandise to fashion illustrators in the advertising department. This tag, attached to the sample, shows how the garment or accessory can be shown to the best advantage.

prerecorded message. Customers are asked to give their orders in enough detail that they can accurately be recorded by a message-taking device.

In actually tracking the results of the ad, the buyer generally keeps careful records. In large stores a formal report may be required for management. Figure 15-4 is an example of a buyer's report to management on the results of a particular ad. These results are measured in terms of net dollar and unit sales. Buyers are expected to report, usually on a printed form, such points as the number of advertised items in stock before and three days after the ad ran, the number sold, total dollar sales of the department for the three-day period

following the ad, weather conditions, special display efforts, and any other pertinent data that would help evaluate the ad's pulling power.

Both buyers and advertising executives learn from such reports which items and approaches produce the most sales among the customers of the store and department concerned. Thus a sound basis for future planning is laid.

The Varying Responsibilities of the Buyer

Each of the seven basic advertising tasks that have been discussed in the previous section must be completed for advertising to become a reality.

In very small stores, the owner-manager, who is also the buyer, may be responsible for completing every task, and in medium to large stores, the buyer may serve as a merchandise expert whose information helps in the completion of the advertising tasks.

In this section we will take a brief look at the ways in which the sales promotion division and the advertising department in larger stores are organized. Then we will investigate the use of outside agencies and subscription services for advertising. And we will discuss briefly the buyer's responsibilities in stores in which there is no advertising department.

At the conclusion of the chapter, we will examine the ways in which buyers can have an impact on advertising even when they are considered to be acting only in an advisory capacity.

The Buyer and the Sales Promotion Division

Traditionally, in chain stores as well as in large and medium-size department and specialty stores, there is a sales promotion division which is responsible for promoting sales through advertising, display, and publicity. In some stores, personal salesmanship is also considered part of this function. In small stores where there is a relatively modest amount of promotional activity, there is usually a sales promotion manager who is directly involved in managing all of these activities. Where the volume of promotional activity is too large for such an arrangement, an advertising manager and a display manager usually function under the direction of the sales promotion director. The director may personally handle publicity and its close relative, public relations. Very large stores have a publicity manager as well, who supervises special events, the activities of consumer boards, and similar functions. In this case, the sales promotion director, often a vice president, is free for policy-making and for long-range planning.

The chief executive of the sales promotion division is usually responsible for preparing storewide sales promotion plans and budgets in conference with the advertising manager, the display manager, the publicity or special-events manager, the merchandise managers, and, if there is one, the fashion coordinator. Such plans and budgets are based on storewide sales goals, which have been developed from six-month dollar merchandise plans (as explained in Chapter 5).

STOREWIDE PROMOTION PLANS. These storewide sales promotion plans indicate, by specific type of activity such as advertising, display, and special events, the extent to which the store intends to employ each in its effort to produce the total storewide sales planned for the upcoming season. Included in the master sales promotion plan are such regularly scheduled events as Anniversay Sales, White Sales,

and Back-to-School promotions. Also included are other important and timely storewide, divisional, or departmental promotions for Easter, Father's Day, Mother's Day, and similar holidays. Each department of the sales promotion division—advertising, display, and special events—then prepares its own seasonal plan and budget based on the amount of money allocated to it in the storewide promotional budget. This department plan designates in general terms how that money shall be used to implement the master plan.

THE PROMOTION BUDGET. The percentage of planned dollar sales allocated to sales promotion varies from store to store. It depends on the type of store and the policy of the store with respect to the nature and extent of promotional activities it chooses to employ. The percentage of departmental planned dollar sales allocated to sales promotion expense also varies from department to department. This depends mainly on the merchandise involved and sometimes on the extent of local competition as well. Sales promotion budgets for fashion departments are usually higher than those for departments selling semistaple or staple goods. Typically 3–10 percent of sales is budgeted for advertising fashion goods.

By far the largest share of the sales promotion division's budget each season is allocated to advertising, and the major share of the advertising budget is usually allocated to newspaper space.

The Buyer and the Advertising Department

Most chain stores and large department and specialty stores have an "in-house" advertising department. This department is supervised by the promotion manager with the aid of the copy chief and the art director. The benefits of having an in-house advertising department are many, one of the most important being the ability to act quickly on changes in fashion. In-house copywriters and artists also develop a familiarity with the fashion image and the store's target customer.

Because the vast majority of buyers will be working with an advertising department, specific suggestions for dealing successfully with this department so as to have an impact on advertising are given in a later section of this chapter.

The Buyer and Outside Advertising Agencies

Because it is very costly for a store to operate an advertising department, some smaller stores rely on the services of outside advertising agencies. This is particularly true for specialized advertising needs such as the preparation of a direct-mail catalog or a radio or television ad.

Special services are also available for specialty stores such as jewelry stores. Several services produce monthly advertising proofs on a made-to-order basis for "subscribers." The store owner selects illustrations and copy blocks for current merchandise and adds the store's **logo-type.** The "logo," as it is called, is the distinctive type or symbol used to identify the organization.

The Buyer Without an Advertising Department

In the very small store with no staff advertising expert or agency, the owner-manager is in many cases also the advertising specialist. This person often finds that many aids in constructing ads are available free or at little cost. To induce small businesses to buy advertising space, some newspapers may offer technical assistance in preparing an ad. Part of the work on a market trip involves canvassing the possibilities for obtaining suitable advertising material, so that when buyers or owners return to the store, they know not only what merchandise to advertise but also how best to present it in an advertisement.

Smaller stores often use media that larger ones may ignore. The cost of a newspaper ad looms large in the budget of a tiny establishment, so its proprietor often uses less costly media such as direct mail. Considerable use is also made of such resource-provided aids as low-cost statement enclosures, display cards, package enclosures, and the "as advertised in" posters supplied by consumer magazines.

Planning and reporting are less formal in relatively small stores where there is no advertising specialist to concentrate on promotions. Even in the smallest shop, however, good management demands at least a rough guide indicating what is to be spent, in which media, for what merchandise, and with what expectations. A record of ad results also needs to be kept so that past experience can guide future decisions. Often all that is needed is a scrapbook of ads run, with marginal notes on costs and results.

Making an Impact on Advertising

Many beginning buyers feel that their impact on advertising will, at best, be minimal. The advertising department in a large store can provide a valuable service for each department and each buyer. The new buyer should learn as quickly as possible how to work within the existing system. Buyers are supplied with a great deal of information with which they can work, including a calendar of tentative advertising plans for the month, details of last year's ads for the month such as tear sheets of the ads, information about the money that was spent last year, and sales figures on the advertised items. It is the buyers themselves, however, who supply the information and make the basic decisions that initiate the upcoming advertising.

The buyer who is able to intelligently use the information that is supplied will, without a doubt, make better decisions about specific products to advertise, the product features and benefits to stress, the media to select, and the best timing for the ad. The buyers who receive the most benefit from the advertising department are those who meet their deadlines when asked to supply copy sheets, fill out the sheets clearly and carefully, describe the merchandise accurately, include the price of the product and indicate the percentage of reduction if the item is on sale, and clearly explain what they want in the specific ad in question.

The buyer is also responsible for knowing the status of all items that have been purchased for specific advertising. When an ad is scheduled, the buyer should let the sales associates in the area know about the ad so that they are prepared to help the customers find the advertised items and to explain the product features and benefits.

Buyers should develop an understanding of which items are best advertised in each type of media by observing the success of their own ads, researching past experience, and observing the practice of other stores, including local competitors, stores in nearby areas, and, to the extent they can learn from travel and from reading out-of-town newspapers, retailers across the nation.

Reference

1 "Eye-Catching Graphics and Visuals Create Upscale Catalogs with Dreams for Sale," *Stores,* November 1984, p. 57.

Buying Vocabulary

Define or briefly explain the following terms:

Advertising plan	Logotype
Advertising request	Merchandise advertisement
AIDA concept	Outdoor advertising
Broadcast media	Prestige advertisement
Cooperative advertising	Print media
Direct mail	Promotional advertisement
Gross rating points (GRP)	Tear sheet
Institutional advertisement	Transit advertising

Buying Review

1. List seven objectives of retail advertising.
2. Name the two basic types of ads used by retail stores. Describe how they differ and explain why each is used.
3. Explain the AIDA concept in advertising. Give an example of a print media ad that uses this concept to satisfy the requirements for a successful ad.
4. Why do retailers use local newspapers extensively for their advertising?
5. Explain how ads in a national fashion magazine can enhance your store image. How would you go about selecting merchandise for such an ad?
6. Why is direct-mail advertising effective for promoting fashion goods? What is called the "most startling development" in direct-mail advertising? What are two other examples of direct-mail advertising?
7. What traditional forms of broadcast media have been used for many years to advertise fashion merchandise? What innovations have widened the advertising possibilities in this area?
8. Explain the advantages and disadvantages of cooperative advertising for the fashion retailer.
9. What are the seven basic tasks that must be accomplished before any fashion advertising can appear in the media?
10. Briefly explain how a buyer can get the best results from an advertising department in a large store.

Buying Case

You are the buyer in the sportswear department of a large department store in Albuquerque, New Mexico. Today is June 1, and you have a full-page newspaper ad scheduled for June 10 featuring a special purchase of some very popular sportswear items that are sure to "blow right out of the store" at the price you are able to offer them for. The ad is to run in the paper that is read most frequently by fashion-conscious potential customers.

Unfortunately, you have a big problem. At this time it looks as if there is about a 40 percent chance that you will not have the merchandise in stock by the time the ad runs. This is one of the few full-page ads your department will run this season, and you have to make some quick decisions as to what you will do. The advertising department has the time and funds available to prepare only one ad for your department, so you cannot have two ads prepared and decide at the last minute which one to run. They need your advertising request form by 4:00 this afternoon.

It appears that you have several choices: (1) You can choose to go ahead with the ad. Then you can put constant pressure on the vendor, insisting that the merchandise be shipped on time. This may even require a trip to the market in Dallas for an emergency meeting, at which time you could possibly select substitute merchandise that is acceptable. With this solution you probably will not know for sure that the goods are available until the last moment. And there is still a chance that they will not arrive in time. (2) You can abandon the idea of advertising your special purchase because you feel that the risk is too great. Instead, you can have a special sale on existing merchandise in your department. Although you have planned markdowns, you would not normally have taken them all at this time. However, there is a good chance that you will be able to turn over a large portion of your inventory with a full-page "special sale" ad. (3) You can ask the advertising department to prepare a more general ad for your department with a prestige or institutional message. The ad could then mention both your special purchase items and your "special sale." Then you can mark down some of the merchandise in stock and continue to put pressure on the vendor. This middle-of-the-road decision would allow you to hold all of your options open. If the "special purchase" goods do not arrive, you may still be able to run the sale on your current stock and supply customers with rain checks.

Make a decision on the type of ad you will run. You can select one of the three choices presented here or invent your own. Then defend your decision. Describe the advantages and disadvantages of your course of action. If you choose to go ahead with the ad for your special purchase items, explain what you will do if they do not arrive.

Chapter 14

Visual Merchandising

A century ago, merchandise display was the most important, and usually the only way to show customers the goods a store carried. Whether the store was in a major city presenting "the latest from Paris" or a small dry goods store showing a new shipment of bright calico bolts of cloth, display played a major role in selling the stock.

Then advertising took over, bringing the merchandise message out of the store and into the streets. The message went first by remote signing (the sides of barns that later yielded to billboards) and by print through catalogs and newspapers. Later, radio and television became mixed with print advertising as the retailers sought to reach everyone with their messages.

Fifty years ago, display meant dramatic windows, neat housekeeping, and maintenance of inventories. Stores were oper-ating with two major weapons—mass advertising, and qualified, informed sales-people who cared—while display was usually used to announce the arrival of a new season. Daffodils were used for spring, pumpkins for fall, tinsel on trees for the Christmas spirit.

Then came the revolution—the store as theater became the effect that both retail-ers and customers wanted. Seasonal dis-plays gave way to frequently scheduled promotional happenings, such as import fairs, back-to-school promotions com-plete with audio-visual presentations, per-sonalities appearing to sell. Retailing through display became show business! This new exciting effort is called **visual merchandising.** It can be defined as the presentation of merchandise and services to their best selling advantage for maxi-mum customer acceptance. Visual mer-chandising has absorbed and dramatically expanded the interior and window display functions traditionally found in retail stores.

In this chapter we will look first at the role that visual merchandising plays in fashion retailing today. Then we will note some of the important elements of store planning. In the next section of the chapter, we will review some of the basics of fashion display that are still an important part of visual merchandising. Finally, we will examine the ways in which you, as a fashion buyer, can both benefit from, and have an influence on, visual merchandising.

Visual Merchandising and Fashion Retailing

The words "visual merchandising" have become familiar in fashion retailing in the past few years. In fact, the term has often been used interchangeably with the word "display." But times have changed, and so has the meaning of visual merchandising; it is no longer just another expression for display. Today it is a complex combination of store layout, store design, fixturing, construction, mannequin selection, and display. Until recently, store planning and display were the responsibilities of

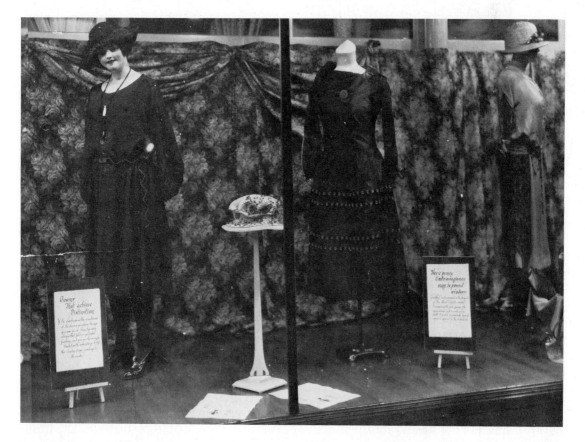

This window display from the 1920s shows a straightforward presentation of merchandise typical of that time.

two very separate groups of people. The display (or visual merchandising) staff handled the planning and execution of both window and interior displays, including the selection and upkeep of mannequins. Store layout, store design, fixturing, and construction were usually handled by store planners—outside architects who specialize in retailing—hired by store management to plan the store before it opened for business. For the most part, these areas were considered finished when the store opened its doors for business. In most stores, the store planning remained as it was for an extended period of time. And when it was changed, store management frequently worked directly with outside specialists, often to the exclusion of the display staff.

Today, these store planning areas, together with display, are an integral part of the visual merchandising. With the new concept of visual merchandising, the store is viewed almost as if it were a theater, and there is continual effort to establish and maintain an image that will set the store apart from other stores with similar merchandise and services. Although the actual store planning work is often done by outside consultants, it is done under the direction of the visual merchandising manager. By consolidating the control for store planning and display, stores are more easily able to plan and carry out store image campaigns.

Some authorities have indicated that approximately 80 percent of the merchandise in any set of directly competing stores is virtually identical. And to make matters worse, the stores are often clustered in malls where the customer's first contact depends largely on the availability of a parking space. This means that it is critically important for a store to create the type of atmosphere and merchandise presentations that will trigger action on the part of customers while they are shopping in the store.

Essentials of Store Planning

Store planning aspects of visual merchandising encompass all areas of the store—nonselling as well as sales-related areas. In this section we will look briefly at two major store planning functions: store layout and store design (which includes both fixturing and lighting).

Store Layout

The **layout** of a store is the plan that allocates a specific location and amount of space to each of the merchandise departments as well as each of the nonselling areas. The layout should support the merchandising plans that have been developed by the store's buyers and approved by management. If the better separates department is expected to increase dramatically in volume and the ladies' coat department is expected to decrease dramatically in sales volume, then logically, better separates is a candidate for increased selling space and ladies' coats is a candidate for decreased space.

In deciding on location and size for both selling and nonselling areas, the store image, customer preferences, layouts of competing stores, and stock capacity are some of the important factors that should be taken into consideration.

In the recent major renovation of the anchor store in a New England mall, the retailer reorganized its store layout to bring the store into line with current customer preferences. This called for moving menswear from the first floor to the second so that it would conform to the traffic predominance in the rest of the mall. It also called for dividing women's sportswear into two types and price structures, the expansion of junior misses, the creation of a petites department, and the elimination of the piece goods and needlework department.

Location and size can be critical factors in the success of a given department because, as you learned in Chapter 8, departmental success is evaluated on the basis of sales per square foot of selling space. (This measure is determined by dividing the department's total net sales for the year by the number of square feet of selling space.) The goal of each department is to have an increase in the number of sales per square foot over the preceding year. The layout changes planned by the store mentioned above were made with the end objective of increased sales per square foot of selling space. And all of the renovation costs were calculated in such a way that they could be allocated per square foot of selling space.

Store Design

The **store design** is the decorative style used by the store to convey the image that it wants to project to the customer. Another word frequently used for this decorative style is **decor**. Store design includes the selection of such nonselling furnishings as carpeting, wall coverings, murals, dividers, pictures, and planters. It also includes the choice of selling fixtures such as shelves, display racks, counters, and mannequins. Another important consideration is lighting. All of these factors work together with store layout and display to help create the desired fashion image.

A spacious interior with a high, vaulted ceiling and polished hardwood floors, streamlined display fixtures, and freestanding displays create an image of elegance for the high-fashion merchandise in this specialty store.

Here is an example of how a store upgraded its fashion image with the aid of an outside specialist. The strategy is one that departs somewhat from the trend of increasing current stock and minimizing reserve stock. The huge-capacity, densely positioned floor fixtures that were found in this store have been replaced with a fixture that gives more than twice as much exposed wall footage. Face-out fixtures that hold fewer garments but are tastefully designed and photomuraled have also been added. The effect is definitely away from the store's former appearance of merchandise that is packed in and toward a chic fashion look. The store design has not only yielded improvements in sales per square foot, it has also resulted in increased stockturn and has encouraged customers to make larger average purchases than they did in the past.

Many stores are launching campaigns to attract more fashion-oriented customers. These campaigns, strongly based on visual merchandising, call for careful coordination of newspaper advertising and direct mail with in-store presentations. Getting and keeping the attention of fashion-conscious customers requires distinctive display fixtures. For example, one store catering to businesswomen had racks for hosiery specially designed to resemble office file cabinets. Some retailers have also invested in customized mannequins.

The effective use of lighting in store design is much in evidence in boutiques throughout the country. Special lighting systems feature low-voltage pin spots that accentuate single items for a dramatic effect.

Although there is an atmosphere of creative exploration in store design, a few basic guidelines still apply. The design should provide cost-effective fixtures and equipment that are easy to care for and flexible enough to allow for further change. The design should carry out the image campaign defined by the store and at the same time contribute to customer convenience and ease of shopping. In addition, the design must not hinder the important job of store security.

Essentials of Store Display

The other, more traditional, side of visual merchandising is **display.** It can be defined as the visual presentation of merchandise. In many cases there is a fine line of distinction between store planning and store display. The fixtures and lighting for a display may be attributed to store planning, while the presence of merchandise for that fixture may be attributed to store display. It is very logical, therefore, that they both be considered integral parts of visual merchandising.

The purpose of fashion display is to highlight a trend, tell a fashion story, or demonstrate just how apparel fashions should be accessorized and worn.

Retailers use display in two forms: window display and interior display. Window displays are created to catch the eye of people passing on the street and to persuade them to enter the store. Interior display is used to encourage impulse buying, to create customer interest at point of sale, to carry out a promotional theme, as well as to enhance the store's decor.

Whereas a newspaper fashion ad is seen at home, on a bus, or in the office, a fashion display is seen by the customer when he or she is inside or just outside the store. By the time people see a display they have already made the preliminary moves of leaving their homes and places of business and of approaching the store. They are already on the retail scene, whether idly strolling by or on an errand. Display, if it is effective, can reap dividends from this proximity by sparking a buying impulse that leads to a sale.

Window Display

To a fashion retailer, a store window is useful for selling merchandise, promoting an idea, or publicizing the store as a place to patronize. Its primary function, in one of retailing's puns, is "to make the passer buy." For this purpose it must be arresting and as dramatic as it can afford to be in the context of the store personality and the merchandise involved. Older stores were constructed with many display windows at street level. Newer, free-standing stores may have only a few or no windows at all. Many stores in modern regional shopping malls have no separate display windows; instead, customers are presented with a sweeping view of an entire selling floor as they approach a store's entrance.

Window displays are designed to convey one of several different kinds of messages to the customer. Window displays featuring fashion merchandise may be designed to show seasonal trends in fashion colors or looks, or to show how to wear specific fashion merchandise to achieve a particular "look," or simply to show what the store has available at various price lines.

FASHION MESSAGES. Windows are an excellent medium for conveying a fashion message. They may be used to dramatize a new color, for example, by showing garments and accessories in a particular springtime yellow, an autumn brown, or a bold print in which a certain color predominates. They can dramatize a new look, skirt length, or season of the year. All of this must be determined ahead of time by the buyer during market visits and planned for when purchases are made.

Because the window should arouse interest and stimulate customers to refresh their wardrobes, the actual styles selected for display are usually more extreme and in earlier stages of their fashion cycle than much of the assortment inside the store. If the window merchandise is not too different from what already hangs in the customer's closets, it cannot be stimulating. Arresting qualities are essential.

A familiar summary of this philosophy is "Show royal blue; sell navy." The royal blue catches the customer's eye, but once inside the store, they buy their familiar, wearable navy. If navy alone had been in the window, their eyes might have glanced off it without receiving the message that it was time to buy some new spring clothes.

HOW-TO-WEAR-IT WINDOWS. Among the most rewarding types of window display are those illustrating how to wear new fashion merchandise. While a few people have a fashion sense that enables them to innovate and to quickly grasp the right way to put together a look, by far the great majority do not. The effective window display answers their unspoken questions and shows them clearly what to do by presenting several versions of a new look. By showing a mannequin dressed in all the elements of that look, and in the surroundings for which the new fashion is intended, a window can give customers an overall picture of the look. It allows customers to judge whether or not they want to wear the new look and, if they do, it gives them confidence that they can achieve it.

At no time do windows do a better job of conveying fashion news than when new color combinations or pattern combinations are introduced. Many of the customers' prejudices against certain colors or patterns can be swept away in an instant when these colors and patterns are displayed in ways that they can relate to their own lifestyle and environment.

Over the past decades, a remarkable number of innovations in dress have swept across the fashion scene. To some extent, their acceptance by consumers of all ages and economic and social levels has been the result of effective displays presented in how-to-wear-it windows.

DIRECT-SELL WINDOWS. Window displays that aggressively attempt to make sales also have an important function in promoting fashion merchandise. Not all customers are concerned with newness and glamour; most are concerned with price as well, particularly in times of economic stress. Thus many customers are drawn by the windows of less expensive stores that feature poster-size signs announcing, for example, that dresses are "all reduced to $29" or that the store is having a "Special! Matching knit hats and gloves . . . $10." Also for the price-conscious customer are the windows that present a veritable cornucopia of items—many kinds and many classifications, arranged with only the thought in mind of showing as much as possible in a small space. Display people who do windows for neighborhood shops of modest size are experts at this; so are the display staffs of shoe, hosiery, and general merchandise chains.

That windows of this type rarely convey fashion excitement does not in any way diminish their importance in the promotion of fashion merchandise. Vast quantities of apparel and accessories are sold as a result of such windows. These windows are the workhorses of fashion window display. The merchandise that they promote, even though it may be at or past the peak of its cycle, constitutes a substantial share of the total volume of fashion goods sold at retail.

PRINCIPLES OF GOOD WINDOW DISPLAY. A window display is a work of art, created with merchandise and fixtures instead of paint, ink, or clay. This is why window displays are usually the work of professionals who know the basic elements of design and understand how to use those elements to achieve specific artistic effects. However, there are also some principles completely divorced from artistic ones to which window displays, if they are to be effective, must adhere.

First, a window display should feature merchandise that is both timely and in current demand. Fashion merchants pick the newest and most dramatic items and looks in their fashion assortments to feature in their window displays. For the merchant selling higher-priced goods, these are the eye-catchers—the styles people have already seen in the fashion news but have not yet had a chance to examine in a store's assortment. For the more moderate-priced merchant, these would be the styles that have gained fairly wide acceptance but are still showing strong popularity.

Next, both the number of items shown and the way they are presented should reflect the fashion image of the store. Stores with higher-priced lines will often put only a single coordinated look or even a single item in a window. That store will use a minimum of props, but both props and background decoration will carry out the "exclusivity" or "prestige" theme. A store with moderate-priced lines, however, will put a number of items in each window to show that they carry a wide assortment of currently popular styles.

Perhaps most important, the items chosen for window displays should be backed by adequate stock on the selling floor. If customers are drawn into a store by an item in a window display, they expect to find in the store's stock a good selection of that item. In higher-priced fashion stores, the assortment on the selling floor does not have to contain a large number of the exact item that is in the window display, but it should contain a reasonable number of items that are similar in their styling and fashion appeal. In more moderate-priced stores, the emphasis should be on having the featured item in a wide variety of styles, sizes, and colors.

Occasionally buyers purchase higher-priced articles just to use for window displays to attract the upscale customer.

Interior Display

Once customers have entered a store, the chances of converting their browsing activities into buying impulses can be increased by an effective combination of store layout, store design, and interior displays. These displays may be point-of-sale efforts at the actual spot where the goods are sold, or they may be displays in such places as overhead ledges, corners, platforms, or entrances to departments. Often they repeat a theme expressed in windows, direct mail, and newspaper or magazine advertisements. In this way they once again drive home the store's fashion message, whether it be the approach of a new season or the opportunity to buy a bargain. In large stores, such displays are again the work of professionals on the visual merchandising staff.

Within a department, however, displays of fashion merchandise are often the responsibility of buyers, their assistants, or the salespeople. Ingenuity, knowledge of the merchandise, and proximity to the point of sale make up for the absence of the professional's touch. In the last section of this chapter we will look at the ways in which buyers can have an effect on visual merchandising.

There are several basic types of interior displays. These include displays that present a coordinated look, displays that suggest merchandise for a specific end use, displays that show a single item or an assortment of items, and displays arranged for easy selection.

VIGNETTES. A product or group of products shown in use in a special small space is a **vignette.** A typical vignette might display a mannequin in a nightgown and matching peignoir, wearing slippers of appropriate style and color and seated on a boudoir chair to complete the suggestion of a woman preparing for bed. The impact of such a display at the entrance to an intimate apparel department is often enough to draw passing customers to its counters or racks.

A vignette shows how the merchandise looks in use.

ITEM DISPLAYS. A single garment or accessory may be featured in an **item display.** The display may be created by putting one piece on a form. Or, several versions of a style—a shoulder bag in several sizes, for instance, or a style of sweater in several colors—may be shown on a display fixture.

ASSORTMENT DISPLAYS. A display that shows, identifies, and prices one of each of the styles currently in a section of stock is an **assortment display.** Such a display is generally used for basic items and permits the customer to make at least a tentative selection while waiting to be served. A classic example is the usual wall display of white shirts behind a men's furnishings counter. The windows of shoe chains follow the same pattern, and their interior displays of slippers, boots, or shoes are also of this type. Scarf departments use assortment display when they fan out their folded stock of each price and type, permitting customers to see the entire color range at a glance.

SELF-SELECTION RACKS. Although they are not usually thought of as such, self-selection racks are definitely a type of departmental display. These should have clearly marked signs and be arranged by size, color, style, or price points. Similarly, the counters and racks that face the aisle can be considered the "windows to the department." In order to emphasize the breadth of the color assortment, several garments, each in a different color, may be displayed on a rack or t-stand. To feature mix-match possibilities, as in sportswear separates, all items of a particular style, pattern, or color may be grouped in one area. The first arrangement says, "Choose from our rainbow assortment." The second says, "See how many components we offer in each color." If the rack is merely a hodgepodge, the implication is that the

The Sesame Street characters in this J.C. Penney's children's department enliven the self-selection display.

assortment is broken or unplanned, as on a clearance rack. In most stores the buyer, within the framework of store policy, decides which message should be conveyed in departmental displays and instructs stock and sales personnel accordingly. It may also be the buyer's responsibility to see that the "windows to the department" are changed frequently to keep customers interested in the department's fashion message.

OTHER TYPES OF DISPLAYS. Interior display makes use of many additional small but effective aids: a counter card, describing the qualities of the goods; a sign atop a rack of clothes, stressing a major selling point; a garment laid open across a

Elston's SIGN REQUEST

DEPT. NO.
& SIGNATURE _____

DATE NEEDED _May 1, 1981_

SIZES	5½ x 7	(7 x 11)	11 x 14	POSTERS	TOTAL 22

DISTRIBUTION:
INDICATE BRANCH,
NUMBER FOR EACH.

MMJ	DMJ .	NMJ	HMJ	FMJ	PMJ	WMJ
4	2	2	2	2	2	2

OMJ	KMJ	AMJ		
2	2	2		

Perfect Gift for Mother
LEAD IN

Easy Care — No Iron Robes
KEY COPY

SELLING POINTS

- *Colorful Prints*
- *Feminine Styling*
- *Sizes 8 – 16*
- _____

$ ___ _18 99_ ___
PRICE

SELLING POINTS
4 POINTS ON 11 x 14 ONLY

HAND LETTERING

EXAMPLE

SPECIAL
SPARKLING GLASSWARE
- hand-blown crystal
- clean lined **$ 00**
- exquisitely cut

APPROVED _____

ALLOW 7 WORKING DAYS, (EXCLUSIVE OF SATURDAY
AND SUNDAY) FOR COMPLETION OF SIGN REQUESTS.
ALLOW EXTRA 3 DAYS FOR HAND LETTERING AND/OR
DISTRIBUTION. WRITE CLEARLY, CHECK SPELLING AND
LIMIT COPY. ALLOW 10 DAYS FOR POSTERS.

Form 14-1. A sign request. The copy on signs displayed in windows and interiors
provides important product information to customers.

lighted, glass-topped counter, emphasizing its sheerness and perfect weave; a sample article attached to a rack of packaged articles, inviting the customer's examination. Attractive displays inside the store as well as large, dramatic windows are all part of the effort to promote the fashion image of the store.

Vendor Aids

Producers of fashion merchandise, from coats to cosmetics, are keenly aware of the selling power of good retail display. Eager to help stores harness this effective tool in behalf of their merchandise, many vendors in the fashion business develop dealer aids which they supply free or at modest cost to stores.

COUNTER AND WINDOW CARDS. Intended to be used in windows, on counters, or with interior displays of the vendor's merchandise, counter and window cards usually name the brand and describe the selling points of the item or brand. Cards of the "as advertised in" variety bear a mounted reprint of the producer's advertisement in the publication concerned. Smaller retailers are generally likely to use these to supplement their display facilities. Larger stores are likely to have a policy against the use of such cards, preferring that all announcements be made in the store's own style. These store-sponsored signs sometimes include posters on which the store's catalog art or other direct-mail advertising is enlarged and reproduced.

FORMS AND FIXTURES. To facilitate the display of specific merchandise, resources sometimes offer stores free or inexpensive forms and **fixtures** on which to display their merchandise. This equipment often bears the brand name of the fashion producer who supplies it. A familiar example is the type of self-selection racks that is provided for packaged bras, gloves, or pantyhose.

The development of self-selection fixtures is a process requiring a large investment in research and design that only a large store is willing or able to make. Smaller stores that do not have capital available for such an investment may willingly use forms and fixtures supplied by vendors who do.

The fixtures developed by vendors generally prove to be very effective in displaying the merchandise, highlighting its sales appeal, and leaving ample space for an orderly supply of stock on the selling floor.

The Buyer and Visual Merchandising

There is no single answer to the question "What is the buyer's responsibility in visual merchandising?" The role of the buyer with respect to visual merchandising varies widely from store to store.

In a Small Store

In a small store, the owner-manager, who is also the buyer, may be the one person in charge of visual merchandising. But this does not minimize the importance of visual merchandising to the store. By rotating merchandise frequently and featuring newly arrived merchandise, the owner-manager can keep the stock looking fresh.

The owner of a small fashion shop in a town of only 6,000 people explained that window display is actually her only effective form of sales promotion. She personally plans and constructs all of the displays in her small window, and she changes the window at least once a week.

The store is located in the center of town and most of her customers must drive past the store daily. The clothes that she selects for the window sell so quickly that she is often forced to change the display after only a few days. Inside the shop, she uses the self-service racks as a form of interior display. Every two or three days she moves merchandise around and regroups it so that the shop will always have a fresh look, and so that customers will see merchandise that they may have missed in another location. When the owner of this small shop makes any store design or layout changes, she and her husband not only plan the visual changes, they actually do the physical work themselves.

In a larger store, the owner-manager may contract with an independent window trimmer who specializes in arranging displays for small fashion stores. Interior displays are usually done by the manager and supervised staff members. Store design and layout changes may be planned by the owner but executed by outside specialists.

In a Chain Store

Visual merchandising presentations for chain stores are designed in their company headquarters many months before they are executed by the individual stores. Store design and layout changes are tested in a limited number of prototype stores before they are made chainwide. Usually these changes are made by store planning specialists under the direction of company headquarters. Similarly, displays for chains are designed months ahead of time also. They are installed either by display specialists who cover certain regional areas, by the store managers, or by the visual merchandising staff within the individual store.

When both window and major interior displays are shipped from company headquarters and installed by the staff of the individual stores, they are very carefully planned, with complete instructions and accompanying sketches. Step-by-step directions specify the merchandise to use, the theme of the display, the background colors and materials to use, the props to select, and the lighting specifications. Usually any signs that are needed are enclosed with the display kit. Although this approach doesn't leave room for creativity at the individual store level, it does help to give the chain a uniform fashion image.

Fashion buyers in chain organizations usually purchase a single classification of merchandise, such as men's sweaters, handbags, or women's blouses. They are often responsible for working with the visual merchandising staff in selecting apparel and accessories to be featured in displays and deciding how to best coordinate fashion looks. Larger department stores and specialty chains employ the services of a fashion coordinator who assists the visual merchandising staff in highlighting current fashion trends and coordinating fashion looks. (In Chapter 15 there will be more coverage of fashion coordination.)

In Department Stores

Department stores generally plan their visual merchandising campaigns as they do their advertising—month by month for up to a year in advance. Store design and layout changes are usually handled directly by the visual merchandise manager, often with the aid of outside specialists.

Fashion windows in stores that have street-level display windows are planned many months in advance, usually when the storewide promotional plans are being drawn up. At that time visual merchandising executives and buyers work together to determine what looks, colors, and other fashion features they wish to promote during the coming season. The display department then draws up a seasonal calendar, based on the storewide promotional plan, indicating the dates on which specific themes and merchandise are to be featured and the number and location of windows assigned to carry selected messages. Departments compete for window space on the basis of how well their merchandise assortments convey the messages or themes the store has elected to promote during a given season.

Windows are rarely assigned to departments on a regular basis, although older stores with many display windows may assign certain banks of windows to certain store divisions on a fairly regular basis. For example, windows featuring ready-to-wear and accessories usually flank the main entrance to a store because of the general interest of customers in these types of merchandise. Household textiles and home furnishings, on the other hand, are often displayed in window areas where there is less traffic. During special sales events, such as White Sales, household textiles may be allotted windows in the areas of higher traffic as part of the store's promotional efforts.

As in the case of newspaper advertising, the store may require from the buyer a form stating what is to go into each window assigned to that department and what signs are to be used with the merchandise. If related items from other departments are used, the buyer or assistant may have the responsibility of selecting and signing for such items and seeing that they are eventually returned to the lending departments. Some stores have either visual merchandising or display coordinators who are responsible for securing merchandise to be used in displays. It may be the buyer's responsibility to work

with this coordinator in selecting appropriate fashion merchandise.

Windows, like ads, are not always used for direct selling. They may be used to set the mood of a season, as are some of the merchandise-free windows featuring animated scenes that large stores install for Christmas. Rather than suggesting specific purchases, these windows remind customers that it is a gift-giving season.

Interior displays in department stores are usually constructed by the professional visual merchandising staff. The sales staff in the department or the buyers may redress mannequins and make other minor adjustments to give an already installed display a fresh look. In many large department stores there may be a special training effort on the part of the visual merchandising staff. The mission is to teach the area managers and salespeople how to create departmental displays that deliver a unique message to customers.

Making an Impact on Visual Merchandising

As you have seen in the previous section of this chapter, the buyer's involvement with visual merchandise varies greatly with the size of the retail organization. In large chains and department stores, buyers sometimes feel that they have very little control over visual merchandising, and as a result, they are not anxious to become involved with it. This may not be the most advantageous approach to use, as a buyer in one large departmentalized specialty store learned. When one of the designers who had regularly been supplying the store with fashions visited the selling floor, he was very disappointed to see that his fashions were not being displayed in a location that suited the prestige of the designer label. As a result, this designer refused to do any further business with the

Focus

Frank Calise: Putting Bonwit Teller's Merchandise Center Stage

The catchphrase of recent years has been "creating theater in retailing." So what better background for a top visual merchandiser than to have been a set designer for the Broadway stage?

That's just where Frank Calise SVM got his beginnings—and where he was "discovered" back in the early 1960s by the display director of a New York City furniture chain, who tapped Calise for his staff. A new career was launched that would find Calise some 25 years later in the position of vice president of visual merchandising for swank Bonwit Teller, New York. The initials, "SVM," for Society of Visual Merchandising, are the professional equivalent of a PhD. Calise earned this designation after extensive training and experience.

Overseeing a staff of 36 creative people in Bonwit's store planning department, branches and sign shop, Calise places his emphasis on in-store visual merchandising. He depends on communication from other departments, saying, "I'm vitally involved. I know what's coming in and what the store is emphasizing. The customer must be aware of this totality of image."[1]

Among the fixtures Calise has designed to create that image are in-store signs held in elegant brass planters, custom-made mannequins finished to look like marble, and mirrored display cases that reflect pink marble floors. Every detail, from choice of color to finishing touches of fresh flowers, is carefully planned with the end goal of selling merchandise, and that ability is the key to success. Says Calise: "Visual merchandising has gained status in the eyes of management because we've matured, not necessarily because we're 'talented,' but because we know how to sell."[2]

Indeed, talented visual merchandisers like Calise have gained status in the eyes of all retailers: In 1985, Calise was named the National Retail Merchants Association Visual Merchandiser of the Year—an honor he compared to "winning an Oscar."[3] Will that success and recognition take time or attention away from the job? One would doubt it. Explains Calise: "Visual merchandisers better find time to see what's around them, so when they give a directive, it's right for the company and customers. It takes years to build a store image and two seconds to tear it down."[4]

1 Dorothy Kellett, "Like Winning an Oscar," *Stores*, June 1985, p. 85.
2 Ibid., p. 80.   3 Ibid., p. 76.   4 Ibid., p. 85.

store. If the buyer had been in close contact with visual merchandising when the store (or department) layout was planned, this problem might have been avoided.

Even though a buyer may not be personally involved with the actual construction of displays, development of the store layout, or selection of wall and floor coverings, it is the buyers who are collectively responsible for selecting the merchandise that is used as the basis of the store's fashion image. The buyer who receives the most benefit from visual merchandising is the one who quickly learns how to work within the store system and then makes a sincere effort to be as cooperative as possible. Buyers should develop a friendly relationship with display department personnel. Personal visits and enthusiastic presentations of exciting merchandise often result in added use of those goods in displays.

One of the major passwords for working successfully with visual merchandising is "communication." If you have a new and exciting fashion look, it must be communicated to the visual merchandising staff, the advertising staff, the salespeople, and eventually the customers. Visual merchandising specialists cannot be expected to keep tabs on fashion trends as closely as you must. It is your responsibility to make sure they do not make mistakes in coordinating the looks they are featuring. You should educate them as to the type of accessories, for example, to use with a new type of dress or coat.

Within your department, you may have

A buyer may suggest accessories that will give a fashion display a coordinated look.

to follow through on the work of the visual merchandising people. If goods are sold off of a display, make sure that it is put back together properly. If a display has been in the area for a few weeks, change the jewelry and accessories, even if the display is not scheduled to be completely redone.

Remember that the racks and counters that face the aisles in your department are your "windows to the department." If store policy allows it, you should constantly look for ways to improve customer appeal and implement those ideas in your department. Move merchandise around to give it a new look, reorganize it into logical and attractive groupings, and mark it down if it is not selling as it should.

References

There were no direct quotes in this chapter, but many of the concept and information came from the following resources:

Lewis A. Spalding, "Getting Visual," *Stores,* June 1984, pp. 22–28.

"Best of Class," *Stores,* December 1984, pp. 37–41.

Lewis A. Spalding, "Anatomy of a Revamp," *Stores,* December 1984, pp. 42–45.

Karen R. Gillespie, Joseph C. Hecht, and Carl F. Lebowitz, *Retail Business Management,* 3d ed., McGraw-Hill, New York, 1983, chap. 10, pp. 136–148; chap. 24, pp. 337–349.

"Display Matters: Mainstreet," *Stores,* December 1984, pp. 58–59.

The Buyer's Manual, NRMA, 1979, pp. 315–343.

Buying Vocabulary

Define or briefly explain the following items:

Assortment display	Layout
Decor	Store design
Display	Vignette
Fixtures	Visual merchandising
Item display	

Buying Review

1. Visual merchandising is no longer just another term for display. Instead, it is a complex combination of several different factors. Name these factors.

2. With the new concept of visual merchandising, the store is viewed almost as if it were a theater. Explain how this concept can be of benefit to the store.
3. What are the two major store planning functions? Describe each of these functions.
4. What is the purpose of fashion display?
5. What are the two forms of display used by retailers? Explain the purpose of each form.
6. Name and give examples of the different types of window displays that are used in fashion merchandising.
7. What are three principles to which window displays must adhere if they are to be effective?
8. Name and describe four major types of interior displays.
9. What are vendor aids? Give two examples of these aids.
10. As a buyer, you may not be personally involved with the actual construction of displays or development of store layout. With this fact in mind, describe how you can achieve the most from visual merchandising.

Buying Case

You are the buyer of the lingerie department in a medium-size department store. You are having lunch with several newly hired buyer trainees who are currently serving as salespeople to fulfill the requirements of their training program. One of the trainees says, "If I had an opportunity to redesign the store, I would cut down on the size of each department and put a nice big stockroom right outside each selling area. Then we could have a generous supply of back stock for each item at our fingertips. I'm sure we could increase sales this way because we would seldom be out of stock and we wouldn't have to walk half a mile to the stockroom."

Do you agree with this recommendation? What are the pros and cons of this idea? Decide exactly what you would say to the buyer trainee. Then compose a probable "conversation" between the trainee and yourself. Your planned conversation should include questions you could ask to help the trainee understand your ideas.

Chapter 15

Public Relations and Publicity

Fashion shows, cosmetic demonstrations, celebrity appearances, and the Macy's Thanksgiving Day Parade are all examples of a powerful sales promotion tool—public relations. **Public relations** is the public understanding and acceptance that is earned when a specially designed program is executed by a business. That program can be as simple as informal modeling of the latest styles by one or two of the store's salespeople or as complex as a full-scale salute to a foreign country by a major department store. In most instances the value that is realized by a store is in direct relationship to the amount of creativity, time, effort, and money that it invests in public relations.

A closely related area of sales promotion that is also very important to the retail store is publicity. **Publicity** is the free and voluntary mention of a firm, product, or person in some form of media. It can include such things as media coverage of store openings, announcements of upcoming store events, coverage of your store's public relations events, radio or television interviews with such people as celebrities who are visiting your store, designers, store managers, and even buyers, articles about fashion trends that mention your store, and feature articles about your store or department.

In this chapter we will examine the goals of both public relations and publicity. Then we will look separately at each of these areas, including the various types of public relations events that are being planned by retail stores today and the ways in which stores are able to successfully obtain publicity.

Finally, we will examine the ways in which buyers can benefit from, and also

All these shoppers came to Marshall Field's when actor John Forsythe visited the store as part of a special promotional event.

contribute to, both public relations and publicity.

Public Relations and Publicity Goals

The ultimate goal of both public relations and publicity is to attract more people to the store and to encourage them to buy the merchandise that the store carries.

As it is with advertising, public relations efforts are both institutional (designed to sell the image of the store) and promotional (designed to sell the merchandise in the store). In the next section, we will give specific examples of public relations efforts that can be considered institutional, others that can be considered promotional, and ones that fall between the two extremes.

Publicity can also be both institutional and promotional. Most often, it is institutional since it is designed to inform peo-

ple of the newsworthy activities of a business. But it can be seen by the customers as promotional if it encourages them to visit a store on a particular day or week to look at and consider buying a specific type of merchandise that is offered by that store.

Public Relations

Almost every store engages in some type of public relations effort. This involvement may be as simple as participation in a charity fashion show that is sponsored and managed by the charity organization or as complex as the Macy's Thanksgiving Day Parade. In some stores, public relations events are known as **special events.**

If you were to look at a representative sample of the events that stores commonly sponsor, you would find that they can be arranged along a continuum. At one end are those events that are primarily a form of institutional promotion, such as the Cancer Cut-A-Thon sponsored by a local hair salon and the Merchandising Student of the Year scholarship that is sponsored by a local department store.

The customers who participate in the Cancer Cut-A-Thon pay for their haircuts just as they would if they visited the salon when there is no special event scheduled. But they are aware of the fact that the money for their haircuts is going to charity. The Cut-A-Thon introduces potential customers to the salon and, at the same time, it impresses them with the charitable contributions that are being made by the salon owner and the employees. If the customers are pleased with the service they receive and with the outcome of the haircuts, it is possible that some of them will return to the salon the next time they need a haircut.

A similar type of goodwill is established when customers know that a store has sponsored a scholarship for a local merchandising student. This fact can be brought to the attention of customers by publishing an announcement such as:

The Town and Country is proud to salute Madison High School Senior Aimee Le-Clerc, who is Madison's Merchandising Student of the Year. Join us for a special awards ceremony in her honor on Wednesday from 4:00 to 4:30 in our College Shop on the fifth floor.

Customers who see an announcement such as this may decide to shop at the store even if they do not know the student and have no intention of attending the awards ceremony. They may be impressed with the fact that the store cares about the further education of local students. In addition, the award may attract many students from the winner's school to the store.

At the promotional end of the continuum would be an event such as a major salute to a foreign country by a department store or chain. The huge salute to Japan presented a few years ago by Wanamaker's in Philadelphia is certainly the type of event that brought excitement to the store, and with the excitement came customers who were eager to buy the Japanese merchandise that the store had imported. The store used transit advertising and 60-second television ads that were three times as frequent as the store's regular advertising. The huge store event featured a Japanese drum corps and two performances of *Madam Butterfly* in the store auditorium. The event was so successful that Wanamaker's planned to buy $20 million worth of extra goods (over and above their normal open-to-buy) for their next major salute to another country.[1] Clearly, the purpose of this type of event is to promote the sale of the store's merchandise. One small store contacted the Canadian Trade Council, which contributed $10,000 plus flags and props for an all-Canada promotion. Manufacturers can help buyers and store owners get such aids.

Typical public relations events include educational programs and demonstrations; advisory boards such as career women's, college, and teen boards; celebrity appearances; fashion shows; trunk shows; and foreign-country promotions. Each of these events is discussed briefly below without positioning it along the continuum between institutional and promotional public relations. These events are only a few examples of the great many that are sponsored every year by retail fashion businesses in an attempt to attract more customers to their stores.

An increasing number of store executives consider it the retailer's responsibility to create an exciting, theaterlike atmosphere for the shopping customer. As a result, the use of special events has steadily increased. Some traditional stores even see these events as a necessity as they attempt to compete with the growing number of off-price stores. A representative from Famous Barr explains that "there's a major show in our downtown auditorium every Sunday; there's a wardrobe consultant in every store—and all of those things are being strengthened."

Educational Programs and Demonstrations

Store-sponsored educational programs can be directly related to the store's merchandise or they can be entirely unrelated. For example, Marshall Field in Chicago recently worked with Buick in arranging a series of seminars for women on preventive auto maintenance. They also cosponsored a series of women's seminars with American Express called "Take Charge." Gloria Steinem, Polly Bergen, and others were there to kick off the week-long event that featured seminars on topics ranging from plastic surgery to travel planning. The series was a huge success, with more than 500 women attending each day. As an added feature, the store coordinated fashion shows with the event.

Typical of educational programs that are closely related to a store's merchandise are skin care and cosmetic programs, hair-styling demonstrations, seminars on selecting the right accessories, and workshops on updating your wardrobe.

Advisory Boards

Some stores select, from among their customers, community leaders to meet several times a year with store principals to discuss the store's role in the community. These leaders give advice on merchandise and services that the store might offer, and suggest ways that the store may contribute even more successfully to community events.

STUDENT ADVISORY BOARDS. A **college board** is a consumer advisory panel made up of at least one upper-class student from each college that is important to the residents in the area of the store. In the back-to-school selling rush, these young men and women serve both as salespeople and as advisors to college-bound customers. They may also be asked to do some informal modeling of the store's fashions.

Teen boards are somewhat similar to college boards, but their activities continue year-round. Although actual sales work may not be involved, teen board members may help the store to engage in other activities. For example, they may help the store to plan fashion events for high school students or encourage the introduction of a fashion column in the school newspaper.

Teen boards, unlike those for college students, often engage in activities beyond fashion merchandising alone. For example, working through their teen boards, stores may sponsor such projects as charm schools and the preparation of fashion columns for school newspapers. Some stores have similar activities for preteens on a more restricted scale.

Accustoming younger age groups to regular store visits increases the likelihood that they will become fashion customers in their college, career, and married years. And the store, having "watched them grow up," is better able to anticipate their wants. It can also encourage them to comment freely to management if assortments or services are lacking.

Both college boards and teen boards can be valuable consumer advisory groups for the store as well as successful sales-support groups. At one time their popularity was nationwide. Now, however, they are more popular in outlying areas of the country than they are in major cities.

CAREER WOMEN. There are also boards composed of career women. Never in the history of retailing has so much attention been paid to the working woman as in the last few years. The reason is obvious. Working women make up a very large part of a retailer's business. Because they are working, these women are out of the house and in close proximity to retail stores. They also have dollars to spend.

In the 1960s, programs existed in a few major department stores. These usually consisted of a career club with a board of directors chosen from the city's leading women in business. Programs, fashion shows, and "how-to" clinics were held on a regular basis for the club members. In return, the members helped the store by offering reactions to merchandise and by suggesting how the store could become more popular with working women.

By the end of the 1970s, career women programs had been started in almost every major store in the United States—from Dayton's, with its Brown Bag, week-long series of meetings, to Saks Fifth Avenue, Foley's, Abraham & Straus, Macy's, Weinstock's, Jordan Marsh, Stern's, and many others. Programs varied from store to store, but among the special services usually offered were famous guest speakers, how-to clinics, fashion shows, seminars, and career guidance round-tables.

One store runs a club for career women which holds meetings devoted to informative programs emphasizing fashion. One club member is chosen by lot every second week to select and accessorize several stock garments she considers ideal for working women. Her selections are then featured in the store's boutique for career women.

Retailers now realize that the ranks of working women are going to swell in the next decade. This extremely valuable market has placed its demands for recognition squarely in front of the country's retailers—who have responded with programs like those mentioned above.

Celebrity Appearances

One very effective way to encourage customers to visit a store is by scheduling a celebrity appearance. Although customers who attend may not shop at the store while they are there for the celebrity appearance, many of them will come back at another time. Other potential customers may not attend the event but they will think better of the store because of it. The opinion that the store is an exciting place to visit may have a "rub-off" value when these customers are ready to shop at some other time.

Fashion Shows

Whether the retailer's store is a high-fashion, big-city salon or a small shop on Main Street, there is nothing that tells the fashion story to customers quite so clearly and dramatically as does a fashion show. The usual presentation employs models, music, and a commentator, allowing the audience to both see and hear about fashion merchandise. Simpler ways of running shows are possible, of course, and some very effective presentations have been done by commentators who simply hold up each item as it is being discussed. The glamour treatment, however, is more likely to draw larger audiences and win more publicity, and this method is the one stores usually like to use.

Such fashion shows may be held to benefit a local charity or to highlight the store's own assortments. In the former case, admission is charged and the proceeds are turned over to a designated charitable organization. In the latter case, admission is free and may be open either to the general public or only to those who have been invited to come.

Fashion shows may be held on a selling floor or in the store's restaurant or auditorium. Or they may be held outside the store, according to the occasion and the facilities required. Some shows feature the fashions of a single vendor or designer; in others the styles of several vendors are modeled. Shows may be general in nature, appealing to a cross section of the store's customers. Or they may be planned for specialized audiences, such as teenagers, college or career men or women, prospective brides, expectant

A celebrity appearance requires elaborate planning and coordination. "Miami Vice Day" at Marshall Field's flagship store in Chicago attracted a crowd of 20,000 people.

mothers, or people with special interest in travel or sports. Sometimes, when a fashion show is held at the request of a school or other organization, the models come from the group's membership.

Ways in which retailers assemble audiences for these shows are as varied as the kinds of shows they stage. If the event is on behalf of a charity, the sponsoring organization sells the tickets and usually offers the services of some of its members as models. If the event is geared to a relatively small, special-interest group, such as brides or expectant mothers, personal invitations may be mailed out. For across-the-board audiences, announcements may be placed in the store's advertising, in its windows or elevators, or on radio broadcasts, inviting all interested persons to attend.

Cooperation in the staging of a fashion show may be provided by a consumer publication, a merchandise vendor, a fiber or fabric producer, or any other organization with a reason to help the retailer convey a fashion message.

Trunk Shows

A **trunk show** is a presentation by a designer, vendor, or vendor's representative of samples of a line. Usually the merchandise is from one of the more expensive lines that the store carries. The show is held in the store department that is featuring the line. The representative brings samples of the complete line to the store, puts on several scheduled showings, and takes special orders from any customers who choose styles, colors, and sizes not in the store's stock. The trunk show is not only a good public relations event for the store, it is also an opportunity for designers or vendors' representatives to pinpoint regional variations in fashion demand and to get customer reaction to the overall fashion philosophy for the line. Trends in demand can be gauged more accurately from face-to-face customer contact than they can from within the narrow limits of a design room or a vendor's showroom. Stores that schedule trunk shows inevitably find that customers who attend feel that they have been accorded special treatment by both the vendor and the store, despite the fact that trunk shows are generally announced in press releases, included in ads, and open to the public.

Foreign-Country Promotions

Large-scale salutes to foreign countries are becoming increasingly popular in major department stores and chain stores. You have already read about some of these events earlier in this chapter. Retailers such as Jordan Marsh, J. C. Penney, Famous Barr, The Broadway, Bloomingdale's, and Neiman-Marcus are planning this type of major promotion on a yearly basis. These extravaganzas often include demonstrations, special exhibits, entertainment, and special merchandise from the country being saluted in every department of the store.

Although this type of promotion takes a great deal of detailed planning and coordination, store officials in these stores who are committed to these events say that they are definitely worth the effort. A major foreign-country salute gives the store an aura of excitement—almost a theatrical feeling. The special entertainment and exhibits attract customers who might not otherwise visit the store, and the imported merchandise, if well bought and displayed, may mean a handsome profit for the store.

Publicity

Since publicity, unlike advertising, is given free by the medium concerned, it

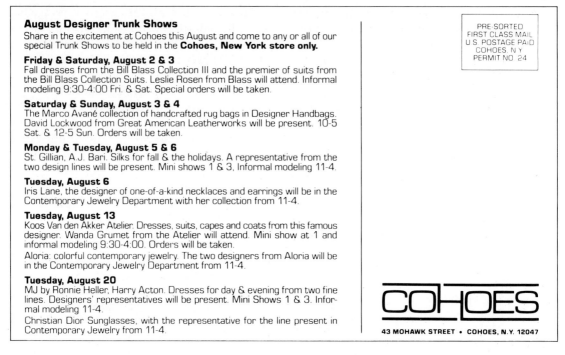

Trunk shows bring a vendor's latest lines to stores located outside the major metropolitan fashion centers.

can bring extremely valuable sales results at little cost. Many retailers, along with entertainers, political aspirants, and authors, now look upon publicity as a vital key to their success.

Paid advertising is placed in a medium at the request of the advertiser, who decides where and when it will appear. In the case of free publicity, however, the medium concerned decides whether or not the material will be used at all, and if so, the amount of time or space that will be allotted to it and what words and pictures will be used.

In the fashion world, vendors or merchants—the major sources of fashion publicity and information—merely make the facts available to the media and suggest how these facts might be presented. They retain the right to specify a **release date,** which is the earliest date that the announcement can be made. Whether the announcement concerns a new and exclusive fashion design or a personal appearance by a well-known fashion figure in a store, the media usually honor the specified release date as a matter of policy.

The way in which fashion news is originated by designers, vendors, and fashion leaders has been discussed in earlier chapters. This chapter is concerned with the efforts of retailers to publicize fashion in general and their own fashion assortments in particular.

Methods of Obtaining Publicity

Retailers call attention to newsworthy developments within their stores or actually create news by causing something newsworthy to happen, as you learned in the public relations section of this chapter. Stores provide selected media with information about such events in hopes they will be of potential interest to the media's audiences. In turn, these media may then devote space or time to telling their readers or listeners about such happenings.

In their attempts to gain publicity, retailers make news available promptly and, preferably, in advance of the expected event. In addition, they refrain from flooding media with information that is not really newsworthy, for to overdo the publicity effort may cause print and broadcast editors to be less cooperative.

Following are several methods of passing fashion news along to print or broadcast media.

PRESS RELEASES. Retailers may issue press releases before or after such newsworthy events as a visit to the store by a designer, the opening of a new department, or the introduction of a new fashion development. A **press release** is a written statement of news that has occurred or is about to occur, specifying the source of the information and the date after which its use is permissible. Press releases may originate with the store or may be provided to the merchant by vendors whose products are involved.

PHOTOGRAPHS. Vendors frequently send directly to newspaper fashion or women's-page editors glossy photographs of a model dressed in one of the styles in the vendor's line. Attached to each of these glossies is a short description of the style, the fabric in which it is made, the color and sizes in which it is available, occasionally some information about the designer, and often the local store or stores where that particular style may be found. Reproduction of such a photograph, accompanied by information on the item,

its fashion importance, and where it may be purchased locally, often results in favorable publicity for both the vendor and the local store customers of that vendor. Unfavorable publicity, however, may result if an editor does not check with the credited local store or stores as to the actual availability of the style and its selling price before printing or broadcasting the related publicity. No customer enjoys making a trip to a store and finding that the publicized style is not in stock, or finding it in stock but at a higher price than stated in the publicity.

TELEPHONE CALLS. Sometimes retailers may alert news media to happenings with only a telephone call. If the store is staging a fashion show to raise funds for charity, a call to the editor of the fashion or women's page of the local newspaper may bring a photographer and a reporter to the show.

FASHION CONSULTATIONS. Fashion merchants often make their expertise available to the media to encourage accurate and stimulating publicity for their stores. Retailers do this by welcoming questions on fashion subjects from the press and answering them as completely as possible, thus encouraging editors to check with them on the accuracy and completeness of fashion news from other sources. Merchants can also achieve some of the same results by being available to speak on fashion subjects before school or consumer groups. In each case, they help stimulate both the public's fashion interest and the assortments of the store the merchant represents.

Media Used

Retail merchants look to both print media and broadcast media when seeking fashion publicity. Most retailers find that the publicity given their activities by local newspapers engenders greater consumer interest than any other media they use. Magazine publicity can be of considerable value but often lacks the news quality and local impact of newspaper coverage. Radio and television publicity also can be very useful, but again, the approach may not be as localized as newspaper publicity. Also, radio or television publicity cannot be preserved for future reference.

NEWSPAPERS. As a consistent user of advertising space in local newspapers, a retailer often gets preferential treatment in obtaining publicity. For maximum effect from publicity, the retailer selects the paper that seems most likely to reach the readers who will be interested in the particular publicity message. Which paper appeals to which group of readers is something the retailer already will have learned in the course of selecting media for advertising.

Newspapers are also generally more receptive to store requests for publicity than are other media because of the frequency of their publication. Fashion editors and lifestyle page editors have daily pages to fill and Sunday features to prepare. They usually welcome information about store events that have local news value.

The local fashion publicity efforts of retail merchants gain strength from such industry efforts as the semiannual press week showings in New York and Los Angeles. If fashion editors or women's-page editors of newspapers have attended either or both events, they have seen the lines of the sponsoring vendors well in advance of their presentation to the public by retail stores. They have brought back with them the vendors' press releases and photographs of styles the individual vendors consider the most indicative of developing trends. Such editors are not only

conversant with fashion trends as a result of their press week experience but have also become somewhat personally involved in helping these trends develop on their local scenes. With this background and this attitude, they are more receptive than they might otherwise be to the fashion publicity efforts of local merchants. Buyers who join fashion organizations such as The Fashion Group (a national professional group of leading women fashion experts) have an opportunity to network with fashion writers, editors, designers, and publicists. This helps the buyers to know the right people to approach when publicity is needed.

MAGAZINES. Fashion and consumer magazines make a practice of showing fashions editorially and mentioning one or more stores as sources for purchasing that merchandise. These mentions are known as **editorial credits.** The decision to offer an editorial credit to a store rests with the publication. The decision to accept or decline the credit is made by the store, which takes the following factors into consideration:

☐ The value to be derived, in terms of publicity among its customers and in the market, from accepting a credit in the periodical concerned. Not every periodical has equal value in these respects.
☐ The confidence the store places in the style that is being considered for credit. If the sales potential of a style does not warrant purchasing, displaying, and promoting it on its own merits, a store will undoubtedly decline the credit. The store may still carry the style but simply prefer not to give it the merchandising and promotional emphasis that the acceptance of a credit requires.
☐ The crediting of other stores. Some merchants prefer not to accept a credit if other stores also are mentioned, or if the other

stores mentioned are of an appreciably different type from their own.

- ☐ The importance of the vendor to the store. A store may accept a credit as a means of strengthening a relationship with a new vendor, or it may decline a credit from a resource not otherwise important to it.
- ☐ The number of concurrent credits the store may have already accepted in other publications. Too many credits around the same time can upset the store's own assortment and promotion plans.

Accepted and acted upon, an editorial mention publicizes the store and its fashion merchandise among readers of the magazine who are within its trading area. Properly managed, such credits enhance the prestige of both periodical and retailer among consumers and producers.

What are some advantages and disadvantages of accepting advertising credit in a vendor's ads?

Advertising credits are also available in most magazines. They are mentions of one or more store names, in connection with the advertisement of a vendor, as the retail sources for the merchandise being advertised. Such an ad might also include the names of fiber and fabric sources or other appropriate producers whose products contributed to the featured item of merchandise. The factors a store considers in accepting or rejecting such a credit are much the same as those considered in the case of editorial credits.

RADIO AND TELEVISION. A retailer who is a consistent user of radio and television advertising sometimes enjoys preferential treatment in obtaining broadcast fashion publicity from local stations, as is also the case with newspapers. And just as each newspaper has special appeal to certain groups of readers, so does each radio and television program or station have special appeal to target groups of listeners.

Retailers become familiar with the nature of such specialization through observing the results their own advertising has achieved. They augment what they have learned from their own experience by studying the research material prepared by each broadcast medium to indicate the number and kind of people who tune in to its programs. Then, to achieve maximum benefit from fashion publicity placed with broadcast media, fashion retailers seek to obtain mentions from those stations and programs whose listeners they believe will be most responsive to their message. Again, networking helps buyers gain the attention of broadcasters in their selling area. With the increasing popularity of cable television, it may be easier for a store to find a local cable station that closely matches the interests of its intended customers than to rely on local network affiliates.

Sources of Public Relations and Publicity

Because public relations and publicity are frequently closely related, the remaining portion of this chapter will combine the two topics. In this section we will take a look at a few of the public relations and publicity responsibilities of the fashion coordinator and the public relations director in a retail store.

Fashion Coordinator

In any retail organization, much of the fashion publicity obtained is a result of the public relations events that are arranged by the fashion coordinator. The **fashion coordinator** or **fashion director** is the store's ranking fashion authority. The duties include such publicity-generating public relations activities as staging fashion shows, in or out of the store, and arranging clinics or demonstrations at which visiting designers or vendor representatives will speak. The coordinator or director may also represent the store as a speaker on fashion before consumer or business groups in the community.

When stores stage promotional events featuring their fashion assortments, the fashion coordinator or director is very much in the picture. After consulting with various fashion buyers, the coordinator or director may suggest the events, organize and supervise them, or simply stand by to see that the fashion story is correctly presented.

Fashion shows for customers may be held in or out of the store, as direct sales builders or as public relations efforts to assist charitable and civic causes. They may be held in branch stores to enhance the fashion images of those stores. They may be formal, using models on a runway, or informal, with models strolling about a restaurant or departmental selling floor.

Stage-managing such fashion shows, as well as coordinating the outfits and preparing the commentary, is usually the responsibility of the fashion coordinator or director, who works in close cooperation with the fashion buyers.

Many other events also may be used to underline the importance of fashion coordination. There may be talks and discussion meetings for customers of a particular type, such as teenagers, home sewers, or expectant mothers. There may be occasions to talk to women's clubs and similar groups outside the store about current fashions and fashion trends that are of special interest to each particular group. In all such cases, the fashion coordinator is usually involved.

The coordinator or director also works with visiting fashion experts in staging their presentations. For example, a producer of active sportswear may send a golf or tennis pro to a store to give a demonstration and to participate in a question-and-answer session with customers. Or a producer of patterns or sewing notions may send a representative to a store to hold one- or two-day clinics. Or a magazine may stage a fashion presentation on a theme it is currently sponsoring. The store's fashion coordinator or director, in agreement with the concerned buyer, makes sure that the presentation is in line with the store's fashion policy, assists in tying in all advertising, display, and personal selling, and helps secure as much publicity as the particular type of event warrants.

Public Relations Director

Many retail stores employ a public relations or special events director and sometimes a staff to work with this person. Despite the public relations title, this person is usually responsible for handling both public relations and publicity. In addition to planning public relations events, probably the task that is performed most frequently by the public relations director is development of press releases informing the appropriate media of newsworthy information about the store's events, ideas, services, and employees. Let's look specifically at the ways in which fashion shows, visits from designers or vendors, and trunk shows are publicized.

FASHION SHOWS. Fashion show publicity is achieved by word of mouth and by informing the press and broadcast media, through direct contact or through press releases, about an upcoming event and why it is being undertaken. Occasionally, fashion shows are so original in some aspect that the publicity lingers long after the fashions themselves have gone. Such was the case in recent years when models on moving escalators displayed the fashions of a famous New York specialty store in a newly opened suburban branch.

VISITS FROM DESIGNERS OR VENDORS. A visit from a designer, a vendor, or their representatives can often help a store earn considerable publicity for itself, for the vendor, and for the particular fashion area involved. Some representatives are capable speakers and appear on local television shows or give press interviews on fashion trends. These fashion authorities may address groups of customers or school groups, act as commentators for store fashion shows, or hold clinics and act as consultants to individual customers.

In periods of economic uncertainty and increased competition, higher-priced vendors or their designers tend to increase the number of their visits to customer stores in large urban areas throughout the country.

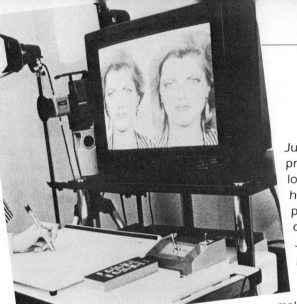

Shiseido: Promoting Cosmetics by Computer

Just as fashion shows have long been a promotional tool for selling the latest looks in apparel, so beauty makeovers have traditionally helped stores to present new looks and products in cosmetics to their customers. Now, the Japanese company Shiseido has been putting a new face on the beauty makeover by means of a sophisticated computerized skin analysis and a makeup simulator.

Shiseido, which began 113 years ago as a pharmacy, is the largest manufacturer of cosmetics in Japan, and third largest in the world, behind American Avon and French L'Oréal. In the United States, the company does a $60 million business in some 800 stores—but its entree into the American market was not all smooth sailing. During the 1970s, the firm was relying on heavy use of the typical promotional vehicles of gift-with-purchase and purchase-with-purchase to boost traffic and sales. It also employed non-English-speaking, kimono-clad beauty "artists" to stage elaborate makeovers for customers. These tactics helped spread recognition of the Shiseido name, but when the promotions slowed down, so did sales.

Then, in 1984, Shiseido took a giant leap into a new era of cosmetics sales by introducing two different computerized services to its cosmetics counter at Bloomingdale's New York. Tying in with the store's massive "Japan at Bloomingdale's" promotion, Shiseido unveiled a Makeup Simulator and a Skin Analyzer, both harnessing the powers of the computer to design personalized skin care regimens and beauty aids.

The Makeup Simulator uses a video camera to project two images of a customer's face. One is the real image; the other can be "painted" by the professional makeup artist to show how the customer would look with a new hairdo, shaping, and makeup. A color print and plan for achieving the new look are given to the customer after the simulation is complete. Shiseido's Skin Analyzer features a "magic wand" that is stroked over a customer's face, instantly providing an analysis of the skin's moisture, texture, and general condition. Again, a personalized regimen for proper skin care is then made available to the customer.

Because of the sophisticated nature of these electronic wonders, Bloomingdale's and Shiseido were able to obtain publicity for the new concept in local media, including *The New York Times*. In addition, a giant television monitor showing the current customer being made over or analyzed drew crowds of customers already in the store to watch the process—and resulted in Shiseido's quintupling its sales during Bloomingdale's storewide promotion.

A year later, sales of the company's cosmetics were still more than double the volume of the previous year for Bloomingdale's, and Shiseido had spread its computerized programs to other stores, including Saks Fifth Avenue and Filene's Boston. And its promotion continued to get publicity, including that most important type: word of mouth. Said Leonard Ichton, vice president for cosmetics at Filene's: "We've seen customers walk away with a computer printout of the topography of their skin and become not just converts but apostles, spreading the word, telling their friends."[1]

1 Bernice Kanner, "Beauty and the East," *New York Magazine*, September 30, 1985, p. 23.
This Focus is based on information from the article cited above and from the following sources:
Anne-Marie Schiro, "The Computer Is a Hit at the Cosmetics Counter," *The New York Times*, October 29, 1984, p. C-14.
Gayle J. Goodman, "A Modern Sense of Beauty," a Shiseido advertisement.

TRUNK SHOWS. Advance announcements about trunk shows are made in press releases and store ads. During and after the event, word-of-mouth publicity inevitably grows out of the customers' excitement over the special treatment accorded them. Further opportunities for publicity may be created by having models show selected styles informally in the store's tearoom, or by showing the line on models at a special breakfast or luncheon show for the benefit of a local charity. Interviews with the visiting vendor or representative may be arranged with print and broadcast media if the vendor is considered an authority on some special aspect of fashion or is otherwise newsworthy.

Maximum publicity benefits result from such vendor visits if the buyer or merchant who is handling the visit discusses the possibilities at an early date with the store's publicity staff. The publicity executives need to know why the visitor is newsworthy and whether they can participate productively in press conferences, television interviews, and other promotional activities. Arrangements for such supplementary appearances have to be made well in advance, not only with the press but also with the visitor. A vendor who knows, for example, that he or she will have five or ten minutes on television may bring along a special group of unusually photogenic style numbers to show, and possibly one or two glamorous models.

Additional Publicity Sources

Two additional sources of publicity for the retail fashion store are vendors and trade groups or associations.

VENDOR PUBLICITY. The fashion publicity efforts of stores are frequently supplemented by the work of the vendors' own publicity staffs. Sometimes the latter channel their publicity efforts through the stores, by making available suggested press releases and glossy photos of the styles they consider important. Sometimes they issue the publicity material directly to the news media, as described above. On occasion, producers may circulate reproductions of magazine pages on which appear either their advertising or editorial mention of their styles. At the same time they point out the local stores that have received advertising or editorial credits.

When such publicity is channeled through the store, the store's buyer, fashion coordinator, and publicity staff have the opportunity to evaluate it in terms of their own scheduled promotional efforts.

TRADE GROUPS AND ASSOCIATIONS. Buyers and merchants who keep in close touch with the industries from which they purchase fashion goods are in a good position to coordinate their own store publicity efforts with those of trade associations serving those markets. Such associations frequently release publicity to print and broadcast media on new developments in their particular areas of fashion and relate these developments to current trends. Some of the fashion industry trade associations have fashion publicists on their staffs or retain the services of public relations firms, such as the one headed by Eleanor Lambert, originator of the New York market's press week.

When an industry trade association launches a drive to publicize its fashion message or its merchandise, or both, the buyer or merchant usually receives in the mail suggestions for tying in with such publicity efforts. These include ideas for press releases, photographs, and recommendations for fashion events. If such material is passed along to the store's publicity staff and discussed with them, it is often possible to work out ways to benefit locally from the national publicity efforts of these associations.

The Buyer's Responsibilities for Public Relations and Publicity

As it is with advertising and visual merchandising, your responsibility as a buyer will vary greatly from store to store with respect to public relations and publicity. Naturally, in a very small store in which the owner-manager is also the buyer, it is this person who will be responsible for these promotional areas. More often, the responsibility for these areas will be with the fashion coordinator or members of the public relations staff. Frequently, however, the buyer is called upon to work with these specialists to make these promotional areas a success.

For a storewide salute to a foreign country, for example, it is the buyer who will actually select and import the goods on which the event is based. When a major event such as this is planned, it calls for careful but aggressive buying of imported goods. If the store does not have enough of the goods it needs to support the event, it will not be a success. Sometimes the buyer travels with the person in charge of organizing the special event to help line up programs such as a visit by a foreign dignitary.

Cooperation is also a key to the buyer's responsibilities when it comes to initiating events and publicity. The buyer may be in the right place at the right time to learn about the availability of a vendor-sponsored event such as a demonstration or exhibit that can be brought into the store. Or it might be the buyer who can make the initial arrangements for a trunk show.

What contributions can a buyer make to the store's sales promotion plans?

When your merchandise is being used for special events such as fashion shows, you may find that you are more closely involved with the event than originally planned. It is important to know how long the merchandise will be used, who is coordinating the fashion looks on the models, and what will happen if the merchandise is soiled or damaged during the show. If a dress or sweater is being featured in a fashion show, you must be sure that a sufficient quantity of that garment is in stock. Naturally, the same holds true for fashions that may be featured in the media as a part of a publicity effort. If the customer comes to your department and finds that the featured item is out of stock, loss of good will and negative publicity may result instead.

In the case of major promotions that may be repeated, you will want to track their success in preparation for next year's involvement. Were you understocked on the promotional items, or were you overstocked? In retrospect what would you have done differently? How much profit can you trace directly to the event? For your own department, was the event worthwhile? If not, how can it be improved for next year?

You will also want to track and report the effects of other public relations and publicity efforts on your department's business. If you find that a specific publicity mention on radio or television has generated business for you, mention the fact to the person responsible for the publicity. If you learn of an opportunity to obtain some free publicity—perhaps a vendor-sponsored event or a cable television promotion that you learn about first— pass this information on to the people who can help the store take advantage of it.

Public relations and publicity are both cooperative efforts. If everyone works together, the store as a whole benefits as well as each individual department. And it is the public relations and publicity areas that can set a department store or specialty store apart from off-price stores that carry the same merchandise.

Reference

1 "Special Events", *Stores,* May 1984, p. 22.

Buying Vocabulary

Define or briefly explain the following terms:

Advertising credits	Public relations
College board	Release date
Editorial credits	Special events
Fashion coordinator (Fashion director)	Teen board
Press release	Trunk show
Publicity	

Buying Review

1. Explain the difference between public relations and publicity. Give an example of each.
2. What is the ultimate goal of both public relations and publicity?
3. As with advertising, public relations efforts are designed both to sell the image of the store and to sell the merchandise in the store. Name these two types of public relations efforts and give an example of each.
4. A trunk show can serve two important purposes for fashion merchandising. Explain what is meant by a trunk show and what purposes it serves.
5. Explain why many store officials believe that foreign-country promotions are worth the effort.

6. Name four methods of passing fashion news along to print or broadcast media so that it can be used for publicity.
7. How might a retailer be successful in obtaining publicity from radio or television stations?
8. What are the major responsibilities of the fashion coordinator or director in retail merchandising? How might this person be helpful in obtaining publicity?
9. How do vendors and trade groups serve as sources of publicity for retail fashion stores?
10. What are some of the buyer's more important responsibilities for public relations and publicity?

Buying Case

You are the chairperson of a committee of fashion buyers from a medium-size department store in Michigan. For the first time in many years, the store's public relations department has organized a college board made up of representatives from each of 10 colleges and universities served by the store and its branches.

The public relations department has asked for your help in planning the first meeting of these college board members. The purpose of this meeting is to gather information that will help both the public relations committee and the buyers plan a storewide salute to France. Your assignment is to gather from the buyers a list of questions to be presented to the college board members and actually to plan the agenda for this meeting.

The major objective of the meeting is to gather information that will help the store plan the type of foreign-country salute that will be of particular interest to the 250,000 college and university students in the area of the store. A secondary objective is to determine how the college board might further assist the public relations department and the store buyers.

Prepare a brief outline of the meeting and a list of at least five questions to ask that will help the store plan the salute to France.

Chapter 16

Personal Selling

Advertising, visual merchandising, publicity, and public relations can help to bring to your store customers who are ready, willing, and possibly even eager to purchase the merchandise you have selected as a part of your buying responsibilities. But those people can walk out without making a purchase if there are no competent and knowledgeable salespeople ready to make the sale. Personal selling is the final essential ingredient for successful sales promotion. If the personal selling efforts of the store's salespeople are not what the customers expect them to be, the sale can be lost.

The people who are responsible for selling your merchandise to the ultimate consumer have an important role in the success of your department or store. To most customers, the salespeople *are* the store. It is rare that customers deal with a buyer or an owner, with an advertising manager or a visual merchandising director, or with the president of the store, but they certainly see and deal with the salespeople. The quality of the contact that customers have with your store's salespeople can mean the difference between meeting your sales goals and missing them. It is essential that these salespeople be "professionals" with a sincere desire to help customers find merchandise that satisfies their needs and wants. Salespeople must honestly believe in the merchandise they are selling and be able to explain to customers how they will benefit from buying it.

As a buyer in a chain organization or large department or specialty store, you will probably not have an opportunity to teach the salespeople who sell your merchandise how to use successful selling techniques, but you will have an opportunity to provide them with merchandise information. If you are in a position to train your own sales personnel, your very presence may act as a morale-booster.

Modern technology cannot replace the effectiveness of professional salespeople.

In this chapter we will look first at the extent of service that is provided in a variety of retail selling situations. Next we will examine the basic steps that must be followed in making a retail sale and the requirements for success in fashion selling. Finally, we will take a look at the ways in which you as a buyer can positively influence the personal selling of the merchandise you were responsible for buying.

Customer Service and Retail Selling

The services that a retail customer expects to receive in a retail selling situation vary considerably from one type of store to another. The level of service ranges from maximum-service selling found in fashion salons to minimum-service selling found in self-service departments or stores. Store management determines the level of service in keeping with its image.

How well salespeople perform has a major impact on how well the desired image is projected.

Maximum-Service Selling

Salon selling is the most exacting type of retail fashion selling and also the type that offers the most extensive service by the retail salesperson. It is most frequently used in stores or departments that offer higher-priced styles in the introductory or early-rise stages of their fashion cycles. In salon selling, little or no stock is exposed to customers' view except that which is brought out by the salesperson for inspection. Close rapport is needed between customer and salesperson if this type of selling is to be successful. An advantage of this method is that once a mutual understanding has been developed, the customer usually comes back to the store to be served by the same salesperson, who understands the customer's wants and how to satisfy them.

Since salon salespeople are likely to develop a personal following of customers who return to them repeatedly and trust their suggestions, many maintain card files on their regular customers. On each customer's card is noted merchandise previously purchased, style and color preferences, sizes worn, price lines preferred, and other pertinent personal information. Salespeople then use these files to inform customers about new styles as they arrive in stock and about other fashion developments. Many specialty stores employ salon selling and encourage salespeople to keep records on their personal followings and to contact those customers whenever new products of special interest to them arrive. Department stores, on the other hand, rarely employ salon selling except in their high-fashion departments.

Focus

Martha: Courting Customers with a Personal Touch

Catering to the *crème de la crème* of wealthy and discriminating customers requires a true art of selling. And that is exactly what Martha Phillips, founder and chairman of Martha Inc. has spent 50 years cultivating and practicing to perfection.

With four Martha dress salons in operation—two in New York and two in Florida—Phillips and her daughter, Lynn Manulis, president of the company, boast a client list that reads like a Who's Who of society: Barbara Walters, Diana Ross, and various Astors, Vanderbilts, and du Ponts are all regular customers who come seeking not just the latest and most elegant fashions but the highly personalized service and care that each Martha salon offers all its clientele.

The epitome of personal selling, Martha provides an atmosphere for shopping that seems almost to come from another age. Customers are greeted by name when they walk through the door and are waited upon by "Miss Martha," "Miss Lynn," or their own personal salesperson, each of whom keeps a record of her clients' sizes, favorite colors, previous purchases, preferred designers, and other pertinent information. Salon and fitting rooms are kept immaculate; merchandise, brought out only on request, is hidden away and filed by garment type, color, size, and designer, frequently pressed and repressed, covered in plastic, and aired once a week.

Because of the stores' deluxe service and attention to its customers, the regulars are fiercely loyal. Said Ivana Trump, wife of renowned real-estate tycoon Donald Trump: "They know me very well. If there's a designer I like or if they see a dress I'd like, they call me and I go quite often."[1] Not only do steady customers spend time at the store, they definitely spend money, averaging at least $1,500 per visit. Martha's top salespeople, who earn a 2 percent commission on everything they sell, often do some $40,000 a day and are disappointed should their individual sales fall as low as the $15,000 range.

In an age where most retailing has adopted varying degrees of self-service as its selling method, Martha is a notable and extremely successful exception, lauded by its suppliers and competitors alike. Said designer Bill Blass: "I don't have another client like that. [M]ost major stores have not a clue how their customers live."[2] And Ellin Saltzman, fashion director of Saks Fifth Avenue was high in her praise: "Martha is brilliant. She runs an incredible business. She knows her customer. She knows how to attract her customer. She buys for her customer and sells to her customer. They service their customers brilliantly. They have superb taste."[3]

1 Michael Gross, "Ladies in Waiting," *Manhattan Inc.*, October 1985, p. 109.
2 Ibid., p. 110.
3 Ibid.

Moderate-Service Selling

Both over-the-counter selling and self-selection selling require a moderate amount of service on the part of the salesperson. Sometimes this service can spell the difference between a customer who buys and one who just looks at the merchandise.

For **over-the-counter selling,** selected portions of the stock are kept in glass display cases, often with some merchandise displayed on top of the cases. Most of the stock, however, is kept on shelves or in drawers below and behind the display cases. Sometimes a free-standing "island" or "square" is formed by three or four glass display cases, with the center of the island or square being occupied by departmental stock and a cash register.

In over-the-counter selling, some merchandise may be available for customers to personally examine. However, salespeople are needed to take other merchandise out of the display cases, off the shelves, or out of the drawers so that a customer can inspect it. This type of selling requires that a salesperson be thoroughly familiar with the departmental stock, well aware of the fashion points and importance of each item, and able to speak tactfully but with authority about differences in quality that exist between similar items at different prices.

Over-the-counter selling is the personal selling method most stores prefer for merchandise that is high-priced (such as fine jewelry), easily soiled (gloves or better lingerie), or fragile (fragrances and some types of costume jewelry). It is also used for merchandise requiring specialized knowledge on the part of the salesperson (cosmetics and shoes).

In **self-selection selling,** merchandise is displayed and arranged so that customers can make at least a preliminary selection without the aid of a salesperson. Open wall racks, T-stands, display shelves, bins, and tables are among the fixtures most commonly used in self-selection departments.

Self-selection does not mean that customers should be ignored until they make a selection; nor does it mean that they should be made to feel pressured by salespeople who are anxious to make a sale rather than help customers find merchandise that they both need and want. Salespeople are responsible for helping customers find merchandise that satisfies their needs, explaining and demonstrating the merchandise, answering customers' questions about the merchandise, checking for styles, sizes, and colors not on the selling floor, assisting in the fitting room if requested, helping customers make a buying decision, and suggesting additional merchandise that can meet the customers' needs. Salespeople who work in self-selection departments can often make a significant increase in their own sales and the sales of the department by becoming proficient in using the basic steps of the sale, which will be covered in a later section of this chapter.

Minimum-Service Selling

In **self-service selling,** customers not only make their selection from the goods on display but also bring their purchases to a checkout counter where they make payment and where their purchases are prepared for takeout. Most self-service operations have stock personnel on the floor to keep the merchandise in order and to check, when requested by customers, for sizes and colors not on display. There are no salespeople as such, however, to give the customer fashion information and advice. In many self-service departments, the only opportunity to provide any service to the customer is at the checkout counter.

Self-service is the selling method most favored by discount operations and others whose low prices require that services be held to a minimum. Self-service techniques, however, may be employed by stores of the traditional type in some of their fashion departments, particularly those handling prepackaged, brand-name goods, such as pantyhose and brassieres.

Although self-service is usually equated with savings and bargain opportunities, this method of selling fashion is not used exclusively for low-priced merchandise,

closeouts, and "distress" merchandise. Both medium-priced and high-fashion goods have also been sold successfully by this method.

Steps in the Retail Sale

Most retail sales presentations can be viewed as having a series of eight sequential steps. As you read the list of steps below, keep in mind that sometimes a similar selling technique may be used by your vendors as they sell their merchandise to you.

1. Preparation for selling
2. Approach
3. Determining customer needs and wants
4. Presenting merchandise
5. Answering objections
6. Closing the sale
7. Suggestion selling
8. Goodwill gesture

Preparation for Selling

As far as the buyer is concerned, this step may be the most important one in the sale. The buyer cannot be present during the actual one-on-one contact between the customer and the salesperson, but the buyer definitely can play a major part in preparing both the salesperson and the department for the sale.

Preparation for selling includes the gathering of merchandise information, the study of customer buying motives, the gathering of information about community and store events, and the physical preparation of the department.

MERCHANDISE INFORMATION. Fashion salespeople need to know all of the fashion points of the merchandise they have been assigned to sell. They also need to know what fashion really is, how it works, and what the current fashion trends are and the direction in which they are going. Those who sell apparel need to be knowledgeable about the fitting of garments and the characteristics of the materials used. Whatever is being sold, salespeople should be able to guide customers in selecting related apparel and accessories, both in their own and in other departments, that will achieve the desired look. Above all, fashion salespeople need an appreciation of the fashion values of merchandise, so that they can state the price of the merchandise with confidence and respect. In a later section of this chapter we will look at some of the ways in which salespeople can be given the merchandise information that they must have to do an effective selling job.

CUSTOMER BUYING MOTIVES. In Chapter 2, you learned that customer buying motives can be measured along a continuum that runs from operational satisfactions to psychological satisfactions. Operational buying motives are those derived from the physical performance of the product. Psychological satisfactions are those derived from the customer's social and psychological interpretations of the product's performance. Many of the customers who buy fashion goods do so for motives that are closer to psychological than operational satisfactions. In preparation for working with customers, the professional salesperson not only must gather as much merchandise information as possible but should look beyond the physical features of each product and discover what that product can do for the customer. A designer suit isn't just well made and smartly tailored; it is elegant and stylish, and conveys the look of success for the wearer. A pair of boots is not just practical, warm, or made of beautiful leather; it represents fashion leadership, confidence, and prestige. A familiar adage among

salespeople is "Sell the sizzle, not the steak." As the buyer of the merchandise, you are the store's resident expert on the item you have selected. You have the responsibility to pass both merchandise information and an understanding of psychological satisfactions derived from that merchandise on to the salespeople. You can do this through face-to-face meetings, bulletins, videotapes, or flash reports.

COMMUNITY AND STORE EVENTS. The successful salesperson is aware of such things as store ads that feature the department's merchandise, fashion shows that may have included items from the department, and publicity mentions locally, regionally, or nationally. To have confidence in the salesperson, the customer should be able to see that he or she is aware of all that is happening to affect the department and its merchandise.

PHYSICAL PREPARATION OF THE DEPARTMENT. Salespeople should be constantly aware of the physical appearance of the department. Merchandise should periodically be put back in order, displays should be checked and fixed if necessary, and housekeeping should always be impeccable.

The Approach

The use of the right kind of approach when greeting a customer can spell the difference between being able to complete the rest of the steps of the sale and being stopped by the customer. The approaches that are typically used in fashion selling are the greeting approach, the personal approach, the service approach, and the merchandise approach.

GREETING APPROACH. The simplest approach to use is the greeting. A simple "Good morning," "Good afternoon," or possibly just "Hi" is a pleasant way to acknowledge customers and make them feel welcome. Often customers will answer the **greeting approach** by explaining why they came to the store if the salesperson waits a few seconds before saying anything else. This gives the salesperson a chance to continue with the rest of the steps of the sale.

PERSONAL APPROACH. The **personal approach** is used when the salesperson knows the customer's name. "Hello, Mrs. Wong. How are you today?" "Hi, Mr. Wilson. I see that your son received a scholarship to State University. I'll bet you're really proud of him."

SERVICE APPROACH. The least satisfactory of all approaches is the **service approach.** It consists of a question such as "May I help you?" or "May I serve you?" This approach is usually the earmark of an untrained salesperson. Whenever the salesperson asks a service question that can be answered with a yes or no, it is very easy to receive the answer "No thank you, I'm just looking." Customers are so used to answering with this automatic response that some of them recite it even if they do need help. Other customers feel as if the salesperson who says, "May I help you?" is really asking, "Are you ready to buy something in my department?" This can make the customer feel pressured and uneasy. The service approach should be avoided in fashion selling.

MERCHANDISE APPROACH. The best approach to use in a fashion department is the **merchandise approach.** It is used when the customer is looking at or touching a particular item of merchandise. "That sweater is machine-washable." "Aren't these spring colors pretty?" If a man is looking at women's scarfs you might say, "It looks as if you're shopping for a gift." If the particular item of merchandise is very popular you might say, "These folding raincoats are very popular. We've sold a lot of them in the last few days."

Determining Customer Needs and Wants

The salesperson should sincerely try to find merchandise that satisfies the customer's needs and wants. This is possible only if the salesperson is able to determine what these needs and wants are. Careful questioning, listening, and observation must be a part of the salesperson's selling skills.

The salesperson should encourage the customer to engage in a two-way conversation that will reveal these needs and wants. After the approach, the customer may say something such as "Yes, these colors are really nice. But what I was really looking for was a sweater in kelly green." If you have kelly green sweaters in stock, you can ask, "What size are you looking for?" If you don't have kelly green sweaters in stock, you might ask, "What do you plan to wear the sweater with?" If the sweater is going to be worn with a dark green skirt, you might be able to show the customer a mint green sweater that will satisfy her needs just as well. It is possible that the customer never thought of choosing mint green. Another possibility is that the customer will buy the mint green sweater because it is a style that she really finds appealing.

Presenting the Merchandise

These nine basic guidelines help salespeople present merchandise effectively [1]:

1. Show only three items of merchandise at a time. As the customer expresses dislike for an item, remove it from the counter.

2. Point out the obvious features of the merchandise. This helps to focus the customer's attention on each item.

3. Talk about the psychological satisfactions (or benefits) that can be derived from the merchandise.

4. Handle the merchandise with care and respect. It will seem more valuable in the customer's eyes if you treat it as such.

5. Let the customer participate in the sale. Put the merchandise into the customer's hands. Have the customer try it on and look in the mirror.

6. Appeal to the customer's senses. Make sure the customer feels the merchandise, smells it if appropriate, and touches it. Describe what the customer should be noticing. "See how lightweight this lining is—but it is still warm enough for the coldest weather."

7. Point out the hidden features. If the item has hand-sewn seams, custom-made buttons, or leather-lined buttonholes, for example, mention them to the customer and show them at the same time.

A knowledgeable salesperson can point out features of the merchandise that will make a customer more aware of its value.

8. Be enthusiastic about your merchandise. You should honestly believe that this is the best merchandise for the customer and that it definitely does satisfy a need that the customer has. If you are excited about the merchandise, your excitement will be passed on to the customer.

9. Show the medium-priced merchandise first and work up or down from there according to the customer's interests. Avoid asking how much the customer wants to spend because the answer can prevent you from showing merchandise that the customer could be interested in.

Answering Objections

Customers are not always prepared to buy the merchandise they have been presented without voicing some objections. The salesperson has to use logic and additional merchandise knowledge to overcome these objections.

Customers may voice sincere objections based on a factor such as their need for the product, the product's suitability, or the price. They may also voice excuses, which are reasons for not buying that cover up the real objections they have.

The customer who says, "I'm not sure this shirt will wash well," is voicing a sincere product objection. The customer who says, "Oh, I don't know. I guess I'll go home and think about it awhile," is covering up a real objection that he or she does not want to voice.

The first step in handling objections (and excuses) is to listen carefully. Ask the customer to further explain the objection. Then one of the following techniques can be used to overcome it:

YES . . . BUT. Agree with the customers' objections but present another point that they may not have considered. If the customer says, "The lightweight soles on these shoes don't look as if they will wear well," the salesperson might answer, "Yes, I wondered about that too, but I've been selling them for over a year now and I haven't had one complaint on the way that they wear."

REVERSE ENGLISH. The salesperson can sometimes restate the customer's objection and make it a reason for buying the product. If the customer says, "This jacket looks like it will need cleaning every time I wear it," the salesperson might say, "The material is specially treated to resist soil, and if it does get dirty, it can be washed right in your washing machine."

SUPERIOR POINT. Another way of overcoming objections is to suggest a fact that outweighs the objection. If the customer says, "This skirt isn't fully lined," the salesperson might say, "You're right, but it does go beautifully with your sweater and it is $20 less than a fully lined skirt."

Closing the Sale

Sometimes customers will hesitate to buy because they need some help in coming to the buying decision. This help can be in the form of a simple either-or question: "Do you like the red one or the blue one?" "Would you like this to be cash or charge?" "Will five pairs be enough or will you need more?" "Do you want to take the coat with you or would you like to have it sent?"

Suggestion Selling

Before the sale is completed, the salesperson should make an attempt to sell additional related merchandise. The last step of the sale is called **suggestion selling.** It is often a service to the customer because the additional merchandise is actually needed in order to fully enjoy the product that is being purchased. With shoes there could be shoe polish or shoe trees. With fabric there should be thread, needles, buttons, zippers, and patterns. With a new shirt there could be a tie.

The suggestion selling attempt should *not* be made with the words "Will that be all?" when both the salesperson and the customer are standing at the cash register. This question asks the customer to quickly think of any other item he or she might need before the sale is rung. Instead, the salesperson might say, "I'd like to show you a tie that would really go well with that shirt," or "We have shoe polish that matches your shoes perfectly." This type of approach is not high pressure, and it will often result in an additional sale. The salesperson might also want to mention another item of merchandise that just arrived at the store or an item that is on sale. A suggestion of this type can be seen by the customer as a service.

Goodwill Gesture

When the sale has been completed, the salesperson should not let the customer just walk away without a friendly word. Naturally, salespeople should always say, "Thank you." They might also say something such as "I'm sure you'll enjoy your new coat," or "Have a nice weekend," or "Let us know how you like your boots next time you're in the store." Even in a self-service store or department, this personal touch can be provided by the cashier. The goodwill gesture should not be reserved only for customers who buy. People who do not make a purchase are entitled to the same type of courteous treatment. "Have a nice day. Stop in again."

Requirements for Success in Personal Selling of Fashion

It is vital to the success of fashion merchandising that salespeople, the ultimate and most personal contact between the store and the customer, have the appearance, manners, speech, grounding in fashion information, and approach to their work that will enhance the store's relationship with its customers.

A buyer or merchant seeks certain essential attributes in fashion salespeople. Selling is greatly aided when salespeople have developed such personal qualities as:

☐ Attractive appearance, scrupulous cleanliness, businesslike dress, and careful grooming.

☐ Good manners and good business etiquette.

☐ Animation, alertness, and promptness in attention to customers.

☐ Ability to form a quick estimate of customers and their preferences, as well as a sympathetic appreciation of their problems.

☐ Ability to speak well, a pleasing voice, a lively and intelligent expression, clarity of speech, and a knowledge of when to talk and when to listen.

☐ Orderliness in thinking, talking, working; accuracy in handling records, reports, and other paperwork.

☐ A good memory for faces and names.

☐ A friendly, tactful manner and, above all, sincerity.[2]

Training of Fashion Salespeople

While some retailers believe that the best fashion salespeople are born with the talent, the fact is that most sales personnel develop their expert abilities through training and perseverance. To sell any

"I'll tell you what it does. It speaks for a you otherwise unspoken for."

An effective salesperson can tell the customer why the merchandise is a good buy for him.
Drawing by Modell; © 1985. The New Yorker Magazine, Inc.

type of merchandise, a salesperson must be well acquainted with the qualities, values, and uses of the goods. Selling fashion merchandise requires that the salespeople know the fashion picture as a whole and the significance of those elements that directly concern the specific merchandise they are selling. Some of the most knowledgeable fashion selling today takes place in boutiques, where each new fashion style is seen as part of a total fashion look that appeals to each boutique's customers. Only when salespeople understand the total fashion look can they explain to customers how its various elements are related to one another and how they may be coordinated to create currently acceptable styles.

Not all salespeople can be expected to be expert fashion consultants. But it should be clearly recognized that lack of fashion and merchandise information on the part of salespeople causes considerable customer dissatisfaction. When salespeople acquire such fashion information from the buyer, from fashion publications, from employee fashion shows, and from fashion training bulletins, they are better equipped to serve as consultants to customers. When salespeople radiate certainty and fashion authority, customers buy with more confidence.

Training in Small Stores

In small shops, informal training of salespeople goes on in the course of the day-to-day operation of the business. Fashion points of the merchandise are explained to the sales personnel by the buyer or store owner as the goods come into stock. In the relatively small store, that buyer or store owner often is on the selling floor for much of the day and can answer any questions posed by customers and salespeople alike.

Frequently, salespeople in small stores are invited to view lines shown by visiting representatives of the store's resources and to express opinions with respect to the salability of the merchandise. They may be encouraged, moreover, to ask questions and to discuss the merchandise with vendors or representatives. The latter, in turn, may be asked by a store owner or buyer to hold meetings with the sales staff to discuss fashion features of the line each represents. Such a presentation often is made to all salespeople in the store, not only those who sell in the department that handles that vendor's goods. Smaller stores are more likely than large ones to ignore departmental barriers and to train their salespeople to sell in all departments. Their salespeople are thus able to help customers to assemble their entire outfit—ready-to-wear, inner wear, furnishings, or accessories—to achieve a desired look.

Training in Multiunit Store Organizations

In large, departmentalized stores, fashion training is more formalized than it is in small stores. Seasonal fashion reports, in the form of illustrated leaflets or color slides or closed-circuit television shows, are prepared by the store's training department in conjunction with the fashion coordinator or director and are shown to salespeople in all of the firm's store units. Buyers, and sometimes merchandise managers, hold meetings for salespeople upon their return from market trips, to report on the fashion trends they observed and to describe the merchandise they have purchased. In each department, the buyer or assistant holds weekly meetings at which the sales staff is told about scheduled advertising for the upcoming week, the fashion points of the merchandise to be featured in these ads, and anything else that will help them be more informed and fashion-conscious in their selling.

In chain organizations, the fashion coordinator or director usually prepares a seasonal summary of fashion trends in both ready-to-wear and accessories. This summary is sent to all stores in the chain at the start of each season. In addition, the central buyers of fashion goods alert the appropriate fashion department managers in the various units of the chain to current fashion developments. The medium commonly used is a fashion bulletin, which features sketches of items, swatches of the materials in which they come, and detailed descriptions, including colors and sizes available. Still another form of fashion training takes place when new styles are sent by the central buying office of the chain into some or all units for testing

In large retail organizations where buying is centralized, the buyer may not have personal contact with the sales staff. Videotaping or filming a presentation allows such a buyer to communicate product information to the salespeople.

purposes. Pertinent information about the fashion features and selling points of the merchandise is sent along with the merchandise.

Use of Employee Fashion Shows

One of the most effective devices for briefing a fashion sales staff is the presentation of a special fashion show. The employee fashion show may be as formal and elaborate as one staged for customers. It may instead be a show taped in the parent store for future viewing in the branches. Or, it may be casual, using salespeople as models and substituting give-and-take conversation for prepared commentary. This type of show involves salespeople in an effective personal way. In some cases, it may consist simply of fully dressed and accessorized mannequins, displayed with explanatory signs in employee lounges or cafeterias. The basic idea, however, remains the same: to show concretely what lines, colors, or combinations of the two

are expected to prove acceptable to the store's customers and to call attention to points of difference between last year's or last season's styles and those of the new fashion season.

Employee fashion shows in a large store are likely to be planned and carried out by the fashion coordinator or director or any buyer whose fashion sense and knowledge have the respect of the store staff. Shows are also often carried out, on a less ambitious scale, by buyers of related departments for the benefit of their combined sales forces. For example, a group of accessories buyers might work with a dress or coat buyer to explain how the new season's millinery, scarfs, belts, or jewelry can be combined effectively with new styles and colors in apparel.

Use of Vendor Aids

Obviously, it is to the interest of vendors of fashion merchandise to do what they can in order to maintain a high level of retail salesmanship on behalf of their merchandise. Among the steps they may take to assist stores in this area, vendors give talks, (sometimes at breakfast meetings that they host), distribute promotional literature, and demonstrate products in use.

Talks to salespeople may be given by the vendors' sales representatives who call upon buyers. Often these talks are given in meetings held before the store opens, but sometimes a vendor may invite the entire sales staff, the buyer, and other store executives to dinner and an evening meeting outside the store. The vendor's presentations made at such evening meetings are often quite elaborate, with charts, slides, films, or modeling.

Sales literature in the form of brochures is often given to salespeople for study and reference. Typical examples of such literature might be a coat manufacturer's booklet on how to care for a leather coat or jacket, a fiber or fabric producer's leaflet about a new textile development, a foundation maker's explanation of figure types and how to fit them, or a lingerie or hosiery producer's color chart.

Many vendors train representatives to instruct salespeople in the use and benefits of their products. Demonstrators visit stores to conduct customer clinics, to assist in the training of salespeople, or both. The representative of a cosmetic line, a hairstylist, and the instructor sent from a fiber or fabric source to explain the use and care of new products are typical visiting demonstrators. Some demonstrators become regular members of a store's staff. These appear to be in the store's employ but are paid, at least in part, by the producer, who trains them to sell and stock a firm's goods. In large stores, representatives of major, nationally advertised cosmetic brands are likely to be permanent demonstrators.

Other Sources of Information

Retail selling efforts are also of vital interest to others who may be several steps removed from direct contact with consumers. These include fiber sources, both natural and synthetic; leather and plastic processors; fabric finishers; associations dedicated to publicizing the merits of fibers, fabrics, leathers, or other fashion materials; and consumer periodicals. From these outside organizations may come a battery of aids for training salespeople. These might include talks and demonstrations, exhibits, leaflets, and film and slide presentations.

Everyone in the fashion business, from the producers of fibers to the makers of finished goods, has a vested interest in improving the quality of retail selling. The reason is plain: If goods move only sluggishly across retail counters, the supply lines all the way back from retailer to manufacturer to source of raw material become choked with unsold goods. Often, fashion salespeople seem to be the focus of all eyes in the trade. Unless they perform their function well, little merchandise is sold to customers. And nothing happens in the fashion business until something is sold.

In addition to all those who cooperate in the training of retail salespeople at no charge to the merchant, there are also professionals who sell their training services. Some come into stores where they hold rallies and workshops on the art of selling and generally try to stimulate people to sell more goods. Others offer film presentations to achieve the same ends. Although these services are usually concerned with retail salesmanship in general, their impact upon fashion salespeople is as important as upon those selling other types of merchandise.

The Buyer's Responsibility for Sales Training Content

The extent of a buyer's responsibility for the salesmanship in his or her department depends, to a large degree, upon the size and type of the store. In departmentalized stores, the buyer or department manager shares the responsibility for salesmanship with the training department. It is the duty of the training department to teach all new employees such things as store systems and procedures. These can range from dress code, to proper execution of a salescheck, to instruction in the store's security rules. Only when this training is complete is the new salesperson sent to the selling floor. From this point on, the training of the salesperson involves specific merchandise and is handled by the department head or buyer. The training department is no longer involved, unless some storewide effort is launched to accomplish a general aim—to curtail errors, to foster courtesy to customers, or to promote increased sales, for example.

In smaller stores, on-the-job supervision of salespeople is the responsibility of the buyer. But in major department stores and multiunit stores, supervision is generally handled by the department manager or group manager. The buyer sends merchandise information and fashion news on a daily basis to these intermediaries, who then share it with the salespeople. In these very large and complex retail stores, the buyer is involved with orders, projections, EDP printouts, and meetings—the many aspects of keeping goods moving through many departments in many branches. Such a buyer may never visit sales personnel in the branch stores. Thus it is necessary for the buyer to depend largely on written communications for contact with the salespeople.

The Delivery of Merchandise Information

As the fashion authority for a department, the buyer is the primary source of information about merchandise carried in the department. The buyer is expected to alert the sales force to current and anticipated trends and to indicate how they will affect sales prospects.

The buyer is also expected to relay to the sales force information about the quality and value of the department's merchandise assortment. Specific selling points of an item should be pointed out, emphasizing to the salespeople the features that might make the merchandise more desirable to individual customers.

Sometimes buyers may also have to teach salespeople how to arrange the merchandise in stock: how to fold slips, how to place dresses on hangers, or how to replace shoes in boxes. Or, they may have to point out to salespeople the most effective way to display merchandise to a customer. For example, they might show salespeople how to demonstrate the many ways in which a customer can wear a scarf.

The Dissemination of Selling Tips

Because of their fashion expertise, buyers can also provide salespeople with effective selling tips. They should supply facts relating to the use and care of merchandise which the sales force can then pass on to customers. Or they may coach salespeople on proper size and fit.

Buyers may also tell salespeople what related items—even from other departments—to suggest in order to enhance customers' enjoyment of a purchase. For instance, they may show how a dress neckline may seem to be more flattering if just the right kind of jewelry or scarf is suggested for wear with it. By briefing salespeople on such suggestions, buyers make it easier for them to close the sale on a major item of apparel or on an important accessory. Moreover, it helps salespeople to impress upon customers the idea that the store is a headquarters for fashion advice.

Training Methods Used by Buyers

The salesperson may be the ultimate link between the store and the customer, but it is the buyer's training and supervision that makes that salesperson a strong, productive, and profitable link for both store and customer. Today, more part-time salespeople are employed in fashion departments. More branches are being opened and store hours are being extended. Buyers have less and less time to devote to the selling floor. As a result of these changes, the proper training of salespeople has become an increasing problem. In order to convey needed merchandise information to salespeople, buyers or their assistants employ a variety of techniques.

Departmental Meetings

Each week, usually before the store opens, buyers, their assistants, the department managers, or the sales managers hold departmental meetings to review new or incoming merchandise and upcoming ads, to give pep talks, and to report any departmental problems or changes. Ideally these are discussion meetings, but often the pressure of time makes them a series of rapid-fire announcements. Some fash-

ion stores, to dispense with formality or avoid the atmosphere of a stereotyped, dull session, use instead a daily five-minute "huddle" just before the opening bell.

Fashion Shows and Reports

In addition to what may be done on a storewide basis, buyers may present fashion shows for their own salespeople to bring out the fashion and selling points of the department's merchandise. They may also provide informal market reports, written or oral, telling their salespeople what they have seen and heard on their latest market trip, what fashion trends appear to be shaping up, and what they have purchased for future delivery.

Miscellaneous

Leaflets, clippings, and other matter related to the department's merchandise may be posted on conveniently located bulletin boards. Also commendation for special selling achievements, appropriate announcements, and bits of cartoon humor may find their way to such bulletin boards.

Other training media may include posted reprints of ads that have been run or preprints of ads that are to be run by the department, as well as posted or circulated printed material, such as fashion magazines and information received from vendors.

No matter how dramatic or handsome the merchandise is, a well-informed, enthusiastic, attentive salesperson can show and demonstrate the goods to make them even more appealing.

References

1 Based on Marilyn Mathisen, *Apparel and Accessories,* Career Competencies in Marketing Series, McGraw-Hill, New York, 1979, p. 224.
2 Paul H. Nystrom, *Fashion Merchandising,* The Ronald Press, New York, 1932, pp. 187–188.

Buying Vocabulary

Define or briefly explain the following terms:

Greeting approach

Merchandise approach

Over-the-counter selling

Personal approach

Salon selling

Self-selection selling

Self-service selling

Service approach

Suggestion selling

Buying Review

1. Explain the statement "To most customers, the salespeople *are* the store."
2. Name the three different levels of service that can typically be found in retail selling situations and give an example of each.
3. Name the eight steps in the retail sale.
4. Describe your responsibilities as a buyer with respect to merchandise information.
5. What is the least satisfactory of all approaches in a retail selling situation? Why?
6. What is the best approach to use in a fashion department? Why?
7. What are the nine basic guidelines for presenting merchandise?
8. What are three techniques for overcoming objections?
9. What is meant by suggestion selling? Give one example.
10. Name three techniques used by buyers to convey needed merchandise information to salespeople.

Buying Case

You are an experienced buyer in a small department store. The store is arranged for self-selection selling.

One of your responsibilities is participating in the training course planned for the new assistant buyers. For this group of buyer trainees, you have been assigned to help with the training session on personal selling.

During the session, one of the more outspoken trainees makes the following statement: "I really think there is very little room for personal selling in a store like ours. If we do our job and select the merchandise that the customers want, it will sell itself. I would be happy if each salesperson just greeted the customer and then backed off. There's nothing worse than high-pressure selling."

What is your reaction to this statement? How would you respond to it? How might you conduct the remainder of the session to help the trainees gain a better understanding of their personal selling responsibilities?

Case For Unit 4

You have recently been hired as buyer of a new children's wear department in a medium-size departmentalized specialty store located in Zanesville, Ohio, a city with a population of about 32,000. The store has been in operation for more than 15 years, with two branch stores in neighboring towns. However, this is the first time the store will offer children's wear for sale.

The new department, which is scheduled to open in approximately four months, will feature a broad and relatively deep selection of moderately priced, fashionable infants', toddlers', and children's clothing from sizes 4 to 14 for girls and 4 to 20 for boys. One of the unique features of the department is that it will also feature a broad selection of athletic attire and accessories for children.

The store manager has asked you to help him and his sales promotion staff develop a preliminary plan for advertising, visual merchandising, public relations, and personal selling.

The chief competition for this new department is described below:

- [ ] A small designer clothing store with two locations, one in downtown Zanesville and the other in a nearby shopping center. This store offers a limited selection of top-quality designer clothing for both girls and boys, but no athletic attire.
- [ ] A discount clothing store based in Columbus with a branch in Zanesville. This store has a medium-size department with a narrow and deep assortment of children's wear.
- [ ] The small children's departments of several nationally known chain and discount stores located in shopping centers approximately half an hour from Zanesville. These stores also have narrow and deep assortments of children's wear, and although they offer a small selection of children's athletic attire, it is in a separate department.
- [ ] A national chain of athletic attire and sporting goods with a store in a nearby shopping center. This store features a limited selection of athletic attire and no other children's clothing.

The advertising manager has agreed to work closely with you to achieve the advertising goals you desire for your new department. Advertising media options open to you include a morning and evening newspaper, an AM rock radio station, an FM "beautiful music" radio station, and a cable TV channel that serve Zanesville and the surrounding areas. Naturally, however, you are not limited by these media choices. You can also use direct mail and outdoor media.

Visual merchandising will be handled by the store's operations and display staffs under the direction of the store manager. He would like your input on the type of "look" you would like to achieve with your decor and displays. The budget calls for a complete renovation of an area that was previously stockroom area to accommodate the new department. Your suggestions regarding display fixtures, mannequins, lighting, floor coverings, and all other aspects of visual merchandising will be the basis of all the work that is done in this area.

The public relations director wants to schedule a meeting at your earliest convenience to discuss special events for the opening. You should also be prepared to suggest any possible sources of publicity that you would like to have the public relations director pursue.

The store prides itself on personal service to its customers. You will be responsible for hiring and training your own sales staff. The store manager would like to know the criteria you will use in selecting this staff and the type of training you plan to use.

Creating Your Plan

On a blank sheet of paper, create a plan for handling the promotional aspects of your new children's wear department. Your plan should include headings for advertising, visual merchandising, public relations and publicity, and personal selling. Use the information you learned in Chapters 13–16 together with the information provided in this case to plan an effective promotional plan. Include in your plan the resources you will need and the problems you will have to overcome. When you finish, your plan should be appropriate for use at a planning meeting with the store manager and the sales promotion staff.

Appendix A
Careers in Fashion Buying

This appendix summarizes information from literature on the executive training programs of a sampling of major fashion retailers. The career paths shown here concentrate on positions in buying and merchandising. Typically these stores offer the flexibility to move between positions in buying and merchandising and positions in store management.

Some stores require experience in both areas.

For further information about the training programs of these and other retailers, contact the human resources or personnel department of the organizations that interest you. You should also avail yourself of your school's career counseling services.

Retailer	Training Program	Career Path in Buying
Allied Stores Corporation		
Jordan Marsh-New England, a full-line department store based in Boston with stores throughout New England. For further information: Jordan Marsh-New England, Executive Recruitment Office, Box 9159, Boston, MA 02205.	Executive Training Program is 12 weeks: Sales—2 weeks, Sales management I—4 weeks, Buying office—2 weeks, Sales management II—4 weeks. Includes on-the-job training and weekly seminars. Evaluation by supervisor at end of each assignment. Management Development Program provides specialized courses for graduates of the Executive Training Program. Assistant Buyer Internship available to college students October 1 to December 31 with option to continue through mid-January. One-week orientation followed by work in buying office under direction of a buyer. Program includes visits from school coordinator.	Senior Manager ↑ Merchandise Manager ↑ Assistant Store Buyer ↑ (Central Office) Buyer ↑ Divisional Sales Manager/ Operations Manager ↑ Assistant Buyer ↑ Sales Manager ↑ Executive Trainee

Retailer	Training Program	Career Path in Buying

Associated Dry Goods Corporation

L.S. Ayres & Co., a department store based in Indianapolis, IN, with stores in Cincinnati, OH. For more information: L.S. Ayres & Co., Executive Recruitment, 1 West Washington, Indianapolis, IN 46204.

Training and Development Program—a 10-week program to prepare for an initial position as a sales manager. Experience in each of seven operating divisions. Training group participates in a special project assigned by CEO and senior executives. L.S. Ayres and Associated Dry Goods seminars are open to Ayres executives throughout their careers.

Senior VP, General Merchandise Manager
↑
VP, General Merchandise Manager
↑
Divisional VP, Merchandise Manager
↑
Divisional Merchandise Manager
↑
Buyer
↑
Senior Assistant Buyer
↑
Assistant Buyer
↑
Sales Manager
↑
Trainee

BATUS, Inc.

Saks Fifth Avenue, a departmentalized specialty store based in New York, NY, with branches throughout the U.S. For more information: Director of Internal Relations and College Placement, Saks Fifth Avenue, 611 Fifth Avenue, New York, NY 10022.

New York Central Merchandising Program—a 6-month program of classroom instruction and work experience, including the following assignments: Selling—2 weeks, Sales floor administration—6 weeks, Merchandise office A—8 weeks, Merchandise office B—8 weeks, placement as assistant buyer.

Executive VP, Merchandising
↑
Senior VP, General Merchandise Manager
↑
VP, Associate General Merchandise Manager
↑
VP, Merchandising Manager
↑
Associate Merchandise Manager
↑
Buyer
↑
Assistant Buyer
↑
Assistant to Merchandise Manager
↑
Executive Trainee

Retailer	Training Program	Career Path in Buying
Federated Department Stores		
Abraham & Straus (A&S), a department store based in Brooklyn, NY, with branches in NY, NJ, and Philadelphia. For further information: Abraham & Straus, Executive Recruitment Director, Brooklyn, NY 11201.	Executive Training Program, an assistant buyer training program, is 10 weeks, including on-the-job experience in a buying office with merchandising assignments in two different departments, weekly seminars, and scheduled workshops. Supervision and guidance from assigned personal sponsor, buyer with whom trainee has worked, and executive development specialist. Placement as assistant buyer after training, with responsibility for a merchandise classification, within approximately 6 months.	General Merchandise Manager ↑ Merchandise VP ↑ Divisional Merchandise Manager ↑ Divisional Group Manager ↑ Buyer ↑ Associate Buyer ↑ Department Manager ↑ Assistant Buyer ↑ Executive Trainee
Bloomingdale's, a department store based in New York, NY, with stores in NY, NJ, CT, MA, MD, PA, VA, TX, FL, and IL. For more information: Director of Executive Placement-K, Bloomingdale's, 1000 Third Avenue, New York, NY 10022.	Merchandising trainee assignment to a department on selling floor in flagship store; progress review and new placement assignments by manager of Executive Training Squad. Each trainee is assigned to a training counselor. Classroom training in merchandise math, purchase order management, consumer buying, forecasting, buying concepts, merchandise presentation, business writing.	Vice President ↑ Central Divisional Merchandise Manager ↑ Store Divisional Merchandise Manager or Buyer ↑ Central Associate Buyer ↑ Department Manager ↑ Central Assistant Buyer ↑ Assistant Department Manager ↑ Trainee
Burdine's, a Florida department store based in Miami. For further information: Burdine's, Executive Recruitment, 22 East Flagler Street, Miami, FL 33131.	Entry position as department merchandiser provides a combination of classroom training and practical experience.	General Merchandise Manager ↑ Divisional Merchandise Manager ↑ Buyer ↑ Associate Buyer ↑ Merchandise Liaison ↑ Department Merchandiser

Retailer	Training Program	Career Path in Buying
Sanger Harris, a department store based in Dallas, TX, with stores in Tulsa, OK, Tucson, AZ (Levy's), Albuquerque, NM, and Forth Worth, TX. For further information: Sanger Harris, Executive Personnel, 303 North Akard, Dallas, TX 75201.	Executive Training Program is 3 weeks of classroom training plus 6 months of 1-day follow-up programs. On-the-job training under sponsorship of a divisional manager. Store Intern Program for college and university students: 1-day (8-hour) orientation focused on cash register operations, 8-hour company orientation, 10- to 12-week selling assignment with meeting with store manager and with other interns. Tour of distribution facility.	General Merchandise Manager ↑ Divisional Merchandise Manager ↑ Merchandise Group Buyer ↑ Buyer ↑ Senior Assistant Buyer ↑ Assistant Buyer ↑ Trainee
R. H. Macy & Co., Inc. Macy's New York, a full-line department store based in New York, NY, with stores in NY, CT, FL, and TX. For further information: Macy's New York, Executive Development, 151 West 34th Street, New York, NY 10001.	A combined classroom and on-the-job training program: 1st week—classroom work and independent projects, 2d week—experience as a sales clerk, 3d week—under supervision of a sales manager, 4th week—classroom training, 5th to 7th weeks—buying office experience and seminars, 8th to 10th weeks—assignment to a second sales manager in a different line from first assignment, 11th week—sales support assignment, 12th week—a series of workshops. Quizzes, projects, and evaluations by supervising sales managers and buyers throughout training.	Senior VP, Merchandising ↑ Merchandise Administrator ↑ Buyer ↑ Group Manager ↑ Assistant Buyer* ↑ Sales Manager* ↑ Trainee
Macy's New Jersey, formerly Bamberger's, a full-line department store based in Newark, NJ, with stores in NJ, NY, PA, DE, and MD. For further information: Macy's New Jersey, Executive Development, 131 Market Street, Newark, NJ 07101.	Similar to Macy's New York	Similiar to Macy's New York

*These two positions are reversed in two other divisions of R. H. Macy & Co., Inc.

Retailer	Training Program	Career Path in Buying
R. H. Macy & Co., Inc.		
Macy's Atlanta, combining the former Atlanta-based Davison's division and the Kansas City, MO-based Macy's Midwest, is now based in Atlanta, with branches in GA, SC, OH, MO, and KS. For further information: Macy's Atlanta, Executive Development, 180 Peachtree Street, N.W., Atlanta, GA 30303.	Similar to Macy's New York	Similar to Macy's New York
Macy's California, a department store with branches throughout northern and central California and Reno, NV. For further information: Macy's California, Executive Development, Stockton at O'Farrell Street, San Francisco, CA 94108.	Similar to Macy's New York	Similar to Macy's New York
May Department Stores		
Kaufmann's, a Pittsburgh, PA-based department store with stores in PA, OH, and WV. For more information: Kaufmann's, 400 Fifth Avenue, Pittsburgh, PA 15219.	One-week store orientation followed by two merchandising assignments in different departments, each for 5 weeks, under supervision of a trainer buyer. Weekly seminars and written assignments. Promotion to acting assistant buyer on successful completion of 11-week training program.	VP and General Merchandise Manager ↑ Divisional Merchandise Manager ↑ Branch Store Divisional Manager ↑ Buyer ↑ Department Manager (1½ to 2 years) ↑ Assistant Buyer ↑ Trainee (6 months)
Melville Corporation		
Chess King, a national chain of young men's fashion specialty stores headquartered in New York City. For more information: Chess King, Manager, Personnel Services, 500 Eighth Avenue, New York, NY 10018.	Skills Training Program is a 6-month program, with operational functions in Phase 1 and management skills in Phase II. Initial placement as assistant manager includes intensive training. Buying career path specialization begins with merchandise planner position; buying is centralized.	Merchandise Manager ↑ Buyer ↑ Assistant Buyer ↑ Merchandise Planner ↑ Store Manager ↑ Assistant Manager

Retailer	Training Program	Career Path in Buying
JCPenney, originally a mass-merchandiser, now repositioned as a national department store chain, headquartered in New York City. For further information: JCPenney Company, Inc., College Relations Manager, 1301 Avenue of the Americas, New York, NY 10019.	Assistant Buyer Training Program—graduates of 4-year colleges are hired as assistant buyers. New associates (as employees are called) receive a Personnel Department orientation. Assistant buyers receive on-the-job training from the buyers to whom they report; occasional rotation of assignment exposes the assistant buyer to new lines. An ongoing program of workshops for assistant buyers sharpens their skills and improves their knowledge of management. Corporate Management Development Programs are available as the associate advances to higher positions.	Merchandise Manager ↑ Buyer (15 to 20 years) ↑ Associate Buyer (8 to 15 years) ↑ Assistant Buyer (5 to 7 years)
Woodward & Lothrop, a privately held department store chain based in Washington, DC, with stores in MD and VA suburbs. For further information: Woodward & Lothrop, Management Placement, 10th and F Streets, N.W., Washington, DC 20013.	On-the-job training assignment combined with workshop sessions.	Vice President ↑ Divisional Merchandise Manager ↑ ⎡ Divisional Merchandise Controller Divisional Merchandise Coordinator Buyer ⎤ ↑ ⎡ Merchandise expeditor Control Analyst Merchandise Analyst Assistant Buyer ⎤ ↑ Management Trainee

Appendix B
Mathematics for the Fashion Buyer

Just as there is a language of fashion, there is a language of buying and merchandising. This language uses numbers to communicate about dollars, units, and percentages. A basic knowledge of mathematical interrelationships of profit factors is essential to profitable fashion buying and merchandising.

The major purpose of this appendix is to present calculations frequently used in fashion buying and merchandising. Although various electronic systems and machines are used in business today to handle mathematical calculations, these machines and systems can do only what they are programmed to do. They cannot think! Thinking remains the responsibility of people.

Math Refresher: Working with Percentages, Fractions, and Decimals

A **fraction** is a way of expressing a part of a whole quantity, such as ½ of the class, ⅛ of a pie. The number above (or to the left of) the line is called the **numerator** and the number below (or to the right of) the line is called the **denominator.** The line in a fraction means "divided by"; ¾ means 3 divided by 4.

A **decimal** is also a fraction whose denominator is a power of 10 (for example, 100, 1000, 10,000). The number of places to the right of the decimal point shows the value of the denominator. One decimal place means tenths; .3 = ³⁄₁₀. Two decimal places means hundredths; .75 = ⁷⁵⁄₁₀₀. Three decimal places means thousandths; .245 = ²⁴⁵⁄₁₀₀₀₀.

For example, U.S. currency is expressed in hundredths.

$$\$.10 = \frac{10}{100} \text{ dollar.}$$

$$\$1.00 = \frac{100}{100} \text{ dollar.}$$

Percent means out of one hundred. It is just another way of expressing a fraction whose denominator is 100. The % sign replaces the denominator.
Examples:

$$1\% = \frac{1}{100}$$

$$1.8\% = \frac{1.8}{100}$$

$$42\% = \frac{42}{100}$$

$$42.5\% = \frac{42.5}{100}$$

$$100\% = \frac{100}{100}$$

$$150\% = \frac{150}{100}$$

Converting Percentages, Decimals, and Fractions

To change a fraction to a decimal, divide the numerator by the denominator. In the

case of a repeating decimal, carry the quotient to four decimal places and round to three decimal places. All money amounts should be rounded to cents (two decimal places).
Example:

$$\frac{.25}{4 \overline{) 1.00}}$$
$$\frac{8}{20}$$

¼ =

Example:

⅗ =

$$\frac{.4285}{7 \overline{) 3.0000}}$$
$$\frac{2\ 8}{20}$$
$$\frac{14}{60}$$
$$\frac{56}{40}$$

To change a decimal to a percent, move the decimal point two places to the right and add the % sign. Where necessary, add or take away zeros.
Examples:

.75 = .75 = 75%

1.25 = 1.25 = 125%

.05 = .05 = 5%

.400 = .400 = 40.0% or 40%

37.6 = 37.60 = 3760%

.376 = .376 = 37.6%

To change a percent to a decimal, move the decimal point two places to the left and drop the % sign. Add zeros if necessary.
Examples:

5% = 05. = .05

.5% = 00.5 = .005

37.5% = 37.5 = .375

75% = 75. = .75

100% = 100. = 1.00

.05% = 00.05 = .0005

Multiplying and Dividing When Given Percents

It is advisable, when multiplying or dividing in problems where percents are given, to convert percents to decimals, rather than attempting to work with complex fractions.

MULTIPLYING BY PERCENTS.
Example:

Multiply 8.68 by 32%.

Procedures:

1. Change percent to decimals by moving two places to the left and dropping the % sign.

32% = .32

2. Multiply the two numbers, disregarding the decimal points for a moment.

868 × 32 = 27776

3. Count off the number of decimal places in the two numbers being multiplied and count off the same number of places from the right in the final answer.

8.68 × .32 = 2.7776 (4 decimal places)

FINDING 100%, 10%, OR 1% OF A NUMBER.

100% of any number is the number itself.

100% of 614 = 614

100% of 28.32 = 28.32

To find 10% of any number, merely move the decimal point, wherever located, one place to the left. If there are no numerals to the left of the decimal point, add a zero.

Examples:

$$10\% \times 8.75 = .875$$
$$10\% \times 9 = .9$$
$$10\% \times 321 = 32.1$$
$$10\% \times 1650 = 165$$
$$10\% \times .31 = .031$$

To find 1% of any number, move the decimal point, wherever located, two places to the left.

$$1\% \times 75.9 = .759$$
$$1\% \times 72.04 = .7204 \text{ or } .72$$
$$1\% \times .51 = .0051$$

FINDING (MULTIPLYING BY) A FRACTION OF 1%. The simple way of finding a fraction of 1% is as follows:

1. Find 1% of the number.
2. Then divide the answer by the denominator of the fraction.

Example:

$$1600 \times \tfrac{1}{4}\% = ?$$
$$1\% \times 1600 = .01 \times 1600 = 16$$
$$16 \div 4 = 4$$

DIVIDING BY PERCENTS.
Example:

Divide 87.50 by 37.5%.

Procedures:

1. Change % to decimal by moving the decimal point two places to the left and dropping the % sign.

$$37.5\% = .375$$

2. $.375\overline{)87.50}$

Clear the decimals in the divisor (.375) by moving the decimal point to the far right. Move the decimal point an equal number of places to the right in the dividend (87.50). If necessary, add zeros in the dividend.

$$.375\overline{)87.500}$$

3. Place the decimal point in the quotient (answer) over the decimal point in the dividend.

$$375.\overline{)87500.}$$

4. If final answers call for amounts of money (as in $87.50 divided by 37.5%), carry out to cents and round out cents (not dollars) by adding 3 zeros to the right of the decimal point.

$$\begin{array}{r} 233.333 \\ 375\overline{)87500.000} \end{array}$$

5. If final answer has a third decimal figure of 5 or more round up the second decimal figure. If the third decimal figure is less than 5, drop it. $87.50 \div 37.5\% = \$233.33$

When to Multiply and When to Divide in Problems Involving Percentages

To solve a problem which calls for an answer in percents (the relationship of one number to another expressed as a percentage), divide by the whole amount (usually the larger number).
Example:

34 is what % of 360?

$$\begin{array}{r} .094 \\ 360\overline{)34.000} \\ 32\ 40 \\ \hline 1\ 600 \\ 1\ 440 \\ \hline 160 \end{array}$$

$$0.94 = 9.4\%$$

To find a percentage or partial amount of a given number, multiply the number by the percentage.

Example:

$$12\% \text{ of } \$25.00 = \$25.00 \times .12 = \$3.00$$

To find the whole amount (100%) when you know the partial amount and its equivalent percentage, divide the percentage into the number that represents the partial amount.
Example:

Find 100% if 12% is 15

$$\begin{array}{r} 125 \\ .12\overline{)15.00} \end{array}$$

To find what percent or portion one number is of another, divide. Reminder: Express the answer as a percentage, carried out to 1 number past the decimal. To do this, calculate your answer to 2 numbers past the decimal point. If the second number past the decimal point is 5 or more, round up the first decimal number. If the second number past the decimal point is lower than 5, do not change the first decimal number. Drop the second decimal number in your final answer.
Example

75 is what % of 180?

Suggested procedures: If you know how to work with ratios, set up your ratio as follows:

$$\frac{75 \text{ (the partial amount)}}{180 \text{ (the whole amount)}} = \frac{X \text{ (the partial \%)}}{100 \text{ (the total \%)}}$$

$$\begin{array}{rl} 180X = 7500 & 41.66 \\ X = & 180\overline{)7500.00} \\ & \underline{720} \\ & 300 \\ & \underline{180} \\ & 1200 \\ & \underline{1080} \\ & 1200 \end{array}$$

$$X = 41.66\% \text{ or } 41.7\%$$

or

1. Set up a fraction with the partial amount (75) as the numerator (top number) and the whole amount (180) as the denominator (bottom).

$$\frac{75 \text{ (partial)}}{180 \text{ (whole)}}$$

2. Divide the bottom number into the top number $\frac{75}{180} = 180\overline{)75.}$ and add 4 zeros after the decimal point before you begin to divide.

$$180\overline{)75.0000}$$

3. Divide.

$$\begin{array}{r} .4166 \\ 180\overline{)75.0000} \\ \underline{72\,0} \\ 3\,00 \\ \underline{1\,80} \\ 1\,200 \\ \underline{1\,080} \\ 1200 \\ \underline{1080} \end{array}$$

4. Convert your decimal answer to its percentage form by moving the decimal point two places to the right and adding the percentage sign.

$$.4166 = 41.66\% \text{ or } 41.7\%$$

To find the percentage of the "whole amount" when the whole amount and the percentage rate are known, multiply. Reminder: In final answers that deal with amounts of money, answer to the nearest penny. Therefore, carry out answer to three decimal points and if the third decimal point number is 5 or more, round up the second decimal point number; 10.656 = 10.66)

Example:

What is 32.5% of $960?

Suggested procedures:
If you know how to work with ratios, set up your ratio as follows:

$$\frac{32.5}{100} = \frac{x}{960}$$

$$100x = 960 \times 32.5 = 31200$$

$$x = \$312.00$$

or

1. Convert the percentage to its decimal form by moving the decimal point two places to the left and dropping the % sign.

$$32.5\% = .325$$

2. Multiply the amount given ($960) by your decimal number.

$$
\begin{array}{r}
960 \\
\times\ .325 \\
\hline
4800 \\
1920 \\
2880 \\
\hline
312000
\end{array}
$$

3. Total up the numbers of decimal places in the numbers you are multiplying (960 × .325 has 3 decimals) and count off the same number of places from the right in your final answer.

$$312000 = \$312.000 \text{ or } \$312$$

To find the whole amount (100%) when the partial amount and its equivalent dollars are known, divide the partial amount by the percent.
Example:

Find 100% if $144 equals 16%

Suggested procedures:
If you work with ratios, set up your ratio as follows:

$$\frac{16\ (\text{partial }\%)}{100\ (\text{total }\%)} = \frac{144\ (\text{partial amount})}{x\ (\text{whole amount})}$$

$$16x = 14400$$

$$x = 900$$

or

1. Convert your percentage to its decimal form by moving the decimal point two places to the left and dropping the percentage sign.

$$16\% = .16$$

2. Divide your converted percentage (16% = .16) into its equivalent given number.

$$.16)\overline{144}$$

and remember to clear your divisor (.16) of decimals by moving them the necessary number of places to the right and also moving the decimal place in your dividend (the "inside" number, 144) by the same number of places, adding zeros if necessary.

$$.16)\overline{144.00}$$

3. In final answers that deal with amounts of money, carry your answer out to dollars and cents. Therefore, before beginning to divide, add three zeros after the decimal point in order to round out cents. If the number in the third decimal place is 5 or more, round up the number in the second decimal place ($88.385 = $88.39).

$$
\begin{array}{r}
9.00 \\
.16)\overline{144.00000} \\
144 \\
\hline
\end{array}
$$

Mathematical Formulas and Concepts

The following sections review the formulas and concepts that fashion buyers use to plan purchases and analyze the results of their buying decisions.

Figuring Profit

Basic factors that affect profit and loss are:

1. *Net Sales* (operating income). To find net sales,

Gross Sales — Customer Returns and Allowances = Net Sales

2. *Cost of Merchandise Sold.* To find cost of merchandise,

Billed Cost — Cash Discount + Inward Freight + Workroom Costs = Cost of Merchandise

3. *Operating Expenses.* To find operating expenses, simply add all expenses, such as rent, electricity, salaries, phone, and maintenance.

To figure profit or loss using these factors, first calculate gross margin, the difference between net sales and cost of merchandise.

Net Sales — Cost of Merchandise

= Gross Margin

The formula for calculating profit is

Gross Margin — Expenses = Profit (or Loss)

The factor to which all other factors are compared is net sales, and the comparisons are expressed as percentages. Net sales always equals 100%. To find the percentages of each of the factors:

$$\frac{\text{Total Cost of Merchandise \$}}{\text{Net Sales \$}} = \text{Cost of Merchandise \%}$$

$$\frac{\text{Gross Margin \$}}{\text{Net Sales \$}} = \text{Gross Margin \%}$$

$$\frac{\text{Expenses \$}}{\text{Net Sales \$}} = \text{Expense \%}$$

$$\frac{\text{Profit or Loss \$}}{\text{Net Sales \$}} = \text{Profit or Loss \%}$$

Pricing the Merchandise

To make a profit the retail buyer must determine the proper price for the merchandise that is sold in his or her department or store.

There are three major dollar factors involved in the pricing of merchandise. They are as follows:

The Cost Dollar is what a buyer pays a vendor for the merchandise.

The Retail Dollar is what a buyer prices merchandise to sell to the customer.

The Markup Dollar is the difference between the cost dollar and the retail dollar. When planning this, buyers take into consideration what they need to plan in order to have a gross margin large enough to cover the expenses and still produce a profit.

$$\begin{array}{ll} & \text{Cost of Goods \$} \\ + & \text{Markup} \qquad \text{\$} \\ \hline = & \text{Retail Price} \quad \text{\$} \end{array}$$

Given any two of the basic pricing factors, the third can be calculated in both dollar amounts and percentages. Therefore:

Retail $ = Cost + Dollar Markup

Markup $ = Retail — Cost

Cost $ = Retail — Dollar Markup

In actual retail practice, however, the markup dollars are converted into percentages of the retail price for comparison and analysis. Therefore:

$$\text{Markup \%} = \frac{\text{Markup \$}}{\text{Retail \$}}$$

Initial Markup is the first markup placed on merchandise. This markup can be planned in advance. It is the difference between the cost price and the *first* retail price placed on merchandise.

Maintained Markup is the difference between the cost price and the *final* retail price at which the merchandise is sold. The maintained markup must be large enough to cover expenses and provide a profit.

The following formulas are for the various buying and pricing situations that occur in fashion buying and merchandising:

Figuring markup percentage when cost and retail are known

$$\text{Markup \%} = \frac{\text{Markup \$}}{\text{Retail \$}}$$

Figuring retail when cost and initial markup % are known

Retail = Cost
$$\overline{100\% - \text{Markup \%}}$$
(Cost Complement)

Figuring cost when retail and initial markup percent are known

Cost $ = Retail $

× Cost Complement (100% − Markup %)

Repricing the Merchandise

One of the most common price adjustments is the lowering or reduction of the original retail price.

Figuring the Dollar Markdown

Original or Present Retail $
− New Retail $ = Markdown $

Figuring Markdown Percentage

$$\text{Markdown \%} = \frac{\text{\$ Markdown}}{\text{\$ Net Sales}}$$

Retail Method of Inventory

This is the way buyers keep track of their stock. It is called a book or perpetual inventory. They record everything in this book inventory. To find the book inventory:

Opening Inventory + Additions to Stock (Ins) − Withdrawals from Stock (Outs) = Book Inventory

Always remember to start with the opening inventory figure.

Ins = Opening Inventory
Transfers In
Purchases
Returns from Customers

Outs = Sales (Gross or Net)
Transfers Out
Returns to Vendors
Employee Discounts
Markdown

Subtract the outs from the ins to find the book inventory.

To find an overage or shortage (in dollars) subtract book inventory from the physical inventory.

Physical Inventory − Book Inventory = Shortage or Overage

If the physical inventory is *larger* than the book inventory, you have an *overage.*

If the physical inventory is *smaller* than the book inventory, you have a *shortage.*

To find the overage or shortage percent

Overage or Shortage $
$$\overline{\text{Net Sales \$}}$$

= Overage or Shortage %

To estimate your overage or shortage in dollars

Net Sales $ × Overage or Shortage %

Physical inventory automatically becomes the next opening inventory.

Dollar Planning and Control

Turnover: The degree of balance between your sales and your stock. Shows the number of times an *average stock* has been sold and replaced. Turnover rate can be preplanned.

$$\text{Turnover} = \frac{\text{Net Sales for Period}}{\text{Average Stock for Period}}$$

(To calculate average stock, total all stocks and divide by the number of stocks totaled.)

Stock-Sales Ratio: Shows a *specific* stock planned to achieve a planned sales figure for an individual time period.

$$\text{S-S Ratio} = \frac{\text{Retail Stock for Time Period}}{\text{Sales for Time Period}}$$

Planned Purchases at Retail:

　　Planned EOM Stock
　+ Planned Sales
　+ Planned Markdowns
　　───────────────
　= Planned Total Requirements for Period
　− Planned BOM Stock
　　───────────────
　= Planned Purchases at Retail

Planned Purchases at Cost:

Planned Purchases at Retail

　　× Cost Complement (100% − MU%)

Open-to-Buy at Retail:

Planned Purchases at Retail for Period

　　　　　− Merchandise on Order

BOM Stock (Beginning of Month):

Planned Monthly Sales × Stock-Sales Ratio

Average Stock (When planned sales and turnover are known):

$$\frac{\text{Planned Sales for Period}}{\text{Turnover Rate}}$$

Reminders:

The EOM (end-of-month) stock figure automatically becomes the BOM (beginning-of-month) stock figure of the following month.

When the term *average* stock appears, it means that more than one stock figure must be used and divided.

Terms of Sale: The Different Discounts

A **discount** is a deduction, expressed as a percentage, that is subtracted from the billed cost of goods.

A **quantity discount** is a percentage deducted from the billed cost of goods when a *stipulated* quantity is purchased.

Billed Cost $ × Quantity discount % =
　　　　　　　　　Quantity Discount $
Billed Cost $ − Quantity Discount $ =
　　　　　　　　　Final Billed Cost

A **trade discount** is a percentage or a series of percentages that are deducted from the *list price*.

List Price $ − Trade Discount $ =

　　　　　　　　　Billed Cost $

In calculating trade discounts in a series, you may use any one of the following formulas to find the final billed cost in dollars.

Direct Method:

　　　　List Price $
　　　× Trade Discount %
　　　= Discount $

　　　　　List Price $
　　　　− Discount $
　　　　= Cost $

　　　Cost $
　　× Discount %
　　= Discount $

Cost $
− Discount
= Final Billed Cost

Complement Method: In this method you subtract the trade discount percentage from 100% and get the complement of the trade discount percentage.

List Price $
× Complement of Discount %
= Cost Price $

Cost $
× Complement of Discount %
= Final Billed Cost

"On Percentage" Method:

Complement of Discount %
× Complement of Discount %
= Product of Complements

List Price $
× Product of Complement
= Final Billed Cost

A **cash discount** is a percentage deducted from the billed cost if payment is made within a *stipulated* time. Eligibility for a cash discount depends only upon the time element. Cost prices which have quantity and/or trade discounts may also have a cash discount.

Billed Cost $ Billed Cost $
× Cash Discount %   − Cash Discount $
= Cash Discount $ = Final Billed Cost

When the cost of goods is found by deducting a series of trade discounts, you take the cash discount on the final billed cost.

Dating means there is a specified time period for the payment of an invoice. Dating is usually accompanied by a cash discount. Together, they are expressed as a single term of sale. There are many different types of dating:

COD Dating: Cash on delivery. Invoice must be paid upon delivery of merchandise.

Regular Dating: Discount period is calculated from the date of the invoice.

Extra Dating X: Calculated from the date of the invoice with specified extra days granted during which the discount may be taken.

EOM Dating: End of month. Discount period is calculated from the end of the month in which the invoice is dated.

ROG Dating: Receipt of goods. Discount period is calculated from the date the goods arrive, rather than the date of the invoice.

Advanced or Postdating: The invoice date is advanced so that additional time is allowed for payment to be made. The discount period is calculated from the advanced dating.

Net Payment: Net payment dates are dates on which an invoice *must* be paid! The invoice may be subject to interest charges if not paid by net payment date.

Anticipation is an *extra* discount. It is taken in addition to any regular or other discounts which apply. Anticipation is usually combined with the cash discount percentage when calculating discount. The Accounts Payable Department, rather than the buyer, is responsible for computing the amount of anticipation.

Glossary

Adjustments See **Customer returns and allowances.**

Ad valorem duty A charge added on to the declared dollar value of foreign merchandise levied as a percentage of dutiable value. (See also **Duty.**)

Advance orders Regular orders placed for delivery sometime in the future, rather than for immediate delivery.

Advanced dating An arrangement whereby an invoice is dated from a specified future date rather than from the date the invoice is prepared.

Advertising The paid use of space or time in any medium. This includes newspapers, magazines, direct-mail pieces, shopping news bulletins, theater programs, catalogs, bus cards, billboards, radio, and television.

Advertising credit A mention of one or more store names, in connection with the advertisement of a vendor, as being the retail source(s) for the merchandise advertised.

Advertising plan A projection of the advertising that a store intends to use during a specific period of time (such as a season, quarter, month, or week) in order to attract business.

Advertising request A form prepared by a buyer stating when and where an ad is to appear and how much space is to be used. The form also requires a brief factual description of the style(s) selected for advertising and of what is important and exciting about the goods from the customer's standpoint.

AIDA concept The series of tasks including attracting the customer's attention, developing interest, creating desire, and securing action.

Allowance See **Discount.**

Anticipation An extra discount granted by some manufacturers for the prepayment of their invoices before the end of the cash discount period.

Apparel manufacturer A firm that performs all the operations required to produce a garment.

Assortment See **Merchandise assortment.**

Assortment display A display created by showing, identifying, and pricing one of each of the styles currently in a section of the stock.

Assortment plan A comprehensive and detailed listing of all items making up an assortment by type and price line.

Average gross sale Net sales of a department divided by the number of sales transactions during the same period.

Back order Order placed by a buyer for a shipment or part of a shipment that was not filled on time by the vendor.

Balanced assortment An assortment in which types, quantities, and price lines of merchandise included in inventory during a given period of time are closely matched to the demand of target customers.

Basic stock An item of merchandise that should always be kept in stock throughout a season or year because of consistent demand.

Beat-Last-Year book Daily sales record with subtotals showing sales to date and comparing sales to those of the previous year at the same time of year.

Behavioral segmentation Grouping of consumers according to either their opinions of specific products or services or their actual rate of use of these products or services.

Best-selling price lines Those limited numbers of price lines within an assortment that account for the greater share of the department's dollar and unit sales volume.

Blanket order An order that covers the delivery of merchandise for all or part of a season. The buyer places requisitions against the order as merchandise is needed.

Book inventory The dollar value of inventory that should be in stock at any given time as indicated by the store's accounting records.

Boutique A shop associated with few-of-a-kind merchandise, generally of very new or extreme styling, with an imaginative presentation of goods. French word for "shop."

Brand Identity of a manufacturer or distributor of an item.

Broad and shallow assortment Selection of merchandise that offers a wide variety of styles but only limited sizes and colors in each style.

Broadcast media Radio and television (including cable television) viewed as a means of advertising.

Buyer A person whose responsibilities involve the selection and purchase for resale of a category of merchandise sold by a retailer to consumers.

Buying motivation Why people buy what they buy.

Buying on consignment Placement of an order with the privilege of returning unsold goods by a specific date. (See also **Consignment selling.**)

Buying plan A general description of the types and quantities of merchandise a buyer expects to purchase for delivery within a specific period of time. Sets a limit on the amount of money to be spent.

Cash discount The percentage or premium allowed by a manufacturer off an invoice if payment is made within a certain specified period of time.

Cash on delivery (COD) Agreement between buyer and seller that the buyer will pay in cash upon receipt of merchandise.

Central buying An organization in which all merchandise buying activity is performed from a central headquarters with authority and responsibility for the selection and purchase of merchandise in the hands of a central buying staff.

Central merchandise plan A form of central buying in which distribution of centrally ordered merchandise to individual stores is made by the distribution department following a plan that allocates specific quantities to each store unit.

Chain organization A group of 12 or more centrally owned stores, each handling somewhat similar goods, which are merchandised and controlled from a central headquarters office (as defined by the Bureau of the Census).

Charge-back A store's invoice for claims against and allowances made by a vendor.

Claim See **Charge-back.**

Classification An assortment of units or items of merchandise which are all reasonably substitutable for each other, regardless of who made the item, the material of which it is made, or the part of the store in which it is offered for sale.

College board A customer advisory group composed of college students who inform store management of the store's image among their peers and also serve as salespeople, customer advisors, and sometimes models in clothing departments that sell to their age group.

Commissionaire (pronounced "ko-me-see-ohn-air") An independent retailer's service organization usually located in a major city of a foreign market area. It is roughly the foreign equivalent of an American resident buying office.

Compound duty A combination of ad valorem and specific duties. (See also **Duty.**)

Confined style(s) Styles that a vendor agrees to sell to only one store in a given trading area. See **Exclusivity.**

Consignment selling An arrangement whereby a manufacturer places merchandise in a retail store for resale but permits any unused portion, together with payment for those garments that have been sold, to be returned to the wholesale source by a specified date. (See also **Buying on consignment.**)

Contract buying An arrangement in which a "development sample" of an item is made up so that it can be copied or adapted for sale at a price more advantageous to producer and customer. This type of buying is commonly used by chain organizations and mail-order firms, and often in foreign buying as well. (See also **Specification buying.**)

Cooperative advertising Retail advertising, the costs of which are shared by a store and one or more producers on terms mutually agreed to.

Cost of goods sold The amount of money paid for merchandise (including freight, discount, and workroom charge) sold during a specific period of time.

Coverage The maximum quantities to which each items's stock should be built after each regular stock count. Expressed in terms of either a certain number of weeks' supply or a specific number of units, or both.

Cumulative discount A type of quantity discount based on volume of business done with a resource over a certain period of time. See **Quantity discount.**

Customer returns and allowances Refunds or partial refunds made to customers when merchandise is returned; also called **Adjustments.**

Cutting ticket An indication in specification buying of the quantity of a style that the buyer is ordering. Manufacturers require a minimum cutting ticket based on their break-even point in production.

Dating The length of time a vendor gives a buyer to pay for goods purchased. Includes **regular dating,** which allows a discount for payment within a stipulated time; **EOM** (end-of-month) **dating,** which allows a discount for payment within 10 days of the

month in which the invoice is dated; **ROG** (receipt-of-goods) **dating,** which allows a discount for payment within 10 days of receipt of goods in the store; and **extra dating,** which allows a specified number of extra days for the buyer to pay the bill and earn the cash discount. (See also **Cash on delivery [COD]** and **Advanced dating.**)

Decor The decorative style used by a store to project an image to the customer; also called **Store design.**

Demographic segmentation Division of a market into groups according to such characteristics as age, family composition, sex, occupation, income, and level of education.

Department store A store, as defined by the Bureau of the Census, that employs 25 or more people and sells general lines of merchandise in each of three categories: home furnishings, household linens and dry goods (an old trade term meaning piece goods and sewing notions), and apparel and accessories for the entire family.

Designer brand A labeling of merchandise associating it with a "name" designer.

Direct expenses Those expenses incurred as a direct result of the operation of a specific department and which would cease if that department ceased to exist. Examples include costs of buying trips, advertising, and salaries of salespeople.

Discount A reduction in the list or quoted price given to a buyer by a vendor; also called an **Allowance.**

Discount store A departmentalized retail store using many self-service techniques to sell its goods. It operates usually at low profit margins, has a minimum annual volume of $500,000, and is at least 10,000 square feet in size.

Display The nonpersonal, visual presentation of merchandise. (See also **Visual merchandising.**)

Distributor In a central merchandising plan, a person who divides the merchandise ordered by a buyer into the quantities needed by each store unit.

Divisional merchandise manager The supervisor of the buyers for a number of related departments.

Dollar merchandise plan A budget or projection, in dollars, of the sales goals of a merchandise classification, a department, or an entire store for a specific future period of time, and the amount of stock required to achieve those sales.

Dollar open-to-buy See **Open-to-buy, dollar.**

Drop ship Shipment of merchandise by a manufacturer directly to a unit of a retailing firm that has placed the order through its central buying office.

Duty A charge added by a national government to the declared monetary value of foreign merchandise.

Economic ordering quantity (EOQ) A system whereby, when the stock for an item reaches a predetermined level, a reorder is automatically triggered.

Editorial credit The mention, in a magazine or newspaper, of a store name as a retail source for merchandise that is being featured editorially by the publication.

Exclusivity Allowing a store sole use within a given trading area of a style or styles. An important competitive retail weapon.

Expenses Money spent to run a business, including such items as salaries, rent, advertising, and utilities.

Eyeball control See **Visual control.**

Fashion A style that is accepted and used by the majority of a group at any one time.

Fashion coordination The function of analyzing fashion trends in order to ensure that the fashion merchandise offered is appropriate in terms of style, quality, and appeal to the target customer.

Fashion cycle The rise, widespread popularity, and then decline in acceptance of a style. **Rise:** The acceptance of either a newly introduced design or its adaptations by an increasing number of consumers. **Culmination:** That period when a fashion is at the height of its popularity and use. The fashion then is in such demand that it can be mass-produced, mass-distributed, and sold at prices within the reach of most consumers. **Decline:** The decrease in consumer demand because of boredom resulting from widespread use of a fashion. **Obsolescence:** When lack of interest has set in and a style can no longer be sold at any price.

Fashion forecasting A prediction of the trend of fashion as determined by the prevailing elements in all the fashion industries. Supplied by fashion coordinators as often and in as much detail as management requires—usually on a 6-month or seasonal basis.

Fashion image That aspect of a store's image that reflects the degree of fashion leadership the store strives to exercise and the stage of the fashion cycle that its assortments represent.

Fashion merchandising Refers to the planning required to have the right fashion-oriented merchandise at the right time, in the right quantities, and at the right prices for the target group(s) of customers.

Fashion merchandising policy A long-range guide for the fashion merchandising staff of a store, spelling out the store's fashion aims, standards of quality, price ranges, attitudes toward competition, and any other elements that may be considered pertinent.

Fashion retailing The business of buying fashion-oriented merchandise from a variety of resources and assembling it in convenient locations for resale to ultimate consumers.

Fashion theme The central subject chosen for a coordinated approach by specified fashion departments in their merchandise assortments.

First cost The wholesale price of merchandise in the country of origin.

Fixture display   A form, stand, rack, or other piece of equipment on which to display merchandise.

Flash sales reports   Daily reports of sales, by department, developed from the unaudited sales checks and cash-register tapes for the previous business day.

FOB (Free on board)   Designation of a point at which ownership changes from vendor to buyer and designation of who (vendor or buyer) will pay shipping charges and from what point. Includes **FOB factory,** which means the buyer pays all transportation charges and owns the goods from the moment they are shipped; **FOB destination,** which means the vendor pays transportation charges and owns the goods until they reach the place designated by the buyer (the store or warehouse, for example); **FOB shipping point,** which means the vendor pays any crating necessary for sending the goods to a place where they are turned over to a transportation company; **FOB destination, charges reversed,** which means the vendor owns the goods until they reach the buyer but the buyer pays transportation charges; and **FOB destination, freight prepaid,** which means the goods become the possession of the buyer as soon as they are shipped but the seller pays the freight charges.

Franchise operation   A contractual agreement in which a firm or individual buys the exclusive right to conduct a retail business within a specified trading area under a franchisor's registered or trademarked name.

Function   A major area of responsibility with an organizational structure, for example, the merchandising function.

General merchandise manager   Head of the merchandising division in a retail organization.

General merchandise stores   Retail stores which sell a number of lines of merchandise—apparel and accessories, furniture and home furnishings, household lines and dry goods, hardware, appliances, and small-wares, for example—under one roof. Stores included in this group are commonly known as mass-merchandisers, department stores, variety stores, general merchandise stores, or general stores.

General store   An early form of retail store which carried a wide variety of mainly utilitarian consumer goods.

Geographic segmentation.   Division of a market into cities, counties, states, regions, or rural areas.

Greeting approach   Initiating a conversation with a customer by saying, "Hello," "Good morning," or another welcoming phrase.

Gross margin   The dollar difference between net sales for a period and the net cost of merchandise sold during that period.

Gross rating points (GRP)   The percentage of the population in a particular area that can be expected to see an outdoor advertisement.

Group purchase   The purchasing from a given resource of identical merchandise by several stores at one time so that all participants may share in the advantages of a large-volume purchase.

Hot items   Items, new or otherwise, that have demonstrated greater customer acceptance than was anticipated.

Income statement   A summary of the transactions of a business over a specific period of time; it indicates net sales, cost of goods sold, gross margin, expenses, and profit; also called **Profit and loss statement.**

Indirect expenses   Those expenses that do not directly result from the operation of an individual department but are shared by all departments of a store, such as compensation of top management executives, utilities, maintenance, insurance, and receiving and marking expenses.

Initial markup   The difference between the delivered cost of merchandise and the retail price placed on it when it is first brought into stock.

Institutional advertisement See **Prestige advertisement.**

Irregulars Goods having defects that may affect appearance but not wear.

Item display A display featuring a single item or several versions of a single style.

Job lot buying Buying an assortment of merchandise that a vendor has been unable to sell at regular prices and therefore offers at a reduced, usually flat price.

Key resource A producer from whom a department has consistently bought a substantial portion of its merchandise in past seasons; also called a **Prime resource.**

Landed cost The cost of foreign merchandise at the store after importation from abroad; it is the cost upon which retail price is based.

Leased department A department ostensibly operated by the store in which it is found but actually run by an outsider who pays a percentage of sales to the store as rent.

Letter of credit A document issued by an American bank to a foreign producer at the request of an American retailer that is the producer's customer; when the merchandise is ready for delivery to the United States, the producer presents the letter of credit to a bank in the foreign country and is paid by that bank, which charges the account of the American bank representing the store.

Licensing An arrangement whereby firms are given permission to produce and market merchandise in the name of a licensor, who is paid a percentage of sales for permitting his or her name to be used.

Licensing agreement A contract whereby the licensor usually agrees to pay the licensee a royalty for use of the licensee's name.

Line An assortment of new designs offered by manufacturers to their customers, usually on a seasonal basis.

Manufacturer See **Apparel manufacturer**

Markdown The dollar difference between the previous price and the reduced price to which merchandise is marked.

Markdown percentage The dollar value of the net retail markdown taken during a given period, divided by the dollar value of net sales for the same period.

Market representative A specialist who covers a narrow segment of the total market and makes information about it available to client stores.

Market segmentation The dividing of the total market into smaller customer groups which include those customers who have similar characteristics.

Market trip A visit by a buyer to a city, district, or building complex where many vendors offer a category or related categories of merchandise for sale.

Marketing The performance of business activities that directs the flow of goods from producers to consumers.

Marketing process The series of activities involved in converting raw materials into a form that can be used by ultimate consumers without further commercial processing.

Markup The difference between the wholesale cost and the retail price of merchandise (sometimes called "markon" by large retail stores).

Merchandise advertisement See **Promotional advertisement.**

Merchandise approach Greeting a retail customer who appears interested in a particular item of merchandise with a comment about the merchandise.

Merchandise assortment A collection of varied types of related merchandise, essentially intended for the same general end use and usually grouped together in one selling area of a retail store. **Broad:** A merchandise assortment that includes many styles. **Deep:** A merchandise assortment that includes a comprehensive range of colors and sizes in each style. **Narrow:** A merchandise assortment that includes relatively few styles. **Shallow:** A merchandise assortment that contains only a few sizes and colors in each style.

Merchandise journal See **Purchase journal.**

Merchandising The planning required to have the right merchandise at the right time, in the right place, in the right quantities, and at the right price for specified target group(s) of consumers.

Merchandising policies Guidelines established by store management for merchandising executives to follow in order that the store organization may win the patronage of the specific target group(s) of customers it has chosen to serve.

Mom-and-Pop store A small store run by the proprietor with few or no hired assistants.

Monthly stock-sales ratio The relationship between stock and sales that indicates the number of months that would be required to dispose of a beginning-of-the-month inventory at the planned rate of sales for the month.

MOR The Merchandising and Operating Results report issued by the National Retail Merchants Association, compiling stock-sales ratios of comparable retail firms.

Narrow and deep assortment A selection of merchandise in which there is a limited number of styles, but those selected are stocked in all available sizes and colors.

National brand A nationally advertised and distributed brand owned by a manufacturer or processor. Offers consistent guarantee of quality and fashion correctness.

Negotiation process Exchange of ideas between buyers and sellers for the purpose of coming to a mutually satisfying agreement.

Net sales All the sales that have been made for a specific time period minus customer returns and allowances.

Number or style number A specific version or variation of a style.

Off-price buying Buying of manufacturers' overproduction at deep discounts for the purpose of offering consumers low prices on name-brand fashion merchandise.

Off-shore production Domestic apparel producers who import goods either from their own plants operating in cheap, labor-rich foreign areas or through their long-term supply arrangements with foreign producers.

Open order Order placed by a resident buying office with the name of the manufacturer filled in by the resident buyer when the best resource has been determined.

Open-to-buy, dollar The dollar value of planned purchases for a given period minus the dollar value of all orders scheduled for delivery during the same period but not yet received.

Open-to-buy, units The units of planned purchase for a given period minus the units on order for delivery during the same period but not yet received.

Operational satisfactions (customer) Those satisfactions derived from the physical performance of a product.

Organization chart A visual presentation of the manner in which a firm delegates responsibility and authority within its organization.

Organizational structure The arrangement of work and assignment of the people who have the responsibility and authority to do that work within an organization.

Outdoor advertising Paid messages promoting a business, a service, merchandise, or an idea in outdoor signs, either standardized or not, or on public or commercial transportation vehicles and in stations.

Over-the-counter selling An arrangement whereby selected portions of stock are kept in display cases, shelves, or drawers, and salespeople are needed to take this merchandise out for customer inspection and to complete a sale.

Overstock A selection of merchandise on hand that exceeds its planned size

Patronage motives (consumer) The reasons that induce consumers to patronize one store rather than another: why people buy where they do.

Percentage of stock shortage to sales An inventory result used to evaluate a buyer's performance by comparing a stock shortage established by physical inventory to sales figures.

Periodic stock count control A unit control system in which stock is counted and recorded at regular intervals and the results are used to compute sales for the intervening period.

Perpetual control A unit control system in which purchase orders, receipts of merchandise, and sales are recorded for individual style numbers as they occur, and stock on hand is computed.

Personal approach Greeting a customer by name, possibly with a cordial comment about positive personal news in the customer's life.

Physical inventory The value of inventory on hand as determined by taking a physical count.

Planned purchases The term used to indicate the amount of merchandise that can be brought into stock during a given period without exceeding the planned inventory for the end of that period.

Planner Supervisor of a plan establishing the needs of individual stores within an organization that uses a central merchandising plan.

Policy A settled, clearly defined course of action or method of doing business deemed necessary, expedient, or advantageous.

Pre-retail The practice of indicating on each purchase order the intended retail prices of all items being ordered.

Press release A written statement of news that has occurred or is about to occur, specifying the source of the information and the date after which its use is permissible.

Prestige advertisement An advertisement that "sells" the store as a good place to shop, rather than its specific merchandise. Also called **Institutional advertisement.**

Price agreement plan A buying arrangement in which merchandise is ordered by a central buying office, which prepares a catalog from which managers of store units can order directly from the manufacturer.

Price change form A special form required for reporting all upward or downward revisions in retail prices of merchandise in stock.

Price line A specific price point at which an assortment of merchandise is regularly offered for sale.

Price lining The practice of determining the various but limited number of retail prices at which a department's or store's assortments will be offered.

Price range The spread between the lowest and the highest price line at which merchandise is offered for sale.

Price zone A series of somewhat contiguous price lines that are likely to have major appeal to one particular segment of a store's or department's customers.

Prime resource See **Key resource.**

Print media Newspapers, magazines, direct mail, outdoor advertising, or any other vehicle for presenting advertising messages in print.

Prior stock Proportion of old to new goods.

Prior stock report A report that summarizes information about the amount of stock still on hand in each of a number of prior seasons.

Private label or store brand Merchandise which meets standards specified by a retail organization and which belongs exclusively to it. Primarily used to ensure consistent quality of product as well as to meet price competition.

Private label buying Developing merchandise to specification or altering standards and specifications of national brands to create and sell merchandise that is unique to the store.

Profit Money left after merchandise offered for sale has been purchased and expenses of running the business have been paid.

Profit and loss statement See **Income statement.**

Promotional advertisement An advertisement that endeavors to create sales of specific items; also called **Merchandise advertisement.**

Promotional buying Purchases of goods for resale during special events or sale-price promotions.

Psychographic segmentation Division of the market according to customer lifestyles.

Psychological satisfactions (consumer) Those derived from the consumer's social and psychological interpretation of the product and its performance.

Public relations Execution of specially designed programs by a business to earn public understanding and acceptance.

Publicity The free and voluntary mention of a firm, brand, product, or person in some form of media.

Purchase journal A monthly or semimonthly report listing all invoices for merchandise received, transfers or merchandise in and out, and returns to or claims against vendors that have been entered in a department's book inventory during a given period; also called **Merchandise journal.**

Purchase order A contract between a store and a vendor to purchase certain specified merchandise under certain specified conditions.

Quantity discount A price reduction predicated upon purchase of a number of units stipulated by the vendor.

Quota A limit put upon articles entering a country by its national government.

Receiving apron A sequentially numbered form on which complete information about each shipment of merchandise received is recorded.

Regular buying Buying merchandise to sell at regular established price lines in a store's merchandise assortment.

Regular or stock order Order placed by a buyer directly with a vendor, giving time, amount, and shipping instructions.

Release date The earliest date on which a publicity announcement can be made.

Reorder An order for an additional quantity of previously ordered goods.

Reporting services A business that publishes news about retail marketing and fashion merchandising.

Reserve requisition control A form of periodic stock count control in which stock on the selling floor is considered sold and only the reserve stock is counted.

Resident buying office A service organization located in a major market area that provides market information and representation to its noncompeting client stores. **Associated:** One that is jointly owned and operated by a group of independently owned stores. **Private:** One that is owned and operated by a single, out-of-town store organization and which performs market work exclusively for that store organization. **Salaried or Fee:** One that is independently owned and operated and charges the stores it represents for the work it does for them. **Syndicate:** One that is maintained by a parent organization which owns a group of stores and performs market work exclusively for those stores.

Resource Vendor, source of supply; also called **Supplier.**

Resource structure The group of vendors from whom a buyer purchases merchandise.

Retail method of inventory A method of inventory evaluation in which all transactions affecting the value of a store's or department's inventory (such as sales, purchases, markdowns, transfers, and returns-to-vendor) are recorded at retail values.

Retail reductions All reductions that occur in the retail value of the inventory, including merchandise markdowns, discounts allowed to employees and other special customers, and stock shortages.

Retailing The business of buying goods from a variety of resources and assembling these goods in convenient locations for resale to ultimate consumers.

Return-to-vendor A store's invoice covering merchandise returned for cause to its vendor.

Sales per square foot The number of square feet of selling space of a department divided into the department's total net sales for a period; used to evaluate a buyer's effectiveness.

Sales promotion The coordination of advertising, display, publicity, and personal salesmanship in order to promote profitable sales.

Salon selling The most exacting type of personal selling: Little or no stock is exposed to the customer's view except that brought out for the customer's inspection by the salesperson.

Sample-test-reorder technique Buying of a broad and shallow selection of a new fashion, to gauge customer reaction, followed by a substantial quantity reorder of favored styles and markdowns and clearance of unpopular styles.

Season code A code indicating the month and season of receipt of merchandise. The code appears on the price ticket of an item and is used to determine how long the item has been in stock.

Seasonal discount Price reduction offered to a buyer for purchasing merchandise out of season.

Seconds Factory rejects having defects that may affect wear.

Selection factors The various characteristics or components of an item of merchandise that influence a customer's decision to purchase.

Selective distribution Limitation of the retailers in a trading area to whom a vendor will sell based on their common pricing and fashion level.

Self-selection selling The method of selling in which merchandise is displayed and arranged so that customers can make at least a preliminary selection without the aid of a salesperson.

Self-service The method of selling in which customers make their selections from the goods on display and bring their purchases to a checkout counter where they make payment and their purchases are prepared for takeout.

Service approach Greeting a customer with the question "May I help you?" is considered a poor approach because it invites a negative response.

Shop A small store or area within a large store that is stocked with merchandise for special end-use purposes: intended for customers with specialized interests.

Signature brand Private label merchandise endorsed by a well-known personality.

Silhouette The overall outline or contour of a costume. Also frequently referred to as "shape" or "form."

Special event An occasion involving a promotional event, sale, or other event featuring specific merchandise or prices.

Special order buying Placement of an order by a buyer for a particular style in a specific color and size.

Specialty store A store that carries limited lines of apparel, accessories, or home furnishings (as defined by the Bureau of the Census). In the trade, retailers use the term to describe any apparel and/or accessories store that exhibits a degree of fashion awareness and carries goods for men, women, and/or children.

Specification buying See **Contract buying.**

Stock on hand (OH) Units, dollar value, or both of each price line of each classification on hand during the time when new purchases are planned.

Stock on order (OO) Units, dollar value, or both of each price line of each classification on order for delivery during the time when new purchases are planned.

Stock overage The condition existing when the physical inventory is greater than the book inventory.

Stock-sales ratio (monthly) The number of months that would be required to dispose of a beginning-of-the-month inventory at the rate at which sales are made in (or planned for) that month.

Stock shortage The condition existing when the book inventory is greater than the physical inventory.

Stock turnover The number of times that an average stock of merchandise (inventory) has been turned into sales during a given period.

Stockkeeping unit (SKU) A single item or group of items of merchandise within a classification to which an identifying number is assigned and for which separate sales and stock records are kept.

Store design See **Decor.**

Store image The character or personality that a store presents to the public.

Store layout A plan that allocates a specific location and amount of space to each merchandise department and nonselling area in a store.

Stylist The title given to persons employed to study consumer demand, who help buyers select and coordinate their assortment in line with this demand. Early title of fashion coordinator.

Suggestion selling The offer of additional merchandise that will go with or enhance items the customer has already decided to buy.

Supplier See **Resource.**

Taking numbers Writing an adequate description of each style the buyer is considering for purchase, including style number, size range, available colors, fabric, wholesale price, and any other relevant details.

Target market The group or groups of customers a store wishes to attract.

Teen board A customer advisory group composed of local high school students; often members of DECA (Distributive Education Clubs of America).

Terms of sale The combination of allowable discounts on purchases and the time allowed for taking such discounts.

Trade discount A single discount or series of discounts from the manufacturer's list price (which is often the suggested retail price).

Transit advertising Print ads placed on transportation vehicles and in subway and train stations and at terminals.

Trunk show A form of pretesting that involves a producer's sending a representative to a store with samples of the current line, and exhibiting those samples to customers at scheduled, announced showings.

Unbranded merchandise Goods without a label of established significance; may not identify the manufacturer.

Unit control Systems for recording the number of units of merchandise bought, sold, in stock, and on order, and from which a variety of reports can be drawn.

Unit planning Projecting sales and beginning-of-the-month inventories in terms of units of merchandise by classifications and price lines.

Variety store A store carrying a wide range of merchandise in a limited number of low or relatively low price lines.

Vendor See Resource.

Vignette A display showing a product or group of products in use.

Visual control A form of periodic stock count in which a rack or bin is assigned to each style, size, or classification, and a periodic visual check is made to see whether one of these bins or racks looks too empty or too full. Involves no use of records. Sometimes called **Eyeball control.**

Visual merchandising Everything visual that is done to, with, or for a product and its surroundings to encourage its sale. This includes display, store layout, and store decor.

Want slip A form on which a salesperson reports a customer's request for something that is not in stock.

Warehouse and requisition plan A form of central buying in which store managers may requisition the quantity of an item they need for their customers; often applied to staple stock.

Working the market Preplanning a market trip to maximize productivity by budgeting time and arranging order of appointments, and then following the plan.

Index